WICKED CITY CHICAGO
From Kenna to Capone

Curt Johnson and R. Craig Sautter

december press

A special issue of December Magazine,
comprising vol. 37, no. 1, 1994

Wicked City Chicago by Curt Johnson and R. Craig Sautter

ISBN 0-913204-31-5
Library of Congress Catalog Card Number: 93-73785

Manufactured in the United States of America

Photo credits will be found on p. 380

Cover by Lee Wallek

Published by December Press
Box 302, Highland Park, Illinois 60035

They tell me you are wicked and I believe them, for I
        have seen your painted women under the gas lamps
        luring the farm boys.
And they tell me you are crooked and I answer: Yes, it
        is true I have seen the gunman kill and go free to
        kill again.
And they tell me you are brutal and my reply is: On the
        faces of women and children I have seen the marks
        of wanton hunger.

—Carl Sandburg, from "Chicago"

What is life? It is the flash of a firefly in the night. It is the breath of a
buffalo in the wintertime. It is the little shadow which runs across the
grass and loses itself in the sunset.

—Crowfoot's last words

Books by Curt Johnson

Novels
Hobbledehoy's Hero
Nobody's Perfect
Lace . . . . (novella)
The Morning Light
Song for Three Voices

Anthologies
Short Stories from the Literary Magazines
   (with Jarvis Thurston)
The Best Little Magazine Fiction: 1970
The Best Little Magazine Fiction: 1971
   (with Alvin Greenberg)
Writers in Revolt: The "Anvil" Anthology
   (with Jack Conroy)

Nonfiction
How to Restore Antique and Classic Cars
   (with George Uskali)
The Forbidden Writings of Lee Wallek
*Green Isle in the Sea: An Informal History of the
   Alternative Press, 1960-85* (ed. with Diane Kruchkow)
The Mafia Manager: A Guide to Success
Wicked City Chicago: From Kenna to Capone (with
   R. Craig Sautter)

Reference
Who's Who in Writers, Editors & Poets, biennial
   (ed. since 1985, with Frank Nipp)

Books by R. Craig Sautter

Expresslanes Through the Inevitable City (poetry)
Smart Schools, Smart Kids (with Sally Reed and E. B. Fiske)
*Floyd Dell: Essays and Reviews from "The Friday Literary
      Review," 1909-13*
Wicked City Chicago: From Kenna to Capone (with Curt Johnson)

CONTENTS

ILLUSTRATIONS

PREFACE

What Floyd Dell wrote in 1912 still holds true:

> One reason for knowing the history of Chicago is that the history of Chicago is the history of the Middle West. And the history of the Middle West is, to a larger extent than the school textbooks have ever permitted us to discover, the history of the nation.

This book was written as an attempt at self-education in the history of Chicago, and also as an attempt to find the parallels between individuals who achieve power, and the circumstances determining that kind of success. As to the latter aims, the principal discovery of the writer has been that there is no new thing under the sun. Additional discoveries can be found in the last chapter.

Wicked City is intended for the general reader. So far as I was able to learn, the facts given as facts are what is known or believed, and I embroidered them as little as necessary. The best surmise—my own or someone else's—is labeled as such. The Bibliography gives my sources, without which, of course, this book could not have been written, and I thank the authors of those materials for their labors. Mistakes and erroneous assumptions in the text are mine.

A reader of this book in typescript objected that there were instances of racism and sexism in it. Where I agreed, and could, I corrected those passages, but the people, events, and attitudes described in *Wicked City* existed and transpired over a period from roughly 1880 to 1931, a 50-year span that is already more than 60 years gone at its closest approach. Chicago—and the United States—was in that period what we would today term both sexist and racist. (Except for its sometime concealment, the situation has scarcely changed.) It is not possible to write about those people and events, I think, wholly in terms that some would today call "politically correct" (PC).

It should be remembered that goats don't have puppies; that is, there is a majuscule difference between recording and endorsing. Some passages or language in this book may still cause the PC reader to wince, but to write about 1880-1931 Chicago with an overprint of 1990s-sterilized language would, in my opinion, give offense to the truth of those times. Words have their consequences, of course, but these are minuscule, I think, compared to actions.

Moreover, in most neighborhoods of Chicago today—in Logan Square, to take one example—should you start talking about the badge of political correctness, some guy in a gold hat is liable to respond, "Bah-dges? We ain' got no bah-dges. We don' have to show you any steenkin' *bah-dges*!" or thereabouts. And he will be much closer to life as it is lived than the professor from Evanston or Hyde Park flashing a PC badge.

In many instances, politically correct 1990s language isn't going to help matters much, anyway. To use a perhaps far-fetched example (but perhaps not so far-fetched), if you are a homeless Ojibway eking out an existence in Chicago's Uptown—so low on the social scale of the city that you don't even know of, much less regret, Michael Jordan's retirement from basketball—I don't think you'd feel all that much better about your prospects in life were you to be told that General William Tecumseh Sherman's much-admired 1869 opinion had been revised to: "The only good Native American is a dead Native American."

And of course the question about political correctness that should always be asked is: Whose politics?

Perhaps it is best to settle for something close to the warning given by Mark Twain in the "Notice" he prefixed to his rambling, purposeless, apolitical story of two rafters on the Mississippi:

> Persons attempting to find a motive in this narrative will be prosecuted; persons attempting to find a moral in it will be banished; persons attempting to find a plot in it will be shot.

Persons attempting to find political correctness in *Wicked City*, then, will be sentenced to copy out the First Amendment 20 times. When they have done this, then they will be shot. If you are pro-PC in language but wish to avoid such a fate, you may substitute words of your own choosing for the author's ("lightning bug," say, if he used "lightning" and it offended you). No hard feelings on my part, I assure you.

In addition to the writers upon whose work I drew, I want to thank Jeanette Frances Esposito, a truly remarkable lady, for her indispensable help in writing about her father. For his editorial help and encouragement, I want to thank—as always (41 years of it now)—Frank Nipp. For their help on this project or over the years on others, I want to thank Bob Connelly, Betty Axelrod Fox, John Houlihan, Mark Johnson, Kathryn E. King, Diane Kruchkow, Randy Lane, Tom Legge, Vivien Leone, Florence Hamlish Levinsohn, Phyllis Magida, Christine Newman, Harlan Olafson, Joyce Olafson, Sally Reed, William F. Roemer, Jr., and Beth Winefield. I want also to thank Daniel J. Olas and Sharon Lee for their assistance. For his many valuable suggestions, I am indebted to Kenan Heise. I only wish Bud Dressell, Jeff Marks, Bob Wilson, Bill Bergstein, and Jack Conroy were still here to thank.

Most especially I want to express my appreciation to a tough cookie and lovely woman by name of Rochelle, who for 15 years never lost faith in this book—or, anyway, waited for it that long.

I would also like to thank my co-writer, R. Craig Sautter, who for this book has taken the career of Theodore Dreiser, with which I was familiar, and the subject of jazz, with which I was not, and given me insights into each.

Last of all, I want to thank Jim and Donna Benson, who have supported me in many ways—some of which they don't even know about, perhaps—for lo! these many years. Without their encouragement, this book could not have been accomplished.

—CLJ

Little Italy family, Chicago, 1890s

Charles Tyson Yerkes

TITAN

For Johnny Torrio, calculating gangster, the springboard to success in his chosen vocation was a monopoly on Chicago's vice. For Charles T. Yerkes, devious financier, the springboard was a monopoly on Chicago's traction. In their hard-edged, relentless pursuit of the dollar, Yerkes—the organizer of Chicago's street railways—and Torrio—the organizer of Chicago's underworld—were cut from the same cloth, though Torrio's swatch was soaked in blood. The two men had completely different personalities, but each, with similar methods, successfully wooed the same goddess: Wealth.

This is their story and also that of other men and women who lived when they did, and Chicago's story during that time, but it is chiefly Johnny Torrio's—and that of his protege, Al Capone. We begin with Charles Tyson Yerkes, however, by indirection to find direction out.

Like most early Chicagoans, he came from elsewhere—and he was devoted to the pursuit of wealth, and power, and beautiful women. Possession of the first, of course, was the edge.

Throughout his life, Charles Tyson Yerkes, Jr., garnered wealth for himself and his backers with seeming ease, making alliances where he had to—and could—and acquiring enemies along the way. And throughout his life he had an appreciative, freebooter's eye for women as well. Some years he paid lawyers as much as $150,000 to protect him from the consequences of his liaisons.

Born in Philadelphia the son of a Quaker bank president, he left school at 15 to work as an office boy in a grain-commission house. He started his own stock brokerage house at 22, at 25 went into banking, specializing in blue-chip bonds. At 34 he went to prison.

A panic on the Philadelphia Stock Exchange—induced by market confusion in the aftermath of the Chicago Fire of 1871—found him overextended and unable to deliver money he had received in the sale of City of Philadelphia securities.

1

Pardoned after serving seven months of a 33-month sentence, he speculated successfully during the Panic of 1873 and two years later, backed by the Philadelphia financiers William L. Elkins and P. A. B. Widener, he seized control of Philadelphia's Continental Passenger Railway Company, its stock soaring to $100 from $15 as a result. With his profits he paid off his criminal shortfall to the city, even though the City Council had already passed a resolution forgiving this debt.

When his first wife, mother of their six children, divorced him, he relocated west to Fargo, North Dakota, with a second wife, but small-town living did not suit the couple and in 1881, with just $40,000 in capital of his own, Yerkes came to Chicago.

Through his connections with Widener and Elkins of Phila-delphia, he quickly established credentials in Chicago's LaSalle Street financial community and, after some initial ventures in gas and electricity stocks, he took an option on the North Chicago Street Railway for $1,750,000. A year later he acquired the West Division Railway Company, his objective now clear: to gain a monopoly of all Chicago traction.

His principal supporters in achieving this objective, Widener and Elkins, were immensely wealthy Easterners who determined the growth of public transportation not only in Philadelphia and Chicago, but also in Baltimore, Washington, D.C., and Pittsburgh. Because of the scope of their successes, Widener and Elkins, together with New Yorkers Anthony C. Brady, Thomas F. Ryan, and William C. Whitney, were jointly known as the Traction Ring.

For a dozen years from 1886 on Yerkes devoted most of his considerable energies to his monopolistic objective, and during this time he irrevocably fixed the pattern of Chicago mass transit: Poor service always, and at rush hours fewer seats than passengers. As he explained: "It is the straphangers who pay the dividends."

With shrewdness, cunning, and force of personality; through continuous stock manipulation; and never without back-door political dealing and bribery, Yerkes constructed a purposely tangled maze of companies that facilitated his kind of large-scale financing. Nor was it happenstance that directly or indirectly he controlled most of the companies that contracted for his projects, nor that those companies' billings were astronomical. Nor that every contractor who did work for him kicked back part of the padded charges.

Yerkes could be disarmingly plainspoken. "The secret of success in my business," he once confessed, "is to buy up old junk, fix it up a little, and unload it upon some other fellows."

His business acumen not only enriched himself and others, it also brought about the change in Chicago transit from horse-drawn cars to cable cars, and by the mid-'90s he was introducing trolley systems to the city and building an elevated system, the downtown branch of which was known as "The Loop," after the smaller streetcar route that was there earlier.

From well-furnished second-floor offices at North Clark, corner of Division, in the North Chicago Street Railway Building (the rear portion of which was a horse and streetcar barn), Yerkes ultimately capitalized his many separate lines at nearly $120 million, three-fifths of which was "water." That is, 60 percent of the stock did not represent assets, nor was it backed by earning power. His pyramiding personal fortune was a textbook example of the axiom that when you have enough of the right kind of business acumen, it is not only the straphangers who can be made to pay dividends.

He built a magnificent Chicago mansion for himself and his wife and, in 1893, a million-dollar palace on New York's Fifth Avenue—as an Eastern retreat and seraglio. In his Chicago home his wife could amuse herself at a piano that cost $1,700 and from his mansion he was often taken to work in his $1,000 carriage. But he and his wife were never admitted to Chicago's highest society, and that rankled with the second Mrs. Yerkes. That did, and her husband's ever-roving eye. (When Yerkes paid $80,000 for a gold bedstead once owned by the King of Belgium, a Chicago Club member inquired, "What's it stuffed with, pubic hair?")

Even though the Yerkes were not acceptable to Mrs. Potter Palmer and the rest of Chicago's haut monde, this did not prevent Chicago's socially élite husbands from joining Yerkes in his predatory business forays whenever they could smell a profit, though meanwhile they kept close watch on the rascal's attentions to their wives and daughters.

But in 1896, out of long-nursed malice, they decided to force him into bankruptcy. The confrontation took place in the home of meatpacker Philip D. Armour.

Yerkes entered the Armour parlor almost jauntily, even though he knew that the merchants and bankers gathered there had decided to rid their city of him by calling in the loans for which he had pledged most of his holdings as collateral.

"Well, well, gentlemen," he said pleasantly, "this is the damned biggest collection of straw hats I ever saw at a funeral." He almost smiled. "Looks like I'm no good. Already busted, eh? A bad egg, a menace to conservative business and all that, eh?"

"Yes, Yerkes," someone replied, "that's it, you are."

"My loans will be called? My stock sold tomorrow?"

"That is right."

"All right, go ahead," he said quietly. "You want a selling of stock, you want the damnedest exhibition of stock selling you ever saw in your lives? Go ahead. But . . . if the Stock Exchange doesn't close down, *your* banks all will." And he turned and left.

In their eagerness to destroy a man they considered a dangerous pirate, the upright men of money had forgotten that he could retaliate with the aggregate strength of the Traction Ring and bring down all of LaSalle Street with himself. "Let Mr. Yerkes alone," counseled Marshall Field, one of those present, "and he will come to his own end."

Yerkes' business dealings were carried out by accepted Chicago methods—connivance with and corruption of the ruling politicians—though executed more boldly and sometimes more ruthlessly than his rivals. If a Yerkes' transit line needed a tunnel under the Chicago River, he sent word to the aldermen on his payroll in the City Council—the Grey Wolves—and somehow the city's interests were found to coincide with his own. On a smaller but still significant scale, if money had to be passed to jurors in a personal-injury suit against one of his lines, somehow a willing bailiff could always be found. (This was often necessary; accidents at railway crossings were frequent and the city had a far greater than normal population of cripples as a result.)

He bought favors wherever possible; his Chicago mansion, his collection of rare jewels, his racing stable, and his art collection (each painting selected in Europe by Yerkes himself and including works by Rembrandt, Rubens, Hals, Corot, Reynolds, Turner, Botticelli)—all this and more was assessed for tax purposes in Chicago at a grand total of $7,000. But as the *Chicago Times* editorialized, this was a benefit enjoyed by all the wealthy citizens of Chicago: "The Chicago system of taxation," it concluded, "is systemized crime against the poor. . . .The trusts, the corporations, the millionaires of Chicago pay taxes on less than one-tenth of the value of their enormous accumulations of wealth, while the small property owners are being taxed on from one-half to one-third of the value of their humble possessions."

Yerkes dealt through such politicians as Alderman John Powers of the Nineteenth Ward, "Little Mike" Ryan, "Foxy Ed" Cullerton, and occasionally the pair from the First Ward, "Bathhouse" John Coughlin and "Hinky Dink" Kenna, as well as U.S. Congressman William Lorimer, a onetime streetcar conductor who had become head of Cook County Republicans.

Chicago's newspapers continually attacked him and his business operations, their anti-Yerkes bias probably due as much to their owners' personal animus, and to the fact that Yerkes' connections were in the East, as to his methods, which were not that different from those of almost all of Chicago's other men of commerce. For his part, Yerkes returned the editors' dislike—they annoyed him—but only once was provoked to respond. Learning that certain revelations about his private life were to be printed, including innuendoes about his wife, he called on the editor-in-chief: "The publication of that article will hurt me. . . .I shall be down and out. There will be nothing for me to do. . . .I also inform you that if you publish it, I, myself, personally, will kill you for sure! Good morning." (The article never appeared.)

Because of the newspaper reports of his financial plunderings, Yerkes' reputation with the public was the worst of all Chicago's robber barons. In his 1894 book *If Christ Came to Chicago!* the crusading English journalist William T. Stead wrote: "As the man said when asked if the fox had stolen the goose, 'I would not like to say what I cannot prove, but I saw a good many feathers around his nose as he left the yard.' Mr. Yerkes' nose is well-feathered, indeed."

In addition to the allegiance of the Chicago City Council, Yerkes had also purchased that of the state legislature in Springfield, and in 1895 that body passed bills giving his 12 traction franchises renewals that would have permitted them use of the streets of Chicago without payment for the next 99 years—the "Eternal Monopoly" bills.

Illinois' beleaguered Governor John Peter Altgeld vetoed these bills despite Yerkes' offer of a half-million-dollar bribe to sign them—after which Yerkes said of Altgeld, sincerely, "I admire *that* man." His admiration, however, did not preclude his joining other Chicago financiers and industrialists, who for their part had been angered by Altgeld's pardon of three men convicted in the Haymarket Square case in '93 and his siding with the Pullman workers in their strike in '94, in seeing to it that Altgeld was branded in the public eye as an enemy of the commonwealth. Altgeld was not elected to a second term in 1897.

His successor, John R. Tanner, signed a bill offered by the legislature that authorized the Chicago City Council to extend Yerkes' franchises for 50 years with no payment to the city, but by now the powerful enemies Yerkes had accumulated in 17 Chicago years joined their opposition with that of the Municipal Voters League, one of the city's infrequent and almost always ineffectual reform movements, and he was forced to mount a highly expensive counterattack in an attempt to have a second 50-year bill passed after the first was defeated.

But despite this costly effort, and despite the philanthropies he made to buy public favor—an electrically lighted fountain for Lincoln Park, for example, and the world's largest refracting telescope (later installed at the Yerkes Observatory on Lake Geneva in Wisconsin) to the University of Chicago—the citizens rose against him.

The Municipal Voters League posted thousands of city corners with placards reading "YERKES THE BOODLER" in banner-size letters, the city's newspapers repeated and elaborated on this and other charges, ministers denounced him from their pulpits, and at mass meetings of the citizenry it was half-seriously proposed that he be hanged. ("Boodling" was the use of public money for private gain.)

Mayor Carter Harrison, Jr., then in his first of five terms, vowed he would "eat my fedora hat" before he would permit Yerkes to win. ("Tell me, Mr. Mayor, what do you want, anyhow?" "Mr. Yerkes, . . . there is not enough money on God's footstool to induce me to vary my position in the slightest degree.") When the second bill reached the Council, a mob carrying guns and rope nooses marched on City Hall to monitor the voting. The intimidated aldermen voted 40 to 23 against.

His plans defeated for good and all by this vote in 1898, Yerkes spoke a stirring farewell to his transit-line workers and in 1899 left Chicago after disposing of his personal holdings to Elkins and Widener for a sum rumored on LaSalle Street to be nearly $20 million.

From Chicago Yerkes moved on to New York and London, ending his career on an apparent peak of success in England, where he moved socially in the King's circle and headed the syndicate which dug the London Underground. "And this giant himself," the great American novelist Theodore Dreiser wrote of him, "rushing on to new struggles and new difficulties in an older land, forever suffering the goad of a restless heart—for him was no ultimate peace, no real understanding, but only hunger and thirst and wonder. Wealth, wealth, wealth! . . . Anew the old urgent thirst for life and only its partial quenchment. . . .The lives of two women wrecked, a score of victims despoiled. . . ."

Yerkes died, age 68, on December 29, 1905, in New York City, where he had been living alone and ill in hotels, estranged from his second wife because of his involvement with a married woman *and* her daughter. His fortune, which had been estimated at between $30 million and $70 million, was found to total only slightly more than $2 million, and most of this was dissipated in the litigation of his estate.

His name is now long forgotten but in his time—because of a decade-long portrayal of him by Chicago's journalists as *the* master boodler—Chicagoans blamed him for almost every misfortune their city suffered (as in the 1930s, with more justice, they were to blame Samuel Insull).

He cheated and stole from his fellow citizens but Charles Tyson Yerkes was still the least hypocritical of the early dynasts, and at odds with them for this and because of his open, reckless manipulation of capitalism's rules for overt conduct. ("Let us take the land anyway and apologize afterward," was his instruction in one transaction. A century earlier Frederick the Great had enunciated much the same rule of conduct: "Take possession first and negotiate afterward.")

In his honesty (by his code) and lack of principle (by conventional standards), Yerkes was the precursor of the gangsters who made Chicago their duchy in the next century. His piratical ruthlessness epitomized the fortune-making methods of Chicago's dynastic upperworld and foretold what its underworld's leaders—in their way—would be like; what any of the system's leaders had to be to prevail.

WHY NOT?

A gambler and a whore, probably. . . . Chances are good that the first male settler along the bogs and sloughs of the mud town named from the Ojibwa for wild onion—*checagou*—was a fugitive from the law, probably a gambler; and that its first woman settler was a whore. The annals do not record this, but the odds are. . . .

The annals do record that in the 17th century, long before a town sprang up, while the Jesuit missionary Jacques Marquette was preaching to the Indians, one Pierre "The Mole" Moreau was selling them firewater.

The annals also record that during the Civil War the city had 200 houses of prostitution, exclusive of the services available at the rear of its hundreds of saloons, that 2,000 soiled doves—or "gamahucher specialists," as they were also called—walked its downtown streets, and that a game at cards or dice or a sporting wager could be found in its every saloon or tavern.

Following the war, Rodger Plant's Under the Willow resort for gamblers, prostitutes, and criminals at Wells and Monroe had window-shades with gilt lettering asking citizens "WHY NOT?"—a question that Madame Lou Harper and other bawdy house madams such as Carrie Watson, Vic Shaw, Kate Anderson, Annie Stewart (who shot and killed a police constable for cheating her at cards—and was acquitted), Rose Lovejoy, Lizzie Allen, Effie Hankins, the Everleigh sisters, and hundreds more were to answer after their fashion for the next half century.

Essential to the workings of vice in Chicago were John "Bathhouse" Coughlin and Michael "Hinky Dink" Kenna, the First Ward's Democratic aldermen. (There were two aldermen to a ward at the time.) Prostitution was prohibited by law in Chicago but condoned by the authorities as a necessary evil, as it was in most other larger U.S. cities. When Chicago's segregated vice district, the Levee, moved south to make room for more legitimate businesses in the city's increasingly crowded downtown, the city legislators thoughtfully redistricted to bring the Levee

7

once more within the purview of the Bath and Hinky Dink.

From its earlier boundaries of Lake Michigan, the Chicago River, and 12th Street (today, Roosevelt Road), the First was doubled in size southward to 29th and, at its western limit of Canal Street, into a key-tab to 31st.

The original Levee—probably so named by nostalgic riverboat gamblers who frequented its dives—was only a few blocks square, stretching along Custom House Place from Polk to Harrison, but it gradually enlarged year by year. The new, south Levee ranged either side of the cobblestones of Wabash and Clark from 18th Street to 22nd. Chicago's Tenderloin (where the choicest cuts of graft were obtainable) was the nation's largest.

The slums of Little Italy in the Nineteenth Ward adjoined the First Ward, but the First itself boasted splendid Michigan Avenue mansions, fine hotels, restaurants, theaters, an opera company, a symphony orchestra, giant department stores, the Monadnock Building and the Masonic Temple, the city's financial temples on LaSalle Street, marble-pillared City Hall—and river wharves, Clark Street hovels, and the Levee dens themselves. The Levee's working population consisted of thousands of gamblers, bums, thugs, jackrollers, pimps (called "cadets"), madams, harlots, and thieves—including the hot-tempered pickpocket/saloonkeeper Mickey Finn, who would advertise and serve his namesake knock-out potion to unsuspecting patrons and then rob them in a back room, taking everything, including clothes and shoes.

In the Levee could be found debauchery to satisfy every man's heart's desire: faro joints, dice joints, policy stations, gyp auctions, arcades, hock shops, opium dens, peep shows, dance halls, plain and concert saloons, burlesque houses, and brothels to cater to every taste at rates scaled to every bill clip and coin purse. The Everleigh Club was at the luxury end of the scale, the cribs of Bed Bug Row (a dime or two bits a slommock) at the lowest, with houses such as Saratoga, Victoria, Sappho, Black May's, Silver Dollar, House of All Nations, The Library, Why Not? and dozens more in between, including that of Kitty Plant's (Rodger's daughter), where two ponies performed in circuses nightly.

A commission of concerned Chicagoans investigated Chicago's vice situation in 1910: it estimated that there were 27,300,000 paid-for couplings annually. (The entire city's population—man, woman, and child—was 2,185,283.) Gross income from prostitution was estimated at $30,000,000, with half of this going to politicians and police. More than 5,000 full-time prostitutes worked in Chicago and on weekends 10,000 more freelanced. (Simple economics: A girl made $6.00 a week for six days full-time in store or factory; Saturday night and Sunday morning in the Levee brought her four to five times that.)

Testifying before the commission, a small-time madam with just one employee related that her cottage averaged 200 customers a week. Accused of being a white slavedriver, she responded indignantly "When the girl is rushed, I help out."

At another session, a self-employed bawdy basket, middleaged and overweight, testified that nightly she accompanied 30 men to her third-floor room. "Why, that's terrible!" a woman commission member exclaimed. "Yes—those stairs are killing me" was the reply, giving to posterity a punchline for all occasions.

The investigating commission published its findings in a 311-page report. When other cities requested copies, the U.S. Post Office banned the volume from the mails as obscene.

From the myriad pleasure domes of the Levee, the personally circumspect, even puritanical, Kenna and Coughlin, acknowledged Lords of the Levee, exacted regular tribute. In addition to weekly payments based on ability to pay (that is, cash intake, but roughly as follows: small houses, $25 weekly; large houses, $50 to $100 weekly, plus $25 weekly if drinks were sold; poker and craps, $25 weekly per table), there was also a schedule of fees for legal work. For stopping an indictment of grand larceny against a panel house (wall panel slides open, arm emerges, hand removes valuables from clothes discarded by guest), the charge was $500; for pandering, $1,000; for harboring a girl, $2,000.

The Bath and the "Little Fellow," as Hinky Dink was also known, were able to provide protection because, through their control of the First Ward vote, they had men beholden to them in every city, county, state, and federal office, and they controlled the jobs of city workers as well, including inspectors and police—and because, as aldermen, they were in a position to grant reasonable favors to the respectable businessmen of the city.

Entrepreneurial aldermen could count on a routine take of $15,000 to $30,000 a year over and above the stipend of $3.00 per Council meeting they received from the city. Special votes purchased for non-routine matters brought anywhere from $8,000 to $100,000 each, depending upon their importance and the alderman's.

Coughlin and Kenna went along coolly and competently with most of the requests the financiers of Chicago made and were willing to pay for—zoning variances, permits, tax reductions, licenses, city services, connecting bridges, and such-like amenities—but they did not support Charles Yerkes' 50-year traction franchise bills. Not that they scrupled against profiting from a robber baron's difficulties, but rather, as Bathhouse explained to Mayor Harrison, they preferred to stick to the small stuff: "There's little risk and in the long run it pays a damned sight more."

Bathhouse John was big, bluff, goodhearted, outgoing, bumblingly voluble, and a bizarre dresser; besides scores of garishly colored waistcoats, for example, his wardrobe included a bathing suit of baby blue with heart's-blood polka dots. He published bad poetry about Chicago in the newspapers and in his public statements he seemed, at times, simple-minded. Once, in private, Mayor Harrison asked Kenna if Bathhouse was crazy or just full of dope. "No," Hinky Dink replied, "John isn't dotty and he ain't full of dope. To tell you the God's truth, Mr. Mayor, they ain't found a name for it yet."

Kenna was his partner's opposite—small, glum, quietly dressed, closemouthed, aloof, shrewd, and down-to-earth. Asked the meaning of the legend "In Vino Veritas" lettered above the mirror in the smaller of his two bars, he answered, "It means that when a man gets a snoot full he gives his right name." (After meeting him, the British writer H. G. Wells wrote, "Now, Alderman Kenna is a straight man, the sort of man one likes and trusts at sight, and he did not invent his profession. . . . Whenever you want to do things in Chicago, you must reckon carefully with him." Wells also said that he would "as soon go to live in a pen in a stockyard as into American politics.")

At Kenna's Workingman's Exchange on Clark Street, which had a 100-foot bar (two inches less than 100 feet, actually, but still the world's longest bar), patrons got "The Largest and Coolest Schooner of Beer in the City" (one pint, nine fluid ounces for five cents) and the best free lunch in town, no orchestra, no women, and no selling to minors. Here for more than 20 years the derelicts, hobos, and jobless of the First Ward ate and drank for a nickel. More, Kenna found jobs for the down-and-out and rescued them from trouble with the police.

He also told them how to vote, and in 40 years he never lost a primary or an election in the First Ward. He and the Bath compiled this record by marshaling the ward's Party workers on election day to chain-vote its railroad hands, stevedores, tramps, thugs, thieves, cadets, rounders, and any other warm bodies that might be available. The Democratic slogan in the First Ward on election day was "Vote early and often." The floaters were taken to a polling place and given genuine (purloined), already-marked ballots. These they deposited in the ballot box and the blank ballots they had received on entering the polling place were then turned in for a fee (50¢ or a dollar), to be marked and voted at a different polling place, whereupon the procedure was again repeated. The correctness of each ballot cast was thus ensured.

Above the Workingman's Exchange was the Alaska Hotel where the down-and-out or dead drunk could flop to sleep the night and waken in the morning to scrub the saloon floor below, polish brass, and shine schooners. Their reward was a dinner pail of pick-me-up known as "a rub of the brush" made from the slops of beer, wine, and liquor sold the night before. In usual times the Alaska could accommodate 300 men, but on election eve it made room for twice that many.

They were a seemingly unlikely pair, the Bath and the Little Fellow, to wield the power they did and for so long, but a highly effective and increasingly wealthy pair. For that matter, the City Council itself was a sometimes preposterous legislative body. Once, for example, Alderman Little Mike Ryan, during deliberations over a proposal that the city purchase six gondolas for its Lincoln Park lagoon, asked his colleagues, "Why waste the taxpayers' money . . .? Get a pair of them, and let nature take its course."

And year in, year out, election to election, there was always the haunting question of the honesty of the Council's elected members. As expressed by a colleague, Alderman Nathan Brewer, however, this question should have haunted no one. "There are only three aldermen in the entire 68," Brewer stated, "who are not able and willing to steal a red hot stove." The journalist William T. Stead wrote "We shall probably not err on the side of charity if we admit that there are ten Aldermen on the Council who have not sold their votes or received any corrupt consideration for voting away the patrimony of the people . . . but ten righteous Aldermen out of sixty-eight are not sufficient to save the City Hall from the reproach of being under the dominion of King Boodle." His concluding characterization of Council members was: "Swindlers and scoundrels sitting in the center of the whole machine and treating their duties and their trust as means by which they can fill their own pockets."

It was Hinky Dink Kenna who organized First Ward vice and elections—and the celebrated First Ward balls—and it was Bathhouse John Coughlin who, accompanied by two police officers, made morning inspection and supervisory rounds to see that all was as it should be with First Ward constituents.

To those who lingered in the streets in the Italian neighborhood around Polk and Clark, the strapping Coughlin would call out, "*Salute! Buon giorno!*" a greeting borrowed by him from "Big Jim" Colosimo, the collector for the "protective association" through which the Bath and Kenna carried out their responsibilities to the illicit commerce of the Levee.

Colosimo is the man who brought Johnny Torrio to Chicago, and Torrio brought Alphonse Capone.

George M. Pullman

Marshall Field

DYNASTS

Of a morning, the merchant prince Marshall Field liked to be driven to within a block of his giant, Corinthian-columned department store; there he would step down from his carriage and stroll leisurely the rest of the way, inspecting his emporium's display windows. "Give the lady what she wants" he once admonished a clerk, and this instruction became the establishment's watchword.

Field was a courteous, affable, courtly, serious, mild-looking, industrious man, a churchgoing Presbyterian with strikingly cold blue eyes. He arrived at his office promptly at 9:00, closed his desk promptly at 4:00.

FIELD, MARSHALL   (1835-1906). Beginning life as a Massachusetts farm boy, Field came to Chicago in 1856 to work as a clerk in a dry goods store at a salary of $400 a year, half of which he saved. A pioneer of new merchandising methods, he and Levi Z. Leiter bought Potter Palmer's store in 1865 and it became Marshall Field and Company. He donated substantial sums to the Field Columbian Museum (now Field Museum of Natural History) in the city in which he prospered.

In his first years in Chicago, Field worked 18 hours a day and knew the cost and price of every item his employer, Potter Palmer, offered. When he went into business for himself—with partners—he reduced his own hours but continued to pay close attention to detail, and he set up a rigid organization in the company, with clear lines of accountability. But even before he became established as the premier dry goods merchant and largest taxpayer in the country, he looked about for other ways of making money. While dry goods were the basis of his fortune, his ultimate immense wealth was realized through investments in bank stock and downtown Chicago real estate. (A saying of his day was that if you were smart enough to eat soup with a spoon, you were smart enough to get rich on land in Chicago. On the other hand, the emperor of U.S. banking, J. Pierpont Morgan, who knew the youthful

Field in Massachusetts, and stayed overnight with Field whenever he was in Chicago, once asked rhetorically if Field did not have "the keenest financial mind of any man in the country.")

Field's advice to those who wished to emulate his success was succinct: "Merchants who keep their business well in hand, sell for cash, and pay for goods at short time, taking advantage of all cash discounts, keep good habits, and pay strict attention to business rarely fail."

Field never praised his employees and he paid them low wages—clerks *and* partners—and never a cent more than he had agreed to pay them, no matter how well they performed. He did not keep partners long. His most capable and innovative associate, H. Gordon Selfridge, after completing an extensive and profitable program of improvements he had proposed in the retail operation, asked that the firm name be changed to Field, Selfridge and Company, a request that Field ignored. "If it is not done," Selfridge said, "I shall have to sever my connection with the house."

"Selfridge," Field replied to his most valued aide, "the connection is severed right at this instant."

At each year's end he held a dinner in his home for his partners to celebrate the past year's successes. Over after-dinner brandy each year he would make a simple, stark announcement to the assembled company of close associates: So-and-so—seated at his left down the table, perhaps—would not be with them to celebrate at the holidays next year. So-and-so had not measured up the past year and his services would no longer be required by Marshall Field and Company.

The English journalist William T. Stead observed that:

> Old residents in Chicago have told me how when each fresh department was added to Marshall Field's stores it was as if a cyclone had gone forth among the smaller houses which were in the same line of business. When Marshall Field opened any new department, say of cutlery or hardware or millinery, jewelry, etc., or what not, he would run it at cut rates so as to give him the command of the field, contenting himself with the profits of the other departments. Against such a power, so concentrated in turn against each detachment of the enemy, or the competitor, nothing could stand. . . . So it has come to pass that Chicago is honeycombed from end to end with elderly men who twenty years ago had businesses of their own in retail stores by which they expected to make a living of their own and to have a comfortable competence on which to retire in their old age. They reckoned without their Marshall Field, however. . . .

When Field was starting out on his own with Leiter, the reaper king Cyrus Hall McCormick had the opportunity to become a financial partner, but declined. McCormick was at heart a tinkerer, not a financier—though a great part of his own fortune, like Field's, came from investments, most of them in real estate. McCormick's expressed formula for achievement was not one easily imitated, if indeed it was decipherable; he observed that "indomitable perseverance in a business properly *understood* almost insures ultimate success."

McCORMICK, CYRUS HALL (1809-84). Born in Virginia, McCormick came to Chicago in 1845 with only $60. He established a factory to manufacture the mechanical reaper and within a few years was a millionaire. McCormick's philanthropies included Presbyterian Theological Seminary of the North West (now McCormick Theological Seminary).

The reaper not only made Cyrus Hall McCormick a millionaire; it also played a major part in the North's victory in the Civil War: its mechanical efficiency on the flat farm lands of the Middle West did the work of half a million men away in uniform. (It took three hours to gather a bushel of wheat by hand; ten minutes by reaper.)

A stout, ruddy, bearded man of great persistence, McCormick fought his many competitors with constant litigation, widespread advertising, yearly field days on which his reapers were pitted against other makes, easy credit, and by giving good service on a superior product that he supported with a money-back guarantee. Through the decade of the '70s he sold 10,000 reapers and binders a year—and in 1879 built a huge sandstone mansion at 675 Rush Street in Chicago, a home so mammoth that it contained a 200-seat private theater.

He was a stubborn and parsimonious millionaire, given to fits of long-lasting temper. When charged what he felt was an unjust $8.70 for excess luggage while traveling, he sued the railway and fought the suit in court after court for 18 years, finally winning in the Supreme Court, his wife and himself the only living parties to the original claim.

His favorite meal was hot mush and cold milk. When he took his family to dine elegantly at the Palmer House, he insisted on a special rate. (Potter Palmer gave it to him, noting that "75¢ does not pay me the actual cost of the dinners.") In his later years, crippled and stooped by rheumatism, he became more crotchety and would fire household servants on the spot if he felt they were impertinent. The traction titan Charles Yerkes was of the opinion that McCormick was "an insufferable prick."

McCormick's claim to being the sole inventor of the reaper was always open to question, even among members of his own family. But he instituted assembly procedures in his factory that foreshadowed mass production, his sales methods placed hundreds of thousands of reapers in fields where before the wheat had rotted, and he worked hard on improving farm machinery all of his life. He also worked his employees hard, including his brothers, and for low wages—and like all of Chicago's dynasts of America's Gilded Age was puzzled when the employees were not grateful, and angered when they tried to organize for more.

During the tense summer of 1877, when there were riots in the city—part of a nationwide strike effort by railroad workers protesting wage cuts—Marshall Field volunteered the use of his delivery wagons to transport policemen from one trouble area to the next. Three men were killed and eight wounded in a demonstration at a Burlington RR roundhouse, and the next day ten strike sympathizers were killed at the Halsted Street viaduct. Federal troops direct from the Indian Wars were marched in to restore order.

Albert R. Parsons, a blacklisted typesetter and brother of a famed Confederate general, had urged the strikers on. He was arrested and brought to the mayor's office and advised to leave town. "Why, those Board of Trade men," said the mayor, "would as soon hang you to a lamp post as not."

In 1878, Field, McCormick, and other churchgoing Board of Trade men subscribed secretly to a fund to furnish Gatling guns and uniforms to the Illinois National Guard. This was done, as McCormick's agent wrote in his report, to prepare for "what danger if any was to be anticipated from the communistic element in the city."

The next year, the meatpacker P. D. Armour broke a butchers' strike in his Packingtown plant by telling reporters, "We have two large houses in Kansas City and another in Milwaukee, where we can do this work cheap—for half the price we can here. Chicago can see this business killed if she likes." At the same time, Armour was working at a transaction in pork at the Board of Trade from which he netted a quick $2 million.

Armour's credo for commercial success was simple, if somewhat contradictory: (1) Pay your debts; (2) collect your debts; (3) never injure anyone; (4) never forgive anyone who injures you; (5) buy out or destroy any competitor whose products are better than your own.

Up at 5:00 and at work by 7:00, Armour employed 20,000 men across the country and owned 5,000 freight and refrigerator railroad cars, as well as storage plants, grain elevators, and a fleet of lake-going ships. He did a $100 million business a year in packing and owned stock in a number of rail lines to protect the shipping of livestock to his plants, but he delighted in trading on the commodities market, and made most of his fortune there.

On one of his forays into the Board of Trade pits he clashed with the eccentric son of one of Field's former partners who had determined he would corner the world market in wheat, cash and futures. For six months, using his father's money and credit, the young man bought—as Armour looked on and also bought, and then sold to the young man, Joseph Leiter, as the price of wheat continued up. In early December Armour was obligated to deliver three million bushels to Leiter in 30 days. The wheat was in Duluth, the waterways were frozen tight, and there was no storage space for it in Chicago, supposing it got there.

An Armour associate gave this account of what happened:

> "By working immense gangs of men in three shifts day and night, here on Goose Island in 28 days Armour built the largest grain elevator in the world; and meanwhile with ice crushers and tugs he broke the ice and kept open the Soo, brought down the grain and on Christmas Day delivered to young Leiter elevator receipts for all wheat sold by Armour to him."

The young man had by that time contracted for over 70 million bushels, sending the price of wheat so high that in Europe the poor could not afford bread. Armour continued to supply wheat, an avalanche of selling began, and the corner was broken. Young Leiter lost $2,500,000 of his father's money. Armour profited by the same sum.

A 250-pound, pugnacious-looking six-footer, chop-whiskered, overbearing, Armour professed the Congregationalist faith. A reporter once asked him why he did not retire, since he had made far more money than anyone would know what to do with. "Because I have no other interest in life but my business," he replied. ". . .I do not love the money; what I do love is the getting of it, the making it."

ARMOUR, PHILIP DANFORTH (1832-1901). A principal founder of Armour and Company, one of the world's largest meat-packing firms, Armour was born in Stockbridge, New York, and came to Chicago from Milwaukee in 1875. He donated money to found Armour Institute of Technology, which later with the Lewis Institute and, much later, the Institute of Design became Illinois Institute of Technology.

Armour's fortune had its basis in his meat-processing operations in Packingtown. The residents of Chicago's Packingtown—the tenement jungle that sprang up around the 345-acre Union stockyards—slaughtered and processed livestock by the tens of millions annually. Because of the low wages paid for this work, the children of Packingtown were often forced to scavenge food for the family from Packingtown's garbage dumps.

On the community's Whiskey Row were hundreds of ramshackle saloons, side by side, block after block; at Whiskey Point, another 200. (At the saloons, workers could get a free lunch if they bought a drink.) From the yards came the all-pervasive stench of livestock manure and sausage-making, and black, oily smoke belched ceaselessly from the plants' smokestacks. Bubbly Creek, an arm of the Chicago River at the southern boundary of the yards, was an open, stinking sewer.

The novelist Upton Sinclair described living conditions back of the yards: "There were four such flats in each building, and each of the four was a 'boarding house' for the occupancy of foreigners—Lithuanians, Poles, Slovaks, or Bohemians. . . . There would be an average of half a dozen boarders to each room—sometimes there were 13 or 14 to one room, 50 or 60 to a flat. . . . Very frequently a lodging house keeper would rent the same beds to double shifts of men." The rooms, said Sinclair, were "unthinkably filthy."

P. D. Armour walked to his LaSalle Street office from his home at 2115 South Prairie, an avenue of grandly ornate structures. Within a range of five blocks on Prairie Avenue, 40 members of Chicago's very exclusive Commercial Club had their homes. Two blocks north of the Armour home, at 1905 South Prairie, was the $100,000 residence of Marshall Field, and two blocks north of Field, at 1729 Prairie, was the $250,000 brownstone castle of George M. Pullman, the sleeper-car king.

Some mornings Field would alight from his carriage at Pullman's corner to walk the rest of the way to the Loop with his neighbor, who had offices in the Pullman Building at the southwest corner of Michigan and Adams. Pullman went to his offices dressed in silk hat, Prince Albert coat, striped trousers, and patent-leather shoes, a costume he wore with an air of pomposity and superiority toward his fellow men—though not toward Field, of course, who sat on the board of the Pullman Palace Car Company and held the largest block of its stock.

Pullman was fond of calling an underling into his office and beginning an interrogation by saying, "The most disappointing thing in my life is to be surrounded by men so incompetent and shortsighted."

Field, Armour, and Pullman would often lunch together at the "Millionaire's Table" of the Chicago Club. On the 5th of May, 1886, their conversation could only have been about the bombing the evening before at Haymarket Square. About these events Field is known to have said, "The police have acted nobly and deserve the highest commendations of all good citizens."

HAYMARKET BOMBING (May 4, 1886). During a meeting at Haymarket Square in Chicago, Illinois, to protest police tactics against strikers at the McCormick-Harvester plant, a bomb was thrown. In the ensuing disturbance, a patrolman and six workers were killed, 200 wounded. Eight anarchists were found guilty of inciting to murder. The resulting trial aroused strong anti-labor feelings nationally.

The year before, following a strike at the McCormick factory, Marshall Field had proposed to the Commercial Club that its members sponsor a U.S. military base near the city, since federal troops had proven their worth in keeping the peace during labor unrest. (Chicago's men of business at that time used the Pinkertons—a force of private detectives—to break unions.) The Commercial Club membership—limited to 60 men of "clear thinking and high ideals"—donated 632 acres of land on the north shore of Lake Michigan, and Fort Highwood, later renamed Fort Sheridan (by General Sheridan himself), was established in 1887. (A group in the rival Merchants' Club then gave land further north for the Great Lakes

Naval Training Station. Chicago was henceforth secure by land and lake.)

Now, following the Haymarket bombing, it was rumored that Field was holding secret conferences with other business leaders to make sure that the Haymarket leaders were hanged. It is certain that he went to City Hall and demanded that the mayor repress free speech in the interests of public safety. The mayor demurred, and Field responded, "Mr. Harrison, we represent great interests in Chicago."

At Haymarket Square, on Randolph Street between Desplaines and Halsted, 2,000 workers had gathered to protest the killing of six of their fellows by the police the previous afternoon. (McCormick plant guards did the killing; the workers had struck for increased wages and an eight-hour day.) Samuel Fielden, a teamster, was addressing the crowd in the rain when a column of 200 police arrived. Their commander ordered the crowd to disperse. The speaker replied, "We are peaceable," and climbed down from his stand and at that moment in the darkness a bomb was thrown, killing one officer and injuring 60 more. The police opened fire, wounding some of their own and killing at least 6 of the crowd and wounding possibly 200.

The person who actually threw the bomb was never found, but eight men were selected to be indicted for murder from the hundreds rounded up by the police. All were found guilty in a trial whose judge, Joseph E. Gary, enunciated the unique principle under which they were condemned: "Whoever advises murder is himself guilty of the murder that is committed pursuant to his advice."

Seven were sentenced to death by Judge Gary—two of whom had not been present at Haymarket Square the night of May 4th. (The eighth, whose crime was owning stock in a radical newspaper, was sentenced to 15 years in prison.) One of the seven sentenced to death was Albert Parsons, the blacklisted typesetter who had been told to leave town in 1877. Parsons, who had escaped Chicago after the bombing but returned of his own volition for the trial, charged that the jury had received $100,000 from Chicago millionaires. Then he made a declaration: "We plead for the little ones, we plead for the helpless, we plead for the oppressed, we seek redress for those who are wronged, we seek knowledge and intelligence for the ignorant, we seek liberty for the slave—we seek the welfare of every human being." The Illinois Supreme Court upheld the death sentences.

The governor was willing to commute the sentences, however, provided that the civic leaders of Chicago approved. Fifty upright men of commerce gathered for this extralegal life-and-death hearing and Marshall Field introduced his spokesman, the State's Attorney, who argued that those who roused the rabble deserved death. The 50 then cast their votes.

The man who had called the meeting for the governor and spoken for clemency said, "Afterwards many of the men present came around to see me singly and said they . . . would have been glad to join me . . ., but that in face of the opposition of powerful men like Marshall Field, they did not like to do so, as it might injure them in business, or socially."

On November 11, 1887, four of the seven were hanged, a fifth having already killed himself in his cell. On the gallows, Parsons cried out, "Let the voice of the people be heard!"

George M. Pullman did not intend that there should ever be labor problems in his model town of Pullman. There he was going to show that "such advantages and surroundings made better workmen by removing them from the feeling of discontent and desire for change which so generally characterizes the American workman, thus protecting the employer from the loss of time and money consequent upon intemperance, labor strikes and dissatisfaction which generally result from poverty and uncongenial home surroundings."

PULLMAN, GEORGE MORTIMER (1831-97). Born in Brocton, New York, Pullman came to Chicago in 1855. With a background as a cabinetmaker and construction engineer, he supervised the raising of many of Chicago's downtown buildings out of the mud, then developed the first railway sleeping car suitable for use in long-distance travel, then the dining car, then the parlor car. In 1867, he organized the Pullman Palace Car Company. In 1880, he built a factory south of Chicago and around it the model town of Pullman, Illinois.

Pullman was a perfectionist and a self-confessed humanitarian. "It was my father's chief desire," he said, "that I should do something for humanity." What he did was hire an architect named Beman to design a model town for his workers. (Beman asked that the community be named after himself. Pullman was willing. "We'll take," he said, "the last half of your name and the first half of mine. . . .") The town was situated 10 miles south of Chicago on 3,500 acres Pullman owned beside Lake Calumet, whose breezes, he was sure, "would produce 10 percent more work." Opposite the factory—whose tall clock tower on the red brick machine works dominated the town—were 1,800 brick homes of "Dutch" design, and an arcade with theater, public library, hotel named after Pullman's 13-year-old daughter Florence, retail shops and stores, a post office, a bank, two churches, and a school. There was a huge recreation field for the town's 9,000 dwellers—three-fourths of whom were foreign-born (Scotch, English, Irish, Dutch, Scandinavian, German)—and a park with a bandstand. Except that its ruler's sandstone castle was far to the north on Prairie Avenue, it was an archetypical medieval town, populated by serfs.

No beer gardens or saloons were allowed—though there was a private bar in the Florence Hotel for George M. Pullman's personal guests and visitors. Pullman would fire an employee who dropped a piece of paper in the street and failed to pick it up, and any tenant could be evicted from his home on 10 days' notice for any reason. No labor organizers were permitted within the town's limits; no improper books were permitted in the library or improper plays in the theater. "I shall try and benefit humanity where it is in my power to do so," Pullman avowed.

When the theater was formally opened he brought an invited audience of wealthy men and women out from Chicago in six lavish Pullman cars through a heavy snowstorm (the private train making one stop at 18th Street for the Pullmans, a second at 22nd Street for his Prairie Avenue guests) to hear a lecture on the sanctity of the model town of Pullman. "Everywhere is utility, order, cleanliness, and beauty," noted the lecturer. ". . . They must help children, women, and men to grow into sweeter, whiter, nobler, and more productive manhood."

Pullman revenues were scaled to return a 6 percent profit to the Pullman Palace Car Company; rents were 15 percent higher than equivalent housing in Chicago. Residents bought their gas and water from the company, which got it from Chicago, water at four cents per thousand gallons, sold at ten cents to tenants; gas was bought at 33 cents per thousand feet, sold to tenants at $2.25 per thousand feet. The annual fee for use of the public library was $3.00 for adults, $1.00 for children; only 250 families could afford to belong. Even the sewage from the workers' homes was put to profit by George M. Pullman; he had it pumped to his 140-acre farm, where it was spread on the fields as fertilizer. The Presbyterian minister who leased one of the town's two churches from the company ($300 a month) preached a sermon on George M. Pullman, using as his reverential text, and intending to be complimentary, "Thou has made him a little lower than the angels."

On paydays, money owed the Pullman Palace Car Company for rent, gas, water, provisions, and any other bills due was deducted from what the employee had earned. Heads of families, thus, sometimes got only three or four cents in cash on payday.

In 1893 Chicago held its World's Columbian Exposition to celebrate the 400th anniversary of Columbus' discovery of America. The 686-acre fairgrounds was called the "White City." The winter of the Exposition year in the White City, as the whole of Chicago was by then calling itself, was known as the "Black Winter." One of the nation's recurrent financial panics and depressions had struck and in Chicago people went hungry and died from the cold. Democratic political clubs organized soup kitchens in the winter of '93-'94, and City Hall sheltered 2,000 homeless each night. The 6,000 saloonkeepers of the city fed 60,000 hungry, jobless men a day, even when the men could not afford the nickel beer that was the customary prerequisite of a free lunch. This cost the saloonkeepers $18,000 a week.

The Pullman Palace Car Company laid off a third of its work

force and wages were cut 30 percent to 40 percent for the rest, though rents in Pullman City remained the same as before. On payday, some workers got nothing and others went into debt to the company. Over the winter workers would faint at their jobs from hunger. Finally, a delegation of 43 workers was sent to discuss these conditions with George M. Pullman.

He refused to meet with them, but fired them all and the next day evicted them from their homes.

A group of workers met in a nearby town and there organized a local branch of Eugene Victor Debs' new American Railway Union (ARU). Back in Pullman they recruited more members and demanded restoration of their former wages. When this demand was quickly refused, 3,000 of them went out on strike on May 11th.

George M. Pullman shut down his plant. "I don't know how long the strike will last," he said. "Financially it is a good thing for the stockholders."

PULLMAN STRIKE (May-August 1894). When the members of the American Railway Union struck in sympathy with Pullman Palace Car Company workers, it was established by the U.S. courts that the courts had the power to issue orders and injunctions in labor disputes affecting the public interest. President Grover Cleveland sent federal troops into Chicago to protect the mails, and following violence and extensive property damage, the courts ordered all strike activities stopped. When Eugene Debs, head of the union, refused, he was held in contempt of court and jailed.

By the end of the first week of the strike, 151 Pullman families were begging for food. The Democratic mayor of Chicago sent thousands of dollars of groceries to the town, paid for out of his own pocket. The strike chairman at Pullman said, "We do not expect the company to concede our demands. . . . We do know that we are working for less wages than will maintain ourselves and families in the necessaries of life and on that proposition we absolutely refuse to work any longer."

Twice Pullman declined to submit the dispute to arbitration—arbitration urged on him by many Chicago civic leaders and the mayors of 56 U.S. cities. The national Republican Party strategist Mark Hanna, hardly known for his pro-labor sentiments, raged that "a man who won't meet his own men halfway is a goddam fool!" Reminded that Pullman had built his workers a model town, Hanna replied, "Model shithouse! Go and live in Pullman and find out how much Pullman gets selling city water and gas . . . to those poor fools!"

The ARU sent Pullman a note pleading with him to meet with the strikers. He refused to open the note. By June 22nd, the ARU had lost its collective patience and delegates to its annual convention (held in Chicago), acting on instructions from their locals, voted unanimously to boycott all Pullman cars beginning on the 26th. "We shall absolutely insist on order," Debs promised.

Though no violence had as yet occurred, U.S. Attorney General Richard Olney—a founder of the General Managers' Association (GMA), a strikebreaking combine of 24 railway lines—obtained a court order July 2nd enjoining the union from interfering with the U.S. mails or interstate commerce. The railroads then attached unnecessary Pullman cars to trains so that ARU members would not handle them—and would thus technically be interfering with the mails and interstate commerce.

On July 2nd, also, over Illinois Governor Altgeld's protests, President Grover Cleveland ordered U.S. troops from Fort Sheridan marched into Chicago. On July 4th the troops pitched their tents around public buildings and along the lake front. Marshall Field, the Pullman Palace Car Company's largest stockholder, publicly expressed his thanks for their presence. When rioting began, railroad cars were overturned and burned—some by gangs of hoodlums hired by the GMA.

By the 9th, the troops had quelled the rioting, but 12 men had been killed and $685,000 worth of property had been destroyed. Without federal intervention, George M. Pullman might have been forced to arbitration.

Debs was indicted on the 10th and, leaderless and starving, the strikers capitulated. When late in August the Pullman plant reopened, new employees had to sign a pledge they would never join a union, and all ARU members rehired were required to surrender their union membership cards.

Many were not rehired—some 1,600—and Governor Altgeld journeyed to Pullman's town to ask George M. Pullman to permit them to return to their jobs. Pullman instructed a vice president to show the governor the wonders of the model town. Altgeld found to his horror that 6,000 people were without food, four-fifths of them women and children. Altgeld returned to Springfield and wrote Pullman asking him to cancel all rents from October 1 and to rehire his workers. Pullman refused to accept the letter until it was forced on him by a National Guard officer, then said he could do nothing.

After six months in prison, Eugene V. Debs was released; he came out a confirmed socialist. Governor Altgeld, who had pardoned the surviving Haymarket prisoners the year before because on investigation he had found that their jury was packed, their judge prejudiced, and that none of the accused had been shown to be guilty, finished out his term as governor knowing his political career was at an end.

George M. Pullman died three years after the strike at his model town. Because it was feared discharged workers might try to take revenge, he was buried beneath reinforced concrete and steel. He left a fortune of $21,000,000. (His bequests to his twin sons, however, were for only $3,000 a year, since "Neither has developed a sense of responsibility. . . .") Cyrus Hall McCormick had died a dozen and one years earlier, leaving a fortune of $10,000,000 to his wife and children. P. D. Armour died in 1901, four years after Pullman, leaving a fortune of $31,000,000, and Marshall Field in five years more, his death seemingly hastened by grief over the mysterious death of his son, who it was rumored had been killed either by his own hand or in scandalous circumstances.

When Field died in 1906, he left a fortune of $120,000,000, most of it to his two grandsons under terms that made it probable their shares would grow to $300,000,000 in their lifetimes. (The stock of the trust company that was to oversee the grandsons' wealth shot up six points on the day Fields' will was read.)

Of Field, the *New York Times* eulogized: "What a typically American career it is! . . . What is the use of talking about proletariats and classes in the face of such an object lesson that the hopes of American life are still as open as they ever were?" . . . True, but not as intended.

The early dynasts' huge fortunes were amassed at the expense of others, from the labors and, often, the misery of millions whose lives the men of great wealth owned but gave no slightest thought to, neither their joys nor their sorrows, nor their deaths after lives of grueling work and shattering disappointment.

The legacy of the dynasts was that the people of the Great Grey City began to dimly see this at last. The legacy was cynicism and bitterness. For half a century millions of men and their families lived in poverty, starved, perhaps turned to crime, but certainly died to build the fortunes of the dynasts. In less than half a century the city had progressed from "Give the lady what she wants" to "Let the voice of the people be heard!"—though how that voice was to be heard would perhaps not have been predicted by most social theorists.

When in 1886 Marshall Field told Chicago's mayor "We represent great interests in Chicago—," the mayor interrupted him. "Mr. Field," he said, "any poor man owning a single small cottage as his sole possession has the same interests in Chicago as its richest citizen."

But this was either the practiced cant of the politician or heroic wishful thinking. Every poor man in Chicago knew it was very far from so. It was clear to every poor man in Chicago that the rich were in alliance with the politicians of the city to exploit and defraud him; he knew this as well as he knew the pattern of calluses on his palms. He knew that he and his family lived on the crumbs from the tables of the wealthy. First the rich, then the politicians—and, finally, the gangsters, all of them looting the city and its citizens. This was the legacy of the dynasts of the Gilded Age.

THE BUILDERS

In 1795, after their defeat at the Battle of Fallen Timbers the year before (outnumbered two to one by "Mad Anthony" Wayne's troops), the Indians relinquished 25,000 square miles of their Midwest lands, including six square miles "at the mouth of the Chickago River emptying into the Southwest end of Lake Michigan where a fort formerly stood."

Their Miami chief, Little Turtle, said it was okay by him for the white man to take the six square miles at the mouth of the Chickago River; he didn't have any use for it. Out of the six square miles came Chicago's First Ward.

In 1812 most of the garrison of a new fort built there, Fort Dearborn, was massacred by Pottawatamies. Captain Billy Wells distinguished himself in the garrison's defense before he was seized, beheaded, and had his heart torn out and his blood drunk to acquire his bravery. (That could still happen to a person on Wells Street.)

Captain Wells had grown up in Little Turtle's family. The Indians were especially angry because the garrison, anticipating an attack, had dumped its whiskey stores in the river. The fort was burned.

The town of Chicago was incorporated out of the mud on both sides of the river 21 years later, August 4, 1833. Its area was one square mile; its population was about 300 people.

On September 28, 1833, 8,000 Ojibwa, Ottawa, and Pottawatamie Native Americans ceded 5 million acres east of the Mississippi to the white invaders for less than 2 cents an acre. In August of 1835, the Indians—inspired by the contents of hundreds of jugs of whiskey—held a final, howling, fearsome, ceremonial war dance along the river (beginning at Rush and Kinzie) and then left Chicago to journey west, as the treaty declared they must.

Land prices soared in early Chicago. A parcel outside the town limits bought for $5,500 in 1833 sold for $100,000 three years later. Forty acres within the limits bought for $450 in 1833 sold for $200,000 three years later. The fur trader Gurdon Hubbard (called Pa-pa-ma-ta-be, "Swift Walker," by his Pottawatamie friends) had picked up two lots at LaSalle and Lake for $66.66. In 1836 he sold them for $80,000. (Part of Hubbard's trail to Danville later became State Street, that great street.)

The population of Chicago increased to 4,000 by 1836. (The population of St. Louis in 1836 was 15,000; of Cincinnati, 40,000.) The land speculator's credo was "Buy by the acre, sell by the foot."

The town was incorporated as a city on March 4, 1837. Its first mayor was William Ogden, a land speculator, who brought to Chicago its first professional architect, John Mills Van Osdel, to design the Ogden family home in the center of a block bounded by Rush, Erie, and Ontario streets and North Wabash Avenue.

Most of early Chicago was barely above river level, which is why its residents called it Mud Town. Streets and the river itself were fouled with filth and refuse, and polluted water seeped into dwellings. The center of the city might as well have been a bog. In 1852 a cholera epidemic took 630 lives; in 1854, 1,424 lives from a population of 35,000. (By then, Cincinnati's population was 115,000; St. Louis's, 80,000.) It was decided that for reasons of health and growth the city's ground level would have to be raised 6 to 12 feet and sewers constructed. The humor had long before faded from signs in the streets saying "No Bottom Here" and "The Shortest Road to China."

Work began on the herculean project in 1856 and continued for almost two decades; 1,200 acres were raised. The river was dredged and mud and sand from its bottom was dumped on the streets, hand-packed, and graded. This effectively lowered business store fronts out of sight beneath the street level. Contractors elevated many of the buildings to the new level. Some buildings had their second stories converted to first floors. In seven weeks, the young engineer George M. Pullman, with 500 men turning 2,500 jackscrews half a turn (a quarter inch) at each whistle blast, raised the five-story Tremont House hotel at Lake and Dearborn eight feet without a single crack to its brick walls.

A *Harper's Magazine* reporter gave this description of the city at this time:

> It was one of the shabbiest and most unattractive cities of about a hundred thousand inhabitants anywhere to be found; but it had more than trebled its size in ten years; the streets were mud sloughs, the sidewalks were a series of stairs and more or less rotten planks, half the town was in process of elevation above the tadpole level, and a considerable part of it was on wheels—the moving house being about the only wheeled vehicle that could get around with any comfort to the passengers. The west side was a straggling shanty-town, the north side was a country village with two or three "aristocratic" houses occupying a square, the south side had not a handsome business building in it, nor a public edifice of any merit except a couple of churches, but there

were a few pleasant residences on Michigan Avenue fronting the encroaching lake, and on Wabash Avenue. Yet I am not sure that even then the exceedingly busy and excited traders and speculators did not feel that the town was more important than New York. For it had a great business. Aside from its real estate operations, its trade that year [1860] was set down at $97,000,000, embracing its dealing in produce, its wholesale supply business, and its manufacturing.

During the Civil War the city, having an Illinois lawyer as President, waxed intensely patriotic and sent 22,000 of its boys off to war, 3,000 to be killed, thousands more maimed. There is no record of any of its leading merchants enlisting, though many were of fighting age (Pullman, 29; Marshall Field, 26; Philip Armour, 29; Potter Palmer, 34). Very few of their class did in the country: a substitute could be bought for $300. The merchants did their bit for the North, however, selling to the Union Army all the goods and provisions it could pay for.

In Camp Douglas on the city's South Side, 6,129 Confederate prisoners of war died out of 20,000 held there. When Lincoln was assassinated, his body lay in its coffin at John Van Osdel's Court House and a quarter million Illinoisans shuffled past it to view their slain President and no one said a muttering word. Some found the silence eerie.

By 1870 Chicago's population was 300,000, nearly equal to that of St. Louis and surpassing Cincinnati's. Then came the Fire starting on Sunday, October 8, 1871, destroying half the city, leveling a swath four miles long and two-thirds of a mile wide, demolishing 18,000 buildings and homes (including all of the city's commercial structures), and leaving 100,000 homeless.

The father of a young Harriet Monroe drove her downtown after the Fire. She later wrote of that sad trip: "And everywhere around us, and northward as far as the eye could reach, nothing but charred ruins, with only the castellated water tower rising intact high above the ghostly devastation."

Ministers told their congregations the Fire was the visitation of the Lord aroused by the wickedness of the city. (Some estimates put 1 in 10 of its population working either as a bawd, a thief, or a gambler.) And, true, Joseph Medill of the *Tribune*, during the hard times of 1867, had forewarned Chicagoans they would have only themselves to blame for a catastrophe: "Too many are trying to live without labor and too many squander their earnings on intoxicating drinks, cigars, and amusements. . . ."

By 1880 the city had amazingly recovered to become the third largest city in the United States—population more than half a million—and by 1890 it had doubled this and was the second largest U.S. city—population 1,099,850. St. Louis was far behind with a population of only 451,770, and Cincinnati had more or less been left at the post with only 296,908. As Carl Sandburg was later to say, Chicago had become hog butcher to the world, stacker of wheat, player with railroads, and the nation's freight handler—a city of big shoulders.

In the years immediately following the Fire, it was said that Chicago architects and builders measured their work not by the number of jobs but by the mile. Within six weeks of the Fire in 1871, for instance, building began on 318 structures. In the two decades after the Fire $300 million was spent on construction. Land in the Loop soared to $900,000 a quarter acre; the barriers of Lake Michigan to the east, railroad tracks to the south, and the Chicago River to the north and west put this premium on Loop land.

The style that prevailed initially was that of the Paris of the Second Empire (an empire that had just been destroyed in the 1870 Franco-Prussian War). Van Osdel designed the Palmer House hotel in second Empire. The British writer Rudyard Kipling called it "a gilded and mirrored rabbit warren." It became Chicago's best-known hotel.

Second Empire was followed by Greek Revival and quasi-Victorian, and then Henry Ives Cobb designed a huge, dark, Gothic castle for Potter Palmer as a residence at 1350 on a street that was to be called Lake Shore Drive. The mansion cost Palmer $1 million. He had developed State Street for merchants after the Fire. The development he now promoted around his mansion established the north side as another place besides Prairie Avenue for Chicago's rich to live—the Gold Coast. The first large dance held in the castle's ballroom in 1885 was in effect acknowledgment of the 59-year-old Palmer's 36-year-old wife, Bertha, as leader of Chicago's high society.

William LeBaron Jenney's 1884 nine-story Home Insurance Building on the corner of LaSalle and Adams is considered the world's first iron-and-steel framed structure, and by some the first skyscraper. Its walls, partitions, floors, and roof were hung from its skeleton of metal girders, beams, and columns. Jenney had been a captain under Grant and Sherman in the Civil War. His office trained many of Chicago's architects, including Martin Roche and William Holabird, who as partners in 1899 built the 13-story Tacoma on the corner of LaSalle and Madison, the first skyscraper to have its skeleton riveted in place, which shortened construction time. Buildings were being built higher because land was so expensive—and because Elisha Graves Otis had invented the passenger elevator and it was finally being utilized.

The partnership of John Wellborn Root and Daniel Hudson Burnham built the 10-story Montauk Building on West Monroe in 1882. It was the first structure to rest on a floating foundation, a raft of steel and concrete. Its façade was free of the pillars and other ornamentation of earlier times. Its look was functional. It was the world's first building to be called a "skyscraper."

Burnham and Root's Monadnock Building on West Jackson Boulevard, opened in 1892. It was the last great building in the ages-old tradition of masonry construction. To support the weight of its 16 stories, its walls were seven feet thick at their base. It, too, had a plain façade free of curlicues and frills.

The firm of Burnham and Root built 216 houses, 39 office buildings (27 in Chicago's Loop, but including New York's Flatiron Building), 23 railroad stations, 16 apartment buildings, 10 hotels, 9 schools, 7 warehouses, 5 stores, and 3 hospitals. In 1885 they built the impressive Rookery (leading lawyers had their offices in it) on South LaSalle, and in 1892 the 22-story Masonic Temple on the corner of State and Randolph, the highest office building of its time.

Their Masonic Temple was considered a Chicago School structure. The firm of Adler and Sullivan was also a leader in this school. Dankmar Adler was born in Germany in 1844. He served under Sherman in the Civil War. From 1871-78, he and the carpenter-builder Edward Burling erected 100 structures in Chicago. Louis Henri Sullivan, born in 1856 in Boston, studied architecture there and then in Paris—in Paris after working six months for Jenney in Chicago in 1873. He went to work for Adler as a draftsman in 1879, became his partner in 1881. Their greatest commission together was the 10-story Auditorium on Michigan Avenue.

The Auditorium's cornerstone was laid in 1887; the building was completed in 1889. In it, Adler's self-taught and unmatched proficiency in acoustical engineering was displayed to its fullest, as was Sullivan's genius with the use of arches and decoration. The latter, expressing Sullivan's imaginative ornamental style, did much to create Art Nouveau, a style that dominated in the U.S. and Europe to the end of the century.

Italian artisans laid 25,000 square feet of marble mosaic in the building—50 million pieces. Total cost of the structure was more than $3 million. With a masterful engineering feat, Adler solved the problem of building the higher, heavier, 17-story tower without it settling more than the 10-story main building. He devised an ingenious mathematical formula enabling him to pile the necessary pig iron and brick in the lower stories of the tower as it was raised so that it, with its greater final weight of 15,000 tons, would settle equally with the main building. The ballast was progressively removed from the tower as it rose beyond 10 stories.

The Auditorium was the first new building in the whole world to be electrically lighted and the first to be air-conditioned. Its gold and ivory theater seated 4,237, with room for another 3,000 on special occasions, making it the largest opera house in the world. The stage could be extended to form the nation's largest ballroom. The theater's acoustics were so perfect that a normal conversation on stage could be heard in the top gallery, half a block away and five stories up. It had the 17-story tower, hotel accommodations of 400 rooms, 136 offices, shops, restaurants, banquet rooms, and a long and ornately decorated bar. It was elegantly simple, supremely functional, and exquisitely ornamented. (Today it is the campus of Roosevelt University and also houses the Auditorium Theater.)

The Chicago School consisted of the men who pioneered high-rise building, though the term was also applied to those who looked not to Europe and the past for inspiration but to nature and the spirit of democracy—at least according to its most articulate member, Sullivan:

> . . . when we know and feel that Nature is our friend, not our implacable enemy . . . then it may be proclaimed that we are on the high-road to a natural and satisfying art, an architecture that will soon become a fine art that will live because it will be of the people, for the people, and by the people.

One of the few Eastern architects whose work was unreservedly admired by the Chicago School was Henry Hobson Richardson, especially his red-stone Romanesque masterpiece, the Marshall Field Wholesale Store, built in 1885 on the block bounded by Adams, Quincy, Wells, and Franklin streets. It was starkly functional and also beautiful--characteristics of the best of Chicago School structures.

At the time of completion of the Auditorium, Chicago, New York, Washington, D.C., and St. Louis were competing to become the host city to the 1892 World's Columbian Exposition to commemorate and celebrate the 400th anniversary of Columbus' discovery of the New World. Chicago's bravado and bunkum, its proud boasts and grand exaggerations of its suitability for the task, led Charles A. Dana of the *New York Sun* to tell his readers to ignore "the nonsensical claims of that Windy City." (There you have it.) In 1890 Congress designated Chicago as the official site of the Exposition, or World's Fair as it was also called. The planners named John Root architect-in-chief of the fair and Daniel Burnham construction chief.

At the behest of Chicago's Mayor Harrison, Mike McDonald, the city's lord of gamblers and thieves, assembled the pickpockets, sharpers, gambling house proprietors, and con men of the metropolis and laid down strict rules for working the fair's visitors. Pickpockets, for example, would not be allowed at the entrances to the grounds; thus money would be preserved to be spent inside. McDonald also set forth the scale of protection fees: 40 percent to 60 percent or more on net, this (less McDonald's cut) to police and politicians. Trust everybody, but cut the cards.

In advance of the fair, Chicago businessmen raised the rent 300 percent on their property occupied by madams. Cost of protection was also raised. Mary Hastings, a First Ward madam (who boasted that no one could suggest an act too disgusting to be performed in her house—one of her boarders had a glass eye, presumably), complained that the price of bribery was getting out of hand. To which a police captain replied in hurt anger, "Why damn you! What are you made for but to be plundered?"

Six hundred and eighty-six acres of scrubby ground and swamp-land, Jackson Park, on the lake south of the Loop was selected as the fair's site by Root in consultation with the fair's landscape architect, the noted Frederick Law Olmsted (NYC's Central Park, Stanford University's campus). The architects set to work on their designs for the various main buildings and then, on January 11, 1891, the 41-year-old Root died of pneumonia. Burnham redoubled his own efforts. He first confirmed Root's appointments of five Chicago architects, including Adler and Sullivan, and five from the East for the fair's design board. With Burnham's approval the official architectural style of the fair was deemed to be Classical, not Chicago School. He told a stunned Sullivan that now was a time "to work up a big business, to handle big things, deal with big businessmen." Thus, a classical Roman idiom for the 19th-century Midwest fair.

The Exposition Ball—grand march led by Bertha Honoré Palmer to the music of John Philip Sousa's band—was held on the night of October 20, 1892, and on October 21 Harriet Monroe's "Columbian Ode" was read to the Vice President of the United States, governors, ambassadors, other dignitaries, and the 500 artists of the World's Columbian Exposition. Miss Monroe—a poet and writer and the late John Wellborn Root's sister-in-law—had vexed the fair's planners by demanding and receiving $1,000 for her ode since, as she pointed out, other contributors to the fair were being paid for their labors; why not a poet?

Then, when the *New York World* printed her ode on its front page, she sued the newspaper for theft of literary property, another impertinent and unprecedented action. She won in court: $5,000, plus lawyers' fees and court costs. She would have sold NY rights to the *World* for $200.

Ten thousand workers labored to complete what was coming to be called the White City (whitewashed lath and plaster), with the low total cost for grounds and buildings estimated at $20 million, the high at $40 million. When it opened on May 31, 1893, the tiny White City used three times as much electricity as all the rest of Chicago. It was a lagoon-studded dream of Rome—and a few miles away were the hotels of Pack-ingtown and the flimsy tenements of Little Italy. (And it was truly a White City. Blacks were excluded totally from the work force, and eating and restroom facilities were provided for them only at the Haiti Building.)

On opening day, Bertha Honoré Palmer, whose husband had given $200,000 toward erecting the Woman's Building—this edifice to house a display of the achievements of women had been his wife's inspiration—guided a delegation through the structure (designed by a 21-year-old Boston architect, Sophia Hayden, with murals by Mary Cassatt) and spoke briefly, mentioning the abuses and injustices suffered by women, a state of affairs she said that with other women, including her Chicago friends Jane Addams of Hull House and Frances Willard of the Women's Christian Temperance Union, she hoped to live long enough to see corrected. She began her talk by saying "Even more important than the discovery of Columbus, which we are gathered together to celebrate, is the fact that the [government] has just discovered women." She spoke of the necessity for the acknowledgment of women's rights and deplored women's exploitation and forced dependence. She concluded with, "We now dedicate our Woman's Building to an elevated womanhood, and we know that by doing so we shall best serve the cause of humanity."

The Woman's Building was Sophia Hayden's first commission. It was also her last. The first woman to receive a degree in architecture from the Massachusetts Institute of Technology, she lived another 60 years but never got another chance to practice her profession, that is, was never again asked to build a building. Burnham at first expressed doubts that a young woman architect could function well on a construction site, but after meeting Hayden he said, "She could soon be at the head of a lucrative business."

Hayden and Mrs. Palmer disagreed over use of the building's interior, however, and Mrs. Palmer transferred artistic control of it to a woman who listened more closely to her wishes. In appealing her case to Burnham, Sophia Hayden suffered a nervous breakdown and had to enter a rest home.

She appeared at the dedication of the building opening day, however. On one wall of her Woman's Building was a magnificent Cassatt mural titled "Modern Woman." The wall beneath it carried the two-word inscription: "Sophia Hayden."

At a meeting of the American Historical Association held at the fair, a professor from the University of Wisconsin, Frederick Jackson Turner, read what came to be recognized as one of the most influential papers ever given in his field; its title was "The Significance of the Frontier in American History." Turner's thesis was that the presence of the frontier in America had generated a new and unique kind of energy—"And we have now exhausted the last American frontier."

Awed by the mechanical marvels displayed at the fair, the historian Henry Adams wrote: "Chicago asked in 1893 for the first time the question whether the American people knew where they were driving." Inspired by the White City, the children's writer L. Frank Baum transformed it into the Emerald City at the end of the Yellow Brick Road in the Land of Oz.

Mrs. Palmer acted as hostess for visiting dignitaries during the exposition. When Eulalia, daughter of King Alfonso of Spain, came to Chicago to celebrate the 400th anniversary of Columbus' discovery made on behalf of her royal forebears, Mrs. Palmer had a suite expressly decorated for her at the Palmer House, and arranged a grand reception for the Infanta at the Palmer mansion. When the royal personage was called for at the Palmer House, however, she asked the emissary, "Your Mrs. Palmer—is she the innkeeper's wife?" The Infanta, it must be said, had been drinking.

But when she was told that this was true, in a manner of speaking, Princess Eulalia said she could not possibly go to such a person's home. She was finally persuaded to go, arrived very late, behaved boorishly, and left early and very rudely. Mrs. Palmer, outwardly unruffled, urged her 200 guests to continue to enjoy themselves. She did not comment on the Infanta's behavior, then or ever. Her husband was enraged.

Finley Peter Dunne, who wrote for the Chicago *Evening Post*, would tell his readers about the bartender Mr. Dooley. Mr. Dooley understood the Infanta's position:

> "Aristocracy, Hinnisy, is like real estate, a matther iv location. I'm aristocracy to th' poor O'Briens back in th' alley, th' brewery agent's aristocracy to me, his boss is aristocracy to him, an' so it goes, up to the Czar of Rooshia. . . . I don't want ye iver to speak to me whin ye get rich, Hinnissy." "I won't," said Mr. Hennessy.

In addition to its main exposition buildings with their 160,000 exhibits from all over the world, the fair had a Midway Plaisance that ran between 59th and 60th streets to Washington Park. Here could be found a giant, 2,100-ton Ferris Wheel (the first), named after its Illinois inventor. During the Exposition, 1.5 million rides were sold on it at the high price of 50¢ a ride. There were also the first motion picture show, alligators, camels, a chamber of horrors, Wild West marksmen, the hootchy-cootch belly dancer Little Egypt, and much, much more. Some of the largest crowds queued up before the beer tent; it featured a new German beer, Chicago's own Berghoff. Twenty-seven million people visited the fair before it closed on October 31, a figure approaching half the U.S. population of 63 million.

With all it had, what the fair did not have was Chicago School architecture, with the exception of Sullivan's Transportation Building. With its "Golden Doorway" of five arches, the Transportation Building generated more interest than any of the other main buildings. It looked like a gorgeous enclosure for exhibits—trains and cars—which is what it was, not the Roman senate chambers.

Almost 30 years after the fair, Sullivan gave his opinion of the Exposition's use of the Classical Style:

Thus architecture died in the land of the free and the home of the brave—in a land declaring democracy, inventiveness, unique, daring enterprise and progress. Thus ever works the pallid academic mind, denying the real, exalting the fictitious and false. The damage wrought by the World's Fair will last for half a century from its date, if not longer.

In 1899 Thorstein Veblen had put much the same thought more economically: "The office of the leisure class in social evolution is to retard the movement and conserve what is obsolescent."

A young Frank Lloyd Wright worked on the drawings for the Transportation Building, one of his last jobs for the firm of Adler and Sullivan. Born in 1867, Wright studied engineering for a year at the University of Wisconsin, then pawned some of his father's books for fare and set out for Chicago. Twenty years old, he first worked as a draftsman in the city for $8 a week. When he heard that Adler and Sullivan needed draftsmen for their Auditorium project, he went to Louis Sullivan and showed him his drawings. Sullivan assumed they'd been traced. When Wright assured him they were original and Sullivan seemed impressed, Wright asked for a job at $25 a week, and got it.

Within a year Wright was given his own office, began to design dwellings for the firm, and became Sullivan's chief assistant. He was the sole architect, with Sullivan's supervision, for the $25,000 Charnley House at 1365 Astor Street, erected in 1891. The decoration was Sullivanesque.

To pay for a house he had designed and built in Oak Park for his own growing family, Wright accepted several dwelling commissions on his own—three by his own admission, probably six or more. He had a five-year contract with the firm which prohibited such outside work. When Sullivan learned of it in May 1893, he called Wright into his office. Sullivan's Irish was up and the association ended. The two men did not speak to each other for more than 15 years.

The World Exposition's overseer, Daniel Burnham, in 1895 began the project for which he would be longest remembered—his master plan for "The City Beautiful," a vast undertaking that would do for Chicago what he had done for the fair: bring order to it. His dream envisioned a city with broad new thoroughfares through its crowded sections, a civic center of grand plazas, triumphal arches, and public buildings on a gigantic scale near the lakeshore, galleries, museums, theaters, parkways all along the lake front, industrial zones, a comprehensive, citywide park system, a consolidation of all railroads into one yard with just two terminals, forest preserves to the west, outer-city highway circuits, and much else. He may or may not have said, "Make no little plans; they have no magic to stir men's blood . . .," but in promoting his plan to businessmen he did say, "In city planning there is no limit to be fixed."

34

By 1907 he had gotten the members of the Chicago Commercial Club to back his ideas and in 1909, after almost 15 years of arduous research and promotion, Burnham formally presented "The Chicago Plan" to the city. Parts of it have been carried out; other parts remain proposals. Possibly the only factor Burnham failed to provide for in his plan was the great mass of the people of Chicago. When, for example, a broad new thoroughfare is put through a crowded section of the city, the people who live there are dispossessed. Perhaps the plan would have worked well in classical Rome or Second Empire Paris, but at the time of its presentation in Chicago, it was objected by many that it was in reality a scheme to tax the poor for improvements desired by the rich.

What is sometimes forgotten when discussing Chicago's great 19th-century architectural accomplishments (most now razed, many of their sites now parking lots) is that most of the city's population did not live or work in those structures. They couldn't afford to. Life was hard for most of Chicago's people—as it is for most of the world's people throughout history—even for those considered well off by the poorest.

Mr. Dooley in 1898 told of a contractor who worked for the Sanitary District. (Established in 1889 to deal with the city's waste, the District had the flow of the Chicago River reversed so that Lake Michigan flowed into it, shoving Chicago's sewage toward St. Louis.) Dooley's parable is worthy of Sartre or Camus ("drift" is sand, gravel, clay and boulders left by ice age glaciers):

> ... He thought he was biddin' on soft mud, but he sthruck nawthin' but th' dhrift. But he kept pluggin' away. "'Twill soften later," he says. Th' ingineers tol' him he was a fool. Twas dhrift all th' way through. He rayfused to listen. He knew he'd come to th' mud th' nex' day or th' nex' so he wint on an' fin'lly he got through an' made a good, clane job iv it. He looked back on his wurruk an' says he: "I knowed it was dhrift all th' time, but if I'd let mesilf think that what was ahead was as har-rd as what was behind I'd thrun up th' job an' broke me con- thract," he says. .... So it is with us. We've all taken a conthract to dig through th' glacial dhrift. We know its glacial dhrift. We know its glacial dhrift to th' ind, but we make oursilves think 'twill come aisy wan iv these days. So we go on, with pick an' shovel, till th' wurruk is done an' we lay it down gladly.

Dooley's contractor did not live in a mansion on Prairie Avenue or the Gold Coast, or go to work in the splendid skyscrapers of the Loop. He lived in Bridgeport in a modest home, raising a family, and went to work in a ditch. And he was, comparatively, well off.

The poor of Chicago lived and worked in slums. They were meant to live at the subsistence level because they would then be more likely to be a tractable, captive work force. The shanties and tenements of Greek Town and Little Italy and Packingtown were built to *be* slums and the shifting mix of nationalities that lived in these enclaves was meant by their landlords to *be* slumdwellers. In fact, George M. Pullman's model town had a section built specifically as a slum for those of his employees who did not earn enough to rent better housing.

Burnham's plan was not devised for the benefit of slumdwellers, much as he may have liked to think it was, but for the cliffdwellers of the city and their rich cousins on the Gold Coast, its white-collar workers and its silk stockings. . . . All his life Burnham had wanted to become a millionaire.

In 1894 the firm of Adler and Sullivan completed the Chicago Stock Exchange, a 13-story skyscraper on the corner of LaSalle and Washington. It had a powerful façade, but its special glory was Sullivan's designs and ornamentation for the ironwork in the elevators, stairwells, and lobby. Louis Sullivan could wave his pencil and turn a doorknob or kickplate into a masterwork of Art Nouveau. Nor did his filigree ever violate the structural integrity of a building.

The panic of 1893 brought on a nationwide depression that of course affected the architectural profession. In 1890 Adler and Sullivan had built the 10-story Wainwright Building in St. Louis, a major expression of their solution to creating skyscrapers, and in 1895 they completed the 12-story Guaranty Building in Buffalo, New York. Nationally and internationally they were famous as a team, but in 1894 their commissions did not cover expenses and in 1895 no new commissions came into the office at all. To his partner's surprise, Dankmar Adler quit the architectural profession in mid-1895 and went to work at a large salary as sales manager for an elevator company. After 16 years of working with Adler, Sullivan was alone. He felt betrayed.

Frank Lloyd Wright, another traitor, was building innovative houses throughout the Midwest—"prairie houses" designed to merge easily with the heartland's landscape. This was in accordance with the aesthetic convictions taught him by Sullivan: True architecture comes from natural forms, from the environment in which it stands.

Wright called his Prairie Style "a city man's country house on the prairie." By 1910 he had designed 60 of them in Illinois alone, many in the Chicago suburbs, especially Oak Park and River Forest. The prairie house's horizontal lines hug the ground. It has widely projecting eaves (just as had Sullivan's Transportation Building), and interior spaces designed on a flowing, open plan that often converged on a hearth.

In public architecture Wright in 1904 designed the landmark Unity Temple for Oak Park. It had a square sanctuary for worship and a fellowship hall with kitchen, sewing room, and classrooms joined to but still isolated from the sanctuary. The membership could not afford to build in stone so Wright used reinforced concrete, a relatively new material then, for walls, roof slab, and ornament, together with stained glass and wood. The temple was noble and solid, "For the worship of God and the service of man" (Wright's father was a Unitarian minister).

In 1913 he designed an indoor-outdoor pleasure palace near the University of Chicago on the South Side, the Midway Gardens. It combined an open-air café, a band shell, and a large winter garden. This was Frank Lloyd Wright's dance hall, and it had Cubist sculptures among its decorative features.

Wright lived on through a private life tinged with scandal and scarred more than once by tragedy, and a professional life that saw him become in his lifetime an American artistic deity. In 1956 at the age of 89 he brought plans to Chicago that had to be displayed on a 26-foot-tall canvas. "This is The Illinois, gentlemen," he said to reporters. "The Illinois will be one mile high, contain 528 stories and have an occupancy of 100,000 people and space for parking 15,000 cars and 100 helicopters. In it will be consolidated all government offices now scattered around Chicago." . . . Don't laugh—it could happen yet.

In 1959 he died in his sleep, age 92. The year before, the membership of the American Institute of Architects had ranked him as "the greatest American architect of all time" and listed his Robie House and Falling Water homes as among the 10 "all-time best" works of American architecture.

When Louis Sullivan found himself alone (as he himself termed it in his *Who's Who in America* sketch) he was at the height of his powers. In 1897 he completed the 13-story Bayard Building in New York City. It was said that it was his favorite skyscraper. Certainly it had the most elaborate exterior decoration of any of his tall structures. But after the Bayard Building he had only one more major commission, the Schlesinger and Mayer Department Store (now Carson Pirie Scott), a classic of modern commercial design and his last important Chicago work. It was begun in 1899, completed in 1904. After it, his larger commissions came chiefly from small-town banks: Owatonna, Minnesota (1906), Cedar Rapids, Iowa (1911), Grinnell, Iowa, and West Lafayette, Indiana (1914), Sidney, Ohio (1917), Columbus, Wisconsin (1919), each a Sullivan lapidary gem but too few in number to keep him either busy or solvent. He was stubborn and dogmatic and he would not compromise his principles to gain a client. Tastes were changing, too; his skills at decoration and ornament were not in demand.

When he was not drinking more than was good for him, he wrote about his life and beliefs: *Kindergarten Chats*, a series of articles, at the beginning of the quarter-century of drought, and *The Autobiography of an Idea* at its close.

He married in 1899 at the age of 43. The bride was 20. She left him in 1909. About the same time, he reconciled with Wright.

"I am in excellent health," he wrote in 1917, "but the bottom has dropped out—the future is blank." In 1918 he left the Auditorium offices in which he had worked and created for almost 30 years for offices at 431 South Wabash, rent $50 a month. He wrote to Wright: "I simply have to 'lay to' every once in a while from sheer exhaustion due to too much corroding anxiety. . . ." Wright had sent him a check to meet his office and hotel rents. So dire was Sullivan's situation that he tried to land a job with the post office, but failed.

He tried to sell off his last possessions. Wright sent another check but not in time to prevent Sullivan's landlord from twice locking him out of his office. He moved to the Cliff Dwellers, a literary club's gathering place, where they gave him free space. He wanted to go with Wright to Japan and work with him on Wright's Imperial Hotel commission, but Wright did not ask him.

His fees for the Farmer's and Merchant's Bank in Columbus, Wisconsin, enabled him to take an office again, but it was located far south of the Loop. A European school of architecture almost hired him to be its head, but that fell through, as did a number of possible commissions. His only work was designing a pedestal for a statue and a few remodeling jobs. He wrote to Wright in Japan, "I am in a very serious situation; indeed it is now a sheer matter of food and shelter." Wright sent him a check.

In 1923 he wrote an article for *The Architectural Record* on the competition for the new *Chicago Tribune* building. He called the Gothic Revival winner a "dying idea," the second-place design of Eliel Saarinen "resonant and rich, ringing amidst the wealth and joy of life"—opinions concurred in by almost all later critics. He wrote a second article for the *Record* on Wright's Imperial Hotel in Tokyo. He called it "the high water mark thus far attained by any modern architect. Superbly beautiful it stands, a noble prophecy."

He was suffering from dilation of the heart and in January of 1924 he put himself under the care of a doctor who lived within walking distance of his lodgings, a hall bedroom at the Hotel Warner, 29th and Cottage Grove. Overindulgence in strong coffee throughout his adult life and having to lay to with a bottle too often had so shortened his breath that he had to pause to catch it after stepping up from street level to the sidewalk. By the end of March he was under the care of a nurse.

He died, age 67, in his sleep, destitute and with no heirs, on April 11, 1924—just at the time the wooden overcoats of the gangsters came into fashion in Chicago and LaSalle Street discovered that stock market speculation was the royal road to wealth. In its obituary the *New York Times* called him "The dean of American architects," but in human terms he had fallen about as far as a man could from the heights he'd attained. The one thing he hadn't lost was his integrity.

In the 500 years since Columbus discovered the New World,

there have been only two American architectural geniuses: Louis Henri Sullivan and Frank Lloyd Wright, and to the very end of a long life Wright never referred to Sullivan except as his *"lieber Meister."*

To appreciate the grandeur, the elegance, the simple stateliness, and the beauty of Sullivan's work, it is not necessary to search out one of his still-standing monumental buildings. It is only necessary to go to Chicago's Graceland Cemetery and view the small Carrie Eliza Getty Tomb there, which he designed in 1890.

Form ever follows function.

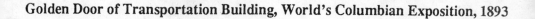

Golden Door of Transportation Building, World's Columbian Exposition, 1893

Immigrant Italian railroad workers, Butte, Montana, 1904, above. The boxcars were living quarters from early spring to late fall. Below, immigrant Italians in Chicago *taverna*

GUAPPO

Giuseppi Esposito—Chicago's "Diamond Joe" of its Roaring Twenties, its "King of the Valley"—relished the wearing of pure crystalline carbon: diamond rings, diamond stickpins, diamond shirt studs, and a belt with his initials "J. E." bejeweled in the buckle. He called the diamond on his stickpin "the moon"; that on his finger, "the sun." A display of diamonds, he believed, showed the stranger what kind of man you were. In this he was like his countryman *compare* in Chicago's under/overworld, Big Jim Colosimo.

As the Valley's unofficial mayor, Diamond Joe—or "Dimey" or "Don Peppino," as he was also called—accepted his place of leadership in Chicago's Little Italy as his due, guarded it, enjoyed its privileges, helped his countrymen through it, and was proud he had it—*Grazie a dio*. In his later years, he was a portly, affable man, dark and forceful, a dispenser of favors and money, a quick-to-laugh, playful man, a man of rough charm yet stubborn and easy to anger. His style appealed to his countrymen.

He knew the people to know in his world and used them—Big Jim Colosimo, John "The Fox" Torrio, Alphonse Caponi, the Terrible Gennas—as they used him. There is an understanding in such matters: you do favors and carry out certain undertakings for others and, in return, you have their backing. Quid pro quo.

Giuseppi Giachino Esposito was born April 28, 1872, the second of three children, in Acerra, a village in the Campania region of Italy 7 miles east of the great bay of Naples, 120 miles below Rome, 25 miles above Salerno, with *Monte Vesuvio* looming midway between the village and Salerno. Rebuilt about 217 B.C. after being destroyed by Hannibal in the Second Punic War, *Acerrae* (as it was called by the Romans) two millennia later was a small agricultural village where Giuseppi's father, Giachino, made a living for the family by cultivating mulberry trees. He fed the leaves to domesticated silkworms, steam-killing the worms at the

41

chrysalis stage, unwinding the cocoon filaments, and twisting them to produce a yarn. This cottage industry had been introduced to the Campania a century before but it had done little to alleviate the chronic poverty of the region.

At the time Giuseppi Esposito was born the south of Italy was still a backward, almost feudal society. Ninety-nine percent of its people were landless, at least three-fourths were illiterate. A tradition of despotic rule, conspiracies, and brutal seizures of power remained strong in the region, dating back to the Middle Ages when the *signori* and their *condottieri*—for-hire professional soldiers—were the law and their power was limited only by the possibility of provoking their subjects to revolt.

Sometimes called the most mysterious city in Europe, called by southern Italians the City of Seven Wonders, and situated on one of the most beautiful bays in the world, Naples (*Napoli*) was the intellectual leader and financial capital of the south. With almost half a million inhabitants it was also the largest city in the kingdom, but its slums, surrounding villages such as Acerra, and rural districts were afflicted with poverty, disorder, brigandage, and violence. Just seven years before Giuseppi's birth, 5,000 peasants of the region were slaughtered during an abortive revolt against their masters.

Even those who did own a small plot of land could not make a living from it and had to work as tenants or laborers on the large estates. In the late 19th century the poor of Naples and its surrounding villages had only two means by which they could hope to better their miserable living conditions: emigration or crime. Neapolitan crime was a highly organized activity, organized by the secret brotherhood of the Camorra. Unlike the Mafia in Sicily, which began as a nationalist movement, the Camorra was from its inception a league of blackmailers, smugglers, thieves, and assassins.

Differences were often resolved by murder, a tradition that also dated back at least to the Middle Ages, following the grand example of Ferrante, King of Naples. Learning of a plot against his life by the barons of Apulia in 1486, Ferrante invited the barons to a banquet at his castle in Naples to announce the betrothal of his niece to the son of one of the plotters. Once they were in his castle and seated for the banquet, he had his guests killed.

The strength and solace of Neapolitans in the wretched circumstances of their lives came first from their families, and then from music, from religion, from wine, and from the local cuisine—much of the time enjoyed out of doors at singing and dancing contests or other celebrations with family and neighbors. Street musicians, hurdy-gurdy men, and peddlers pushed brightly painted market carts and sang of their wares of food, drink, and cheap toys on the narrow streets of Naples and its surrounding villages, streets that were garlanded with colored lanterns during the frequent processions of religious relics and banners for the festivals of patron saints. The custom of *passeggiata*, or promenade, was also observed in the villages: men and women strolling in the square to gossip and to see and be seen.

After centuries of bare survival, two folk traditions had emerged: the necessity of mutual respect between individuals, and contempt for constituted authority. Partly because differences were often resolved by murder, life expectancy for males in the year of Giuseppi's birth was only 35 years. There was no justice for a Neapolitan except as he enforced it himself, and from this it followed that even brigands—perhaps especially brigands—must be men of the highest principles: honor, vengeance, solidarity.

Neapolitans kept their word, kept their silence, never cooperated with the legal authorities, and accepted as fated the ever-present danger of death. By holding to these principles they earned respect and avoided bringing shame to their family or themselves. Their principles were about all the poor possessed.

Giuseppi Esposito grew to his teens in the straitened circumstances common to Acerra. The Espositos had a small house near a narrow stream called *La Bocca Dela Signora*. Behind the house were the mulberry trees, some lemon trees, and the garden.

As was the custom, Giuseppi's mother nursed him till he was three years old. Big for his age, the infant had a long head, large, liquid-brown eyes, black, straight hair, and an olive skin. As a boy he was hot-tempered, loud, rough, stubborn, and happy, qualities he retained throughout his life. He was a poor loser, a hard, angry fighter, and a hard worker—outside of school. He preferred hunting in the forests with his uncle, who trained him as a marksman, or helping his parents in the garden to any other pursuits besides playing and roughhousing, or swimming off the great crescent dunes of the Neapolitan beaches. By the time he was 13 he had completed less than three years of village school.

One day in his thirteenth year his mother, Theresa, set out a lunch of bread and cheese for herself, her husband, and her younger son and was awaiting the return of her husband, Giachino, who had gone that morning to a neighboring village. The oldest son, the favored Gatano, was living in Naples, attending La Scala di Mattalone to prepare for a career in the army, and the daughter, Maria, was at a friend's.

Theresa poured herself a glass of wine and then, in raising it to her lips, spilled it down the front of her dress. Frightened by what she took as a bad omen, she ran to the door and called to her son, "Giuseppi, Giuseppi—something has happened!" And it was at that instant, at twelve noon, so the story is told, that mother and son saw the horse that pulled the family cart galloping toward them down the oleander-bordered dirt road. Behind the runaway animal bounced their cart, and twisting and bumping beside it in the dirt and dust of the road, tangled by one leg in the reins, was the body of Giachino.

On his father's death, Giuseppi had to assume responsibility for the family, since his older brother was in Naples at school. The 13-year-old took a job as a helper to a village baker. His wages were paid in bread as well as lira and this and the produce they could grow in the garden, selling some of it, supported the Espositos and paid for the older brother Gatano's schooling. The family also sold mulberry leaves to other silk farmers, and at harvest time Giuseppi worked as a laborer for farmers of the region, sunrise to sunset, seven days a week, as long as the harvest lasted.

On one of his harvesting ventures he fell to quarreling with a friend, Jacobus di Presio, a dispute that ended with di Presio slashing him with a knife and running off. It was the first quarrel Giuseppi was involved in that left him with a wound. Forty or so years later he chose to even the score.

When he was 17 he and Gatano, then a high-living officer in King Umberto's army, arranged to sell the family's stand of mulberry trees. With some of the money received Giuseppi opened his own bakery in Acerra. The peasant women and their daughters came carrying trays of dough on their heads which he baked into loaves for their families.

By 18 he had attained his full height. Slim, strong, dark-haired, and handsome, Giuseppi *fatta una bella figura*—cut a swath in public. He was what was called in Neapolitan dialect a *guappo*, a dandy. He enjoyed both his work and his customers, who often encouraged his attentions. His behavior might be described by the verb *pavoneggiarsi*—to strut like a peacock—behavior considered endearing by most of the villagers, especially the women. When he found a chance, Giuseppi, even at work, returned their good opinion in a tangible way. If a woman so favored neglected to remove his mark before leaving the bakery, the twisting streets of Acerra saw her return home with a large white handprint on thigh, or flank, or breast, or buttock.

He liked plump women, plump like his mother. "Why do you want two loaves of bread?" he might ask his more buxom customers. "You have already stolen two."

Giuseppi would then approach the customer more closely. "Two loaves," he would say sternly, at the same time thrusting his hands against the front of the woman's dress. "Here, and here!"

As the head of the Esposito family, however, Giuseppi was a strict and watchful guardian of his younger sister, Maria. One day a peasant woman buying bread said to him teasingly, "Gio, a very handsome man is here from America. You remember Juan? The girls are wild for him. Your sister is there, in the square, too, Gio."

His temper flaring, Giuseppi ran to the square where he found a dozen young women clustered around a well-dressed young man seated at the table of an outdoor café. The young man was describing the wonders and delights of America to his enthralled audience.

Giuseppi shoved his way into the group and took his sister roughly by the arm.

"What have I done, Gio?" she asked, beginning to cry as he pushed her ahead of him to their home.

"What has she done?" the mother asked.

"Went to see some *buffone* from America."

The next day the young man called to apologize to Signora Esposito for the embarrassment he had caused her daughter.

"I would like to be introduced to your son," Juan said. "I do not blame him, for if I had such a truly beautiful sister like your daughter, I would have responded just as he did. I would, Signora, like to call on your daughter while I am here if that is permitted."

That evening Juan apologized to the master of the house, Giuseppi, for the effrontery he had shown in speaking to the young women of the village, but in particular for—by the very audacity of his presence in the village—causing a shadow to be cast on and darkening the spirit of Giuseppi's sister, the beautiful one, not that anyone or anything for very long could possibly do that, but—on the other hand, had he known that by merely coming to visit his birthplace, Acerra, he—

"*Basta*," Giuseppi said, "What is your name?"

"Of course, of course: Juan—Juan Delaurentis. I would like to call on your sister. If that were by the remotest chance possible, unworthy though I am so much as to—"

"What do you do?"

Juan explained that he made shoes, that he was an artisan— *artigiano*—a craftsman of leather for the foot, and that in America such work was highly prized by the rich, and highly paid, very highly paid.

Even though Giuseppi recognized in Juan's speech, and his high-starched collar and cuffs, his white spats over high-button shoes, the trappings of a fellow guappo, Delaurentis was given permission to call on Maria Esposito. Three weeks later the two were married and two days later Signor and Signora Delaurentis embarked for America on a ship on which Juan had a month earlier had the remarkable prescience to book return passage for *two* to the land where everyone was highly paid, the land of bread and work, *pane e lavoro*.

In little over a year Giuseppi joined them. He had listened to the agents—the *padrones*—sent to Italy from America to recruit laborers for the States, and to their promises of high wages, and that, and the possibility of adventure in a strange land, appealed to him. But he did not like to think of leaving his mother or his birthplace.

Emigration from Italy had started in the north. In the south the people were more deeply attached to their home villages—their *paesa*—despite the poverty in which they lived. But under the monarchy the black-haired southerners were treated less as equal partners with the blue-eyed, blond northerners than as a colony to be exploited, and as year followed year of this policy southern Italians began to weaken in their resistance to emigration, especially as they were swayed by the grandiose promises of the padrones.

The padrone system came into being with the shortage of labor in the United States that resulted from the Civil War. In 1864, by act of Congress, employers in the United States were given the right to import foreign workers under contract. The peasants of southern Italy were among the earliest beneficiaries of this U.S. Congress-given right. Agents were sent to the Kingdom where they overcame the peasants' fear of leaving the known for the unknown by offering them work at what by Italy's standards were awesomely high wages. The agents were the padrones. They furnished passage to the United States for the emigrant and took care of him upon landing until he went to labor on the job for which he had contracted from one to three years of his future.

Southern Italy had few trade unions or cooperatives to help its laboring population and, as Baron Sonnino told the Italian parliament in the late '80s, in its 20 years of existence the king's government had produced not one effective measure to improve conditions for the impoverished southerners. Worse, since the middle '80s southern Italy had been experiencing an economic depression even more pronounced than was usual for it. After the harvests of some years, olives, citrus fruits, and other produce brought less in the marketplace than it cost to raise them. At the same time, the price of the grain on which the peasants depended rose steeply. The women of Acerra were more and more baking their own bread, less and less bringing the dough to Giuseppi Esposito, no matter his pleasing attentions.

Each year half a million of Giuseppi's countrymen left Italy to work in the United States, or Argentina, or Brazil. Giuseppi had considered the move, but always there were his responsibilities in Acerra to consider. It was his older brother, Gatano, the educated one—the *galantuomo*—who made up his mind for him.

On a day in 1895 Gatano came unexpectedly to the bakery, wearing his uniform but there was no insignia on it and he was not wearing his officer's cap. He fell to his knees in front of his younger brother and a tear trickled down one cheek.

"Get up!" Giuseppi shouted. This was shameful.

"It was not my fault, Gio," Gatano said between sobs. "I drank a little when I was on duty, everyone does, but they took away my rank. I am not in the army."

For several moments Giuseppi stood there silent, his hands at his sides, his brother on his knees before him. Then Giuseppi clenched his fists and threw both hands in the air. "*Basta*!" he said. "Ten years I work so that our mother can be proud of you and now, because you swill like an animal—*disgraziato*!"

The three of them said their farewells amid hundreds of other families bidding goodbye to hundreds of other voyagers who would soon be sleeping steerage in the holds and on the hatches of the ship as it steamed toward America. The black smoke of Vesuvius hung in the distance.

Giuseppi embraced his weeping mother, kissing her cheeks, her eyes. "I will make money," he promised, "and I will send it to you. And I will send for you when I have saved enough."

He turned to his brother. "If you work, there is enough to live on," he said. He could smell the sour odor of stale wine on his brother.

He stepped nearer. "You had better take care of our mother," he said, "—or I will kill you." He put his arms around Gatano and pulled him close.

He released his brother. He embraced his mother one last time and then picked up the satchel that contained his belongings and turned to the gangplank of the ship that would take him to the golden land.

Decades later in the Valley—Chicago's Little Italy—the old Italian men had a saying. "If we put *our* hands in a sack full of money, we come out with shit. But if Diamond Joe puts *his* hand into a sack of shit, he comes out with money."

For many years in the New World it did work that way for Giuseppi Giachino Esposito—Colosimo's friend, Torrio's friend, the Gennas' friend, Capone's benefactor—but one Chicago pre-election dusk it did not.

Guappo, of course, is the Italian from which came the American pejorative for an Italian, *wop*.

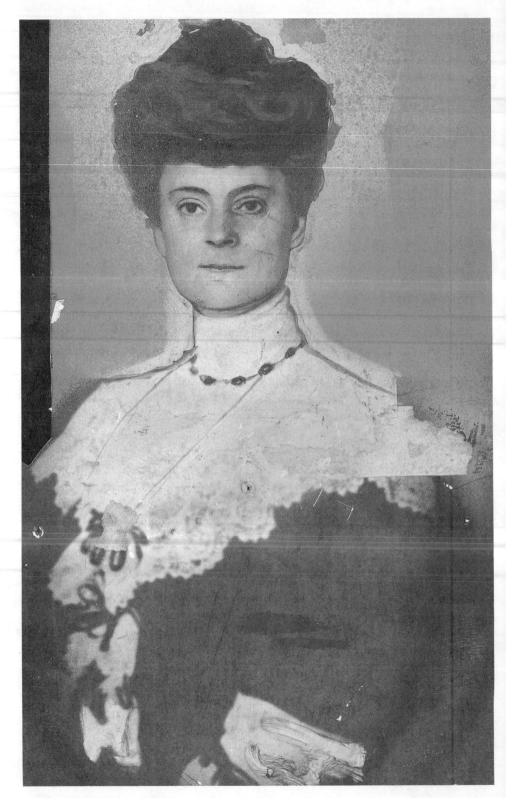

Anita McCormick Blaine

SILK STOCKINGS

William Hale Thompson, Jr., was born on May 14, 1867, in a Boston mansion. His father's family had extensive land holdings in New Hampshire wrested from the King of England, and the great grandfather, Ebenezer Thompson, after playing a prominent role in the Revolutionary War, was a presidential elector for George Washington. William Hale's father served on Admiral Farragut's staff during the Civil war. His mother, Medora Gale, came from a pioneer Chicago family. Her father was one of the 38 incorporators of the town.

In 1869 the Thompsons moved from Boston's Beacon Street to Chicago's South Sangamon Street. The senior Thompson set up in the real estate business and after the Great Fire in 1871 grew prosperous from it. He was elected to the Illinois legislature as a Republican. There he sponsored the first Illinois measure for the prevention of cruelty to animals. His oldest son, Billy, attended the Charles Fessenden prep school but preferred by far riding his pony about the neighborhood with his friends, the Pike brothers, playing cowboy and Indians, and leading raids north and south into the tough Irish neighborhoods where rich kids were hated and had to fight their way out.

The summer he was 14 Billy Thompson was thrown into the lock-up after an altercation that followed his galloping his horse full tilt across a Chicago River bridge on his way to a make-believe skirmish with Indians in Lincoln Park. When his father got him released at 2:00 in the morning he told the boy he was going to find a boarding school to send him to, for the discipline of it.

Young Bill protested. He told his father he wanted to go out west and become a cowboy. He got a job clerking in a grocery at Peoria and Madison that paid $9.00 a week, and persuaded his father to agree that if he saved $7.00 a week from his wages he could go west in the fall, at his own expense.

Anita Eugenie McCormick was born on July 4, 1866, to 56-year-old Cyrus Hall McCormick and his 30-year-old wife Nettie Fowler McCormick. Anita's infant years were spent in a New York Fifth Avenue mansion from where her father oversaw his investments in mines, the Union Pacific and other railways, and land companies. (Cyrus McCormick's annual income from rents in the late 1860s was $95,000, this in addition to $250,000 a year from his reaper company.) The Great Chicago Fire of 1871 prompted Anita's father to move back to Chicago and the wellspring of his fortune, the McCormick reaper works.

The son of a Virginia farmer and blacksmith, Cyrus McCormick was involved in Illinois Democratic politics, and deeply involved in encouraging missionaries and guarding Presbyterianism from the modernists. In Chicago the family attended the Fourth Presbyterian and Anita was enrolled in the Misses Grant's seminary. At 12, as a result of a family trip abroad, she was sent to an Englishwoman's pension boarding school in Neuilly, France. She was the only boarder there. "Rather lonely," she wrote.

In 1879 the family moved into its 675 Rush Street Chicago mansion, a residence felt to be eclipsed in grandeur only by the Potter Palmers' on Lake Shore Drive. Anita's mother was an overprotective and stern taskmaster. She shut her children inside a closet when she felt they needed punishment, made them record the minutes they spent brushing their teeth and dressing, and attempted by Bible reading, morning prayers, and cautionary instruction to improve their morals. Anita's older sister, Virginia, was subject to seizures of weeping and hysterical prayer and was an insomniac and sleepwalker.

Cyrus McCormick was the first U.S. manufacturer to guarantee his product, the first to sell it at a fixed price, and the first to give customers time to pay. One of his workers said of him:

> "In spite of his temper and drivin' ways, . . . the grandest old feller ever lived. He knew how to get spirit into his men. . . .No white-collar boss but right out on the job, workin' hard with his sleeves rolled up on some new gadget that had gone wrong. He knew machines like his own mother. While he was livin' we had one boss—and if anything went wrong, you could go right to him and get it fixed up. In these new days of big companies, you have a dozen bosses—and where are you? With old Cy we knew."

Cyrus McCormick died in 1884, age 74.

Eighteen years old, his daughter Anita had a dream after his death. His body was lying on his bed. He opened his eyes and held his arms out to her and she ran to him. "'Oh, my father,' I said, 'how terrible! But oh I love you *so much* and that tells you my whole story.'"

Not yet 15, but six feet tall, Bill Thompson arrived in Cheyenne, Wyoming, during the Black Hills gold rush. The town was booming; it was also his dream come to life. Cow ponies stood at hitching rails up and down Main Street, cowboys strolled from saloon to gambling hall, and painted women slouched in doorways. The young man had left Chicago with $80. Three days after arriving in Cheyenne he was down to 80¢. He got a job as helper to a ranch cook and spent half his remaining change on a cookbook, since he had never cooked in his young life.

His work at the 101 Ranch on Wyoming's Chugwater and Horse creeks required that he rise at 3:00 in the morning to rebuild the fire, haul water, fetch wood, and help prepare breakfast and bake the day's supply of fresh bread. By the time the cowboys were up he was ready to begin his full day's work. He loved the life. When winter arrived his father had to order him home.

He spent the next six years working outside of Cheyenne, and he learned the skills of a cowboy. He stayed in Chicago only three months of each year, attending classes at the Metropolitan Business College. His boyhood friends went on to Yale and Harvard and Princeton for their further education.

In 1888 his father wired him that he had bought a ranch outside Ewing, Nebraska, and Bill was to go there to manage it. Bill Thompson, 21, rode east out of Cheyenne at the head of a short string of cow ponies to follow the Union Pacific rails to Ewing (which he could not find on a map).

He located Ewing, and his father's 3,800-acre ranch southwest of town on Goose Lake. The new manager fit in at once with the veteran hands, both at working and at carousing. In his second summer he laid out three barroom adversaries in Ewing with a pool cue. He also tended to ranching, buying yearling steers in Kansas City or Omaha, fattening them on Nebraska feed, and selling them in Omaha, Sioux City, or Chicago. At the end of his first three years the Ewing operation had a profit of $30,000.

His father died in 1891, leaving an estate of $2 million. After the funeral his mother told Bill he couldn't go back to Ewing. "Your father expected you to carry on."

When she was 14 Anita McCormick wanted to "bring Jesus' love to the poor people." While out walking with a cousin they saw a little girl enter a dilapidated house on Huron near Clark. They knocked and asked the woman who answered if the little girl went to Sunday School. They bought goods for a small dress, had a seamstress make it, and took it to the woman. "She said she had asked her husband and he said it would be alright. I suppose he knew Papa's name. So the little girl had the dress and is going."

Anita's 27-year-old brother, Cyrus, Jr., with a degree from Princeton, was head of the McCormick works at the time of the Haymarket bombing there in May 1886. After the trial and conviction of the Haymarket eight—seven sentenced to death—mother Nettie McCormick told her son Cyrus, Jr., that they had "together done what we could to uphold liberality and fairness in our dealings with the laboring classes . . . and where the issue is one of principle, we have been unwilling to surrender, whatever might be the cost."

Twenty-year-old Anita had concerns of her own. "Is it end enough," she wrote her mother, "just to try to round and broaden ourselves as much as possible, and develop our faculties to their highest extent?" She anguished over her older sister's breakdown as well. After the elder Cyrus McCormick's death, Virginia began locking herself in her room, wandering the mansion at night pounding on doors, and climbing out windows to walk on the roof. Her mother did not want to put her into an institution, for then Chicago society would *know*. Her mother gave way to fits of weeping and praying. Anita felt like "lying down to sleep, or even to die if I could get away from everything."

She "came out" in 1887, an attractive brunette. Before the Bachelors and Benedicts dance on New Year's Eve, the dinner served was clams followed by asparagus soup, iced salmon with mayonnaise and iced asparagus, frogs' legs "a la poulette," roast squabs on toast, new potatoes, and beans. A breather of orange and pineapple sherbet in Jamaica rum preceded broiled woodcock, peas, and tomato salad. Claret, sherry, and apollinaris water accompanied the meal; dessert was individual ices and strawberries, followed by coffee in the drawing room.

In 1888 Anita fell in love with Emmons Blaine, son of James G. Blaine, the "Plumed Knight," Republican candidate for U.S. President in 1884. Before the wedding in 1889, mother Nettie gave the groom a timetable of Anita's menstrual schedule and cautioned her daughter to abstain for 10 days following her period. (Mother Nettie had once drawn aside a bride-to-be who was an orphan and warned her to beware of the "pitfalls between her eager feet.")

The newlywed Blaines lived in Baltimore until Emmons took a position as assistant general manager of the Baltimore and Ohio Line, when they moved to Chicago to live in the Rush Street mansion while mother Nettie was in Europe. From there mother Nettie sent Anita detailed child-carrying and -bearing instructions, ending with "Please Darling, burn this as soon as you have read it." On August 29, 1890, Anita gave birth to a son.

A year and a half later her husband was ill and the marriage was no longer as happy as it had been. Anita blamed herself. "Oh God, help me to live in others and out of myself." In June 1892 Emmons attended the Republican National Convention to help his father regain the nomination. Their efforts failed and Emmons returned to Chicago and died within the week. His wife was 26.

There was not much for Bill Thompson to do at his late father's real estate offices. The staff there did it all well enough themselves. So Bill started going about town with his boyhood chums, the Pike brothers, and with them spent much time at various Levee resorts.

Gene Pike, a graduate of Yale, was a member of the Chicago Athletic Club, so Bill joined, too. As a member of its Chicago Athletic Association (CAA) he learned to play water polo. The CAA teams competed with other private clubs and teams from Ivy League and Midwestern schools, and with "Big Bill" as its captain the water polo team fought its way into the finals of the national championships. It lost, but Bill starred.

He played baseball, won the handball championship of the CAA, won swimming and diving trophies, put on aerial trapeze exhibitions, won the club billiards championship. He was a natural, and never more so than at left tackle on the CAA football team.

In 1894 the football team beat Princeton and Dartmouth. By 1896 Bill was captain and coach. He recruited former college stars and by Thanksgiving Day the team was to play the Boston Athletic Club for the national championship. The night before the game it was charged that a CAA member had provided free meals for six CAA players, a violation of American Athletic Union rules.

"Fellows," captain and coach Bill said, "there's only one thing to do. We want the championship but we've got to expel those men."

Without those men, Chicago held the Boston team scoreless and won the game and championship. Captain Bill was lauded as the beau ideal of pure sportsmanship.

He was now living with Gene Pike in the Metropole Hotel, not far from their Levee haunts. He seldom visited the real estate offices. Gene Pike ran for alderman in the Second Ward in 1899 and won election as a Republican to the City Council. Pike suggested that Bill run for the other aldermanic post in the ward, but Bill declined. He was more interested in sailing his boat, the *Myrone*, at the Thompson estate in Oconomowoc, Wisconsin, where he was vice-commodore of the yacht club, whose membership was other Chicago millionaires. Pike's idea was being discussed one afternoon at the Chicago Athletic Club when a member offered to bet Pike $50 that Bill would never run because he was afraid of getting beat. Thompson stood up, looked the man squarely in the eye, and said he'd cover that bet himself.

When the World's Columbian Exposition closed in 1893, there

were 200,000 unemployed workers in Chicago. At Christmas the widow Anita McCormick Blaine gave 125 sacks of provisions to neighborhood children after their school principal had vouched for the "worthieness" of their families.

Mrs. Blaine had a home for herself and her son built at 101 East Erie, 50 feet from mother Nettie's front door, a block from brother Cyrus's house. Thermometers were installed in each room of the house and Emmons Blaine, Jr., was not allowed to enter a room unless it was at the right temperature for him. Tile drainage was placed in the lawn so Em could run barefoot without getting his feet wet. To further safeguard the boy's health, he was given cold baths, a bland diet, and had the consistency of his bowel movements recorded. His mother consulted many physicians over what she considered to be the precarious state of her son's health until she found one who confirmed her feeling that he was a delicate child.

Anita's two younger brothers were at Princeton, her older brother Cyrus was managing the reaper works under what his mother considered her direction—Nettie was also monetarily aiding missionaries—and Anita's older sister was in the custody of nurses. Anita had heard of Colonel Francis Wayland Parker and the accomplishments of his Chicago Normal School on Chicago's far South Side. She and the Colonel agreed that instruction should foster "the tendency of the soul toward freedom" and in 1896 she entered her son in the Colonel's school, then persuaded the Colonel to establish a branch on the North Side, closer to her and Emmons.

In 1898 Anita pledged $5,000 a year for five years to establish a College for Teachers. In 1899 she opened an office on Monroe Street— to which she was driven in her carriage down Michigan Avenue—to administer the trust for a large, innovative private school she and Colonel Parker planned to found, the Chicago Institute. Mother Nettie approved: "You are doing a great and estimable good to your race."

Anita pledged $400,000 for land, building, and equipment and $95,000 a year for seven years for support, but actual costs proved to be half again as much and by mid-1901 the plans had been broadened to include a merger with progressive educator and philosopher John Dewey's Laboratory School at the University of Chicago. In 1902 Colonel Parker died and in 1904 Dewey angrily left the University of Chicago for Columbia. As it was, Anita's philanthropies were exceeding $100,000 a year.

When he was 11 and in the bathtub her son Emmons asked his mother why "ladies always sit when they pee-pee." His mother told him that women's bodies are made differently than men's.

"Are they? I didn't know that."

"Yes, I'll show you mine."

"And all the divineness rose in me," she wrote of that occasion, "and I felt as if rising out of my body as I slipped off my gown and my vest and stood there a moment—very simply—and all the wonder, how and whether was gone, while my child looked all at me just as ever, interested in what I had said but not any more—just loving simple interest, not a thought beside, and we had it together."

Big Bill Thompson announced his candidacy for the Republican nomination as alderman of the Second Ward the day after the Everleigh sisters opened their Club doors for the first time. Thompson's support was expected to come from the people in the ward's "silk stocking" precincts, those of wealth and privilege who lived in fine homes on Prairie Avenue and Grand Boulevard. Blocks away to the west were the fancy houses, saloons, and gambling dens of the southward-tending new Levee, and the tenements and factories. The silk stocking constituency had become annoyed by the encroachment of Levee denizens into their view and the boldness of the Everleigh Club's opening seemed a portent of worse to come. Thompson's announcement that he would run seemed to the wives of the wealthy an answer to their call for reform and law and order.

Curiously for a reform party, the Republicans met in Freiberg's Hall, one of the Levee's most notorious dives, to decide on their nominee. "Fellows," Big Bill said to his associates in the Grand Old Party, "I aim to be a first-class representative of this fine ward. What the Second Ward needs is decent streets and enough lights to protect the citizens from holdup men." He was chosen by acclamation, and Ike Bloom's waitresses ambled in and set 'em up for the thirsty statesmen, drinks on Big Bill—the good stuff, 20¢ a shot.

The silk stockings distrusted the Democratic candidate—most were Republicans—and Big Bill ensured his popularity with the rougher element of the Second Ward by the intelligent but exhausting campaign strategy of visiting every one of the ward's 270 saloons and buying drinks for their patrons. He spent $175 a day; made no speeches. The city's newspapers endorsed him as a sterling sportsman and successful real estate executive.

The respectable businessmen of the Second Ward closed their stores on election day and manned the polls for Thompson. Democratic aldermen Bathhouse John Coughlin and Michael Hinky Dink Kenna of the adjoining First Ward, in a tactic puzzling to some, did not help the Second Ward's Democratic candidate as they easily could have by sending in sluggers and chain voters, and Big Bill was elected, 2,516 votes to 2,113.

The new alderman, however, took little interest in his responsibilities, though at a newspaperman's suggestion he did introduce a bill that established the first city playground (in a black section of the ward at 24th and Wabash), a measure that started a national playground movement. When Big Bill did appear in the Council's chambers it was noticed that the Little Fellow, Alderman Kenna, often conferred with him, asked his advice even, flattered him, jollied him along, so to say.

On October 11 a redistricting ordinance was introduced in Council to redefine the city's ward boundaries. Both of the Second Ward's reform aldermen, Pike and Thompson, voted "Aye." The ordinance was passed 43 to 23. It extended the First Ward boundaries past 22nd Street in what had been the Second Ward, far enough to bring the lucrative new Levee into Coughlin's and Kenna's domain.

On December 21 an amendment was offered that extended a bit more of the First as far south as 31st Street. Once again aldermen Pike and Thompson voted "Aye." In effect—and inexplicably—the two young reform Republicans had voted themselves off the map. Their bachelor apartment in the Metropole Hotel was now within the confines of the First Ward.

The Second Ward's businessmen were stunned and outraged. "We wanted to separate the bad and good parts of the ward," Big Bill explained—lamely—to a mass meeting of his silk stocking supporters. "We didn't realize. . . ."

Pike announced he would retire from politics when his term expired. But as it dawned on the 33-year-old Thompson how he had been duped and humiliated he grew angry and vowed to fight, to run against John Coughlin in the First Ward when his own Second Ward term ended. This threat afforded the Bath and the Little Fellow some small amusement. As the *Chicago News* pointed out to the purest exemplar of sportsmanship in Chicago, "a man cannot commit political suicide twice."
. . . As the Italian saying has it, *Lavar la testa all'asino e acqua persa*—Washing a donkey's head is a waste of water.

But more of the disparate lives of these two children of wealth anon.

BROTHER THEO

Sarah arrived in Chicago in the summer of 1883 with her three youngest sons and a determination to reunite her scattered and wayward family. Her elder daughters, Mame, Emma, Theresa, and Sylvia, and brother Al had some years before left their Evansville, Indiana, home to escape its grim poverty and their father's fanatically religious ways. Two of the girls had found salvation in the arms of prosperous men. The other two returned to live with their mother and three younger brothers in a small apartment across the street from a beer garden on rundown West Madison Street.

Sarah's oldest son, Paul (who went by the name of "Dresser"), was making a reputation for himself in New York City as an actor and song writer. Paul would eventually become rich and famous with more than 100 popular tunes such as "My Gal Sal," "I Believe It, for My Mother Told Me So," "The Sidewalks of New York," "The Bowery," and other sentimental favorites that included what became Indiana's state song, "On the Banks of the Wabash" (lyrics by brother Theodore). But the little money Paul was sending home in 1883 provided only small help for his hard-pressed mother and her brood.

Sarah's son Theodore was the tenth of the surviving Dreiser children, 12 years old in 1883, growing taller and more awkward by the month. He was called "Theo." Deeply inward and thoughtful, he was moody, shy, and often withdrawn. He had known cold and hunger in Indiana and his strict, Germanic upbringing led him to fear the very pleasures in life he secretly desired—the girls who tormented and tantalized him, the wealth of the rich. In Indiana he had been prone, as well, to ecstatic dreams and mystic encounters with the beauties of nature. Down home he was used to rising early on summer mornings to walk the country roads with his dog, inspecting the lush fields, the flowered trees,

---

This chapter was written by R. Craig Sautter.

the fleeting skyprints of scudding clouds.

Now in Chicago, also known at that time as the "City of Rats," he was physically and intellectually groping for his identity, and his moods and fascinations were magnified by his first taste of a city, stirred by the exotic voices of many languages, the anxious and excited faces of immigrant and rural newcomers. He was both dazzled and delighted by the spectacle of flagrant violations of the moral teachings of his rigid Catholic childhood. In Chicago there was a freedom he had never experienced before. Here was a morality that he had been taught was evil, but that he could see was pervasive and real. Here there was a suitcase filled with forbidden stories. As a student in Catholic schools back in Indiana he had taken beatings for his wild imagination, his unauthorized reading, and his unwillingness to submit to strict discipline. So he was immensely excited by the hurly-burly of the streets and he took in and stored deeply as much as his wide eyes could encompass.

The raw energy of Chicago provided a hypnotic side show from dawn when the weary workers rose, to after sunset when lovers wandered recklessly from drinking establishments to hotel rooms. During the summer he spent in the ramshackle West Side neighborhood, the young Dreiser encountered hard-drinking immigrants and sullen workmen, brazen thieves and fancy panderers, worn-out street walkers and glamorous madams, amateur actors and professional musicians, and thousands of exhausted immigrants who toiled against steep odds for mere survival.

He sold newspapers on the streets with his younger brother Ed and ran through the neighborhoods with the local band of toughs, but one of his favorite pastimes was to retreat to the comfortable quarters of his oldest sister who lived unmarried, a kept woman, contemptuous of, but beholden to the man who provided ease and finery in exchange for her person. "When a girl leaves her home at eighteen, she does one of two things," Dreiser philosophized years later. "Either she falls into saving hands and becomes better, or she rapidly assumes the cosmopolitan standard of virtue and becomes worse." In the case of his sister, the latter was evidently the case. But he loved her and saw certain advantages to her arrangement, and he somehow realized that she had been forced to her compromises.

What young Theodore witnessed in the situation of his sisters stimulated his already girl-crazed consciousness and showed him the pleasant reality of an everyday kind of vice he rarely read about in books. Indeed, the city's lusty ways were a kind of portent of the primal role that sexual drives would play in his own life and fiction in years to come. Even at 12 he was aware that sex was a mighty force. Dreiser's adult fiction would explore the fate of his sisters and thereby assault the boundaries of what contemporary literary convention accepted. He would write about the real lives of real people whose destinies were intricately wound up in the forces he saw at work then as a lanky, gawky lad. The moralists of the nation said that young girls had an ethical responsibility to turn away from the evils a city afforded, to take respectable work or marry. Even though he was only 12, Dreiser saw that the choices were not that simple. Lives were easily wrecked by hunger and destitution and sex and greed and by the inability of an honest person to find work at a fair wage, or any work at all.

He would state this uncomfortable determinist reality against the conventional assumptions of free will and individual moral responsibility proclaimed from the nation's pulpits. His fictional illustrations brought upon him the wrath and fear of established society, which tried to ban his books and caused publishers to fear to print them. In the early 20th century, with his abundant honesty, perception, and deep compassion. Theodore Dreiser would become a literary liberator for a nation that had outgrown its cultural puritanism.

But that was years away. In 1883, Chicago proved too inhospitable for even the indomitable Sarah, and the Dreiser family was forced to retreat to Warsaw, Indiana, 120 miles east, not far from her family home in Silver Lake. The skinny boy, who would grow into a big-boned, slightly cockeyed, powerful man with a magnetic yet brooding personality, was now deprived of the bazaar of sensations Chicago offered. Instead, he withdrew into his own imagination and the ready escape of novels by Mark Twain, Harriet Beecher Stowe, Tolstoy, even those of Indiana's General, Lew Wallace. He fell in love with literature.

In Warsaw, Theodore benefited from a few years of public education and the encouragement of his teachers. He spent luxurious hours reading under a great oak tree in a front-yard hammock of his family's rooming house. He was mystified by the small town beauties of the opposite sex whom he was too uneasy to approach. He loved to wander the country lanes that led to surrounding lakes and meadows or lie along the banks of the Tippecanoe River and there engage the cosmos that amazed him.

Yet Chicago's voice echoed in his soul and by age 16, after quitting high school and then failing at farm work, Dreiser was back on Chicago's West Side in a cheap room, fending for himself, working as a dishwasher in a gritty Greek restaurant on Halsted Street.

Fortunately, he had so impressed his Warsaw English teacher, Mildred Fielding, now a Chicago High School principal, that she rescued him from his wage slavery. She knew that despite his poor command of grammar and tortured syntax, her pupil had a born storyteller's gift for observation, characterization, and narration—and a deep well of human sympathy. She gained his admittance at Indiana University, located in the small downstate intellectual oasis of Bloomington, and paid $300 for a year of his study. The university was the oasis; Monroe County was hard, rocky, and poor.

Indiana University's student population of 600, many of them from rural backgrounds of relative material advantage, made Dreiser feel academically and socially inadequate. He was mismatched by his poverty with the well-bred coeds and gentlemen scholars of the classic limestone campus, but the interlude gave him a glimpse of finer paths to glory than dishwashing, and also several months to think, unhampered by drudgery. Hurt by the experience, he chose not to risk a second year of college, fearing he would waste his benefactor's hard-earned money.

Instead, he returned for a third try in Chicago, where his family had reassembled. But soon his mother's death, the direct result of years of grinding impoverishment the family was still trying to escape, brought him to considerable grief. Within a year the constant bickering of his sisters drove him from what was left of his family. Now he sought solace in the arms of women his own age.

Finally, he landed work as a bill collector. But as winter approached, his desire for a fancy coat led to an embarrassing try at petty embezzlement and dismissal in lieu of arrest. All the while his mind was churning with images, theories, and aspirations he could not ignore.

"To me Chicago at this time seethed with a peculiarly human or realistic atmosphere," he said. "It was something wonderful to witness a world metropolis springing up under one's very eyes." He tried capturing his feelings in short pieces he wrote, then decided he would become a newspaperman and dash about the city recording all sorts of exciting episodes. He hounded the editors of Chicago's many papers for a job as cub reporter and finally got his chance with the *Chicago Daily Globe* when the 1892 Democratic Convention came to town.

Once on staff he had very little idea of how to do the job, and little notion of how politics actually worked. But he accidentally met a Southern senator who had been a newsman once himself, who took a liking to him. The senator pointed him toward a meeting at the Richelieu Hotel where the Eastern money men and Tammany Hall gang were deciding to back Grover Cleveland's nomination for a second, split-term. Adlai Stevenson of Illinois would be the Vice Presidential candidate. Dreiser phoned his scoop to an amazed editorial office, beating out a pack of veteran reporters from his own and rival papers.

When the Democrats left town, Dreiser was kept on at $15 a week. And when his editors began to entrust him with weightier assignments, Theo moved to better quarters on Ogden Place, overlooking Union Park. At six feet, one inch, but just 137 pounds, with a center hair part, and decked out in high-collared white shirt, checkered pants, natty suit coat, fedora, and gold-rimmed spectacles (an outfit he would have termed "trig"), Dreiser amused many whose stories he covered. His editor, John

Maxwell, occasionally called him "loony," but Dreiser saw himself as "crazy with life, a little demented or frenzied with romance and hope."

The clumsy, mainly self-taught intellectual was learning to write by studying the essays of Carlyle and Emerson, though at his best he never approached their ease of prose. He contemplated the bitter but persuasive truths of Schopenhauer and his philosophy of pessimism. His editor, John Maxwell, advised him to "wise up" on the predatory nature of the work world and "never to trust anyone." He urged him to follow the examples of Dickens, Balzac, and Zola and to capture as much detail as he could in every account he wrote, a prompting Dreiser followed with a vengeance when he took to fiction.

He was learning to direct the passion of his observations into effective news features that probed the tragedies of the people who tramped Chicago's streets by exploring their emotional predicaments. He was assigned to write about the hideous slums that ran down Halsted Street to the river, from Madison to 12th Street. The scenes he witnessed caused him to question the benevolence of any God. He saw that the fate of individuals was linked to hidden circumstance and irresistible forces of nature; that people were directed by powers over which they have little control; that society as an outgrowth of nature necessarily permitted the strong to prey on the weak. He saw that Chicago itself was such a force.

Once he discovered that he could write, he found he could turn out volumes on any subject. His editors concluded that, comic as he might sometimes appear, Theodore Dreiser had what it took to succeed as a writer, and "not just of the ordinary news variety."

It was probably to this Chicago stay that Dreiser's imagination later returned as he sketched the city that Sister Carrie encountered on her first visit in August 1889:

> Chicago's . . . many and growing commercial opportunities gave it widespread fame, which made it a giant magnet, drawing to itself, from all quarters, the hopeful and the hopeless—those who had their fortune yet to make and those whose fortunes and affairs had reached a disastrous climax elsewhere. . . .The sound of the hammer engaged upon the erection of new structures was everywhere heard. Great industries were moving in. The huge railroad corporations had seized upon vast tracts of land for transfer and shipping purposes. Streetcar lines had been extended far out into the open country in anticipation of rapid growth. . . .There were regions open to the sweeping winds and rain, which were lighted throughout the night with long, blinking lines of gas lamps, fluttering in the wind. Narrow boardwalks extended out, passing here a house, and there a store, at far intervals, eventually ending in the open prairie.
>
> In the central portion was the vast wholesale and shopping district, to which the uninformed seeker for work usually drifted. It was a characteristic of Chicago then, and one not generally shared with other

cities, that individual firms of any pretension occupied individual buildings. The presence of ample ground made this possible. It gave an imposing appearance to most of the wholesale houses, whose offices were upon the ground floor and in plain view of the street. . . .The entire metropolitan center possessed a high and mighty air calculated to overawe and abash the common applicant, and to make the gulf between poverty and success seem both wide and deep.

Tens of thousands of girls like Dreiser's first fictional heroine, Carrie, had to work in the sweatshops of the city, and upon their labor and general mistreatment the great industries rose, thrusting their architecture skyward in an impressive show of temporal authority. By its very nature, the city presented not just a physical but a moral challenge to the system of benevolent values preached in the distant home towns of the girls and immigrants who worked for Chicago's dynasts.

Dreiser would eventually examine these emerging issues and note with precision how the millstones of urban life seemed to crush so many good but unfortunate men and women, while others of far less sympathetic character were catapulted to power and wealth. His pensive and raw depictions of human sorrow, struggle, and fortune would push beyond America's literary technique of "Realism" as practiced by its refined Eastern champions such as William Dean Howells or the cynical Chicagoan and "genteel realist" Henry Blake Fuller. Dreiser the novelist would portray the city true to its rugged and alluring appearance and individual reality. His work would eventually fashion the very notion of Chicago literature for the 20th century and inspire a tradition of American "Naturalism" that would run deep through the work of other Chicago writers such as Sherwood Anderson, Ben Hecht, James T. Farrell, and Ernest Hemingway, up through Richard Wright, Jack Conroy, Willard Motley, Nelson Algren, and Saul Bellow.

But this was all yet to come. The apprentice city reporter was still learning how to write. His *Globe* editors gave him more space for his elaborate and philosophical commentaries. They recognized the depth of his natural insights. He even briefly became the paper's star reporter when a series he wrote on fake auction houses that bilked their rural customers led to arrests.

In the fall of 1892, when Dreiser was still only 21, one of his editors, John T. McEnnis, a hard-drinking but talented writer from St. Louis, recommended him to the prestigious *St. Louis Globe-Democrat*. At that paper Dreiser got off to a good start with several sensational stories of railroad accidents and political scandal, but when he was ordered to cover conflicting assignments, he made the careless error of filing reviews on three plays he had not yet seen, basing his critiques on publicity releases. When all three troupes were delayed by a storm that washed out the roads and Dreiser's reviews appeared anyway, his editor-in-chief was ridiculed in competing papers. Too chagrined to return to the paper, Dreiser managed to catch on with the *St. Louis Republic*, a paper inferior to the *Globe*.

While on a *Republic* assignment to cover the World's Columbian Exposition in Chicago, he met his future wife, a teacher, Sara (Sally) White, his senior by four years, who hailed from modest wealth in Missouri, He was taken by her attention and attractiveness and perhaps her name that recalled his mother and her profession that recalled the few pleasures of his youth. He started a troublesome courtship that continued for six years, during which the two lived mostly in different locations. Their eventual union proved a temperamental mistake from the start. Dreiser constantly pursued other women for the sexual companionship his wife failed to provide and he soon came to resent and fear her. She refused to divorce him, but they legally separated in 1912. She demanded obedience from him. Not until her death in 1942 would Dreiser feel "free" again, as he wrote in a short story with that title. He then married Helen Richardson, with whom he had lived the past 23 years.

In 1894, with the encouragement of his brother Paul, Dreiser decided to work his way East where it seemed all serious writers migrated sooner or later. In Toledo he became friends with the city editor of the *Blade*, Arthur Henry, who gave him a few assignments and shared hours of barroom conversation and speculation. But restless to reach New York, Dreiser pushed on to Pittsburgh, practicing his trade there for a few summer months at the *Dispatch* before finally reaching his artistic mecca. His brother escorted him to all the grand sights of Broadway, but Theo was too intimidated by the city to ask for newspaper work, even though he had established himself as a journalist in the Midwest. He was also intimidated by Paul's success as America's leading songwriter and his growing stage career.

He returned to Pittsburgh to save as much as he could before returning to New York. It was during this second Pittsburgh stay that he began reading T. H. Huxley and the revolutionary theories of Charles Darwin and Herbert Spencer. These put a final spike through the heart of his Catholicism and brought together his own ideas of a brutal force behind human struggle and survival. Spencer's theories "left me numb, my gravest fears as to the unsolvable disorder and brutality of life eternally verified."

He withdrew into himself. He tried New York once again. Paul was on the road, acting, and Dreiser's sister Emma and her children with whom he lived were in dire economic straits. Emma's husband, like Hurstwood, the anti-hero of *Sister Carrie*, was "played out . . . weary of the game and drifting." Theo was given a try-out by the *New York World*, Joseph Pulitzer's scandal-screaming paper, but was paid by the copy inch, not a salary as he had hoped. The editors gave him routine, petty assignments gathering facts for higher-paid rewrite men.

One afternoon he sat in City Hall Park, outside the offices of the *World*. "About me on the benches of the park, even in the gray, chill December weather, was that large company of bums, loafers, tramps, idlers, the flotsam and jetsam of the great city's whirl and strife. . . . It was then the idea of Hurstwood was born. The city was so huge, so cruel."

The sights he witnessed on his beat (police station, morgue, Bellevue Hospital) sickened and depressed him, as did the entire atmosphere of the *World* with its constant warfare between employer and employees and among the staff itself. He could take no more and left, not knowing what he would do next. With his transcontinental quest suddenly at an end, he became despondent. He began to drink heavily, and soon entered the ranks of the homeless men who haunted the Bowery with its "endless line of degraded and impossible lodging houses, a perfect whorl of bums and failures . . . a pathetic street."

In the spring his brother Paul came back to the city, sought him out, resuscitated him, and secured him an editorial job on a music magazine associated with his own music publishing company. Theodore was both grateful and ashamed, but he worked hard to learn his new trade. After a few months, his feet back on the ground, he also turned to freelancing articles to magazines such as *Success*. Some were profiles of famous men of industry and commerce such as Marshall Field and other Chicago civic captains. Through these characterizations he further developed skills that proved useful to his fiction when he later chronicled the life of the traction magnet Charles T. Yerkes. For the *New York Call* he wrote on topics ranging from living conditions in the slums to unemployment. His articles often celebrated individualism and feminism.

Not until 1899 did Dreiser attempt another return to Chicago—but this time in fiction, his still untested frontier. Journalism and magazine work had taken him to the shore, but what of that magical land beyond? While vacationing with his wife at the 14-room home of his by now close friend Arthur Henry on the banks of the meandering Maumee River outside Toledo, Dreiser attempted his first short story, "McEwen of the Shining Slave Makers." A journalist sitting on a park bench suddenly finds himself transported into the deadly warfare between armies of red and black ants, a bizarre scenario that existentially presages Kafka's "Metamorphosis." The tale allegorically warns of the devastation to result when the world's armies go to war, as happened a decade and a half later. Henry was enthusiastic about the story, Dreiser uncertain and outwardly dissatisfied, but that fall *Ainslee's*, a popular national magazine, began buying his short fiction. Suddenly his vague ambitions in fiction, his admiration for Rudyard Kipling, the British journalist turned short story writer, his years of reading, all made a career in letters seem possible.

A few months later, Arthur Henry moved to NYC and nagged Dreiser into starting a novel in competition with his own effort. Almost begrudgingly Theo turned to a task that quickly consumed him. "Finally, I took out a piece of yellow paper and to please him wrote down a title at random—Sister Carrie," Dreiser said years later. "My mind was blank except for the name. I had no idea who or what she was to be. I have often thought there was something mystic about it, as if I were being used, like a medium." Then his thoughts returned to Chicago and the lives of his sisters. He found it easy enough to write 2,000 words a day longhand, the pages dropped recklessly to the floor as he followed his memory and imagination. By the spring of 1900 he was ready to take his massive and unconventional manuscript of 240,000 words—twice the length of popular novels of the day—to publishers.

He didn't expect a welcome reception, and for a while didn't get one. But then young Frank Norris read his manuscript for Doubleday, Page & Company. Norris was the author of the highly successful *McTeague*, and soon would gain even greater fame with *The Octopus* and then *The Pit* (set in Chicago), which probed the greed and treachery of grain speculation. Norris called *Sister Carrie* the best manuscript he had read at the firm and equal to any novel he had ever read. On his recommendation, Dreiser received a contract for publication.

Like Dreiser's own sisters, his heroine Carrie falls into the hands of a man who protects and uses her, one Charles Drouet, a traveling salesman, a drummer, who sweet-talks her on her first train ride into Chicago from her Wisconsin home. Drouet subsequently preys upon Carrie's vulnerability when she falls ill and loses her $4.50-a-week job. He puts her up in his apartment on Ogden Place across from Union Park, where Dreiser had lived.

But in time Carrie is charmed by a man of higher social distinction than Drouet, one George Hurstwood, a restaurant proprietor who lives with his family in a fashionable section of Lincoln Park. The middleaged Hurstwood, entranced by Carrie's simple, youthful charm, commits theft and takes her to Canada. After getting caught and repaying most of the stolen money, Hurstwood moves Carrie to New York City where the couple rapidly descends into the poverty the city offers unprepared newcomers.

These are Carrie's thoughts when Hurstwood first proposes she come with him, sentiments scandalous to any turn-of-the-century reader:

> She went over the whole ground in Hurstwood's absence, and discovered little objections that had not occurred to her in the warmth of the manager's apartment. She saw where she had put herself in a peculiar light, namely that of agreeing to marry him, when she was already supposedly married. She remembered a few things Drouet had done,

and now that it came to walking away from him without a word, she felt as if she was doing wrong. Now she was comfortably situated, and to one who is more or less afraid of the world, this is an urgent matter, and one which puts up strange and uncanny arguments. "You do not know what will come. There are miserable things outside. People go a-begging. Women are wretched. You never can tell what will happen. Remember the time you were hungry. Stick to what you have."

Few American readers of serious fiction had been exposed to girls who thought or acted like Carrie.

Despite her doubts, Carrie leaves Drouet—and without much regret. In New York, Hurstwood, stripped of his meager social status, quickly declines. In the end, he finds himself relying upon Carrie's sudden and accidental career on the stage, but when that career prospers, Carrie leaves him, too.

The gloomy Hurstwood, sitting in his cheap hotel where he had taken refuge with seventy dollars—the price of his furniture—between him and nothing, saw a hot summer out and a cool fall in, reading. . . . Frequently he saw notices of Carrie. Her picture was in the *World* once or twice, and an old *Herald* he found in a chair informed him that she had recently appeared with some others at a benefit for something or other. He read these with mingled feelings.

For her part, "Carrie had attained that which in the beginning seems life's object,

or at least, such fraction of it as human beings ever attain of their original desires. She could look about on her gowns and carriage, her furniture and bank account. Friends there were, as the world takes it—those who would bow and smile in acknowledgement of her success. For these she had once craved. Applause there was, and publicity—once far off, essential things, but now grown trivial and indifferent. Beauty also—her type of loveliness—and yet she was lonely. In her rocking chair she sat, when not otherwise engaged—singing and dreaming.

And so Carrie ascends to her own indifference as Hurstwood descends into an urban hell that brings on his suicide, a fate that had befallen a news writer Dreiser had known and admired in St. Louis after the writer lost his step in New York.

Before *Sister Carrie* was distributed to bookstores, however, the publisher's wife, a woman of some considerable standing in New York society (publishing was "a gentleman's game" back then) and herself a romantic author, read page proofs and was appalled. How could a woman of Carrie's low character be so rewarded with fame and fortune—and still be unhappy and unfulfilled? How could her earnest lover, Hurstwood, once an upright family man of good business standing, be so crushed by

66

the consequences of a single bad, love-sick decision? The outcomes of the story conflicted squarely with the received values that kept Mrs. Doubleday's social class in power and the lower classes in balance. Thus, the story was immoral. She demanded that her husband break the contract. Dreiser was desolated, but fought back. The upshot was that while review copies were sent out, only a few books were distributed and sales were a scant 650 copies. *Sister Carrie*'s author received less than $100 for his many months of creative labor. His dream of freedom through art seemed just that: a dream.

His wife, alienated and disturbed, returned to Missouri. Dreiser no longer could write even a sentence of fiction. He abandoned work on a second novel, *Jennie Gerhardt*. He rented a cheap room in Brooklyn before drifting into homelessness and drink, a decline not dissimilar to Hurstwood's. Hallucinations haunted him and he contemplated suicide.

Once again brother Paul came to his rescue. He sought him out in the Bowery and wept over his fallen condition. He fed him, gave him money, and shipped him off to a health camp. After a month, Theo recovered enough to take a manual laborer's job with an immigrant railroad crew working along the Hudson River.

Three years passed before he could write again. But then he took up an editorial career, turning away from fiction and the psychic horrors that awaited those who tried to tell the truth. He went into the world of glossy, commercial magazines, where he rapidly soared to the heights of that calling. He briefly became an assistant feature editor of the *New York Daily News* and freelanced for the *New York Tribune*. His reading broadened to include thinkers such as Kant. The promise of his youth was polished into a hard-working professionalism. By decade's end he commanded the Manhattan editorial suites of a publishing empire, earning more than $10,000 a year, an extraordinary salary at the time, as editor of the *Delineator* and two other magazines published by the Butterick Company (a maker of clothing patterns), where he directed a staff of 2,000. He lived in a fashionable Riverside Drive apartment and became a social crusader, even persuading President Theodore Roosevelt to convene a national conference of the National Child Rescue League, which Dreiser had founded. But he faced grief again. In 1906, his mainstay, goodhearted and simple brother Paul, died unexpectedly, and to the surprise of all, penniless.

Meanwhile, *Sister Carrie*, its length reduced a third by Arthur Henry's editing, was reissued in England to flattering critical reviews and by B. F. Dodge in the United States, where it was reckoned as a work of "genius" among those hoping for a radically new kind of contemporary fiction. Then Dreiser's editorial career ended. In October of 1910 his secret affair with the underaged daughter of a fellow employee became known and Dreiser was precipitously put out on the street.

This time he didn't wallow in despair or self-pity. Instead, he took up his pen in a fury. By late spring 1911, he had completed *Jennie Gerhardt*, which was published by Harper Brothers. He pushed on, writing without interruption, and by the fall of that year had finished a veiled autobiography, *The "Genius,"* and launched *The Financier*, the first volume of his projected "Trilogy of Desire," based on the life of Charles Tyson Yerkes, Chicago's traction magnate.

When in December of 1912 Dreiser next returned to the city of his adolescence, he came as a literary hero to a metropolis that was teeming with writers, artists, and performers. They were creating a literary "renaissance" of their own. In 1917, Dreiser's friend, the Baltimore critic H. L. Mencken, was to call Chicago the "literary capital of America" because so many writers of talent had come from the young city.

Dreiser settled in a well-furnished apartment on Lincoln Parkway north of Tower Town where artists and bohemians lived amid slightly decaying mansions of old wealth. For the second volume of his trilogy, *The Titan*, he set about collecting data on the Chicago life of Yerkes. In Dreiser's eyes, Yerkes' fictional counterpart, Frank Algernon Cowperwood, was a prime example of the human species at its strongest and most rapacious. Cowperwood built the very skeletons upon which great cities moved and he made himself fabulously wealthy in the process. As *The Titan* opens, Cowperwood emerges from prison, socially tarnished but still comparatively wealthy. "Here was life," Dreiser wrote of Cowperwood's arrival in Chicago.

> Here was a seething city in the making. There was something dynamic in the very air which appealed to his fancy. How different for some reason than Philadelphia! That was a stirring city too. He had thought it wonderful at one time, quite a world; but this thing, while infinitely worse, was better. It was more youthful, more hopeful. . . .Life was doing something new.

Dreiser both envied and despised Cowperwood, his financial schemes and political manipulations. Yet Dreiser's prose is expansively reflective in its examination of the man himself and his socioeconomic vision. Cowperwood surrounded himself with great luxury, beautiful women, and fine art. He made himself a man of immense power who bought and sold politicians, businesses, and mistresses. But Dreiser saw Cowperwood as ultimately "prince of a world of dreams whose reality was sorrow." And he saw the common man Cowperwood manipulated as "but an innocent fly caught in the strands of a horrific spider's web."

Dreiser spent long hours digging up details on Yerkes' connections, poring over documents in the Newberry Library and interviewing those who had been part of the municipal drama that Yerkes directed in his transit schemes. For amusement, Dreiser crossed over from the Newberry to Bughouse Square to watch and listen to the heated debates there between anarchists and socialists and their opponents. When not researching or writing, he spent pleasant hours in discussion with other writers such as attorney Edgar Lee Masters. Masters had not yet published his *Spoon River Anthology*, which would become the all-time best-selling book of poetry in American history, but he had written Dreiser to express his admiration for *Sister Carrie*. The two writers got on royally and shared more than a few bottles of expensive liquor. Dreiser even brought Masters' poetry to the attention of the Chicago writers who were stirring up the literary establishment, critics such as the young Floyd Dell.

The brash Dell was editor of the radical *Friday Literary Review*, considered the nation's most influential avant-garde periodical. It promoted everything from feminism to divorce to socialism, and cele-brated writers who were, in Dell's opinion, honest and brave enough to speak the truth on social matters, both economic and personal. Dell and his colleagues were setting out the critical boundaries of a new, realistic, modern American literature, but Dell also took time to promote Chicago writers. He took Carl Sandburg's first poems to Harriet Monroe, the guiding spirit of *Poetry*, the nation's first journal devoted solely to that literary art. The poems were rejected, but the next batch, submitted by Sandburg himself, included "Chicago," the work that launched his long career.

Of Dreiser, Dell wrote in *FLR*:

> The poetry of Chicago has been adequately rendered, so far, by only one writer, and in only one book. That book is, naturally enough, that one which Frank Harris declared in the *London Academy* to be "The best story, on the whole, that has yet come out of America," to wit: *Sister Carrie.* . . .It is the most real, the most sincere, the most moving, of all the books with which we have dealt, or are likely to deal. . . .
>
> Mr. Dreiser has not looked to see the badness of the city, nor its goodness; he has looked to see its beauty and its ugliness, and has seen a beauty even in its ugliness. And in doing that he has given us, there is little doubt, the Chicago of the whole middle West—a beacon across the prairies, a place of splendor and joy. . . .

Dell had attracted a strong local network of artist friends and Dreiser circulated in this crowd. After introducing Dreiser to Sherwood Anderson, Dell with Dreiser found a publisher for Anderson's first novel, *Windy McPherson's Son*. Another Dell friend was the mystical and pecu-liar Vachel Lindsay, who performed his poems at the Dells' bohemian parties in an old studio left over from the 1893 World's Columbian Exposition near the University of Chicago campus.

Dell also befriended the beautiful and mysterious Margaret

Anderson. He gave her reviews to write for *FLR* and it was at a Dell party that she announced the creation of her own literary magazine, *The Little Review*, which endorsed anarchism and revolution. She was the first U.S. publisher to print portions of James Joyce's *Ulysses*. She also published the young Ezra Pound, and when she found nothing of interest to print she simply issued a magazine of blank pages. The anarchists Emma Goldman and Ben Reitman scandalized the decent people of Chicago when they lived briefly in Anderson's stark white apartment (barren of furniture except for a piano). All of Margaret's money went toward her literary revolution and when she could no longer afford the rent on her apartment she moved north of the city and set up a tent colony of poets and artists on the shores of Lake Michigan below the cliffs of Ravinia.

Far from this tent colony was the Cliff Dwellers' Club on Michigan Avenue, so called by Hamlin Garland, author of the starkly realist *Main Traveled Roads*. Garland claimed he did not take the club name from his friend Henry Blake Fuller's 1893 novel, which satirized Chicago's new species of apartment building occupants. Garland's own fictional images were rougher, and his tales of terrible hardships among the common folk of Wisconsin established him as an American voice of first rank. At the time of Dreiser's pilgrimage, Garland was the literary lion of the city and the two men got along well (though Garland later denounced Dreiser as a sex maniac).

Another Chicago writer Dreiser socialized with was Henry Blake Fuller, a reserved and introverted man with aristocratic mannerisms. Fuller came from an early Chicago family and had inherited its wealth. His first novels were medieval romances, but when he turned to contemporary Chicago he became a sharp critic of the commercialism that drove the city on its frenzied pace. Dreiser had read and admired Fuller's 1895 satire *With the Procession*, in which Fuller contended that Chicago was the only city ever created with the sole purpose of making money, an opinion Dreiser mainly but not wholly shared. But Dreiser's naturalism pushed beyond Fuller's realism.

In the company of Dell and Masters, Dreiser attended a performance of *Trojan Women* by Maurice Browne's experimental Little Theatre company. He was especially attracted by the actress Elaine Hyman, who portrayed Andromachi, and eventually used her as a model for Stephanie Platow, the young girl in *The Titan* whose beauty and innocence induces Cowperwood to seduce her and sacrifice his power. Although Elaine Hyman was already having an affair with Dell, she succumbed after some coaxing to the older Dreiser and his apparently ageless wisdom.

After a month back in Chicago, Dreiser returned to New York to complete *The Titan*. But in 1914 Harpers stopped its preparations for publication of the book, afraid that its brutal realism would offend the firm's financial backers. Though Dreiser publicly denounced Harpers, he could not reverse their decision and the book first appeared through the English publisher John Lane.

Some of his best years were still ahead; so were some of his toughest battles. In 1925 Dreiser would publish *An American Tragedy*, a novel that still ranks among legitimate candidates for the great American novel. It too raised cries of outrage. Then Dreiser's great work was done. He moved to Hollywood where his books were made into movies. His early novels had defined the American literary landscape for at least the first quarter of the 20th century, some would say for the first half century. In these works he had unflinchingly portrayed the brutal social struggle he had himself known first-hand, and to this had added a psychologically probing perspective and philosophically tempered reflectiveness that took in the whole of human experience. He found within each individual values and feelings worthy of understanding and sympathy. In so doing, he broke the rigid strictures of highbrow culture that ordained that a novel must depict a struggle between upper middle-class characters presented as a mild morality play that would deliver an instructive ethical lesson to readers.

Dreiser also portrayed Chicago itself as a player among primal natural forces of hunger, sex, power, and desire—invisible and devastating. These inexorable powers bent human beings like the summer storms pressing across the long Indian grasses of the prairie. In Dreiser's Chicago, people were compelled to act as they did not so much because of independent or free wills or legitimate ethical choices. Rather, they were victims of chance and the savage biological and cosmic conflicts that cast them to and fro, hardly aware of these factors at work on their lives as they toiled, endured, and fought. Nature was "aimless, pointless, unfair, unjust," Dreiser would eventually conclude. So he wondered what freedom could be found in the web of these forces and circumstances that dictated our lives.

Because he was too ill to complete it himself, the last volume of his modern epic "Trilogy of Desire," *The Stoic*, was put into final form by his younger friend and fellow naturalist, James T. Farrell, and published in 1947, two years after Dreiser's death. He was gone, but his books endured. "American writing, before and after his time," said H. L. Mencken, "differed almost as much as biology before and after Darwin. He was a man of large originality, of profound feeling, and of unshakeable courage. All of us who write are better off because he lived, worked, and hoped."

Minna Everleigh

SISTERS

In the very beginning, the city's pay-for-sin parlors were located on the north bank of the Chicago River near Lake Michigan—the Sands, the area was called. In 1857 William B. Ogden, first mayor of Chicago 20 years before, acquired a clouded title to that land, however, and with the stated purpose of uplifting the young city's morality persuaded the sitting mayor, his friend, Long John Wentworth, to evict the Sands' tenants—who were known by *Chicago Tribune* editorial writers to be "vile and vicious persons." (The Sands property ultimately became Chicago's Magnificent Mile.)

Swept by reform—or greed—from their quarters, the professionals of the Sands relocated, first to Randolph and Wells streets, then one contingent to the near downtown south side Levee, another westward along Madison Street. (A century, plus three decades, later, the two areas are today being rehabbed by big-money developers.) For the frugal, Chicago's early Tenderloin offered establishments such as Noah's Ark (two saloons, six brothels) on Washington street near Halsted, which was owned by the rich and pious alderman Jacob Beidler. At the corner of 19th Street and Armour Avenue (now the southern extension of Federal Street) was Bed Bug Row (four dime and two-bit cribs) and opposite it was The Bucket of Blood saloon. Close by The California, the roughest parlor house in Chicago, on Armour (opposite the Why Not? named out of respect for the windowshades at the notorious Under the Willow), was the New Era Cigar Store, proprietors Mamie and Eva Welch, where a $2.00 tobacco purchase entitled you to up to half an hour in the back room with either Mamie or Eva, your choice. Black May's between Dearborn and Armour had light-skinned black hustlers but only for white clients, and spectacularly bestial circuses. Opposite it was a Japanese house and a Chinese house and on the corner of Archer and Cullerton was The House of All Nations, with whores from all nations (and if they weren't, they could fake it). All Nations had a $2.00 and a $5.00 entrance but the same girls worked both sides.

Until the Everleighs arrived, Chicago's grandest whorehouse was Madame Lou Harper's at 219 South Monroe, established during the Civil war. The 20 girls at Madame Harper's luxury brothel—the Mansion—were elaborately gowned and coiffeured, rates were high, and outside the bedroom doors decorum prevailed. (Carrie Watson started at the Mansion as an 18-year-old virgin, amassed a fortune with her own place at 441 South Clark, and was liberal with monetary gifts to church and synagogue.)

One of Madame Harper's competitors for the carriage trade was Lizzie Allen, who (as 18-year-old Ellen Williams) had come to Chicago from Milwaukee in 1858 to be a whore. She began in the Levee at Mother Herrick's Prairie Queen, went on to Kate Anderson's Senate, and by 1865 had graduated to her own 3-girl sporting house on Wells Street and then to a fine 30-girl house at Clark and Polk.

In 1890 Lizzie built a $125,000 brothel on South Dearborn, furnishing it with mirrored bedroom ceilings, a feature that appealed to country customers brought to Chicago by the 1893 Columbian Exposition. When the Exposition ended, Lizzie leased the premises to Effie Hankins. (Three years later, Lizzie died, aged 56 and wealthy. She was buried in Rosehill Cemetery under a tombstone bearing the words "PERPETUAL EASE," an inscription subject to much rephrasing by her one-time customers.)

The Everleigh sisters, daughters of a Kentucky lawyer, had been raised in a genteel, antebellum kind of Old South atmosphere of servants and private tutors. They married well-born brothers but were physically mistreated, or so they claimed, and abruptly left their husbands to tour with a second-rate theatrical troupe that brought them to Omaha in time for the 1898 Trans-Mississippi Exposition.

With an inherited $35,000 they opened a bordello to accommodate Exposition visitors, and though neither had experience as proprietors—Ada was just 22; Minna, only 20—their venture prospered at $10 and upwards a client.

They took their profits to Chicago and for $55,000 and $500 a month bought Effie Hankins' lease on her successful brothel at 2131-33 South Dearborn—the House of Mirrors built by Lizzie Allen a decade before. On February 1, 1900, after spending almost $200,000 for new furnishings and appointments, the sisters opened their three-story, 50-room bagnio as the Everleigh Club—"Everleigh" from their grandmother's habit of signing her letters "Everly yours."

Elegant, discreet, and well-managed, the Club was a Chicago landmark of gracious living for 12 years. Even at its busiest, the house was said to have about it an air of hushed refinement, perhaps in part because, as Minna said, the sisters were "experienced in the finer shames." (Minna, the more articulate of the two, was also euphemistic: Her preferred verb for the principal act practiced for pay at the Club was "slipping." The rest of the Levee madams called it "Mama and Papa fucking.")

Behind the imposing brownstone façade of 2131-33 could be found six pianos (one a miniature, gilded at a cost of $15,000), three 4-piece orchestras (piano, violin, cello, harp), 12 large reception parlors (soundproofed), each decorated with its own motif (copper, silver, gold, rose, blue, green, Moorish, Japanese, Chinese, music, and ballroom), a library stocked with rare editions of the classics ("That's educating the wrong end of a whore," observed "Bet-a-Million" Gates), a large and sumptuous dining room, a full-scale replica of a Pullman Palace Car buffet, rich carpets, gold-plated spittoons, marble statuary and imported oil paintings, hardwood floors of rare woods in mosaic patterns—and up the mahogany staircase 30 boudoirs, each with mirrored ceiling, at least one marble-inlaid bed of brass and firm-cushioned mattress, gold bathtub or shower (some with both), perfumed aphrodisiac spray, and at least one lady in lacy peignoir.

On very special occasions the sisters would open boxes of live butterflies and let the brightly colored lepidoptera swarm fluttering through the parlors and boudoirs. As an envious rival madam remarked, "No man for sure is going to forget he got his balls fanned by a butterfly at the Everleigh Club." (Possibly. Rooms were redecorated at the Club every year. During one of these redecorations a guest put his hand into some fresh paint. The next day Minna said to a painter, "Come, I'll show you where a man put his hand last night." "If it's all the same to you," was the workman's reply, "I'd rather have a glass of beer.")

The sisters' theory was that "the contemplation of deviltry was more rewarding than the deviltry itself." Of Club customers, Minna once philosophized, "It's not the ladies they like best really. They like cards, they like dice, horseracing best. If it wasn't unmanly to admit it, they'd rather most of the time gamble than screw."

House policy, as set forth by the two bejeweled, pleasant-faced hostesses, had "no time for the rough element, the clerk on a holiday, or a man without a checkbook." The sisters were definitely not in business to attract the tourist who came to town with one shirt and a two dollar bill and didn't change either.

As a matter of house policy, Illinois legislators were admitted free. No alcoholic beverages besides wine were allowed ($12 a bottle downstairs; $15 in bed); no drugs or knockout drops, no rolling of customers; no women guests.

The sisters got their fine wines from Chicago's Chapin & Gore, where their monthly bill ran from $2,000 to $5,000 for imported champagnes. In most months the Club's commercial account at the Fort

Dearborn Bank had a balance of $40,000 or more. (The sisters also kept $200,000 in personal savings accounts at the First Trust and Savings and the Illinois Trust and Savings.) In a good year, their net (in a time of no income tax), after all expenses, including protection payments to police and city officials and state legislators, exceeded $125,000.

The ordinary charge for a paying customer's creature comforts ran to totals of from $150 to $1,000, plus a substantial tip to the lady of the gentleman's choice. The young lady got to keep half of the direct house charge for the use of her flesh, a charge that varied from $10 to $50 and up a patron, depending upon services rendered. A customer's check on its return to him bore the endorsement of an innocuously named, fictitious firm—"Utopia Novelty," for instance—with a Loop bank building address.

Over the years, the Club's guests included—in addition to Chicago's silk-hatted business and financial élite—"Gentleman Jim" Corbett, John W. Bet-a-Million Gates, George Ade, John Barrymore, Stanley Ketchell, Edgar Lee Masters, an entire U.S. congressional committee, Ring Lardner, and the brother of Kaiser Wilhelm II. (When told of his brother's visit to the Everleigh, the Kaiser—King of Prussia, Emperor of all Germany, and the man who in just a dozen years would let slip the dogs of World War I—asked the vintage of the wine served.)

Only twice in its history did scandal seriously threaten the Club. On November 25, 1905, Marshall Field's son, 37 years old, married and the father of three children, died of a gunshot wound. The newspapers reported it as an accident, the *Chicago Tribune*'s headline reading: "MARSHALL FIELD, JR., SHOOTS HIMSELF/*Accident Happens in Dressing Room in Prairie Avenue House While Pondering Over a Hunting Trip*." Field had been shot by a "Betsy"—an automatic revolver—a handgun.

It was believed throughout the city that Field had either committed suicide or had been shot by a whore or a gambler at the Everleigh Club and transported from there to the family home, and that Chicago newspapers suppressed the true account because Field's father was one of their largest advertisers.

About a month after Field's death, one of the Club's girls received a phone call (Calumet 412 was the Club's number), and Minna eavesdropped at another outlet. She heard Pony Moore, a black gambler and saloon keeper, offer the girl $20,000 to testify she had seen one of the sisters shoot Field.

Now, in addition to their regular protection payments to the highly placed, Ada and Minna dispensed cash direct to the working police of the 22nd Street Station (on the premise that when you ate at a restaurant, you tipped the person who served you). Minna called a sergeant so retained and the two of them went together to Moore's Turf and Exchange Saloon at Wabash and 21st.

Moore lost his saloon license; the girl vanished.

The second incident took place in 1910, when one Sunday afternoon, January 9th, Nathaniel Moore, 26, married five years, the son of a Rock Island railroad and corporation millionaire, was found dead in Madam Vic (Emma Ludwig) Shaw's resort at 2014 South Dearborn. Moore, who had a reputation for spending his father's money lavishly for entertainment (once, in New York City, writing a check for $20,000 to pay for a small dinner party, chorus girls his guests), had spent Saturday evening at the Everleigh, being asked to leave about one o'clock Sunday morning when Minna discovered the young man about to accept from one of her girls a glass of champagne that Minna suspected was laced with morphine (a mixture that slowed the heart, inducing sleep—or death). The accused and angry girl also left, finding immediate employment at her trade that same night a block away at Madam Vic Shaw's.

At three o'clock the next afternoon, Minna received a phone call from the girl she had discharged the night before: "They're framing you. They've got a dead body at Shaw's and they're going to plant it in your furnace. It's Nat Moore. . . .It's a dirty trick and I won't let them do that to you."

Minna dispatched a trusted emissary to Madam Shaw's. He demanded to see the body. A group gathered; harsh words, accusations, and denials were exchanged; a girl screamed; and Madam Shaw was at last forced to call in the police. The Monday morning headline of the *Chicago Examiner* read: "NATHANIEL MOORE, SON OF RAILROAD CHIEF, FOUND DEAD IN LEVEE RESORT/*Woman Finds Corpse in Bed; Mystery Will Be Investigated at Inquest.*"

Though Moore always carried large sums of money, only $2.50 was found on his body. The coroner's jury verdict was that he had died of a weak heart. The Everleigh Club was not implicated.

The sisters paid their protection through the usual Levee channels but sidestepped the rule that beverages for their house, as for all houses in the Levee, should be purchased from Solly Friedman. Friedman and his brother-in-law, Ike Bloom, were powers in the Levee, Bloom as the proprietor of the notorious low-life dance pavilion, Freiberg's Hall, at 22nd Street between Wabash and State. The sisters also sidestepped as often as possible the rule that brothel keepers buy their provisions from one of four specified grocery stores. Their independence accounted for much of the animosity felt by others in Levee commerce toward them, and for some of their difficulties over the years.

Protection was paid via Big Jim Colosimo, who delivered the money to the Levee's First Ward political leaders, Bathhouse John Coughlin and Hinky Dink Kenna. (Alderman Coughlin—who had a half interest in the Friedman-Bloom food and liquor store—also had an agency that wrote most of the Levee's insurance, as well as much of that for the First Ward's licit businessmen.) As a gesture of *amicizia*, protection collector Colosimo would occasionally drop by the Club to prepare a spaghetti feast for all on Sunday evening—"Beau Night," when the Club was closed to paying customers and Ada and Minna permitted their ladies' long-term, bona-fide suitors to come courting with candy and flowers.

The sisters looked out for the welfare of their charges in other ways as well. "You have the whole night before you," Minna would tell the girls in a set speech, "and one $50 client is more desirable than five $10 ones. Less wear and tear." She told them to "be polite and forget what you are here for. Stay respectable by all means; I want you girls to be proud that you are in the Everleigh Club."

At the Club, just as years before at Lou Harper's Mansion, the conventional forms of respectable society were observed. Sometimes they even originated there. It was at 2131-33 South Dearborn, for example, that a guest, having carelessly spilled champagne in a courtesan's slipper, gallantly sipped the white wine from it, thus stereotyping that romantic cliché.

Late in 1911, however, in St. Louis, Chicago's Mayor Carter Harrison, Jr., made a speech extolling Chicago's many commercial attractions to a gathering of the Show-Me State's business notables. At the post-address reception, a waggish Missourian handed the mayor an advertising brochure. "Mr. Mayor," he said, "I detected an omission in your list of Chicago's marvels." The brochure bespoke the charms of the Everleigh Club in Minna's ornamental prose; it was illustrated with photographs.

Chicago was at that time in the throes of reformist agitation over the very existence of its sanctioned vice district, the Levee, and as soon as the embarrassed mayor returned home he ordered the Club immediately padlocked—for "its infamy, the audacious advertising of it. . . ." He wrote the order himself and gave it personally to his chief of police, but more than 12 hours passed before the order was carried out. At 12:45 in the morning of October 25, 1911, however, before a disapproving crowd that extended into the street, officers of the law did finally padlock the Everleigh Club. Silk-hatted gentlemen bade their hostesses a last, regretful farewell and mounted waiting carriages. The unexplained but merciful delay had permitted pleasure-seekers one last night of expensive sin.

At closing, Minna ordered champagne for all. "The ship has sunk," she toasted. "She was a good one. Let's give her a hurrah."

It was reported that within 24 hours of the closing, each of the Club's *filles de joie* received job offers from other houses in Chicago and across the country. Ada and Minna had employed more than 600 such young women over 11 years, but after the closing the sisters could not remember very much about any of them. (One of the few who became known outside her trade was Belle Schreiber, one of black heavyweight boxing champion Jack Johnson's white sweethearts; Johnson was indicted by the federal government for transporting her across state lines for immoral purposes. He fled the country and in 1915 lost his title to Jess Willard in Havana, Cuba.)

Disenfranchised and in their mid-30s now, but with more than a million dollars in cash, together with $200,000 in jewelry (and $25,000 in never-to-be-paid I.O.U.s), Ada and Minna took a trip to Europe. On their return six months later, they would have reopened at a new location but were asked to pay more than they thought reasonable and right for protection at the new address—$40,000 a year. They consulted with Colosimo, who told them to try to work it out with Ike Bloom.

Bloom told them, "You have the knack for making everybody sore. . . .Why don't you see Bathhouse John, make a deal, be a good fellow and play ball with the rest of us?. . . .Supposing I call a meeting? You make a speech, say you're sorry—anything. They'll be tickled to death to find you a regular. C'mon, what do you say?"

Minna laughed and said, "I'll go my way and the rest can go hang."

With their gilded piano, they moved to New York City, where they lived in anonymity on Riverside Drive under the name "Lester." In 1948, Minna, age 70, died and Ada relocated to Virginia, living quietly there until her death in 1970, age 94. The Everleigh Club brownstone became a low-rent rooming house shortly after the Club's closing, and in 1933 the building was demolished.

Of their Club's success Minna had said, "We'd never have made it without the cheating married man." Then she added, "And if it hadn't been for the cheating married woman, we'd have made another million."

A young Michael Kenna

John Coughlin (in bowler)

RUFFIANO

One night a year the whores of the Levee's knocking shops had a gala given in honor of their profession, more or less. This event had its origins in benefits held in the 1880s and early '90s for Lame Jimmy, a crippled piano and violin player in Carrie Watson's 60-girl parlor house. Madame Watson characterized the lame professor's benefits as social occasions where joy "reigned unrefined." They ended in 1892 when one attending drunken policeman shot another in a dispute over a doxy and there was a clamor of outrage from reformers.

After long thought—six years—a disappointed First Ward Alderman Bathhouse John Coughlin suggested to his guiding intelligence, the Little Fellow, Alderman Michael Hinky Dink Kenna, that they jointly sponsor an annual evening to replace Lame Jimmy's. Kenna agreed but, seeing an opportunity to do good and spread cheer more abundantly, with the stipulation that they not limit attendance to just 300 or 400 but open their event to the entire underworld of the Levee and to those beholden to them for political favors in the upperworld, as well. Thus, the inaugural First Ward Ball held just before Christmas in 1898, with quotas of tickets Kenna-allotted—in proportion to income—to every prostitute, madam, pimp, saloon keeper, slugger, swindler, thief, merchant, politician, and policeman in the ward, 10 to 12 thousand in all, with the addition of a thousand or more upper-class and celebrity thrill-seekers.

For 11 years Bathhouse and the Little Fellow netted from $25,000 to $50,000 for their political campaign chest from their holiday bacchanals. Of the tenth, in 1907, a *Chicago Tribune* reporter gave as his opinion that "If a great disaster had befallen the Coliseum last night there would not have been a second-story worker, a dip or plug-ugly, porch climber, dope fiend, or scarlet woman remaining in Chicago." At this ball two bands played, three bars dispensed 75 kegs of beer and 200 waiters served 35,000 quarts of it (at champagne prices) and 10,000 quarts of champagne (at nectar-of-the gods' prices). The waiters paid $5.00 each for the privilege of serving . . . and the tips.

The tenth's accompanying orgiastic revels inspired a new clamor by reform elements in Chicago, to which an unrepentant Bathhouse responded: "All right, we'll compromise. We won't let parents bring their children. There!"

The licentiousness of First Ward Balls could not have been predicted from the private habits of their sponsors. "I never go into the houses where the women are," averred Kenna; "Me neither," echoed the Bath. They were long-term married men whose marriages ended for both in the deaths of their wives. When at one of the balls whores in Victoria Shaw's employ arrived wearing blouses, tights, and hip-length silk stockings a scandalized Bathhouse told them to leave and re-costume themselves decently. (Tights were considered indecent, but not wispy Indian, Egyptian, geisha, and gypsy costumes, which were very much in favor.) Still, after midnight many a woman at First Ward balls was hardly costumed at all.

They began to arrive by carriage as darkness fell, having worked a half shift at their places of employment, each group of gowned or costumed lovelies escorted into the Coliseum and to their tables or boxes by the police, a necessary precaution because the entrance was mobbed by the curious and unruly. (Among other events hosted during the year at the Coliseum were the Ringling Brothers, and the Barnum and Bailey circuses and those of the national political conventions.) Hundreds of policemen, ushers, and bouncers watched over the throng inside as it gathered so that the women were not harmed or their jewelry stolen. The dance floor was crowded but few on it were dancing. Fights broke out sporadically and bouncers would blackjack one or more of the contestants who would then be dragged outside to cool off. Two ambulances were kept in readiness at the rear of the huge hall at 15th and Wabash.

Just before midnight Minna and Ada Everleigh, resplendent in grey silks and jewels, arrived in their broughams drawn by matched pairs of bays, followed by hansoms and hackneys with the retinue from the Club. Noting the arrival of the sisters, the Ball's grand marshal, Alderman Coughlin in full dress (which on such a night called for lavender trousers, white dress shirt, white waistcoat brocaded with pink carnations and red rosebuds, billiard-cloth green swallowtail coat, pink gloves, and yellow pumps), shouted, "Clear the dance floor!" and ushers and bouncers cleared the floor of the unwanted as 2,000 Levee whores, madams, and masters, together with the First Ward Democratic Club, Chicago's aldermen, police officials, state legislators and judges, and mayors of surrounding towns made their way to it.

"On with the March!" cried the grand marshal, and the 2,000 linked arms 26 abreast as the band struck up a rousing tune and Bathhouse John, walking backwards and directing the marching assemblage with upraised, waving arms, led them up and down the hall before 10,000 yowling spectators, back and forth, back and forth, as many as 30 times, until finally the Little Fellow called out, "Stop it, Jawn!" and the grand march ended—and the revels began.

The balls had a semi-official song which was sung frequently by the increasingly more drunken crowd as the dawn approached. Its lyrics were

> I love you, I love you, I love you.
> You are the ideal of my dreams.
> I always knew there'd be someone like you.
> I have loved you forever it seems.
>
> For years in my dreams' fondest fancies,
> A vision of your face I drew.
> And I knew, dear, somehow,
> When I met you just now,
> You are the ideal of my dreams.

Josiah Pitts Woolfolk (aka the novelist Jack Woodford) was there:

The denizens would sing this song over and over, band or no band, all evening.

Then a superb fight would start, complete with flashing knives and sometimes gunshot. On occasion it would include practically the entire attendance. For fun men would tear the women's clothes off. Some bawdy old madam finding herself thus denuded would utter shrieks of maidenly embarrassment and call upon heaven to right such an injustice. . . .

It would wind up at six o'clock in the morning with half the celebrators of this Black Mass prone upon the floor; nobody knew whether dead or alive. Men and women would have fallen asleep in ultimate embrace. This was frowned upon. Right-thinking celebrants would shove them, still together, under the booths where they were supposed to have been in the first place, where they continued undismayed to undulate. A few sturdy ones would be wandering around at dawning, having sated themselves with numerous companions of the evening, still singing in general to all: "I love you, I love you, I love you." . . . They weren't mad at anybody, and they were convinced that nobody was mad at them. They were simply screaming to themselves, the world, and each other, impartially: "I love you, I love you, I love you."

In all that lost, staggering, full-throated, heart-sick, happy-one-night throng of Chicago's lowest each year was dark-eyed Jim Colosimo, one of the rabble at the first ball—but, by the last, one of the most powerful men in the Levee.

The system has always had a cardinal rule for success: Secure a place within it where you control others. To gain the power he gained, young Giacomo Colosimo followed the rule: He married the madam who owned the whorehouse.

Giacomo was in his late teens when he arrived in Chicago with his father, Luigi, from Cosenza, in Calabria, southern Italy, after a stop-over in Boston. The Colosimos came in the mid-'90s, Papa Luigi carrying with him a cherished family heirloom—an antique sword whose possession guaranteed that some day, so went family lore, a Colosimo would achieve high position and authority.

Jim began humbly enough. He shined boots and shoes and hawked newspapers, carried water to railroad hands, dug ditches, and he also became adept at picking pockets—the usual first occupations of young males in the Levee. But grander opportunities presented themselves to a youth of qualities and Jim seized upon one of these; he became a *ruffiano*—a pimp. Apparently he lacked the wherewithal or sponsorship to pay off the police properly, however, and they dispersed his little band of six with a rough warning to its ponce.

The chastened youth tried his hand with fair success at black-hand extortion, then took employment with the city at the more socially acceptable task of street sweeping. In allusion to the white uniforms they wore, street sweepers were called "white wings" in turn-of-the-century Chicago. A white wing's broom-and-shovel responsibilities were chiefly to follow after draymen, milk and ice wagoners, street peddlers, and coachmen and clean up after their horses.

Aggressively ambitious, Colosimo was presently made a foreman, from which eminence he organized a social and athletic club. As a foreman he was making $2.00 a day (worker white wings got $1.50 a day; the Irish got the $4.00-a-day city office jobs) and Jim must have felt the need to broaden his horizons. Additionally, it was an easy thing at election time for the *fratelanza*'s founder to deliver his brother *spazzinos*' votes to candidates designated by aldermen Coughlin and Kenna.

For his services, Jim came into the circle of Kenna's and Coughlin's benevolence. They first made him a Democratic precinct captain, which meant that he need no longer fear the attentions of Chicago police; then, one of their collectors of Levee protection money. The muscular Colosimo established his credentials as a collector the first time rates were raised. He brass-knuckled a balking Georgie Spencer (whose house was two doors from the Everleigh Club) and deftly lifted the $300 assessment from her purse while she groaned on the floor.

In 1902, while making his rounds, Big Jim was offered a job as manager of her boarders by Victoria Moresco, a proprietor at Archer and Armour. From Archer south, Armour Avenue was bawdyhouse solid, both sides, for two full blocks. With ten dollars in his pocket and a dozen cherry flips (sherry with the white of an egg) in his belly, a roisterer could "go down the line" far into the night. (Those who did, the next morning "went up with the windowshade.")

Victoria Moresco was middleaged, fat, and no beauty. Jim was half her age, lusty, and handsome. Notwithstanding these disparities, they must have fallen instantly and deeply in love. How else explain that just two weeks after Big Jim began work as manager for Victoria the two were married? Perhaps, as an old Sicilian proverb has it, the pleasure of command *is* sweeter than sexual intercourse.

In any case, the Colosimos prospered. Big Jim opened a second *lupanare* on 22nd Street and Dearborn, the Saratoga, and renamed his wife's the Hotel Victoria in her honor. The two of them acquired other houses outright or gained control of them, and they also ran a number of saloons near to, or connected by passageways, to their bordellos. Their take was 60 percent of their girls' earnings. And Big Jim, as well, continued to be the aldermen's go-between with and collector from other First Ward vice entrepreneurs.

Additionally, with Maurice Van Bever, the biggest contributor to First Ward balls (one of Van Bever's bagnios was on Dearborn next to French Emma's; Emma pioneered *all*-mirror rooms), Big Jim organized a white-slave ring with ties to similar rings in New York, St. Louis, and Milwaukee. Some of the hundreds of women imported into Chicago by Colosimo and Van Bever—and either employed by them or sold to other whoremasters for from $10 to $300 plus a percentage of future earnings—were pros. Others were girls as young as 14 or 15. (In the '90s Mary Hastings, madam of a three-story bordello on Custom House Place—today, Federal Street—lured teenage girls to Chicago with the promise of jobs, had them "broken in"—that is, raped—and sold those she did not use herself to other Levee madams. One of her captives tossed a note into the street: "I'm being held as a slave." A passerby took the note to the police, a reporter wrote a story about the note, and "white slave" entered the language. That's one of several versions of the term's origin; only the details differ. Of course there was a play in the country in 1882 entitled *The White Slave* and a novel *The White Slave* in the 1850s. Why not?)

To recruit a girl in Chicago was not that difficult. The well-spoken, dapper roper would sweet-talk an underpaid sales clerk, waitress, maid, factory girl (they were all underpaid) over a glass of wine or a doped cup of coffee, take her to a resort where the madam would promise the girl 10 times what she was then making, have her brutalized if necessary, and put her to work. The young lady's solace when the blues overwhelmed was opium or cocaine or alcohol, provided by the madam.

The routine in a house was described by the journalist William T. Stead:

In the morning, just before 12, the colored girl served cocktails to each of the women before they got up. After they dressed, they took another refresher, usually absinthe. At breakfast they had wine. Then the day's work begun. The girls sat in couples at the windows, each keeping watch in the opposite direction. If a man passed they would rap at the window and beckon him to come in. If a policeman appeared, . . . the curtains would be drawn and all trace of hustling would disappear. But before the officer was out of sight the girls would be there again. They went on duty fifteen minutes at a time. Every quarter of an hour they were relieved, until dinner time. At five they dined, and then the evening's business began, with more drinking at intervals, all night through, to the accompaniment of piano playing with occasional step-dancing, and adjournments more or less frequent, as customers were more or less plentiful. About four or five in the morning, when they were all more or less loaded with drink, they would close the doors and go to sleep. Next day it would begin again, the same dull round of drink and hustling, debauch and drink, a dismal, dreary, monotonous existence broken only by quarreling and the constant excitement supplied by the police.

They lasted about five or six years in the better houses or in call flats, then gravitated toward Bed Bug Row or another grind house or the streets. Customers wanted young, fresh flesh. The quick toll of years, drink, drugs, and disease made it imperative that a Levee merchant constantly replenish the stock.

Harry Guzik with his wife Alma did a fair share of roping. The couple preyed only on girls already familiar with sex—"charity lays"—though the Guziks maintained not ever to have encountered a true virgin. "They're so dumb," Harry said, "you have to teach them never to give away what they can sell."

Harry and Alma would travel to a small town and scout the beauty shops, stores, hotels, and dances for prospects. A girl would be enticed into bed with Harry, whereupon Alma entered the room, disrobed, and joined them. Their frolic was presented to the candidate as a pleasure everyone should seek, enjoy, and share. After, in a post-coitum tryst, so to say, Alma would take the girl aside and advise her—no matter how much you enjoyed yourself, dear, to ask affable Harry to pay.

On leaving the small town, husband and wife arranged with each of their prospects individually to visit them in Chicago, expenses paid. They said they were never refused. In Chicago, the girl again found herself in bed with the Guziks but this time the trio was joined by one of Harry's friends who, upon leaving, pressed a ten-dollar bill upon both Alma and the girl. A few days later the girl found herself a *puttana* for Big Jim Colosimo at $10.00 a trick—$5.00 to Harry and Alma to a top of $100 plus their expenses. "Once she's laid one guy for money," Harry said, "she's hooked. After that you can put her right into a house and she'll turn over her earnings to you every night. If she tries to hold out, you just slap her around a little."

86

Within half a dozen years of his marriage, Big Jim owned or controlled 200 brothels. They ranged from dark, stinking grind houses to fancy, scented parlor houses. It was said he also controlled the play and profits of the Italian national lottery in Chicago and that he parceled out carloads of grapes to Sicilians in the city and sold the wine they made for him to other immigrants from the Kingdom of Italy—sans the federal tax. And, as an outgrowth of his white wings' social club, he came to rule the Street Laborers Union and the City Streets Repairers Union.

Vice collections for Kenna and Coughlin no longer required his personal intervention. (And he may have begun to wonder whether the aldermen's role in providing political protection was quite as vital as their percentage of the take indicated.) The pimps and madams, gamblers and saloon keepers of the Levee brought the stipulated sums to one of his lieutenants, among whom were Ed Weiss, "Blubber Bob" Gray, "Dago Frank" Lewis, Jakie Adler, Mike Carrozzo, "Jew Kid" Grabiner, and his wife's cousin, Johnny Torrio.

Big Jim was making $50,000 a month from the flesh trade alone—that is, an income of at least $600,000 a year, untaxed, and this when a dollar was a day's wages for a clerk at Marshall Fields'. He built a huge house for Papa Luigi and on Cottage Grove Avenue an even larger one for himself and Victoria, filling them with expensive antiques and art objects of every sort, none of which were in the best of taste. He had two uniformed chauffeurs for his motorcars (the largest available) and a staff of liveried servants in his home.

His broad shoulders were now matched by an equally imposing belly. His black moustache and hair were pomaded. In summer he wore snow-white linen suits; in winter, discordant checks. As an avocation he fenced stolen jewelry, keeping gems he liked for himself. He wore diamond rings, diamond shirt studs, a diamond horseshoe ornament on his vest. He had diamonds on his belt and suspender buckles and on his garters. He carried small leather bags of precious stones, rolling the jewels out on a black felt cloth or pouring them from hand to hand, fascinated by their sparkle and what they meant to him.

He also became a labor agent for his countrymen—a padrone. The first years of the century were the time for it; most of Chicago's southern Italian immigrants arrived then, 30,000 to 35,000. It was the place for it, too. Chicago was centrally located and served as a hub for seasonal workers for the entire country; common laborers—"weak mind, strong back"—were needed everywhere.

The immigrants were unskilled—as Big Jim himself had been—and usually could not speak English. Acting as their employment agent, Colosimo operated in tandem with the Italian bankers. It was through a banker that the call went out for workers for a project. Big Jim's man on the site, the labor boss, oversaw the quarters in which the workers lived, managed the shanty store at which they bought provisions, and interpreted for them. Profits were shared with the banker, but the banker realized most of his own gain through holding the savings of the laborers (sometimes as much as $20 or $25 a month), sending money back to Italy for them, to family or other relatives they hoped to bring over one day, and changing this money from U.S. to Italian currency, a process which usually entailed considerable shrinkage.

Over the winter, employment was scarce for common labor, and so for three or four months the padrone would board his clients in tenements owned, quite often, by the banker, a dozen or more men to a room (just as at job sites their quarters were usually a box car for 12 to 14). If employment over a winter was too regular to furnish this advantage to the padrone and banker, they might see to it that employment became less regular.

In 1910 Big Jim opened a *ristorante* at 2126 South Wabash that became so successful he had to build an addition four years later. The restaurant's walls were covered with green velvet and tapestries and gold-framed mirrors, or murals of Mediterranean vistas. The bar was mahogany and glass; the sky-blue ceilings were decorated with puffy white clouds and cherubim. Gold and crystal chandeliers hung over tables set purposely close at Big Jim's instruction to give his establishment an intimate atmosphere. The dance floor could be raised and lowered hydraulically. Floor shows featured singers, dancers, chorus girls, and early "jass" bands. The wine cellar offered an excellent selection; the food was superb. On the second floor was a suite of rooms for gambling. The genially smiling black-moustached host would casually stake losers to another several $1,000 bills from his well-stocked wallet, and eventually his gambling patrons came to call him "Bank."

Colosimo's Café was the symbolic crown of his triumph in the New World, a triumph foretold by the ancient sword carried by his father across the ocean and halfway across the country to Chicago. Big Jim hung this sword in his office at the back of the café, and the lieutenants and strong-arm thugs he employed swore their fealty to him on a Bible resting beneath it in a ceremony of his own devising.

The Italians of Chicago did not just admire and esteem Big Jim for his success; they revered him. No one could say their own lives in the New World were not miserable enough to want to rise from. As a March 30, 1893, *Chicago Tribune* article about "Foul Ewing Street" put it, the street had

> its own peculiar quality of filth and unwholesome smells and congested Italian population. . . .
> The street is lined with dingy frame houses innocent of paint and blackened and soiled by time and close contact with the children of Italy.

Heaps of trash, rags, and old fruit are alongside the garbage boxes already overflowing.

Every doorstep is alive with children and babies dressed in rags and grime, many of their olive-skinned faces showing sallow and wan beneath the covering of dirt.

Some of the dark-complexioned men sit around tables through the daytime hours and gamble at cards or dice with huge mugs of beer beside them.

The *Chicago Daily News*, reporting on "In the Homes of Italians," observed that "Whole families (and these Italians all have large families) occupied one room" and a pile of melon rinds and decaying bananas was "surmounted by a dead chicken too much decayed for even the unfastidious denizens of this district to stomach."

In a story titled "Life Among Chicago Dagos," a *Chicago Herald* reporter gave as his opinion that "It is not abject poverty which causes such nasty and cheap living. It is simply an imported habit from southern Italy." (The reporter had obviously never seen southern Italy.)

Giacomo Colosimo had fought his way out of such conditions; they knew that Big Jim, as their padrone, would help them fight their own way out.

In return for his help he of course required recompense. This was necessary even in the New World. First was the *bossatura*—the commission paid for the job itself, anywhere from $1.00 to $15.00. Then came the cost of transportation to the job—though it was true that the padrone himself was usually not billed for this by the employer. And there were the weekly or monthly fees that had to be charged. And the rent for shelter at the job—though it was true that the contractor usually supplied this free to the padrone. And then there was the cost of provisions (a cup of coffee and bread on rising at three or four in the morning; sausage or bologna and bread and onion at lunch for the younger men, bread only for the older; cheese, bread, and macaroni, or potatoes, or rice and tomatoes for supper). On provisions the padrone took what surely was the wholly fair markup of 50 percent to 75 percent.

All of these sums were deducted from their wages before they were paid. True, in bad years, the laborer sometimes received, after eight or nine months of 7 days/70 hours of labor a week, only $100-$150 clear—but did anyone hand Giacomo Colosimo a bag of gems when he first set foot in Chicago?

Supper groups at Colosimo's Café could include opera patrons and opera stars such as Lucien Muratore, Mary Garden, Titta Ruffo, Enrico Caruso, John McCormack, Lina Cavalieri, Amelita Galli-Curci, maestro Cleofonte Campanini, and theatergoers and stage stars such as Al Jolson, John Barrymore, Sophie Tucker, George M. Cohan, as well as tables of Levee crime notables sometimes sitting elbow to elbow with second- and third-generation heirs of the dynasts with their parties, and socialites and their escorts from the Gold Coast and the toney North Shore. They all came. "It's tea time in Boston but macaronies time in Chicago," their smiling host would call out. It was fashionable, the food and wine were good, the entertainment was good, you could dance, and it was wicked, wasn't it, possibly even slightly dangerous, with *real* gangsters sometimes there, too?

For a decade the fastidious élite of a city of two million came to see and be seen at Colosimo's Café, and to be greeted by its smiling host, Big Jim—pimp, padrone, white-slaver, black-hander, whoremaster in a white-linen suit.

Italian-American couple, Chicago, 1918, identity unknown

KID BLACKIE

On their tour of Europe in 1925, he bought his second wife, the movie actress Estelle Taylor, a 200-pound blue boarhound. She named it Castor and took it with her almost everywhere they went on the Continent. But because of its size, and claustrophobia, and hair-trigger temper—especially where a possible threat to Estelle was concerned—Castor had to travel in a separate car that followed Jack's. Since Castor disliked traveling alone, he would bite the chauffeurs the Dempseys hired.

Estelle didn't think it right to leave Castor unattended when she and her husband made public appearances, so Jack hired a companion for the dog, an ex-lightweight, Lee Moore. One morning Moore was at the top of the staircase of the Dempseys' hotel with Castor when the dog spied his mistress in the lower lobby. He bounded down the stairs, dragging Moore behind him. The ex-lightweight sustained a broken arm, a broken rib, concussion, shock, and Estelle's everlasting enmity. Jack asked his wife why she was so bitterly against Moore.

"Because he called Castor a son-of-a-bitch," was the reply.

The dog struck back by destroying the wallpaper in Moore's hotel room. (Castor had his own room)

In Paris Castor also chewed up an Aubusson rug and several chairs in the Dempsey's suite, and his own room's drapes. The Dempseys sailed for home when the lawsuit for damages was settled, Castor seasick most of the voyage, Estelle in the ship's kennel with him, cradling his giant head.

They stopped at the Morrison Hotel in Chicago on their way to Hollywood and Castor trapped himself in the hotel's revolving doors and became hysterical, tearing up the lobby when he was released. So at last Dempsey decided they must give the dog up, despite his wife's tears. But none of his friends wanted Castor, knowing the dog's proclivities, and Jack had to pay Moore to take him away. All told, Castor cost Jack at least $10,000.

The Dempsey home in Hollywood had its own 18-hole golf course, a swimming pool, gardens, a bridle path, a ballroom, and much, much more, including the Dempsey bedroom decorated by Estelle in gold and Spanish lace. . . . High living for a 30-year-old whose first job was as a mucker in a copper mine at $3.00 a day and whose first wife was a sometime whore.

William Harrison Dempsey, ninth of 13 Dempsey children, was born June 24, 1895, in Manassa, Colorado. After he completed eighth grade at 16—he had worked long periods at odd jobs while going to school—he left home to seek his fortune as a pugilist. His mother had read a biography of John L. "I can lick any son-of-a-bitch in the house" Sullivan while carrying him and had declared that her son Harry (which is what the family called him), like her hero John L., was born to someday become "the world's champion fighter."

Calling himself Kid Blackie (he had black eyes, blue-black hair), he hoboed from town to town in Colorado, Utah, and Nevada. He would walk into a town's saloon and announce: "I can't sing and I can't dance, but I'll lick anyone in the house." Since he weighed only 130 pounds and had a high, reedy voice, there were many who rose to this challenge. But he also had a wicked left hook—taught him by an older prizefighter brother (who, unfortunately, had a glass chin)—and this remained his money punch his entire career. When the challenger lay stretched on the barroom floor, the hat would be passed for Kid Blackie and unless another challenger stepped forward, Kid Blackie would be on his way. If he found himself losing, as sometimes happened in saloons frequented by older and bigger roughnecks, cowhands, lumberjacks, railroad stiffs, and farmers, he would, he said, "run like hell."

It was the toughest way in the world to earn a living, fighting anybody, anywhere, any time for a few dollars—and it took balls of brass—but as Dempsey later remarked, "They could hit me on the chin with a sledgehammer for five dollars. When you haven't eaten for two days you'll understand." He had hundreds of such barroom set-tos in a few years and dozens of more regular fights in rough mining towns and lumber camps, most of which he won by knockouts, some of which he lost to more experienced opponents—but usually in a rematch came back to beat. It was even said that when a fight was held in a tent, as they sometimes were, and his opponent was good, Kid Blackie would try to back his opponent into the tent's canvas side so that his brother or another accomplice outside the tent, armed with a blackjack, could do what it might take the Kid another round or two to accomplish. (The trick with such a maneuver, of course, is not to let your opponent back *you* into the tent's canvas.)

By 1915 he was fighting out of Salt Lake City. His base there was Commercial Street, the flashy, cheap vice center of Salt Lake, where the Mormons permitted saloons, pool halls, whorehouses, and boxing clubs to flourish. About this same time he substituted for his older prizefighter brother in a match and had to drop the moniker Kid Blackie and assume the name his brother had been using—Jack. (Jack Dempsey, the Nonpareil, a world middleweight champion, considered one of the great fighters of all time, died the year William Harrison Dempsey was born.)

In the summer of 1916, because he now had the reputation of a hard hitter and found it difficult to make matches for himself, he got a manager, Jack Price, with whom he made plans to take his skills to New York City. One evening over beers with Price he met Maxine Cates, who was playing piano in a Commercial Street saloon. As Jack recalled, "When she spoke to me she would lean toward me so that her breasts would strain against her dress. . . . I had never met anyone like her. Sometime later I realized I would never meet anyone like her again."

Price and Dempsey arrived in New York with less than $30 between them, and Jack fought his first fight there June 24, 1916, on his 21st birthday. By now he weighed 160 pounds, but he fought a 215-pounder. The newspapers gave him the decision; the promoter paid $16, which he and Price split. His next NYC bout, which he also won, earned them $43.

It was at this time that one of the sleazy characters who infested prize fighting then, as now, a certain John "The Barber" Reisler, sent a telegram to Price which said that Price's mother was dying in Utah. With Price out of the way, Reisler told the naive and inexperienced Dempsey that he had bought Dempsey's contract (Price and Dempsey had no formal contract) and bullied Jack into agreeing to fight for him by threatening that Dempsey would get no fights in NYC without John the Barber as his manager.

Reisler overmatched Dempsey for a July 14th fight against a good, experienced black boxer who had met top fighters. In the second round Dempsey's opponent broke two of Dempsey's ribs and though Jack lasted the full 10 and made a decent showing, he was bloodied and badly hurt. His "manager" took $400 of the $500 purse and vanished, leaving Dempsey to fend for himself.

Riding the rods, Jack returned to Salt Lake, discouraged, lonely, and physically hurting—and looked up Maxine Cates. She was 15 years older than he was (as he said, "quite an experienced woman"), and after a number of weeks of her comfort and company they were, at her urging, married by a justice of the peace.

When his ribs healed he resumed fighting and with fair success, but early in 1917 he let himself be matched against Fireman Jim Flynn, a war horse who had boxed the best for 16 years. Jack lost to Flynn's experience, technical knockout in one, his brother throwing in the towel.

His marriage prospered equally. By mid-summer Maxine had left him and was working as a prostitute in Cairo, Illinois.

At this low point in his fortunes, Dempsey received a letter from John Leo McKiernan—known as Jack Kearns—asking if he would be interested in acquiring a manager. Receiving a quick affirmative reply, Kearns sent Dempsey a railroad ticket to San Francisco and $5.00 for eating money. "This Kearns, as far as I was concerned, had class," Jack recalled. "Riding *in* a compartment instead of under one!"

Twelve years older than Dempsey, Kearns had been a fair welterweight boxer, a baseball player, a wrestler, a gold weigher in a Klondike saloon, a bouncer on San Francisco's Barbary Coast, a dealer in a gambling house, a saloon keeper, a manufacturer of fire extinguishers, and a promoter of fights and manager of boxers. In his 34 years he had come up against many, many people, and though they might have accused him of a variety of things, having dealt with him, not one of them would have ever accused Jack Kearns of possessing a code of ethics.

Training now in San Francisco under Kearns' management and ballyhoo (frequent visits to city sports rooms, sporting life visitors in training camp daily, stories true and almost true planted with reporters, whatever Kearns could think of to spread the word), Dempsey fought eight times the rest of 1917, these bouts including a win over "Gunboat" Smith, a top-ranked heavyweight left over from the Great White Hope (vs. black Champion Jack Johnson) era.

After the Gunboat Smith win, Dempsey was considered one of the half dozen best heavyweights in the country. It was also after that fight that Jack Kearns became "Doc" Kearns. He told Dempsey it was time they took their campaign east, and in what would become his habitual response, Dempsey replied, "Whatever you decide is okay with me. You're the doctor!"

On their way east they stopped in Denver to pound the drums and by great good luck Kearns happened to see the heavyweight champion of the world, Jess Willard, walking ahead of them. He caught up to Willard and taunted the giant of a man into promising to give Dempsey first chance at his title once Willard was ready to fight again. "I couldn't believe Doc's nerve," Jack said, ". . . he had no fear."

In just three weeks in January and February 1918, Dempsey scored three impressive wins, including a two-round KO of Fireman Jim Flynn, who had TKOd him in one round only the year before. Then he knocked out a young heavyweight contender whose ranking was much like his own—Bill Brennan—defeated Billy Miske in a close match, and KOd two more opponents. And then John The Barber Reisler reappeared, brandishing legal papers claiming he was Jack's manager. Reisler said he would go away for $5,000. Using all his glibness, Kearns persuaded

Colonel Jacob Ruppert, owner of the New York Yankees, to stake him to the $5,000 needed to pay off Reisler so that Jack could go ahead with his scheduled fight against Fred Fulton, the number one contender for Jess Willard's heavyweight championship.

Dempsey knocked out Fulton in 18 seconds of the first round. He was now the number one contender himself, which had been Kearns' objective from the very beginning, back when he first took in the skinny kid who'd just been TKOd in one. He never ceased telling Dempsey he would one day be champion and he never ceased working to make him champion. Perhaps it was a little like he'd once told Jack: "Most folks are willing to believe anything you tell 'em, no matter what. It's all in how it's presented. You gotta sell them good, kid, make 'em buy anything and let them think they got the best end of the deal."

By now Dempsey's ring style had a clear pattern. At the first bell he would leap from his corner and go after his opponent with a wild rush, bobbing and weaving his head and shoulders to make himself harder to hit, trying to end it early. Partly this was instinct, partly it was learned in saloon brawls, partly it was due to fighting so often in California, where prize fights were limited to four rounds and you had to finish your man quickly, if you were going to finish him at all.

After his first rush—cruel scowl, bared teeth, flying black hair, unshaven—he tucked his chin onto his chest behind his shoulder to present less of a target and went to work. He could hit savagely with either hand but his left hook, taught him by his brother and refined by Kearns and trainer Jimmy De Forest, remained his best weapon. Under De Forest's tutelage he also mastered combinations: right to the body, left to the head, right to the body, two left hooks to the head, right to the body. . .

Outside the ring he was sure of himself almost to complacency; he was also reserved and considerate; he claimed to have no temper. Standing in his corner before the start of an important fight, however, he was sometimes so nervous that he wet in his cup. But once the bell rang he was transformed, seized by a demoniacal fury that drove him to maim his opponent if he could. (Even in training he was always damaging his sparring partners.) When he had his man hurt, he kept after him, clubbing him on the way down, standing over him and clubbing him if he tried to rise. He rabbit-punched, kidney-punched, hit on the break, hit low, circled behind a hurt opponent and hit from there—every tactic necessary for survival if he could get away with it. The philosophy was simple: Get *him*, any way you can, before he gets you. . . . And if Dempsey were hurt himself, he became even more dangerous.

Willard, the reigning champion, professed to believe he might kill Dempsey if they fought. But it seemed to the public that Willard looked upon all his challengers with the same low regard, since he would not fight them. He had knocked out Jack Johnson for the title in 1915, defended the title once in 1916 and not since then. But Kearns kept Dempsey fighting after the Fulton victory and Dempsey kept knocking out his opponents in one or two rounds, and finally, early in 1919, the promoter "Tex" Rickard signed Willard to defend his title—choice of foe left to Rickard. Though he thought Dempsey possibly too small, Rickard selected him. Rickard and Kearns knew (and were wary of) each other from the Klondike, where Kearns had worked for Rickard in a saloon Rickard managed.

The fight was held in Toledo, Ohio, on July 4, 1919, temperature that afternoon 106°. Champion Willard weighed in at 245 pounds; challenger Dempsey at 187.

What was the young challenger thinking as he waited in the ring for the bell that would begin the contest between him and the champion who was almost half a foot taller and outweighed him by 60 pounds? He was thinking, "Oh my God, I'm not fighting for the title, I'm fighting for my life." Add to this that just before Dempsey left the dressing room Kearns told him he had bet $10,000 at 10 to 1 odds that Willard would go in one, and you have: "I was downright scared."

When the bell rang Dempsey, uncharacteristically, advanced slowly, and then, in the rest of the first round, knocked Willard down seven times. He left the ring thinking he was the new champion, and that Kearns had won $100,000, only to be called back because the bell had malfunctioned and the round had ended before Willard was counted out. The fight lasted two more rounds. Dempsey broke the champion's jaw, shattered his right cheekbone, shut his right eye, and knocked out six of his teeth. Before the start of the fourth round Willard had to quit. *Now* Dempsey was the heavyweight champion of the world.

But of course there were challengers. . . .

NOBODY'S FOOL

"VICE DEFIES DECENCY. . .First Ward Ball Repeats Annual Revolting Scenes of Shameless Sin," thus, the *Chicago Record-Herald*'s headline on December 16, 1908. "I doubt if any city in the world at any time ever permitted such a disgraceful orgy to be carried on," stated Arthur Burrage Farwell of the Law and Order League, who had attended the ball—as an observer. Among much else, he had observed the ball's grand marshal, First Ward Alderman Bathhouse John Coughlin, restrained from throwing a champagne bottle, then a chair. Earlier in the evening the alderman, with the aid of friends, beat up a newspaper photographer, this desperate indiscretion because the Bath thought he was a target for assassination. "Help! Help! I'm shot!" he cried as the flash powder went off. "They got a bomb."

After the ball was over, prompted by crusading newspapers spurred to the task by newly aroused reform groups, important Chicago Democrats persuaded the Bath and Hinky Dink that it was bad politics to flaunt the Democratic party's ties to vice. And so the eleventh First Ward Ball was the last.

Ten months later a renowned English revivalist, "Gipsy" Smith, led an "army of Christians" 3,000 strong, accompanied by 15,000 spectators, into Chicago's segregated red-light district, the Levee. In front of the Everleigh Club evangelist Smith and his followers knelt in the street and prayed. They then sang "Where Is My Wandering Boy Tonight?"

A darkened Levee received this visitation quietly, suspending operations while the army of Christians offered up its prayers. When Gipsy and his devout followers left, however, Levee proprietors lit up the lights, threw open the doors and, because of the thousands of spectators who stayed on, enjoyed their biggest night ever. "We were certainly glad to get all this business," a straight-faced Minna Everleigh said, "but I was sorry to see so many nice young men down here for the first time."

Possibly inspired by evangelist Smith, 3,000 members of the

Women's Christian Temperance Union marched on City Hall January 27, 1910, and demanded of the mayor that he enforce the city code provisions that forbade operation of a house of ill-fame or assignation. The mayor responded by appointing a prestigious 30-member Vice Commission that a year later issued the bulky report alluded to in an earlier chapter. Vis-a-vis vice and Chicago, the statistics-filled document confirmed what every citizen knew but most would have preferred to ignore: conditions were appalling. Prostitution was a multi-millions-a-year industry, and half the huge gross went to politicians and police. The report also noted that "wealthy and prominent businessmen, whose advice is sought in matters pertaining to the civic welfare and development of Chicago, are leasing their houses for this business." The Commission concluded that "Constant and persistent repression of prostitution should be the immediate method; absolute annihilation the ultimate ideal."

Michigan Avenue was a block east of the Levee's quasi-official boundary, and on October 12 Mayor Harrison ordered the police to close all disorderly flats on South Michigan Avenue from 12th to 31st streets. (This meant closing the Arena, too, a three-story house of assignation at No. 1340 utilized exclusively by Chicago's ultra-wealthy. But of course Justice is blind.) Next came the shuttering of the Everleigh Club on October 25; nevertheless, the reformers continued to press a demand to close all of the Levee's houses of sin.

Coincident with Chicago's resurgent reform movement was a nationwide investigation of the white-slave trade by federal law enforcement officers. (The Mann Act, also known as the White Slave Act, sponsored by Republican Congressman James R. Mann of Illinois, was passed in 1910. It made it a federal offense to aid or abet the transportation of a woman from one state to another for immoral purposes.) In Connecticut a young woman working in a Bridgeport brothel said she had been shipped there from Chicago by Big Jim Colosimo. Before an indictment could be brought, however, the young woman was shot to death, her killers almost—but not quite—identified as two of Johnny Torrio's NYC James Street Boys. Torrio and his boss, Colosimo, were picked up in Chicago and questioned at the Federal Building. Both denied ever having heard of the town of Bridgeport.

Following their release, Big Jim promoted Torrio to the rank of first lieutenant.

Johnny Torrio was brought from Orsara di Puglia, southern Italy, to the United States in 1884 by his widowed mother. Just over two years old, he toddled ashore at the Castle Garden immigration station in a long white dress. In 1886 his mother married Salvatore Caputo. Her husband ran an unlicensed saloon—a "blind pig"—behind a grocery store front at 86 James Street on New York's Lower East Side. By the time he was seven, her son was waiting tables and swamping in the back room of his stepfather's saloon. His entire formal schooling totaled 13 months.

At age 19, as J. T. McCarthy, Torrio managed boxers who fought amateur "exhibitions." (Professional boxing was then illegal in New York.) A J. T. McCarthy pug would win his first three or four bouts (by prearrangement), become a favorite, and lose his next (also by prearrangement)—J. T. McCarthy's money on the underdog. When he was 22 Torrio bought a saloon at James and Water streets and leased a nearby rooming house that he converted into a brothel and a vacant store that he made over into a pool hall. He invited the likeliest prospects among his pool hall customers to follow his detailed plans for burglary jobs, fenced their take, and paid them a percentage. Some were older, most were bigger (John stood only 5 feet 6 inches), but he was the leader of the James Street Boys. He had steely-blue eyes but an innocent, if unsmiling, expression, and he was patient and could hold his anger in check. He didn't give the impression of toughness, but he was. And cagey.

His boys helped Tammany Hall's mayoral candidate win election in 1905—beating up the opponent's supporters and stealing ballot boxes—and he allied them with the mighty Five Points Gang led by Paul Kelly (real name, Paolo Vaccarelli), a former professional boxer. The Five Pointers flourished from the turn of the century till 1920 and Prohibition. They stole, mugged, murdered for hire, acted as strike-breakers, helped Tammany Hall in elections. Kelly, their leader, short like Torrio and outwardly a softspoken, well-dressed gentleman, introduced Torrio to suits, shirts, and ties, and talked of opera and composers with his young disciple. His Five Pointers would come to the aid of Torrio's boys when needed and Torrio's James Street Boys reciprocated, but—unlike Kelly—Torrio did not lead his troops into battle; he felt the leader was too valuable to put at risk unnecessarily.

In 1908 when an armageddon loomed between the Five Pointers and their brawling rivals the Eastmans, Torrio cashed in his James Street properties and opened a saloon in Brooklyn with a dimple-chinned young Sicilian and fellow Five Pointer, Frankie Yale (Uale). Twenty-three-year-old Yale was a blackhander and accomplished professional killer. Perhaps as a joke, Torrio and Yale named their saloon the Harvard Inn. It was on Navy Street, near the Brooklyn Navy Yard, on the Coney Island water-front in an area of wretchedly poor Italian immigrants who had moved in when only slightly less wretchedly poor Irish moved out.

For a year Torrio and Yale sold beer, cheap whisky, black cigars, and white women out of their Harvard Inn, but their principal income came from blackhanding. "Blackhand" was extortion, a Sicilian custom of long standing. The blackhander sent a more prosperous countryman a polite message:

Most Gentle Sir:

      Hoping that the present will not impress you much, you will be so good as to send me $2,000 if your life is dear to you. So I beg you warmly to put them on your door within four days. But if not, I swear this week's time not even the dust of your family will exist. With regards, believe me to be your friend.

La Mano Nero

      The victims usually paid; if they did not, they were usually killed. There never existed a national or international Black Hand Society. Practitioners worked solo or in twos or threes, seldom aware of each other's activities. But given the murder of an Italian, even in the absence of a threatening note, New York City and Chicago police were apt to ascribe the death to the workings of the dreaded Black Hand.

      The showdown battle between the Five Pointers and Eastman gangs anticipated by Torrio took place with disastrous results. Paul Kelly was critically wounded. When he got out of the hospital he abandoned his followers to become a business agent for a rag picker's union. Monk Eastman was sent to Sing Sing state prison for 10 years and most members of both gangs who were not also sent to jail or the hospital went into hiding. Worse, a feared NYC police lieutenant, Joseph Petrosino, took this moment to announce his personal war on black-handers. (Conducting this war, however, he was killed in Palermo, Sicily, a few months later.)

      So it was that when John Torrio's cousin Victoria wrote him to ask if he could come to Chicago, expenses paid, to help her husband in a certain matter, the 27-year-old sold his interest in the Harvard Inn to his partner and got on the train. He knew of his cousin's husband, of course, Chicago's most successful whoremaster, Big Jim Colosimo. And wasn't Chicago the vice capital of the country?

      The "certain matter" had its ironic aspects. Torrio was a blackhander. In his younger days Big Jim Colosimo had been a black-hander. But when Big Jim grew wealthy and powerful he started receiving notes from blackhanders himself, most of which he ignored, though once he had been forced to kill three would-be extortionists, two by strangling with his own large hands. But the situation now seemed beyond his capacity to resolve. These men did not fear him or those who worked for him. Their first request had been for $25,000 and when he didn't pay they stopped him on the street in broad daylight and shoved a gun into his belly. After the street encounter they called him on the phone and raised their demand to $50,000.

      Alone, John Torrio met the trio of blackhanders under the viaduct over the Rock Island tracks at Archer between Clark and LaSalle. He attempted to negotiate with the men—he believed in trying to talk things out—but failed to move them. It was finally agreed he would meet the trio the next night with payment.

The next midnight Torrio arrived in an open carriage. As he came under a streetlight he held up a satchel for the blackhanders to see. Behind him, two of Colosimo's thugs, Joey D'Andrea and Mack Fitzpatrick, crouched at the ready, pistols in hand.

On Torrio's return from the midnight sortie, Big Jim asked his wife's cousin for a full account of what had happened. "I looked back," Torrio replied, "and they didn't wave goodbye."

One of the three survived, however, and asked for Big Jim. A detective took Colosimo to County Hospital and the blackhander looked at his countryman in the white linen suit. In Italian he said, "Colosimo, you traitor! A dying man's curse on you."

Big Jim crossed himself. A dying man's curse was a terrible thing. "I don't know what he's talking about," he told the detective.

The trio had come from Pittsburgh. Their bodies were sent back there after a coroner's jury returned a verdict of murder by persons unknown.

Problem-solver Torrio was installed as manager of Big Jim's Saratoga house. He was not pleased to become a male madam but he was a good administrator and he had thought of an imaginative way to stimulate business. He had the Saratoga's girls dress in gingham rompers, their legs bare to above the knees, with sashes tied in large bows at the back, and bright silk-ribbon bows in their hair. No sooner was his kiddieland for lechers functioning than federal agents found a dozen girls from St. Louis in Levee brothels (the Colosimo-Van Bever circuit) and he was arrested. Van Bever and his wife were convicted, fined, and sentenced to one year in prison but none of Torrio's gingham romperettes would testify against him and he was released. (Colosimo was not even arrested, because, the police said, he "could not be reached.") What galled Johnny Torrio about the incident was that his name appeared in Chicago newspapers.

The propitious death of the young white slave in Bridgeport who had been willing to implicate Colosimo freed Torrio from his onerous duties as a male madam; more, it made him the right-hand man of Chicago's vice king. Sad-eyed, with the beginnings of a paunch, Johnny Torrio did not look especially forbidding. His position, will, and intelligence were to make him so.

Big Jim also conferred upon him the reward of a percentage of the take from all Colosimo brothel and gambling interests. Torrio bought a fire-engine-red motor car and opened a saloon at 2001 Archer Avenue, a whorehouse at 2118 South Federal, and in 1912 he married red-headed Anna Jacobs, a small-town girl from Kentucky. She was 22 and her only connection with the Levee was her husband.

The afternoon of September 28, 1912, a young crusader from

Hammond, Indiana, Virginia Brooks, marched 5,000 men, women, and children north on Michigan Avenue from 16th Street to Washington, then west on Washington and south on State to Jackson Boulevard. The marchers sang "Onward, Christian Soldiers" as they converged on Orchestra Hall for their rally; there, Brooks assailed John E. W. Wayman, State's Attorney for Cook County, for his laxness in enforcing the laws against vice.

Under extreme pressure from Farwell's Law and Order League and a Committee of Fifteen that counted among its number such pillars of the community as Julius Rosenwald of Sears, Roebuck and Company, Chicago's wealthiest citizen, and Harold Swift of the meat-packing family, the live-and-let-live Wayman obtained warrants for the arrest of 135 keepers, owners, and agents of property used for immoral purposes in the Levee. On October 4 he reluctantly ordered raids to begin. The ladies of sin fled their quarters and only 23 warrants were served, but more than 100 brothels were closed.

The next day the Levee's whoremasters formed their own committee. (The madams already had an organization: The Friendly Sisters. If they had a motto, it might have been the slogan of their boarders: "Better to make many men happy than one man miserable.") After the committee met at Colosimo's Café, Johnny Torrio ordered the women of the Levee to put on their most garish clothes and heaviest makeup and go into respectable residential districts and apply for lodging, and to frequent respectable cafés and there make scenes. The harlots did this for three days, then disappeared. But, as intended, their expedition alarmed and worried Chicago's citizens. The rationale behind the Levee had always been that since vice existed, if you confined it to one section of the city, you could regulate it. As a member of the clergy expressed it after the forays ceased, "Let us not scatter evil throughout the city."

The raids were suspended but they had impeded the normally placid flow of Levee commerce. State's Attorney Wayman left office in 1913 and on April 17 committed suicide, presumably as a result of stress and overwork.

Early in 1914 Big Jim Colosimo led a group of Levee business-men in plotting the murder of the head of a newly formed and independent Morals Division within the Chicago Police Department. The man was immune to threats or to the offer of bribes. The plot failed and in its free-for-all aftermath a sergeant detective was killed. The gunman was thought to have been a cousin of Johnny Torrio's, imported from New York City. He had leapt from a fire-engine-red motor car to shoot down the sergeant.

Torrio skipped out of state to Cedar Lake, Indiana, but the police arrested his cousin, and also Colosimo and for an hour before making bail Big Jim was behind bars, the only time in his life he was ever jailed. No witnesses were willing to testify, however, and so no charges could be brought. Torrio returned to Chicago but because of his suspected involvement his saloon license was revoked.

On July 17, 1914, the new State's Attorney—after backing a grand-jury probe into Chicago vice—promised to renew efforts to shut down the Levee. He had the support of Mayor Harrison, and on July 26 a newly appointed captain of the 22nd Street police station ordered Levee resort owners to close or be raided. It appeared that an era had ended; no longer would Chicago have a protected, tacitly condoned vice section. (Between 1912 and 1917, 44 other U.S. cities or states shut down their red light districts.)

But on April 6, 1915, William Hale Thompson was elected Mayor of Chicago. Thompson could be said to have had a first-rate mind, if by that is meant the ability to entertain two contradictory ideas at the same time. "I'll clean up this city and drive out the crooks," he vowed while campaigning on the Republican reform ticket. "I'll make Chicago the cleanest city in the world," he said, but as mayor he proved to be the bully champion of a wide-open town.

While the fate of the Levee's brothels was being decided, Big Jim Colosimo was acquiring call flats and run-down hotels to put to use and converting some of his brothels to dance halls and cabarets, though their primary function remained as before. The Bath's and Hinky Dink's share of vice revenues diminished as the righteous chewed at Chicago's Tenderloin, but with the election of Thompson it shrank to almost nothing. They had opposed Thompson and when he won they lost their decisive influence at City Hall. Given the fate of the sponsors of his career in crime, perhaps Big Jim mused that *Papa se ne fa un altro—* Nobody is indispensable. For all we know, he may have been a sometime chianti philosopher; as his own end was to show, he was slightly more complicated than the brute, black-souled animal he seemed. In any case, over the years he had strengthened his personal ties with sympathetic judges, politicians, and police officers, and now he dealt directly with the new mayor.

The Bath turned his aging energies to his insurance business (First Ward businessmen who needed city permits for this and that placed their insurance with Coughlin's agency or their permits were delayed in the Council—and delayed and delayed), and to the race tracks and his 35 race horses stabled in St. Charles. In 1916 his nine-room Colorado Springs second home burned down and for lack of buyers he had to give away the Zoo Park there that he had spent a million dollars developing. (The zoo's biggest attraction was Princess Alice, an alcoholic elephant borrowed by the Bath from Chicago's Lincoln Park Zoo.) He tried his luck at fattening cattle on his Iowa farm and he tried to grow mushrooms for the market, but lost money at both ventures. In the City Council his demodishly-attired 250-pound bulk sat mainly silent, though now and again he could be flattered into reciting one of his poems (ghosted by a local reporter) for the edification of Council members:

> Dear Paree, O gay Paree,
> Why should I cross the sea—
>> To thee?
> Here by the lake,
> The winds blow soft,
>> My thirst I slake
> Both bold and oft.
> The girls are fair,
> Their smiles are sweet;
> They trip along on twinkling feet.
> *A bas* Paree!
>> Boul Mich for me!

The Little Fellow, Hinky Dink, continued to manage his two saloons and to while away his days at his tiny Clark Street cigar store. He and Bathhouse retained their whisky-selling rights in the Levee, and as a hedge against the future they bought up a million dollars worth of bourbon. (When Prohibition arrived, they sold it for twice the buying price.) They were still treated with respect—though not the obsequious deference of former times—by most of their colleagues, and by Big Jim Colosimo when, as they occasionally did, they took dinner at his café, but their glory days were over.

Four years of savage, terrible war devastated Europe but for Johnny Torrio that war was never fought. The world, after 1918, drunk with gunpowder and blood, sank into an anarchy of disorder and confusion, but not Johnny Torrio. He quietly sent his small army of thugs to call on Chicago's cigar store owners to persuade them to rent their back rooms for use as Colosimo handbooks. The owners were happy to. His red motor car took him to the village of Burnham 18 miles south of the Loop at the invitation of Johnny Patton, the village's boy president. Patton, 25, had tended bar since he was 14 and thought he knew a good thing when he saw it. He showed Torrio a two-story building, the Arrowhead Inn, that straddled the Illinois-Indiana state line. Torrio bought the Arrowhead for $15,000, added a bar to the first floor's restaurant and divided the second floor into small bedrooms. He made Patton manager and hired Burnham's chief of police as a bartender, three village trustees as waiters. The crib-like bedrooms were furnished with Levee lovelies.

A local gambler, "Dandy Joe" Hogarty, proposed installing a gaming room, but before he got Torrio's go-ahead he forgot where he was while being served at the bar and referred to the Arrowhead's owner as a pimp. They found him in a ditch with a bullet in his head.

Burnham's chief of police ruled the death murder by robbers unknown and returned to his duties behind the bar.

The Arrowhead was a $9,000-a-month success from prostitute revenue alone, and Torrio built a second house in Burnham, the Barn, and established a mini-chain of $2.00 houses (the girls' share was 80¢ a trick) south and west of the Loop in South Chicago, Chicago Heights, and Blue Island and south and east in the Indiana towns of East Chicago, Gary, and Whiting. Girls were rotated between houses to provide customers with variety (surely the spice of life) but none crossed the state line—unless, at the Arrowhead, there was a raid. Gas station attendants and cabaret and supper club waiters on roads leading to the houses were hired as lookouts for raiding parties.

The jazz musician Milton Mezzrow played at the Arrowhead in its earliest years. (Jazz was then called "nigger music"—Mezzrow was white—or "whorehouse music.") He was sure that in Burnham there "were more whores per square foot than in any town in the good old U.S.A." Two hundred girls worked eight-hour shifts weekdays, 12 hours straight on Saturdays and legal holidays. Visitors "dropped around to snag a honeymoon between trains." Coming in, customers were lively; leaving, glum. "Sugar plums became salt mackerel fast in that town." There were two shifts, one ending at 8 P.M., the other at 4 A.M. When their shifts ended, the girls stopped by the bar to have a drink, listen to the music, and shed a tear of nostalgia for that time in their lives before the world corrupted them. The No. 1 request of lachrymose whores, including those with "a slap from Mr. Clap," was "The Curse of an Aching Heart" ("You fooled me from the start. . . . You dragged and dragged me down," oh, yes. . . .)

Torrio established his Chicago headquarters in a four-story brick building at 2222 South Wabash—the Four Deuces. The first floor was given over to a bar, the second and third to gambling except for his own small, elegantly furnished office on the second, the fourth to the pleasures of the flesh. Under Torrio's direction, Patton oversaw suburban operations, Dennis "Duke" Cooney the Levee's. Jake Guzik (roper Harry's younger brother) supplied beer to the suburban houses from a small brewery bought by him with money borrowed from Big Jim, the loan recommended by Torrio.

Torrio moved his personal household five miles away from the Levee to 417 East 64th Street. John Torrio's business was satisfying the grosser appetites of man, but he seemed deficient in these himself. He ate sparingly, did not smoke, drink, or gamble, and did not like the use of profane or obscene language. He was totally devoted to his wife.

He arrived early at the 2222 South Wabash headquarters, worked steadily all day (planning, checking ledgers and reports, deciding which girls stayed, which were to be traded, which were to be replaced, administrating, delegating, mediating, issuing orders) and then—much as Marshall Field had—left his office promptly to be home by six. Most evenings he spent in slippers and smoking jacket reading, or listening to phonograph records of opera, following the scores, or playing pinochle with his wife. At home he was not like the commanding, all-business, unsmiling first lieutenant he was at the Four Deuces. Back there all night, as Torrio took his domestic ease, a husky 20-year-old brought by him to Chicago from Brooklyn shuffled back and forth in front of the entrance mumbling to passersby, "Good-lookin' girls inside. Got some good-lookin' girls." This was Alphonse Caponi, steering.

Because Colosimo trusted Torrio—the man was *famiglia*, family, wasn't he?—Big Jim spent most of his time at his café. (His wife Victoria seldom made an appearance there any more.) Big Jim had discovered that there were fashionable women of wealth among his customers who were not repelled by the advances of a notorious gangster. Except for seeing to it that First Ward Italians voted at elections as they were told to, Big Jim enjoyed a pleasurable life devoted to celebrities, food, wine, women, and song: *il dolce far niente*—sweet idleness. He was not looking to expand his empire; he was content. When Torrio urged him to diversify into breweries in 1919 when Illinois law made them illegal, he told his first lieutenant they would "stick to women. That's where the money is. There's no future in bootlegging. Prohibition won't amount to anything."

And then Big Jim discovered *true* happiness—in the love of a good woman. Her name was Dale Winter. She was in her twenties, not half his age. She was pretty, and high-principled. She lived with her mother in a south side hotel and before her friendship with Big Jim Colosimo became known she was the soloist in the South Park Methodist Church choir.

The leader of the five-piece orchestra at his café brought her to Colosimo. Big Jim auditioned the young girl, then hired her to sing at his restaurant. When she performed—a white-gowned, virginal figure under a cone of light—he sat quietly in a chair against the wall and listened; during the other acts he roamed among tables, gladhanding customers. When Dale Winter's act finished, he hurried to the stage to escort her off so she did not have to fend away grasping, drunken hands.

She became a star attraction and moved into her own apartment. He saw her home every night in his Pierce-Arrow. His chauffeur affirmed that Big Jim never went beyond the apartment's front door to say goodnight.

He went horseback riding with her in city parks. He left his wife. He became more moderate in dress, flashed fewer diamonds, grew relatively subdued.

Florenz Ziegfeld, Jr., dined at Colosimo's Café, heard Dale Winter sing, offered her a contract. For a performer, this was the big-time. She refused Ziegfeld's offer; she was studying voice. "I hope to be an opera singer. Mr. Colosimo is paying my tuition."

Big Jim divorced his wife in March of 1920, settling $50,000 on her. "I raised one husband for another woman," Victoria said bitterly, "and there is nothing in it."

The middleaged swain was consumed by thoughts of his youthful singing find. "I love you, I love you, I love you. You are the ideal of my dreams. I always knew there'd be someone like you. I have loved you forever it seems."

He would marry her. When they were man and wife she would not have to sing at the café. "You can rest and study and rest and sing and rest and perform roles at the auditorium," he told her. "That was the thing we were silliest about," Dale Winter said, "my being a great singer some day."

"This," he told his first lieutenant, "this is the real thing, Johnny."

Torrio looked at him. "It's your funeral, Jim," he said.

A man's cradle stands in his grave. The life of an eagle is like its youth: full of peril. And everybody's somebody's fool.

Shoeless Joe Jackson

HARD GUYS

"*I'm forever blowing ball games*," Ring Lardner, Chicago sportswriter, sang as he reeled down the aisle of a west-bound Pullman filled with Chicago White Sox baseball players. "*Pretty ball games in the air.*" The Sox had that afternoon lost a second consecutive game of the 1919 World Series to the Cincinnati Reds. Lardner sang:

> I come from Chi,
> I hardly try,
> Just go to bat and die.
> Fortune's coming my way,
> That's why I don't care.
> I'm forever blowing ball games,
> And the gamblers treat me fair. . . .

One year later, with just three games of the 1920 American League season left to play and the Sox half a game out of first place, Charles Comiskey, White Sox owner, sent a telegram to eight of his players: "YOU AND EACH OF YOU ARE HEREBY NOTIFIED OF YOUR INDEFINITE SUSPENSION. . . ."

Twelve months before, the Sox had gone on to lose the 1919 World Series to the Cincinnati Reds, a team most sportswriters, baseball fans, and gamblers believed Chicago could have beaten easily.

There had been rumors in the fall of 1919, but no one could bring himself to believe them. It argued against a main tenet of American faith: The game of baseball came wrapped in Old Glory; it could not be crooked. But day by day as the odds tilted toward Cincinnati, more and more sportswriters, fans, and gamblers realized that something was wrong. And after the first game, the Chicago gambler Mont Tennes—who controlled the nation's handbook betting—came to Comiskey and told him what many now believed a certainty: The fix was in.

Before Mont Tennes was Chicago's gambling major domo, the

major domo was "King Mike" McDonald, the first person to say "There's a sucker born every minute." Chicago's Michael Cassius McDonald, it was, who said that first, and Mike McDonald, it was, who also said, "Never give a sucker an even break," and "You can't cheat an honest man."

Sure, and wasn't it Mike who originated the joke—long a staple in vaudeville—where someone comes by asking for donations—"Mike, we'll put you down for two dollars, right enough?"

"Who's it for?"

"We're burying a policeman."

"Grand! Here's my ten dollars—bury five of them."

Mike made money during the Civil War by organizing bounty jumpers, men who enlisted in the Union Army for the cash bounty offered, then deserted to enlist again and again. Mike took a commission on each bounty: 50 percent.

He headquartered on the second floor of his four-story saloon, gambling hall, and boarding house, the Store, at the corner of Clark and Monroe. The gambling hall was so huge that one of his partners feared they'd never find enough customers. To which Mike—not P. T. Barnum—replied, "Don't you go worrying about that. There's a sucker born . . ." etc. The Store was for two decades a second City Hall, the gathering place for Chicago's politicians, city officials, sporting crowd, and higher-ups in the underworld.

Mike doled out gambling rights in Chicago—his privilege because he owned and advised its mayors, most notably the Carter Harrisons, father and son. He also owned senators and congressmen. Mike McDonald more or less laid the foundations of Chicago's democratic Party, a structure that lasted 100 years, on through the reign of Richard J. Daley. He could have controlled the city's prostitution, as well, but as one of his friends put it, "A crook has to be decent to work with Mike."

He protected gambling house owners, bunco artists, con men, and brace game riggers. Want to buy a gold brick? See Mike's Tom O'Brien, "King of the Bunco Artists" (solid brass brick with one small plug of gold for the mark's testing). During the Columbian Exposition in 1893 O'Brien made half a million dollars in five months' time.

John L. Sullivan came to Mike McDonald to ask for backing in Sullivan's campaign for a fight with the heavyweight champion, said he'd whip three stockyard bruisers from Packingtown to prove his mettle—three at the same time, bare knuckle. Did and got Mike's backing.

Mike took at least 40 percent of every Chicago gambler's income; Chicago politicians got roughly half of this, part to keep themselves and the rest to dispense to others, always including the police. Mike raked off three-quarters of a million dollars a year from this levy on the city's gamblers, exclusive of what he made conducting his own rigged games at the Store. He was also a partner in a million-dollars-a-season syndicate that controlled gambling at Chicago and Indiana racetracks. The only think Mike McDonald lost out at was marriage. His wives kept running off with other men, including, once, a priest.

After King Mike came "Big Jim" O'Leary, son of the woman who owned the cow that supposedly started the Fire. O'Leary controlled gambling on Chicago's South Side for a decade and from 1904 to 1907 operated on Lake Michigan the first gambling ship in American history. Bathhouse John Coughlin and Michael Hinky Dink Kenna took the First Ward's gambling payoffs; Mont Tennes, the North Side's.

Tennes rented and then supplied to the city's gamblers the wire service that provided race track results and thereby he gained control of many of Chicago's gambling houses. With the election of Carter Harrison, Jr., in 1911, and the subsequent relaxation of police interference with gambling, Tennes extended his control from race-track gambling to roulette, faro, craps, poker and other games. For from 40 percent to 60 percent of the win, Tennes delivered peace with the police.

In 1910 he organized the General News Bureau to supplant the service he'd formerly used to provide race results. With arson and bombs he drove that wire service out of business and became ruler of race-track gambling and allied pursuits nationwide. This was the man who came to Charles Comiskey, White Sox owner, and told him that the fix was in on the 1919 World Series.

After Tennes' visit, Comiskey went to see his manager, William "Kid" Gleason, who told him yes, something was wrong. Then Comiskey called on John Heydler, president of the National League. "Impossible!" Heydler said. "You can't fix a World Series." The two then went together to see Comiskey's one-time friend and now bitter enemy, Ban Johnson, president of the American League. It was 3:00 A.M. and they had to awaken Johnson. "That is the whelp of a beaten cur!" Johnson bellowed (he may have meant "yelp"), and that was that.

Comiskey had panicked. From that night on, till a year later when a Chicago grand jury convened to investigate the 1919 Series and he had no choice, he said nothing. Why? Because Comiskey realized he would destroy the value of his team if he spoke out. And they were his property; he owned those men and their skills.

Two days before the opening game, Jake Lingle, a Chicago crime reporter, had telephoned Sox first baseman Chick Gandil: "The word is out that the Series is in the bag."

"Where'd you ever hear that rot!" was Gandil's indignant reply, though as it happened Gandil himself was the leading Sox conspirator in the sellout—which got its initial purse from the powerful and wealthy New York gambler Arnold Rothstein.

Still, no one had proof, and the idea of a fixed World Series was so nearly unthinkable that a full year passed before a Cook County Grand Jury began investigating. It was then that Comiskey suspended his eight players. Indictments were brought, but then the Grand Jury's records, including the signed confessions of three of the eight players, were stolen from the State's Attorney's office (a theft arranged and paid for by Rothstein).

A second Grand Jury investigation was followed by a second round of indictments and a trial.

On August 2, 1921, the eight accused were acquitted.

That night the jubilant ballplayers went to the Bella Napoli, a new Italian restaurant not far from the Criminal Courts Building on the west side, and partied far into the next morning—together with the jury that had acquitted them. But the just-installed (and first) Commissioner of Organized Baseball, Judge Kenesaw Mountain Landis, immediately banned the eight from baseball for life.

The last survivor of the eight banned players who threw the 1919 series, shortstop Charles "Swede" Risberg, died in 1975, age 81, 56 years after the autumn games that renamed his team the "Black Sox."

Swede never claimed he was innocent, though a few of the others did. One of these, "Shoeless Joe" Jackson, was the batting star of the Series (a record 12 base hits), and maintained his innocence till he died in 1951, age 63. (Comiskey's grandson wired condolences to the widow.) Yet Jackson's was one of the three stolen confessions, and Jackson had taken $5,000 as his share.

Swede Risberg worked on a dairy farm in Minnesota after being banned at the age of 26 from the game he played with consummate skill. He went to live in northern California, ended up running a tavern in Oregon. He died the day the 1975 World Series moved from Boston to Cincinnati, home of the Reds.

"Now Risberg threatens to bump me off if I squawk," Shoeless Joe Jackson said after his testimony to the 1920 Grand Jury. ". . . I've got the idea that after what I told them, old Joe Jackson isn't going to jail. But I'm not going to get far from my protection until this thing blows over. Swede is a hard guy."

Sox owner Comiskey was a hard guy, too. And wealthy. The son of a Chicago alderman ("Honest John" Comiskey), he had had a notable career as a baseball player and as a manager, leading the St. Louis Browns of the National Federation to four straight pennants and two world championships, and rising in salary with them from $90 a month to $8,000 a year.

In 1901, when the American League was formed, Comiskey organized the Chicago White Stockings and with that first team in Chicago he won the first American League pennant. He retired from managing the next year and from then on devoted his energies to the chores of being an owner only; these seemed to consist chiefly of banking gate receipts.

Within a decade, Comiskey was a very wealthy man through his ownership of the Sox. South Side fans thronged his ballpark and in 1910 he opened a new one, Comiskey Park, which included a beautiful, 200-person-capacity lounge in which very important sportsmen could eat their fill, courtesy of management, from tables of pheasant, mountain trout, steaks, roasts, and turkey prepared by Comiskey's private chef; drink their fill of Kentucky sour mash bourbon; and smoke fine H. Uppmann cigars. At this same time, meal allowance for Comiskey's ballplayers was a scant $3.00 a day.

In 1917, Comiskey's White Sox had won the American League pennant and also the World Championship in the Series. In 1918 they were not able to repeat, but attendance continued high, and their pennant in 1919, with even higher attendance, was a splendiferous sixtieth birthday present to their owner.

Comiskey had promised his players handsome bonuses in 1917 if they won the pennant. According to Ring Lardner, the bonus was "a case of cheap horsepiss-tasting champagne for the whole team—that was all."

Their star pitcher, Eddie Cicotte, had been promised a bonus of $10,000 in 1917 if he won 30 ball games. Comiskey had his star pitcher benched—to "rest him for the Series"—when Cicotte's total of wins approached the bonus figure. (Not surprisingly, Cicotte played a major role in the 1919 Series fix.)

Put aside the fact that White Sox ballplayers signed contracts with "10-day" clauses in them; that is, if they were injured, they could be released without further pay on 10 days' notice. Most players in the league at that time signed such contracts.

Put aside the fact that Sox contracts included the "reserve" clause; that is, if a player didn't sign with the team he had played with the previous year, he could not play for any other team anywhere in Organized Baseball. All contracts for all teams at that time had the reserve clause.

Consider as the contributing factor the niggardly wage-scale of Charles Comiskey, wealthy owner.

The key players of the Chicago White Sox made about one-half of what the key players of other American League teams made: star pitcher Cicotte, $5,500 in 1919; Shoeless Joe Jackson, $6,000; Gandil and centerfielder "Happy" Felsch, $4,000 each; Swede Risberg, $3,000, and so on down the roster. These were the rewards of the players in 1919 of a team that just two years before had won the World Championship. And whose owner had grown wealthier each year for the past 20 through the efforts of Sox teams.

And so eight players threw the 1919 World Series.

In 1920, one of them, centerfielder Hap Felsch, said: "I got $5,000. I could have got just about that much by being on the level if the Sox had won the Series. And now I'm out of baseball—the only profession I know anything about, and a lot of gamblers have gotten rich."

Then he added, "The joke seems to be on us."

In 1921 a newsphoto used on sports pages throughout the country showed gambler Arnold Rothstein watching a major league baseball game from the private box of the host team's club owner. Judge Landis, Commissioner of Baseball, was furious and Rothstein ceased to watch baseball games from the private boxes of club owners, or at least to have his photograph taken while so occupied.

In 1922, a petition asking for the reinstatement of one of the eight, "Buck" Weaver, was signed by 14,000 Southsiders in a single day. The petition was taken to Judge Landis in his Michigan Avenue office.

Here is Judge Landis' response to the petition bearers:

> "Gentlemen, I had Weaver in this office. I asked him, 'Buck, did you ever sit in on any of the meetings to throw the 1919 Series?' He replied, 'Yes, Judge, I attended two such meetings, but I took no money and played the best ball I am capable of.'
>
> "So I told him, 'Anyone who sat in on such a meeting and did not report it was as guilty as any of the others. Buck, you can't play ball with us again.'"

Weaver's niece, Marge Follett, remembered the night her uncle came home from his interview with Landis. "It was a long time ago," she said in 1989, "but I'll never forget the look in Uncle Buck's eyes. I've never seen a more broken man in my life. I've cried many tears for Uncle Buck. . . ."

Third baseman Weaver had batted .324 in the Series (third highest) and fielded his position in his usual daring fashion. Always smiling or laughing, edging in from third, taunting the batter, cat quick, George Buck Weaver was the only third baseman in the league that Ty Cobb would not attempt to bunt against. The best-hitting and -fielding third baseman in baseball, he loved the sport and was incapable of playing it except to win.

Still hoping to clear his name, he died in Chicago in 1956, a few days after he cashed his first Social Security check: heart attack or broken heart, take your pick.

In 1928, 46-year-old Arnold Rothstein was shot and killed during a poker game in New York City. Rothstein got his start in crime as a teenager loan-sharking stolen money at 25 percent interest. Monk Eastman collected for him when necessary. A power in the underworld at the time of his death, he was worth $50 million or so but was welshing on a $320,000 poker debt, a circumstance that probably contributed to his murder.

Rothstein had also welshed on promised payments to the Black Sox in 1919. Lardner's song lyrics were wrong in that one particular: The gamblers didn't treat them fair.

In the winter of 1919-20 the civil courts of Chicago's South Side overflowed with litigation re missed mortgage payments, inability to pay alimony, failure to pay ordinary bills. In very many of these cases, the defendants pleaded they had lost their last thin dime betting on the Black Sox.

Big Jim Colosimo

SUCCESSION

Big Jim Colosimo, middleaged, undisputed vice king of Chicago, the wickedest city in North America, wed the love of his life, the young singer Dale Winter in Crown Point, Indiana, on April 17, 1920, and three and a half weeks later, on May 11, he was murdered . . . for within the hollow crown that rounds the mortal temples of a king keeps Death his court.

Colosimo's funeral cortege was led by 1,000 men from the First Ward Democratic Club who trudged four-and-a-half slow-moving miles from the Colosimo mansion to Oak Woods Cemetery followed by 4,000 other mourners, including large delegations from the white wings' Street Laborers Union and the City Streets Repairers Union. Among the honorary pallbearers—most in carriages and motorcars—were three judges, a U.S. congressman, a state representative, an assistant state's attorney, three members of the Chicago Grand Opera Company, and nine Chicago aldermen (who had to walk), as well as luminaries from the Italian-American community, including the head of Chicago's Unione Siciliana, Mike Merlo, together with Big Jim's first lieutenant, John Torrio, and the King of the Valley, Diamond Joe Esposito, the unofficial mayor of Chicago's Little Italy. The politicians and the gangsters, the underworld's leaders and the upper world's most respected officials, joined hands openly for this solemn occasion.

One of the pallbearers was Alderman Bathhouse John Coughlin, who had been the young widow's chief comforter at the wake held in the mansion at 3156 Vernon Avenue. There, because Archbishop (later Cardinal) Mundelein refused the deceased Catholic Church services (Colosimo was divorced), the Bath knelt at the bier and recited Hail Marys and the Catholic prayer for the dead.

According to Ben Hecht, the quintessential pen-wielding Chicagoan, city officials worked in relays on the transatlantic telephone trying to persuade Pope Benedict XV to permit Colosimo's burial in

117

consecrated ground. The connection was bad, the Pope grew irritable, and finally, after five hours, the Supreme Pontiff of the Universal Church hung up on his callers.

"I loved Jim with all my heart," the bereft young widow said, and then voiced an opinion that in coming years was to become familiar whenever leading gangsters were spoken of: "He was a powerful personality. If he had started where the lucky start, he would have been one of the great men of his day."

Levee resort owner Ike Bloom gave the deceased an equally strong endorsement: "Big Jim never bilked a pal or turned down a good guy *and* he always kept his mouth shut."

And so they laid to final rest the man who had come to the land of bread and work from a little hill town in Calabria and risen to eminence and power, just as was foretold.

Johnny Torrio paid all funeral expenses for the man who had given him his start in Chicago. It was an expensive funeral, the nation's first grandiose, ceremonial gangster funeral. *Non torno, vi aspetto*—I will not return, I will wait for you.

On the morning of the day of his death, Big Jim and his wife were in Jim's hugely successful, swank supper club relaxing over coffee after the club had closed. A young man-about-town with his high-society date, returning in the early morning from a party, decided they *had* to have a plate of spaghetti from Colosimo's Café. The doors were locked but Jim had them opened for the two and had spaghetti prepared for them. He invited the couple to sit with him and Dale and for the next hour the four sat together talking quietly. It was the last time that Big Jim Colosimo was ever to have guests to his famous macaronies and gravy.

That afternoon the Colosimos were at home in the mansion preparing to go into the Loop so that Dale could shop. John Torrio phoned: a shipment of bootleg whiskey was expected at the café at 4:00 P.M. Jim left the mansion by himself shortly before the hour—promising his wife to return to take her to dinner—muttering to himself in Italian all the way to the café, according to his chauffeur.

Big Jim entered the café, strode through the lobby, past the cloakroom, phone booth, cashier's cage, and the length of the main dining room to his office. A porter coming up from the basement noticed a stranger entering the lobby just after Jim passed through the dining room.

In his office Colosimo conferred with his accountant and with his chef. Standing beneath his family's heirloom sword, Colosimo asked if there had been any phone calls. There hadn't been, which seemed to disturb him. He returned to the lobby, apparently to wait there for the expected delivery. Some moments after he left his office—at 4:25—his chef and accountant heard two shots.

The accountant found his employer lying in the lobby. The vice king had been shot behind the right ear. The second bullet had buried itself in a plaster wall of the lobby.

The police theorized that the killer had hidden in the cloak room. In the phone booth they found a handwritten note, the handwriting of which they interpreted as follows:

> Swan. I made out the statement. You fill in the rest as you see fit. Tell the man to look out after the drugstore and see that he finds out where to find the stuff for me. Don't keep over thirteen men. If you've got more, ask someone to lay off. Bank.
> P.S. Anything you make over $50 belongs to me.

"Bank," of course, was Colosimo, but the rest of the note mystified the police; for starters, they knew no "Swan." (Had they transcribed "Swan" as "Juan" from the handwriting—for "John" Torrio—they would have been less mystified.) Reflexively, they first suspected a blackhander scheme. Colosimo had reportedly left his Vernon Avenue mansion carrying from $50,000 to $150,000 in cash, none of which was found on the body. But the chief blackhand suspect had spent the day of the murder in jail.

They next sought out Jim's spurned ex-wife, Victoria. But at the time of the killing Victoria had been in Los Angeles visiting new in-laws.

Altogether, they questioned 30 suspects, including Jim O'Leary who had been supposed to deliver the shipment of whiskey, and Torrio and a stubble-faced Alphonse Capone (who, following Italian custom, was letting his beard grow until after the funeral). Uncharacteristically, Torrio's eyes filled with tears during his interrogation. Both he and Capone could prove they were elsewhere at the time of their employer's murder.

The porter described the stranger he had seen enter the café. The description fit New York City's Frankie Yale, whom the police knew to have been in Chicago the week of the murder. New York authorities were asked to pick up Yale and the porter was taken to NYC to view a lineup. Face to face with Yale, however, the porter lost his memory. "The fellow I saw ain't here," he said, and so the murder went into the files as unsolved, though Chicago police were in no doubt as to who had pulled the trigger of the .38 that killed Big Jim Colosimo. Their certainty was reinforced when a rumor circulated in the underworld that Johnny Torrio had paid his former partner $10,000 in cash for the execution. Nothing personal, just business.

Dale Winter learned that because of an Illinois law that did not recognize a marriage contracted within a year of a divorce she was not legally Mrs. Colosimo. As a gift, she received $6,000 from Big Jim's estate—which, mysteriously, totaled only $81,000 in bonds and gems, no cash, though at the very least half a million was expected to be found.

She left Chicago and appeared in the road companies of several popular musicals, at last retiring from the theater and public view in the '30s.

Ex-wife Victoria received $12,000 from the estate, also as a gift, divorced her second husband and left Chicago. Papa Luigi, the women's benefactor, got what remained of his son's estate, which was not all that much after the lawyers pocketed their fees. Big Jim had supposedly hidden several million dollars worth of diamonds near Crown Point, Indiana, but the gems have never been found. Or so it is believed.

Big Jim had been a *testedure*—a hard head—as it was said most Calabrians were. And his infatuation with Dale Winter had diverted him into complacency. He had no interest in exploiting the opportunities of Prohibition, but Johnny Torrio, of course, did.

Amendment Article XVIII to the Constitution of the United States reads, in part: "The manufacture, sale, or transportation of intoxicating liquors within, the importation thereof into, or the exportation thereof from the United States . . . is hereby prohibited." The Volstead Act (formally, the National Prohibition Act) was enacted to enforce this 18th Amendment, and on January 17, 1920, the brains and livers of 105,710,620 Americans were thereafter protected by the Constitution from the further ravages and miseries of alcohol. (An unforeseen and totally unexpected consequence of the 18th Amendment was that the drinking population of the United States greatly expanded after it became law—among males, to females, and to younger and younger segments of the population.)

Before he went about organizing Chicago traffic in evasion of the 18th Amendment, however, John The Fox Torrio put in place the last houses of his network of brothels in metropolitan Chicago. Big Jim Colosimo, content with a lock on First Ward vice, had had to be pressured to go into a few suburban and Indiana markets. Torrio, with violence and bribery—both to town officials and individual citizens—forced the services he provided on Chicago's outlying towns wherever he conveniently could. He opened two more road houses in Burnham and increased hours of business from 16 to 24. In Stickney he opened the Roamer Inn, managed by affable Harry Guzik and wife, Alma, Colosimo's ropers of yore, and he established road houses and flatback houses and combinations of the two in Burr Oaks, Berwyn, Steger, LaGrange, and other west and southwest towns.

It is of historic interest that the Roamer Inn may have been the pleasure dome in which Al Capone contracted gonorrhea in 1925, the first of his social diseases. The Inn was also the scene of a criminal act that ultimately demonstrated the strength of Torrio's political connections. In 1921 the Guziks hired a pretty farm girl as a housemaid, had her raped, and enrolled her as a prostitute. Months later the girl managed to get word to her father and brothers, but by the time they rescued her she was destroyed mentally and physically. Harry and Alma were tried for pandering, convicted, and sentenced to prison. Free on bail while their case was appealed, they asked Torrio for help. Not only did they work for him, but Harry's brother Jake had become Torrio's bookkeeper.

One of Torrio's thugs, a Godfearing, puritanical, educated, humane (all of these) $50 for-hire killer, 54-year-old Walter Stevens, had bribed and intimidated jurors in Illinois Governor Len Small's trial on a $600,000 embezzlement charge (allegedly embezzled while Small was state treasurer). The governor was acquitted. Torrio had Stevens remind Small of past favors and before the State Supreme Court could hand down its decision on the Guziks' appeal, Governor Small pardoned them. (They then opened a new brothel, the Marshfield Inn, south of the city. In the eight years of his incumbency, Small pardoned 8,000 felons.)

The jazz clarinetist Milt Mezzrow, in recalling days and nights at the Roamer Inn sounds echoes of Torrio's trick-stimulating kiddieland innovation a decade before when Johnny The Fox was male madam at the Saratoga:

> The girls we knew were all on the dogwatch, from four to twelve in the morning. . . . They paraded around in teddies or gingham baby rompers with big bow in the back, high-heeled shoes, pretty silk hair ribbons twice as big as their heads, and rouge an inch thick all over their kissers.

A brilliant idea remains forever usable. Mezzrow then describes the mechanics:

> When a john had eyeballed the parade and made his choice he would follow her upstairs, where the landlady sat at a little desk in the hall. This landlady would hand out a metal check and a towel to the girl while the customer forked over two bucks. Then the girl was assigned a room number. All night long you could hear the landlady calling out in a bored voice, like a combination of strawboss and timekeeper, "*All* right, Number Eight, *all* right, Number Ten—somebody's waiting, don't take all night."

Some of the houses were elaborate supper clubs with brothels attached; others—those for immigrant laborers—had a saloon and gambling room on the ground floor, many small, bare bedrooms upstairs. The girls worked in three eight-hour shifts.

In the late summer of 1920, Torrio arranged with Joseph Stenson, a wealthy brewer before Prohibition and scion of one of Chicago's first families, to take over the five breweries Stenson was operating on a small scale in partnership with Terry Druggan and Frankie Lake of the West Side Valley Gang along 15th Street. In return, Lake and Druggan were permitted to join Torrio in an alliance of bootlegging interests.

121

Since Chicago was a beer-drinking city, Torrio decided to first concentrate on the manufacture, sale, and transportation of beer. A barrel cost $5 to brew in Stenson's ostensibly dismantled breweries, and sold for $55. Chicagoans drank at least 20,000 barrels a week: ergo, a million dollars weekly profit to the suppliers, less expenses.

In four years of silent partnership with Torrio, Joseph Stenson netted $48,000,000, and he and his family continued to live on Chicago's Gold Coast—during Prohibition and after—and to reap the deference that residence there was given by those enchanted by high society. For many years reporters and authors of books on the era would not name Stenson but refer to Torrio's partner only as "a prominent businessman."

Perhaps it is sufficient to identify the cast of mind of Chicago's Gold Coast inhabitants—one shared by many of their social inferiors—by giving the characterization of its residents voiced by one of its own, a society matron of the time: "I believe in aristocracy; there is something about leisure, luxury, travel, and an acquaintance with the arts which makes for a kind of superiority in the individual who has had these advantages."

All *right*! (But if right, then Emerson was in his senility when he said, "It is no better to have read a thousand books than to have plowed a thousand fields.")

The silk stockings who lived on Chicago's Gold Coast might for amusement very occasionally go slumming (to Colosimo's Café, for example) but at all other times they took pains to avoid contact with the vulgar, common people. They were leagues above the lower classes and to retain this superiority unsullied they maintained their distance. (Edith Rockefeller McCormick's chauffeur was given written instructions for every trip he drove her, thus eliminating the need for Mrs. McCormick to speak to him.) There could be no equal footing—except, as Joseph Stenson knew, in matters of commerce. Though this was not to be spoken of.

With Stenson's aid, Torrio acquired control of other breweries and a few distilleries, at the same time beginning a series of meetings with the heads of Chicago's various gangs, promising them riches if they temporarily gave up robbery and burglary and their other criminal pursuits to concentrate with him on bootlegging. (Most authorities derive "bootlegger" from *boot-leg*, the upper part of a high boot in which bottles of contraband liquor were smuggled in the 17th century.)

Most gangsters who lived made good money bootlegging, but in the 14 years that Prohibition was the law of the land official statistics give 703 as the number of them killed in Chicago as contending factions struggled and fought for dominance, or survival. The true total was probably twice this official figure. (In a sense, Big Jim Colosimo was the first to go. Among the next was Steve Wisniewski, who in July 1921, was certainly the first to be taken on a "one-way ride"—to Libertyville—that is, driven to an out-of-the way location and killed there. Wisniewski had hijacked a shipment of beer.)

Torrio proposed that Chicago and Cook County be divided into spheres of interest so as to reduce the harmful effects of the price wars—and gun wars—that real competition brought to the marketplace. In this he merely emulated the practice of the legitimate entrepreneurs of corporate capitalism. There already was a rough division of territories among Chicago's bootleggers but boundaries were blurred and in trying to expand their domains gangs often collided violently.

The West Side, between Little Italy and Cicero, was Druggan's and Lake's; the Southwest Side was the province of the "Polack Joe" Saltis-Frankie McErlane gang (the first to use the Thompson submachine gun); part of the South Side belonged to Ragen's Colts, an "Athletic and Benevolent Association" of young Irishmen from the Stockyards, a power in the Democratic Party, and the punks who started the race riot in Chicago in July 1919 that killed 14 blacks and 20 whites and injured 500 more; the far South Side belonged to the O'Donnell brothers—"Spike," Steve, Walter, and Tommy; the West Side with a thumb eastward into Chicago was held by another, unrelated group of O'Donnells—"Klondike," Myles, and Bernard.

There were a few smaller enclaves but the balance of the city—the South and Southwest sides of Chicago and its outlying towns, and the city's center—belonged to Torrio and his organization except for that territory of the North Side belonging to the Dion O'Banion gang, which held the Northeast Side between the North Branch of the Chicago River and Lake Michigan, and that supplied by the "Terrible Gennas" in Little Italy's Little Hell. If a rival leadership was weak, Torrio had his gunmen (with his alliances he now commanded a force of 800 condottieri and mercenaries) take over their territory. If the leadership was strong, he tried to persuade the rival to become an ally of his organization. Sometimes they would, sometimes not. But Johnny The Fox Torrio was a patient man.

Little Italy tenement residents, Chicago

COMPARES

If you are very hungry, you dream of food; thirsty, of water. If you are very poor, money becomes your dream, the solution to all of your problems, the consuming fantasy of your parched existence. The Italian immigrants who lived in Chicago's Little Italy were—the vast majority of them—wretchedly poor, like every other immigrant people who came to the city. . . .

A 1911 survey of living conditions in Little Italy concluded that the situation was one of "overcrowded areas, alleys, tenements, families in outlawed cellar apartments, in dark and gloomy rooms, and in conditions of overcrowding that violate all standards of decency and health." Two years later another study concluded that "The Italian is paying a comparatively high rent for dilapidated, unhealthful quarters. He is living in illegally overcrowded rooms . . . and under conditions which . . . are acknowledged to be dangerous and demoralizing."

Nothing changed, of course, after these reports. Two years after the 1913 study a survey of 16 city blocks surrounding Hull House (Jane Addams' social settlement in Little Italy) reported that the 3,000 children being raised there were "growing up in an environment which is full of menace to their health and to their future civic usefulness." The studies were saying that ordinary life in Little Italy was filthy, dangerous, degrading, nearly unbearable, and an incubator of crime. The dream of the parents of those 3,000 children was of money by which to escape their ramshackle tenements crammed two and three to a lot, wall to wall, front to back.

> She had not rubbed their noses in poverty as a good mother should.
>   . . . money was God. Money could make you free. Money could give you hope. Money could make you safe.
>   Money guarded the lives of your children. Money lifted them out of darkness. Who has not wept for lack of money? Who has not

wept for money? Who comes when money calls? Doctors, priests, dutiful sons.

These are the brooding, resentful thoughts of the heroine of Mario Puzo's excellent short novel *The Fortunate Pilgrim*. The heroine is a middleaged immigrant from Southern Italy trying to raise her family in the United States in the 1920s:

> And money was friends, respectful relatives. A new Jesus could never rise to reproach those with money.
> Not to be rich, but to have money; to have money like a wall to put your back to, and then face the world.
> . . . Money for doctors, money for clothes, money for the oil stove, money for school books, money for Communion suits.

The lack of money—poverty and the misery that it brings—was at its most extreme in Chicago in the area known as Little Hell, so named for the soaring flames that rose from the inferno-like gas works at its river boundary. Little Hell encompassed Sedgwick west to the river and from Chicago Avenue north to Division. Originally settled by Irish, then Swedes, the Sicilians came to its narrow, garbage-strewn streets and ramshackle, overcrowded houses in a wave in the first decade of the century and what had been Kilgubbin, and then Swede Town became Little Hell—aka Little Sicily aka The Sicilian Badlands aka Tenement Town. Less than a mile to the east could be seen Michigan Avenue's fashionable Drake Hotel; a mile to the south, the skyline of the rich and growing Loop.

When it was Swede Town, a puzzled reporter from *Harper's Magazine* in the East, where apparently Vikings were few in number, described its inhabitants:

> —a dish-faced, soft-eyed, light-haired people. They are Scandinavians; but they are as malleable as lead, and quickly and easily follow and adopt every Americanism. In return, they ask only to be permitted to attend a host of Lutheran churches in flocks, to work hard, live temperately, save thriftily, and pronounce every *j* as if it were a *y*.

But then the Swedes moved out, and by the '20s Little Hell had a population of 15,000 first- and second-generation Sicilians, an overworked, underpaid, squalor-ridden people called "wops," "dagos," "guineas," "greaseballs," "ginzos," and held in contempt by all the rest of Chicago because they were dirt-poor and foreigners. Even their compatriots, the continental Italian immigrants, looked down on them—for hadn't the "burnt earth" of *Sicilia* been conquered and occupied many centuries before by the Moors? And *they* came out of Africa. And so, no wonder Sicilians were "the dark ones," eh? Though this inference was

126

never to be uttered in the presence of a Sicilian—just as you never told a Sicilian that there were liars, expert liars, and Sicilians; but it was the truth, wasn't it? And as for treachery—well. . . .

Each street in Little Hell came to be populated by families from a particular village of western Sicily: Larrabee Street, Altavilla; Cambridge, Alimena and Chiusa Sclafani; Townsend, Bagheria; Milton, Sambuca-Zabut. The women were the centers of the families. The woman gave birth to the children and raised them, kept the home. Many also took in piecework, making artificial flowers, knitting lace, cracking nuts and picking nutmeats, counting and packeting cigarette papers. Some worked in nearby small factories at unskilled or semiskilled labor, generally in the garment trade. Wherever they did their work, home or factory, it was at long hours and low wages.

The men were the heads of the families. Like the women, they were hard, willing workers. They were also often shrewd, ambitious, and frequently passionate. But in their island villages they had acquired few skills that were marketable in the New World. If they were able to gain the favor of a local politician, the totally unskilled could become street sweepers, sewer diggers, asphalt helpers, road graders, lamplighters, street repairmen, garbage collectors, park workers, either with the city or with a private firm beholden to the politician. The majority could find jobs only at common, sweat labor as ditch diggers, section hands, hod carriers. Others—more adaptable, quicker, or luckier—became peddlers, saloon keepers, barbers, pavers, quarrymen, teamsters, construction helpers, carpenters, mosaic layers, stonecutters, painters, shoemakers, bakers, tailors.

Little Hell's inhabitants were squalid poor but should good fortune befall one he was prey to blackhand extortion by the least scrupulous of his countrymen. The names of coming victims were obligingly posted on a battered, skinny poplar called "Dead Man's Tree" at 725 Loomis in Little Italy. At "Death Corner" in Little Hell, at the intersection of Oak and Cambridge, on one of whose points stood the parish church of San Filippo Benizi, in little more than a year from January 1, 1910, and March 26, 1911, 38 blackhand victims were murdered. (Between 1910 and 1920 at least 80 killings were attributed to blackhanders in Chicago and 55 warning bombings at the homes of merchants. Came Prohibition, blackhanders found more profitable uses for their deadly skills.)

The Terrible Gennas were brought to Chicago by their father from the port town of Marsala about 1910. The sons were Sam, the oldest, Vincenzo or Jim, Pete, Angelo, Antonio, and Mike, the youngest. Homeless, tempest-tossed—a classic example of the wretched refuse of a teeming shore—they disembarked from a day coach at the Polk Street station to join thousands of their fellow islanders in a search for bread and work. ("I light my lamp beside the golden door.") Their mother was dead; their father found work as a railroad hand at $1.25 a day but died not long after bringing his seven sons to Chicago.

The brothers soon discovered how to get money. Bankrolling their ventures through blackhand extortion, they opened a pool room, a gambling house, a blind pig, and finally, early in 1920, through the influence of Diamond Joe Esposito, unofficial mayor of Little Italy and a political force in the 19th Ward, they obtained a license to distribute industrial alcohol. Their allotments, purchased from government sources, were stored in a three-story building at 1022 West Taylor, a few blocks from the Maxwell Street police station. A very little went to legitimate users; the rest the Gennas redistilled to 180-proof and sold as gin (cut with tap water to 90 proof, flavored with juniper berry extract and smoothed out with glycerine) or colored with coal-tar dye, flavored, and sold through bootleggers as 180-proof bourbon, rye, scotch, you-call-it at $6 a gallon, or 90-proof at $3 a gallon. Their product retained some of its wood alcohol denaturant and this, depending on the level, could cause great pain lasting three or four days, or blindness, or death. Equally unsettling to the thirsty, if a batch of "whiskey" was inadvertently flavored too strongly with the fuel oil used, it apparently triggered insanity.

Despite the abysmally poor quality of their product, however, the Genna brothers fell far short of supplying demand, a problem they solved with aid of financing by Johnny Torrio. Long before Prohibition became law, Chicago's immigrant Sicilians had made their own wine. Neighborhoods would hold wine festivals at which a local priest blessed the wines and each family sampled that made by the others, awards going to the finest. When Prohibition came, some families began distilling their homemade wine to make grappa, a clear brandy, and selling it for $1 a pint.

It occurred to the Gennas and Johnny Torrio that what was possible with grapes and sugar was equally possible with corn and sugar. The Gennas went from tenement to tenement in Little Hell persuading the heads of families to install portable stills in their kitchens or in the back rooms of their stores. Given the Sicilian resolve never to cooperate with the law—and the $15 a day to be earned (ten times what was paid for digging ditches or spiking cross ties)—persuasion was not difficult.

Torrio advanced $150 a week per family in the form of corn, sugar, and yeast and in a short time more than a thousand families were cooking alky. The work was not hard; usually an older family member was given the task: you sat by the still reading and smoking or dreaming or knitting or dozing or sipping wine, kept the fire burning but not too hotly, and called for help to take off the alcoholic distillate in five-gallon tins. On average one home still yielded 350 gallons a week, at a cost to the Gennas of 50 to 75 cents a gallon. The alcohol was picked up by their truckers, taken to 1022 Taylor, redistilled, flavored, colored, and wholesaled at $6 a gallon full strength, or cut with tap water and sold for less.

The brothers had discovered not just how to get money, but how to become wealthy. Their gross rose to $350,000 a month; they netted $150,000 a month. Torrio purchased their product at $3 a gallon for sale in his low-life dives; orders from the rich or hotels, clubs, or speakeasies in the Loop and on Michigan Avenue he filled with quality booze trucked from the East via his old partner, Frankie Yale, or from Canada.

Night and day now over Little Hell—mixed with the reek of decaying garbage, the taste of soot and the sulfurous pall from the gas works—hung the pungent odor of fermenting mash and rich, raw alcohol. With their new and abundant source of income, the men of Little Hell saved for the homes they hoped to find elsewhere, the businesses they hoped one day to open, the trips back to their home villages they hoped to take as successful Americans.

They also joined the Unione Siciliana di Mutuo Soccorso negli Stati Uniti. This fraternal organization, founded by immigrants in the 1880s in New York City and taken over by Ignazio Saietta, also known as Lupo (the Wolf), a blackhander and professional murderer, had long-standing ties to crime and criminals. (Its national president was Frankie Yale, who succeeded to the leadership when Saietta was imprisoned for counterfeiting in 1918.) It was also a low-cost, reliable insurance society that sponsored dances, picnics, banquets, and religious celebrations. It was ardently Italian, even though only Sicilians were members. It had loosely connected branches nationwide and, in addition to its Italian nationalistic fervor, it enthusiastically celebrated American holidays, especially the Fourth of July and Memorial Day. The president of the Chicago affiliate (chartered in 1895) was Mike Merlo; the Terrible Gennas were high in its councils. They aspired to the presidency.

Police at the Maxwell Street station (22nd police precinct, "Bloody Maxwell," as it was called when Irish criminals dominated the district, and termed by the *Tribune* in 1906 "the wickedest police district in the world") every day denied the evidence before their eyes of illegal manufacture of alcohol, and the testimony of their noses. Better yet, they provided escorts for Genna delivery trucks through unfriendly territories, protecting them both from rival gangsters and from possibly unfriendly officers from other precincts. Still better, if they found a kitchen still being tended by someone not on the Genna payroll (the brothers provided them with a list), the equipment was smashed. And if, for pro forma display, a police raid absolutely had to be made on 1022 Taylor, 24-hour notice was given. For this protection, arranged by Torrio and Esposito, the Gennas paid from $10 to $125 a month to some 400 policemen, plus larger sums to five captains and to officers out of the central bureau, plainclothesmen, and detectives assigned to the State's Attorney. Cooperating police also received all the liquor they required at wholesale prices.

Except for Tony "The Gentleman"—who had a say in family decisions on killings but who never himself killed and who designed model homes for his countrymen—the Genna brothers were stereotypical Sicilian criminals: proud, haughty, treacherous, and ruthlessly violent. They were also patrons of Chicago opera, devoted family men, and zealous churchgoers. In their pistol pockets they also carried crucifixes and rosaries.

Their odd-job henchmen were less religiously devout, but equally savage. Foremost among them were Samuzzo "Samoots" Amatuna; Giuseppe Nerone (alias Antonio Spano), known as "The Cavalier"; and John Scalisi and Albert Anselmi, who brought with them from Marsala the belief that bullets boiled in onion juice and water and rubbed with garlic induced gangrene in the target.

Diamond Joe Esposito, King of the Valley, mayor of Little Italy (elected to the office by newspaper reporters), supplied the Gennas with the raw materials of their cottage industry: barrels of corn mash, 100-pound sacks of sugar, yeast, all paid for by Johnny Torrio. Don Peppino, as he was also called (as well as "Dimey"), had arrived in Chicago after spending his first ten years in America in Brooklyn. Curiously, given his closeness with the Gennas, Esposito left Brooklyn because he feared the Sicilians there would kill him if he stayed—one young blackhander in particular, last name Uale.

In 1896 after 20 days and nights at sea in steerage from Naples, Esposito spent his first week in the New World as a baker's helper—6-day week, 12-hour day—a job his brother-in-law the artisan shoemaker had arranged for him. Going home to his sister's Saturday night, his first week's five dollars clinking in his pocket, he saw a sight his 23-year-old eyes refused at first to believe: A derelict propped against a storefront, his feet wrapped in burlap. In this, the land of gold—*infamia*!

Giuseppi tapped the man on the shoulder. In Italian he asked what size shoes the man wore. A shrug in return. Esposito leaned down, tore away the burlap wrappings. Then he removed his own shoes and put them on the man's feet. "*Commodo*?" The derelict shrugged again. Esposito asked him when he'd eaten last. The man stared back at him and Esposito gave him a silver dollar. Sock-footed now, he went home on the trolley.

He worked five years as a baker, saving his earnings. There is the possibility that he worked briefly in Boston as a day laborer, where he may have met a very young Jim Colosimo. With $700, some of it borrowed from his brother-in-law, he bought a saloon from a widow. The saloon—in Brooklyn's rough Navy Yard district—had rooms above it that he rented out or, if a man had no money, let go free for the night.

He would have stayed in Brooklyn—the saloon was making a small profit—but he got into trouble with the young man who supplied beer; a matter of raising the price; unreasonably, Esposito felt. His supplier's cool manner and certainty angered Esposito, so much so that he slapped the man. Fortunately, they were alone. Calmly but with menace in his voice the supplier said, "I'll see you at eight o'clock tonight."

That night Joe's black helper, acting as lookout for him, signaled that the supplier was coming. Joe went upstairs and waited. When the supplier entered with two other men Joe shot at him, missing purposely, then fled, escaping roof to roof in a pouring rain.

The next day he and his supplier adjusted their differences. But of course that was not the end of it. A month or so later Joe's helper told him that word was being passed that "Frankie's marked you." Frankie was a 20-year-old Sicilian blackhander, a member of the Five Points Gang.

For a week Esposito waited in his saloon after closing for Frankie to come for him. One night the Sicilian quietly appeared.

Esposito had him in his sights and was ready to pull the trigger but then he could not. Killing a man for good reason was right, but this would surely go on forever. After Frankie, someone else would be sent. He lowered the hammer and called out to Uale that he was coming down.

They talked, but Esposito could see he must walk away from his saloon. That was his first meeting with Frankie Yale. In later years he got to know him better. He already knew Johnny Torrio, his beer supplier. In a few years he got to know him very well.

In Chicago Esposito opened a bakery at Gilpin and Jefferson, sleeping in a back room there. He prospered well enough to move his business to Vernon Park Place and Morgan, from where he introduced to Chicago the home delivery of bread, from horse-drawn wagons. He also in a few years began to contract for cheese, olive oil, flour—provisions for his countrymen sweating under the sun in the American West. He had got them the jobs there and found tenement rooms in Chicago for their families. He had become a padrone, aided in this by Big Jim Colosimo, whose star was just then beginning to rise in the firmament of Chicago vice.

Esposito's sojourn in Brooklyn had not diminished his appreciation of full-fleshed women, nor his cheery, openhanded, black-mustached charm. At least one of his romantic involvements proved helpful in his business ventures. The lovers spoke Italian: "I have people who want to come here but they have no money." She trusted him: "Joe, you can ask any kind of money, you'll get." In emergencies he could go to her for large amounts in cash, as much as $50,000 when needed, even late at night. Another strong-foot financial support in his business

131

ventures was Jewish, ostensibly a dealer in antiques. His shop on Halsted at Madison, however, was only a front for a notch house in back; prostitution provided the money for lending. Esposito never reneged on a loan, nor any other business or political promise. As a Neapolitan, this was a point of honor for him.

In 1908 he either did or did not shoot a man. The Chicago Bureau of Identification Reg. No. 43602 gives this account:

> On Aug. 19, 1908, Giuseppi Esposito fired one shot at Mack Geaquenta. . . . The bullet struck Geaquenta in the mouth and he died almost instantly. The shooting followed a quarrel over a woman in a barber shop at 244 West Randolph Street where Geaquenta was employed. . .

According to Esposito, he was visiting his sister in Yonkers, NY, at the time the shooting took place. At the trial, ten months later, witnesses had disappeared or could not positively identify him as the killer. Case dismissed: "Slayers not apprehended."

He opened a spaghetti joint at 1048 West Taylor in Little Italy's "Patch," its "Spaghetti Belt" as other Chicagoans termed it. A few tables, some chairs; make the gravy, boil the spaghetti—that's all it took. On Taylor Street it was spaghetti you asked for and spaghetti you got.

His jaunty, confident style cut a wide swath in Little Italy. He attended all of the christenings, weddings, benefits, festivals, funerals, saint's day celebrations. Within a few years, by dint of his dominating personality and the energetic, personal attention he gave to the troubles and concerns of his neighbors he became a man looked to for help and advice beyond that sought from him as padrone, and including that on how to vote come election day. On St. Joseph's day he sponsored a festival to which hundreds of neighbors came each year.

He cultivated the friendship of judges and the Maxwell Street police. He could walk into a courtroom, catch the judge's eye, and in 15 minutes be alone with the judge to straighten out some troubling matter for someone, present somebody's hard luck story. He sent witnesses on vacation during trials. He got revoked licenses back for physicians. Once he got a state's attorney drunk and removed vital papers from the attorney's briefcase. "If Dimey wants it done, it can be done" became axiomatic in Little Italy.

He would arrange for those more adept at speaking the English language than himself to school immigrants for their naturalization exams. A typical exchange:

"All right—what do you do?"
"I work."
"For who? What name?"
(Silence; puzzled look.)

"Listen to me now—what is it that you do?"

"I make a lotta kids."

"No, no, no. Who is President of the United States?"

"Diamond Joe!"

In 1913, age 41 and coming into the full ascendancy of his influence and power, Diamond Joe, King of the Valley, was struck by the thunderbolt—*colpo di fulmine*—love at first sight. His barber was trimming Joe's mustache and telling him about a young, beautiful *ragazza* in his neighborhood who was serenaded on weekends by throngs of young fellows. Such a racket. He was describing the forlorn hope on the faces of the young males who gathered each evening before the tenement in which this gift of God lived—with her 16 brothers and sisters!—when suddenly he lowered his scissors and whispered hoarsely, "There she is—the *bambola*!"

Esposito looked out the shop's window, pulled away the barber's cloth, and was out the door to follow the young woman to her destination (a doctor's office, as it happened), where he introduced himself. For him it was a slightly awkward moment; she was so *young*.

Carmela Marchese lowered her head, spoke her own name and excused herself.

Dimey was mildly disturbed that she had given no indication she knew who he was. . . . But she was only 16, according to the barber. No doubt she was shy. . . . No matter; he must have her. If Dimey wants it done. . . .

The next morning he sent several women to her mother with a message: "Signora Marchese, an admirer would like to come over and ask for the hand of your daughter Carmela."

"Is he a lawyer?"

"Bigger."

"A doctor?"

"*Much* bigger."

"Who the hell is he? The Mayor?"

"*Yeah*! He will be here at seven o'clock."

That afternoon a horse and wagon pulled to a halt in front of the Marchese dwelling and the driver took off a variety of household goods and a tray of expensive foodstuffs and carried them inside.

That evening, shortly before 7:00, Joseph Esposito's automobile stopped in front of the tenement and he debarked to present himself. He and the widow Marchese sat together on the small, dilapidated front stoop. Across the street residents of the neighborhood began strolling past—very slowly, more and more of them as the night progressed. An impromptu passegiata.

After an exchange of pleasantries, Signora Marchese and her guest talked first of Italy and then of events and affairs, including the semi-scandalous, of Little Italy. This desultory gossip continued for nearly five hours, while an increasingly nervous and finally irritated Esposito waited for Carmela to appear.

Signora Marchese was a patient, politely gracious hostess. She and her guest shared the food she had prepared. She did not, of course, serve him the food he had sent. They drank homemade wine together. To Signora Marchese her guest seemed substantial enough, serious enough, friendly enough, respectful enough, *un gran brava persona*. He made a good impression. But. . . .

At least half a dozen times she had expressed her thanks, and that of her children, including Carmela, for the afternoon's gifts, and he had dismissed his generosity as inconsequential, as he should have. And she had been suitably impressed by his diamond stickpin and his large diamond ring, and truly stunned when the Signore took from his vest pocket a red bandana and unfolded it to show her the diamonds it contained, which he told her would be her daughter's. But as midnight neared Signora Marchese's patience was wearing thin. When she went into the tenement for a shawl her daughter accosted her. "Ask him!" Carmela hissed.

Signora Marchese returned to her guest. "Well," she said, "is he coming?"

"What?"

"When is he coming?"

"Who?"

"Your son."

Esposito looked back at her blankly until understanding came to him. Then he replied evenly, "I am the father—and I am the son."

The wedding was held the same year. Before the ceremony Don Peppino shaved his mustache. His dark, handsome face looked younger without it, he felt.

Most of the 19th Ward was invited to the wedding. The contadini of Little Italy and their families—the humble people of no influence and few choices (whose fathers had built the trolley lines from which Charles T. Yerkes enriched himself), the humble people exploited in a hundred ways by their employers, doctors, merchants, bankers, lawyers, landlords, politicians, duplicitous interpreters—they celebrated Don Peppino's wedding for three days and three nights, the festivities costing the groom $60,000 ($40,000 of this for wine). If only for a few days, part of *la via vecchia*—the old way—transplanted to the New World.

A son was born two years after the marriage, a daughter in another four years, a second son in six years more. The marriage was often stormy. He was stubborn and volatile and he did not lose his fondness for other women when he married.

Carmela was just as mercurial as her husband and, as might be expected of one of 17 children, strong-willed. Two of Dimey's pet names for his wife were "Piccerella," by which he meant "Little One," and "Figlia," which translates as *daughter* but by which he meant "Stranger."

He founded and was elected president of Circola Acerra, a mutual benefit society whose 500 or so members came from his birthplace or nearby. He gave away hundreds of baskets of food at Thanksgiving, Christmas, and Easter, and on these occasions he also gave dimes to the children (hence, "Dimey"). When driving down Taylor toward Halsted he would have his driver let him out of the car to "meet my people." As the Marmon crept beside him in the street he strutted along the wooden sidewalk calling out greetings. His people, the people whose votes he could deliver, saluted him in return.

He was active not only in 19th-Ward politics but also in Chicago's labor affairs. Joseph D'Andrea installed him as business agent and treasurer of Chicago Local 286 of the International Hod Carriers' Building and Construction Union. With Anthony D'Andrea, who took over for his brother when Joseph was murdered in 1914, Esposito took control of the Sewer Diggers' and Tunnel Miners' Union as well. He contracted for part of the construction of Union Station and for a subway at Washington and Clinton.

In 1917 at his ristorante on Taylor Street, a certain Cuono Coletta, while drunk (but known to be dangerous cold sober), intruded on a family festa by shooting off the tip of Joe's brother's finger. (As he had promised, Esposito had brought his mother and brother to America.) This unruly behavior so annoyed another patron that he took out his own weapon and blew off Coletta's head. Disgusted by the sight of his pasta sauced with blood, Joe walked away from the place, as he had his saloon in Brooklyn. In 1920, however, perhaps invigorated by his election that April as Republican Ward Committeeman (the only one elected of 35 candidates opposing Mayor Thompson's slate), Dimey tried again, this time at 850 South Halsted with the Bella Napoli Café. Here the decor was elaborate, the menu extensive and exclusively Neapolitan. The Bella Napoli's building also held his office.

By the time Prohibition came and he began supplying sugar in vast quantities to the Gennas' alky cookers, he was a power in the city, a friend of Mike Merlo and of John Torrio, and he had been a close associate of Big Jim Colosimo—all powerful men—and he was an ally of U.S. Senator Deneen and other important politicians and well thought of by many judges and police officials.

He was more than a friend to the young thug Torrio made his first lieutenant when Colosimo was killed. One of the first things Alphonse Caponi did when he arrived in Chicago was to call on Esposito—out of respect. Diamond Joe's Brooklyn saloon had been next door to the house in which the Caponi family lived. The father was *un ubriacone*, a drunk, and Joe had helped the family many times, as he had helped the Genna boys when they were first in Chicago.

Diamond Joe's daughter Jeanette Frances recalls that one of the stories her father liked to tell the family about his years in Brooklyn concerned seeing a gypsy to have his fortune told. The gypsy said he would succeed in America beyond his dreams, but that he would have to travel to achieve this. At first, her father said, he thought by travel she meant his ocean voyage from Naples. But when he was forced to sell his Brooklyn saloon he realized she meant inland, to Chicago.

They could see for themselves the gypsy was right those many years ago couldn't they? Look at him: a man who worked hard, who worked for his people, his family, got money for them.

In American popular music of his time, Jeanette recalled, her father's favorite song was "Look for the Silver Lining." But of course his real love was opera. Johnny Torrio loved opera, too. Didn't he spend his evenings at home studying Verdi's melodies, Puccini's harmonies? Like Joe, too, though—and for the same reasons—he loved money, and single-mindedly pursued it.

As the 1920s began, each man was making more money than they could have imagined in their youth, Esposito perhaps half a million a year, the short, quiet Torrio 20 times that much.

Money was the dream. Esposito and Torrio dreamed of money. The six Terrible Gennas dreamed of money. Colosimo had dreamed of money. In Italy they might have dreamed of money, but just as important there would have been a need for respect, with or without money. In America you could not have respect without money.

Wherever you go, there you are.

POLITICOS

In 1920 in a smoke-filled room in Chicago (Suite 4046, Blackstone Hotel, 13th floor) Warren Gamaliel Harding was selected by Republican Party leaders as their candidate for President of the United States after he swore to them "on his sacred honor and before God" that he knew of no reason he should not stand for that high office. He was elected 28th President by an impressive majority.

During his time in office Harding's Veteran Bureau's chief skimmed profits from war surplus sales, bootlegged drugs to dealers, and took kickbacks from purchasing agents; his Alien Property Custodian took bribes, using Harding's Attorney General's personal aide as bagman; and his poker-playing buddy and Secretary of the Interior accepted a $100,000 bribe to permit an oil company to tap into the U.S. Navy's emergency oil reserve at Teapot Dome, Wyoming.

Had the shapers of destiny in that smoke-filed room in 1920 been told by Harding of his young mistress, mother of his illegitimate child, and of his older mistress, wife to a long-time friend, they might not have given his solemn oath of purity full credence and perhaps none of these malfeasances would have occurred.

Harding was not an impressive chief executive. During Harding's time in office, however, Johnny Torrio was. As partner in 12 breweries and handler of output from 50 more, as well as the Gennas' grain alcohol production and that of several other distilleries, operator of 50 whorehouses and 100 gambling rooms, and supplier to 15,000 speak-easies, he managed his full-service capitalistic empire to a mighty prosperity, and his own income rose to exceed $15 million a year.

It required his full energies each day, assessing problems and risks and opportunities, devising strategies to solve the problems, minimizing the risks, and seizing the opportunities. He had to lay out plans for his subordinates and assign tasks and set deadlines; establish long-term objectives; set policies and establish controls; delegate, appraise performances, adjust to contingencies. It was a tremendous job of management and Johnny Torrio excelled at it. He had a mind that compelled him to make order out of disorder.

While the Pax Torrio lasted in Chicago, the rising tide of Prohibition riches lifted all boats fairly peaceably. It was not until 1923, when Spike O'Donnell was pardoned by Governor Small and he returned to his South Side gang, that large-scale homicide came to the beer-supply rivalries.

Torrio's accomplishments would have been more difficult without the broad grin and slow wink of Mayor William Hale Thompson.

But hadn't Thompson's political career been cut short two decades earlier? Wasn't he humiliated by Alderman Kenna in the redistricting of the First Ward in 1900 and effectively finished as a politician? . . . Well, yes and no.

William Hale Thompson did conclude his first and only term as alderman in near silence. (Outside the Council he captained the CAA's water polo team to a championship and married a secretary from his real estate office.) But then he was taken in tow by the "Blond Boss" of Illinois Republicans, William Lorimer, a former horsecar conductor, a bland, placid teetotaler, and the champion of Charles T. Yerkes' traction projects in the state legislature. Through Lorimer Big Bill met the black-coated, string-tied, bucktoothed "Poor Swede," Fred Lundin, a seller of the temperance drink and patent medicine Juniper's Ade. With his strange get-up Lundin would have been the political cartoonist's spitting image of Mr. Dry if he had worn a stovepipe hat. As a matter of fact, however, his temperance drink, Juniper Ade (concocted from an old Lundin family recipe), was favorably known to mix tastily with gin.

"Give them a show," Lundin advised Lorimer and Thompson. "Forget about the issues. Give them a good time and you get the votes."

Thompson, who had not delivered a single speech in his winning campaign for alderman, was the hit of Lorimer's and Lundin's Cook County tent show. He ran for County Commissioner in 1902 and his bellowing, grimacing, arm-waving tirades stirred the Irish, Swedes, Germans, Poles, and Italians of the city into a revivalistic frenzy. "We've got crooks in the City Hall because we haven't got the guts to throw them out! . . . Put Bill Thompson on the county board and I'll show you clean, liberal government!"

A traveling British journalist had accused Chicago businessmen of underpaying and overworking their shop girls and said that the city "by day is all feverish making money and by night is riotous debauchery." Thompson was, naturally, outraged. He confided to his enthusiastic audiences that when he was out West he had met Britishers and he had become acquainted with their character: "They were all seedy and untrustworthy."

He won election to the commission with the third highest total of votes on the Republican ticket, only a few hundred less than that of Charles S. Deneen who was reelected State's Attorney.

For the next few years Thompson alternated between minor political tasks for Lorimer and water polo and yacht racing. He apparently could not decide whether he wanted to be a rich sportsman or a wealthy politician.

Illinois Republicans were split into two factions; one Lorimer's, the other Deneen's. At issue was power and its patronage. Besides, Deneen had reformist tendencies.

In 1910 the *Tribune* disclosed that Lorimer, from a slush fund of $100,000, had bought his seat in the U.S. Senate by bribing state legislators (who at that time elected senators). Thompson rose to Lorimer's defense, singing in a tin-ear quartet at Lorimer rallies and speechifying that Lorimer was the victim of a plot hatched by Robert R. McCormick of the *Tribune*. (As a youth, McCormick had been an admirer of Thompson until he heard him call to a friend at the CAA pool, "Jesus Christ, was I drunk last night!")

"Bob McCormick represents the trust press that would crush the life out of Chicago," Thompson declared. ". . . He's a Deneen pipsqueak and tool of the public utilities. I'm gonna smash Bob McCormick!"

Running for the Cook County Board of Review, Thompson was himself smashed—by 15,000 ballots—in the primary. The next year his political mentor Lorimer was expelled from the Senate because of his means of entry. At a Chicago memorial service for Lorimer's career, Big Bill draped an American flag over Lorimer's shoulders and apostrophized him as "a loyal, fine, courageous, outstanding American!" Mrs. Lorimer was "A sweet little lady who, through it all, has known the truth and has been steadfast and understanding. How bravely she has suffered!"

His speech made an impression on the Poor Swede, who ventured that "I think we've got a man to go places with. He may not be too much on brains, but he gets through to the people."

Lundin, now a wealthy owner of a patent medicine factory and a thriving mail-order business, proselytized Chicago's precincts on behalf of Thompson for mayor throughout 1913. At the rally to announce his candidacy in the primary, Thompson made it clear that the people would rule: "And with you bossing the job I am going to clean up the dirt of the rotten administration in power!" Speaking to the women of Chicago (the 1914 mayoral primary election would be their first) he cajoled them with "You ladies! You know what goes on. You've been proving that and doing a fine job of it! I tell you I am going to clean up Chicago and I mean it! . . . If I am elected mayor, I will protect the fair womanhood of Chicago!"

He circulated through the city 18 hours a day, all seven days of the week. There were 600,000 Germans and Austrians in the city—its largest ethnic group—and to them he capitalized on his known anti-British sentiments in this first year of World War I. He made vague, extravagant promises at women's teas, held out the prospect of city jobs in all wards, told Chicago's blacks: "I'll give your people the best opportunities you've ever had if you elect me!" and won the nomination by the slim margin of 3,591 votes out of 171,000 cast. His Democratic opponent won his primary race by almost 80,000 votes out of 287,000. Stock Yards gambling king Big Jim O'Leary set odds at 5 to 1 favoring the Democrat, Robert Sweitzer, who had defeated the incumbent Carter Harrison.

Sweitzer spoke derisively of Big Bill. "Who ever heard of him doing anything? . . . I find he is the man who plays with sailboats."

With Lundin directing his every step and drafting his speeches, Thompson denounced his opponent as an errand boy for the Gas Trust. To neighborhood groups he said, "I see no harm in a friendly little drink in a friendly neighborhood saloon." To women he made this specific promise: "I'll appoint a mother to the board of education." To blacks he offered jobs: "And if any of you want to shoot craps, go ahead and do it." He told one and all, "We'll build this great city up. . . . We'll have full prosperity and a full dinner pail."

As the campaign neared its close, mailings went out portraying Sweitzer not only as the Gas Trust's candidate but also as the Pope's candidate and the Kaiser's as well. General disorder and serious brawling punctuated the rallies and parades of both candidates. But the gamblers maintained their cold objectivity; odds swung even more heavily to Sweitzer. On election eve he was 8 to 1. In his last speech before the election, speaking in Chicago's Black Belt on Easter Sunday and referring to Jess Willard's defeat of Jack Johnson that afternoon in Havana, Thompson said, "Only a good cowboy like Willard could beat a good man like Johnson. Tomorrow the cowboy will be on your side."

The number of voters who turned out on April 6 was greater than had ever been recorded in a U.S. municipal election. Sweitzer had 251,502 of them, Thompson 390,691, the largest plurality ever given a Republican in Chicago. Big Bill told his Swedish Svengali, the Poor Swede, "Fred, you're a wizard. You did it all, and I'm not ever going to forget this."

Fred Lundin oversaw patronage and administrative details for the new Mayor and sent daily instructions to him at City Hall. Because he wanted to bring his protegé to national attention and, he hoped, gain him a chance at the Republican Presidential nomination in 1918, Lundin had him close Chicago saloons on Sunday, as city law required. This was a mistake, especially for a mayor who had otherwise espoused a wide-open town. It soured many dinner-pail voters on Big Bill. (And he never did get around to appointing a mother to the board of education.)

". . . I guess the only thing to do is get loaded Saturday if you're gonna try to last till Monday morning," Hinky Dink Kenna advised from his Workingman's Exchange saloon. On the other hand, the Sunday closing order caused the Reverend J. B. Brushingham to wax rhapsodic: "Let me tell you, William Hale Thompson," he told William Hale Thompson, "that a sober, law-abiding people may insist that you be the leader of the nation!"

Another Lundin tactic to bring Big Bill's statesmanship to the fore—now for a U.S. Senate seat since the Presidential bid quickly fizzled—was to have him give his views on the propriety of U.S. entry into WWI—which Lundin strongly opposed. Teddy Roosevelt, with many others, had been urging the youth of America to get ready to fight, and patriotic groups were organized throughout the country to ferret out Imperial Germany's cunning secret agents. In April 1917 President Wilson, who had been "too proud to fight," declared against the Kaiser; "We must fight for justice and right," he said, and went back to the White House and wept.

Crafted by the Poor Swede, this was Mayor Thompson's pronouncement: "This war is a needless sacrifice of the best blood of the nation on foreign battlefields." His view approximated that of Jane Addams of Hull House, who asked, "What right have we to send youth into battle while we keep our safe places by the fire?"—and resembled, inadvertently to be sure, that of the International Workers of the World (founded in Chicago 12 years before). In 1918 in a Chicago courtroom an angry Judge Kenesaw Mountain Landis sentenced each of 15 IWW leaders to 20 years in prison for their stand.

The result of Thompson's public declaration in 1917 was that "Kaiser Bill," "Wilhelm der Grosse," "Burgomaster Bill," "a disgrace to the city," "the laughingstock of America," and "a low-down double crosser" were the milder epithets applied to him, and he was hanged in effigy on the Lake front.

Several months of this abuse prompted Lundin to order the Mayor to reverse engines, so Big Bill issued a proclamation calling on all Chicagoans "to show to our soldiers and sailors who are leaving for the front that our hearts, our hopes, our prayers go with them" (When the war ended on November 11 Thompson would only say, "I'm for America first.")

After he announced he was a candidate for the U.S. Senate, he was soundly defeated in his party's primary, but on November 30 he accepted a solemn call from Lundin and other concerned citizens to run for a second term as mayor. His pro-German views on the war were attacked as well as the corruption, inefficiency, and graft of his first term. (When he entered office the city treasury had a surplus of $3 millon. In 1918 it had a $4.5 million deficit.) His response was, "I'm for home rule,

I'm for reduced gas rates, I'm for the five-cent streetcar fare. I'm for the people and against the selfish interests. Bill Thompson is for you!" and he won the primary by 40,000 votes. It was as if the voters were acting on Lincoln's advice: "If you make a bad bargain, hug it all the tighter."

Thompson's Democratic opponent was again the popular Sweitzer. Lundin decided if his man were to have a chance, he would have to concentrate on winning big in black wards (the Second was now 70 percent black), and Irish and German wards. Thompson had named several blacks to responsible positions in his administration and blacks seemed to like him; the Germans already knew he was not unsympathetic, that he was loudly anti-British; and to secure the further affection of the Irish Thompson declared for home rule for Ireland. He was reelected on April 1 by 21,000 votes (11,000 from the Second Ward). Newspapers throughout the country expressed their editorial astonishment and regret, and offered condolences to the city.

Thompson admonished its citizens to "Be a Chicago booster! Throw away your hammer. Get a horn and blow loud for Chicago!"

If his first term had raised suspicions that there were elements of the bizarre and incompetent in his leadership, his second confirmed there had been. He was tragically slow in quelling the bloody five-day 1919 race riot in Chicago, and he deposed the city's superintendent of schools—who had offended Lundin—with tactics the *Tribune* opined partook of "the restraint of a Hottentot war dance."

At 12:01 A.M., January 17, 1920, the Volstead Act went into effect, prohibiting. (At 12:59 six men broke into two freight cars on a Chicago railroad siding and stole $100,000 worth of medicinal alcohol.) John Torrio had of course been paying City Hall for protection from its police but now he increased these payments. He carried a membership card in the William Hale Thompson Republican Club, and he had contributed heavily to Thompson's reelection fund. Nothing personal, just business.

In June Thompson played host to the Republican National Convention in Chicago, determined to throw over his own state's candidate for President, Frank O. Lowden, who was a leading contender nationally. As Illinois Governor, Lowden had been unkind to Poor Swede Lundin in patronage matters. The Mayor told delegates from other states that Lowden's "word's no good. You can't count on him, believe me." As a result of his machinations, there was the infamous midnight meeting in the smoke-filled room that anointed Warren G. Harding. Thompson assured his followers that Harding would be "one of the great Presidents."

In July Thompson began campaigning for his candidate for Governor, Len Small, who defeated Lowden's choice impressively in the primary and went on to win the November election by half a million votes, swept in by the Harding landslide nationally. On the fifth floor of

City Hall, Thompson exulted. "We ate 'em alive with their clothes on! Put on a big party! Let's show 'em we're all live ones!"

But in Thompson's second term his ship of state began to list badly. A slate of 20 judges he had handpicked for election was defeated. His "five-cent fare" transportation bill—seemingly assured of passage in the state legislature—was voted down while he was a spectator on the rostrum after a downstate senator castigated him for coming to Springfield to pressure its lawmakers. He lost a second libel suit he had entered against the *Chicago Tribune*. His staunch friend and worshipful ally Governor Len Small was indicted for embezzlement of state funds. And State's Attorney Robert Crowe—considered a Thompsonite—opened an investigation into fraud in the obtaining of school funds by Thompson appointees.

When in January of 1923 Mayor Thompson learned the details of the investigation Crowe had been conducting and was then presenting to a grand jury he immediately withdrew his name from consideration for a third term. The next day the grand jury brought in indictments of Fred Lundin and 22 co-conspirators for misappropriation of more than $1 million in Chicago school funds. It was charged that the 23 men had profited from fake contracts, false bids, and rigged prices for supplies, and had resorted to shakedowns of suppliers and accepted bribes; that they had engaged in a conspiracy to defraud the taxpayer.

On August 3, 1923, Warren Gamaliel Harding died (he was succeeded by Vice President Calvin Coolidge), terminating one of the most corrupt administrations in American history.

In Chicago the Democrat William E. Dever was elected Mayor. He vowed reform: "This town will immediately become dry," he declared.

Former Mayor Big Bill Thompson announced he was building a yawl, the *Big Bill*, for an expedition to the South Seas to find tree-climbing fish. "I have strong reason to believe," he explained, "that there are fish that come out of the water, can live on land, will jump three feet to catch a grasshopper, and will actually climb trees."

Torrio offered Mayor Dever's Chief of Police $100,000 a month not to interfere with business. By way of reply the chief padlocked the Four Deuces. (In the basement of 2222 S. Wabash was a tunnel leading to a trapdoor opening out of the back of the building. Troublemakers were tortured in the basement, killed, taken out the tunnel and their bodies dumped in the country. Police knew of at least 12 such murders. They were assumed to be part of Al Capone's duties for Torrio.)

The *Big Bill* got as far as New Orleans in its voyage to the South Seas but Big Bill didn't. He returned to Chicago to plot a new course, hoping it would be for'ard.

143

Spike O'Donnell

John Scalisi (left) and Albert Anselmi

CAPO

Early on in Chicago's annals of alcohol Mr. Dooley observed that "Tis a bad thing to stand on, a good thing to sleep on, a good thing to talk on, a bad thing to think on." Had he foreseen Prohibition, Mr. Dooley might have added that it could also be a license to steal.

By 1923 Chicago had 20,000 speakeasies, 13,000 more—or almost three times as many—as it had saloons the night the Volstead Act took effect. Johnny The Fox Torrio's troops garnered three-quarters of the money made from these 20,000, plus revenues from their prostitution resorts and gambling houses, profit centers Torrio was ever alert to enhance and extend.

As the head man of this widespread organization, Torrio had final say in all matters. The military's chain of command was no more clear cut. The burdens of management had increased. All day out of his office at the Four Deuces, he made decisions, handled problems, gave orders, planned, discussed, considered, delegated, and then usually went home to Anna, frequently spending his evenings taking apart phrases and motives in an opera's music and libretto, sometimes singing to his wife from the score to make a point

At his office Johnny Torrio oversaw the activities of a workforce of roughly 800 men, with a weekly payroll past $25,000 just for the lower echelons. The higher echelons got a percentage cut of their sector's profits. Torrio's chief lieutenant, the young Al Capone, received a 25 percent cut of net. Ninety-five percent of the workforce was foreign-born; most were in their mid-20s up to 30; a great many—proportionately more than in the general population—were thin and wiry (not Capone); most boasted flashy wardrobes—in contrast to their chief, who was short and paunchy, nearing 40, dressed conservatively, and usually did not carry a gun.

A gangster's working hours were usually from 4:00 P.M. to 12:00. After midnight he often partied till dawn, slept till noon. As a close friend to the opposite sex he lacked luster. "Judge," one bootlegger told John H. Lyle, "a guy's a gangster because he loves money and that doesn't leave any room to love a woman."

Torrio's power lay in his ability to provide protection. As he said, "I own the police." Control of the police not only gave his own operations immunity but also worked against his rivals, since the authorities *would* move against them.

The hallmarks of Johnny Torrio's management style were system, efficiency, and foresight. What he intended when he first apportioned territories among contending Chicago gangs was, of course, an eventual monopoly for himself. *Il tempo buono viene una volta solo*—The good time comes but once.

The first open challenge to this master plan came from the far South Side's O'Donnell brothers, out by Bubbly Creek in Kerry Patch. At the onset of Prohibition the oldest brother, Spike ("When arguments fail, use a blackjack"), was serving a ten-year sentence in Joliet State Penitentiary for bank robbery. Without him his three younger brothers drifted, odd-jobbing for Torrio out of the Four Deuces and complaining. Finally in the summer of 1923, after pleas on his behalf by six state senators, five state representatives, and a judge of the Criminal Court of Cook County, Spike was paroled by Governor Len Small. The brothers promptly hijacked several of Torrio's beer shipments.

The Fox tried negotiation. A district police captain was brought in as arbitrator. He suggested that the Stockyards' business be divided. Spike refused. Torrio countered by reducing the price of his Stockyards' beer by $10 a barrel. Spike O'Donnell replied by running beer into territory that had been reserved to Polack Joe Saltis and Frankie McErlane during Torrio's initial syndication, and having his strong-arms beat up proprietors who wouldn't buy from him, and wreck their shops. He also imported a New York City gunman.

Torrio met with Saltis and McErlane and under Torrio's direction McErlane, a portly, smiling, pig-eyed Irishman whose weapon of choice was the sawed-off, double-barrelled shotgun, began to hunt. On the night of September 7, 1923, he and his men trapped five of the O'Donnell gang in a South Side saloon. Four escaped but McErlane blew away the fifth. Ten days later the bodies of two more O'Donnell thugs were found in a ditch, hands trussed behind their backs, shotgun slugs in their backs and chests.

New Mayor Dever was enraged and resolute:

"The police will follow this case to a finish as they do all others. This guerilla war between hijackers, rum runners and illicit beer pedlars can and will be crushed. I am just as sure that this miserable traffic with its toll of human life and morals can be stamped out as I am that I am mayor, and I am not going to flinch for a minute."

146

Torrio and Capone and the O'Donnells were questioned. Nothing was determined. The change had come. After a century of being a rutting and gaming ground, Chicago's vice and crime had metamorphosed into a killing ground slick with blood and alcohol. In that fall of 1923 there were 10 gangland killings; the next year, 16; in 1925, 46; and 64 in 1926 (and these proved to be the slow years). In all that time only five men were brought to trial for these 136 murders and all five were acquitted.

While visiting his mother in Brooklyn in July, Torrio had applied for U.S. citizenship. He gave as his occupation "real estate broker" and stated that he had been a resident of Brooklyn continuously since 1900. A doctor and an undertaker swore to the truth of this statement and that John Torrio was a man of good character. Torrio returned to Brooklyn in early November and gave his oath of allegiance to the United States of America, becoming one of 112,000,000 other U.S. citizens, a tenth of whom were foreign-born like himself. (In 1923 there were 94,000 foreign-born Italians in Illinois, 545,000 in New York State.)

McErlane, taking orders now from Torrio through his field general Capone, kept on the prowl for O'Donnells. The night of December 1st fat, pig-eyed Frankie waylaid two of their truckers. One survived to recite a scenario that does not resemble the devil-may-care derring-do of the one-way ride as later depicted in Hollywood's gangster films:

> Pretty soon the driver asks the guy with the shotgun, "Where you gonna get rid of these guys?" The fat fellow laughs and says, "I'll take care of that in a minute." He was monkeying with his shotgun all the time. Pretty soon he turns around and points the gun at Keane. He didn't say a word but just let go straight at him. Keane got it square on the left side. It kind of turned him over and the fat guy give him the second barrel in the other side. The guy loads up his gun and gives it to Keane again. Then he turns around to me and says, "I guess you might as well get yours, too." With that he shoots me in the side. It hurt like hell so when I seen him loading up again, I twist around so it won't hit me in the same place. This time he got me in the leg. Then he gimme the other barrel right on the puss. I slide off the seat. But I guess the fat guy wasn't sure we was through. He let Morrie have it twice more and then he let me have it again in the other side. The fat guy scrambled into the rear seat and grabbed Keane. He opens the door and kicks Morrie out into the road. We was doing about 50 from the sound. I figure I'm next so when he drags me over to the door I set myself to jump. He shoves and I light in the ditch by the road. I hit the ground on my shoulders and I thought I would never stop rolling. I lost consciousness. When my senses came back, I was lying in a pool of water and ice had formed around me. The sky was red and it was breaking day. . . .

The survivor would not name his assailant.

There were at least ten attempts made to kill Spike O'Donnell. "Life with me is just one bullet after another," he said. ". . . I've a notion to hire out as a professional target." In a few of the skirmishes Al Capone was placed at the scene by eyewitnesses, but they would not testify to that in court.

McErlane's continuing hunt bagged an O'Donnell trucker early in 1924 and then the hired gun from NYC and one of the younger O'Donnells. Finally Spike acknowledged he was outmanned and outgunned. Totally frustrated he complained to a reporter, "I can whip this bird Capone with bare fists any time he wants to step in the open and fight like a man." But he realized the time was past for that and within a year he left Chicago, ending the threat to Torrio's hegemony.

When his offer of $100,000 a month for business as usual to Chief of Police Collins was rebuffed, Torrio offered the chief $1,000 a day to overlook the shipment of just 250 barrels of beer a day, but was refused in this also. Mayor Dever had told his Police Chief, "Collins, there's a dry law on the nation's books. This town will immediately become dry. Tell your captains I will break every police official in whose district I hear of a drop of liquor being sold." Knowing how many police officials he had on his payroll, Torrio was not unduly concerned by the new Mayor's determination. But there did seem to be need of a new command post outside of the city's limits. Half a dozen years before he had perceived the importance and value—because of their malleability—of Chicago's outlying municipal governments and had installed whorehouses and roadhouses in suburban villages wherever feasible. He took out a map.

Six miles due west of the Four Deuces, straight out on Twenty-second Street (now Cermak Road, once called "The Street of Whores") lay the unspoiled town of Cicero. Old Harry Guzik, Jake's brother, and Ike Bloom lived there now, shades of the Levee. The town had a population of 70,000, fifth largest in Illinois, mostly steel mill and stockyards workers and their families. It was a blue-collar town whose residents liked their beer of an evening, prohibited or not. The West Side O'Donnells, Bernard, Myles, and Klondike (no relation to the soon-to-be defunct South Side O'Donnells), supplied Ciceronians their beer, but apart from that there was no other open criminality or vice—except for the hundreds of slot machines owned and operated by a local politician, Eddie Vogel. Eddie took 60 percent on the slots, the saloonkeeper paid his overhead with the rest. Prostitution was opposed by Cicero residents—and the West Side O'Donnells—on moral grounds. The residents lived by the code of "You go home with the guy who brung you," and beer on Sunday. They found meaning in their lives in raising their children to be better in the world than they were. It was a peaceable town.

In October of 1923 Torrio leased a house on Roosevelt Road and stocked it with half a dozen women. Cicero police raided the house and closed it. Torrio opened a second house at Ogden and 52nd, moving in the same six women. Cicero police raided this house and closed it, locking up the girls.

Two days later deputy sheriffs descended on Cicero sent by Cook County Sheriff Peter B. Hoffman and impounded all slot machines they found. Eddie Vogel read the message: No whorehouses, no slots. A meeting was held at the Four Deuces; there were negotiations. Vogel's slot machines were returned, the West Side O'Donnells were given an exclusive franchise for beer along Roosevelt Road and several other sections in Cicero and Johnny Torrio agreed not to bring prostitutes into the town. (That had never been his intention; Cicero was surrounded by his good-feeling resorts.) In return he received permission to sell beer in Cicero outside the O'Donnells' territories and he was permitted to open gambling houses and nightclubs. Almost as important to him, he had his new base of operations for metropolitan Chicago beer running. A lifetime of supporting large-scale, organized vice through bribery and violence had taught Johnny Torrio how to handle reformers such as Mayor Dever, but he needed a headquarters to hang his hat.

With Cicero secured, Torrio, like the loyal and dutiful son he was, took his mother Maria back to Italy, his wife Anna traveling with them on a luxury liner. He also took more than a million dollars in negotiable securities and letters of credit to Europe, where he deposited them in Swiss and Italian banks. He bought his mother an Italian villa where, after an extensive tour of Europe with Anna, he left her with villa, money, cars, chauffeurs, and 20 servants—the richest woman in the province.

Wherever you go, there you are, true enough. And most often you're taken there by the circumstances of your life. Think of an infant brought from the warm, secure place he's known to a strange, cold, dark cavern that pitches and tosses him and hundreds of other crowded bodies without stop for three weeks (an eternity), little enough to eat or drink or breathe, with vomit, noise, and stink all around, then to a place also frighteningly different from what you've known the only two years of your life.

Within five years one of the boy's many chores is to mop the splintered floor of the blind pig his stepfather owns and to tote beer. The people in the saloon are big, loud, laughing, shouting, cursing men. Sometimes they fight and bloody each other. Sometimes when he brings them their beer they talk to him, laugh at him, give him small change. Sometimes they have their heads close over the table talking in low voices and ignore him.

By the time he is nine or so he has pretty much figured out why the men shout, why they whisper. Sometimes he goes on errands for the men, takes things places for them, picks up things for them. Once in a while he stands lookout for them. Once in a while a man is killed and the death is spoken of in the saloon. Or not spoken of. He discovers that some of the men he knows have killed other men.

From the men and from older boys he learns that some women are good, like his mother Maria, but that most are worthless, though still sought after.

By the time he is in his early teens he realizes that he is not going to be very tall or big, but he accepts this without regret. Most of the loudest, biggest men are *gonzos*—simpletons. He knows by then that he can talk as quickly as most of his stepfather's customers, and that he can out-think most of them, too.

He learns that it is possible to foretell that if a person does *this*, then *that* will likely happen, that for matters to fall out as you want them to, it is possible to plan, talk, accommodate, and influence the events of the future.

He learns that fairness is never to be expected. If it is won at all, it must be taken. He learns that the world is unjust and indecent, arbitrary and corrupt, and that all men have a price.

He learns to conceal his pleasure, delight, laughter, disgust, sorrow, boredom, astonishment—for he knows that if you show your emotions to others, you weaken yourself. Above all, he learns to control and conceal his anger. Anger is the wind that blows out the candle of the mind.

His eyes look out, seeing everything, revealing nothing. It is, after all, very simple: You live with wolves, you learn to howl.

Scruples? Worth less than the bucket of filthy water from swamping the saloon floor. In fact, a complete lack of scruples confers distinct advantages in an encounter. Get all you can—no matter how—and keep all you get.

Others? They are worth to the world every bit as much as you yourself are: nothing. He knows that he and everyone else on this earth are subject to the same cruelty and indifference. This being so, what does it matter how you use those who can be of use to you? Or, especially, what you do to those who stand in your way?

You work for what you want, indifferent yourself, not caring about, not thinking about the lives of those you use. In the end, it's all the same.

The man who is soft is a danger to himself. (The man who does not think is a danger to everyone.) Be hard or be down. If you can't sell it, sit on it. Don't give nothing away. And yet. . . .

But picture a man seated at an auction being held of a sunny morning, say, in Chicago's Dewey Hotel on Washington Boulevard: 30-

year-old Johnny Torrio entrusted by his boss, Big Jim Colosimo, to bid on needed merchandise. The stock is broken-in and kept on the top floor of the hotel until the weekly auction; for that it is brought to the floor below. The stock consists of young women, most of them immigrants. At the auction they are paraded naked except for their slippers before the bidders. Most go for about $200 a head. A young man, plying his trade.

In the long evenings he spent at home with his wife, Anna, what did Johnny Torrio find in the opera scores he followed and studied while he listened to recordings of the works? What was he listening for, looking for, as he read the score against the sound? What did his mind's eye picture, his mind's ear hear beyond the gramophone's distorted reproduction? What metaphors, if any, to life—his own, his wife's—was he discovering in Verdi's melodies, Rossini's or Puccini's harmonies? The relationships of lyrics to music, the intricacies of the composer's inventions—what message was he seeking, or finding in them? In the long evenings with Anna what were his thoughts?

Maybe he found in opera another world, one he liked better than the one he inhabited by day. "If we sang most of the time, as they do in operas, our lives would resound, as legends," E. L. Doctorow has written.

> You will notice in classical operas that time moves more slowly than it does before the curtain goes up or after it comes down. . . . If we sang most of the time, as people do in operas, we would stand and arrange and rearrange ourselves. . . , and the volatility of the world would diminish. . . .

Or was opera for Johnny Torrio, just another diversion, like the games of pinochle he and Anna played?

Johnny Torrio was a private man and all we know of him are the consequences of his business decisions and public acts. Wherever you go, there you are, true. But what you are when you get there is chosen by you, and Johnny Torrio chose to be a pimp and arranger of murders.

Where did Johnny Torrio, callous pimp, ice-blooded killer, and ultimately master bootlegger, first meet his wife? How did he introduce himself, explain his line of business to her? What in this short, quiet man drew her to him? How did he woo her? How did he keep her?

For the last question there is an answer, one given in an unguarded, personal moment by Anna herself:

> "You think you know him . . . but you don't. I'll tell you about him. He's a wonderful man. Thoughtful, considerate. Our married life has been 12 years of unbroken happiness. He has given me kindness, devotion, love—everything that a good man can give a woman."

Red Grange

THE WHEATON ICE MAN

Five-eleven, 170 pounds in his prime, and tough as nails. Even as a youth his was the classic Midwest male face: deepset eyes, slight frown, straight solid nose, full lips that turned down at the corners, square jaw. A gaunt, brooding visage that said to others, "Show me," and for himself, "This is me, this is all. It's enough."

He played four sports at Wheaton High 30 miles west of Chicago, and won 16 letters, playing center and forward on the basketball team, all positions on the baseball team, and especially excelled in track—the 100- and 220-yard dashes, the low and high hurdles, and the broad jump and high jump. Each of his high school years he was state champion in a different track event.

The son of a policeman (his mother dead), Harold "Red" Grange played end as a 138-pound, 15-year-old freshman, switching to the backfield the next year. The football team seldom lost in his four years at Wheaton High, one season scoring more than 700 points, with lopsided victories such as 107 to 0 (over a hapless Naperville) not that uncommon.

The team was coached by the school's manual training teacher. If a player got too cocky, the coach would give him the ball at practice and tell the rest of the team to bring him down, ten on one. The experience, according to Grange, taught you the value of teamwork.

In his sophomore year, as a halfback, he scored 15 touchdowns and kicked nine extra points. As a junior he scored 36 touchdowns and kicked 39 extra points, in one game running for eight touchdowns and kicking all the points after. In his senior year—1921—Wheaton lost only one game (a game in which he played only briefly before being knocked out and carried off the field), and it defeated Chicago's All-City Champions, Austin High. During his senior season Grange scored 23 touchdowns and converted 34 point-afters, for a total in three years as a back of 74 high school TDs, 82 PATs—526 total points.

He was also a superb defensive player. (At that time, football's rules did not permit free substitution. If you were taken out in a quarter, you stayed out that quarter, which meant that players had to go both ways: offense and defense.)

When he was 14 a local ice-route owner had offered a dollar prize to any boy who could lift a 75-pound block of ice onto his shoulder. Grange was the only boy in Wheaton who did it and his prizewinning feat also won him a summer job as a helper on an ice wagon at $37.50 a week. He held this summer job through high school and college, eventually becoming a wagon boss at $50.00 a week.

He said he believed that carrying 100-pound blocks of ice up flights of stairs helped strengthen his legs, but in July of 1919 the job almost crippled him. Hopping off a moving wagon loaded with three tons of ice, he fell and rolled under it and one of the rear wheels ran over his left leg above the knee. The leg was saved but he was given only a 50-50 chance of complete recovery. That autumn, however, he was at halfback as elusive as ever.

At the state interscholastic track championships in Champaign his senior year he met Bob Zuppke, the University of Illinois' short, easygoing, canny football coach. (Zuppke invented the Flea Flicker play—still occasionally used to good effect—and once counseled a group he was speaking to: "If you can't do anything well, try to become an executive.") The Little Dutchman, as Zuppke was called, made a highly favorable impression on Grange, as he did on most people. "If you come down to Illinois," Zuppke told him, "you'd have a good chance at making the football team."

Grange matriculated at Illinois in the fall of 1922. He felt that basketball and track were his best sports, however, and that at 170 pounds he was too light to play football in one of the country's toughest conferences, the Big Ten. But at the urging of fraternity brothers he went out and made a freshman team that regularly beat the varsity when they scrimmaged. Besides himself the team had two other future All Americas—Frank Wickhorst (at Northwestern) and Moon Baker (at Navy). The next year that freshman team became the core of Illinois' varsity. (In the '20s college freshmen were ineligible to play in regular-season games.) In his first game—against a rugged Nebraska team—Grange ran for three touchdowns and 208 yards. It was a sensational start to what became a spectacular season. Illinois went undefeated in 1923 and tied Michigan for the Big Ten title. Grange ran for 1,260 yards and 12 touchdowns in Illinois' seven games and the Eastern panjandrum of All-America selectors, Walter Camp, chose him first team.

Grange had great speed and power as a runner, and great football savvy and tackling ability, which made him just as valuable on defense as on offense. His coach Zuppke (who called him "Grainche" except when riled; then he called him "Red") later appraised his skills: "He was the smoothest performer who ever carried a pigskin. He ran with rhythm, every movement of his body having meaning and direction. . . . He came nearer to being the perfect football player than anyone I have ever known." (And Zuppke was a realist, not a person given to empty praise. Once when asked what it took to make an All-America he replied, "A long run, a weak defense, and a poet in the press box.")

Grange gave credit to his teammates. "If blockers knock everybody down," he said, "your grandmother can score." He said he'd learned to twist and dart, lunge and dodge, cut and reverse, fake and charge from observing his dog's moves when he chased it. He also said, "The sportswriters wrote I had peripheral vision. I didn't even know what the word meant. . . . They asked me about my change of pace and I didn't even know that I ran at different speeds. I had a crossover step, but I couldn't spin. Some ball-carriers can spin, but I'd have broken a leg."

The *big* game of 1924 was against Michigan, the top-ranked team in the nation. The Wolverines had a 22-game unbeaten streak and had given up only four touchdowns in all those 22 games. On the eve of the big game Michigan's athletic director, Fielding Yost, said, "Mr. Grange will be a carefully watched young man any time he takes the ball." (Yost had also remarked that "All Grange can do is run," to which Zuppke replied, "Yeah, and all Galli-Curci can do is sing.")

October 18, 1924, was Homecoming for Illinois and the game that day dedicated its new 67,000-capacity Memorial Stadium. Grange took the opening kick-off on his five-yard line, threaded his way through 11 Wolverines, breaking tackles along the way, and was clear at the 40, continuing into the end zone for a touchdown.

Illinois next got the ball on its own 33. Grange—No. 77—was given the ball, cut back off tackle behind good blocking, stiff-armed a linebacker, and continued into the end zone for a touchdown.

The teams exchanged punts and Illinois had possession on its own 44. Grange took the snap from center, headed for the right sideline on an end sweep, reversed direction across the field and continued into the end zone for a touchdown.

Two minutes later Illinois recovered a fumble on the Michigan 44. Grange started around end again, cut back and outran all defenders, continuing into the end zone for a touchdown. In 12 minutes of play he had carried the ball eight times and scored four touchdowns on runs of 95, 67, 56, and 44 yards, a bravura performance it does not seem likely will ever be matched.

After his fourth TD he leaned wearily against a goal post. "I need a breather," he told his quarterback. Joining Zuppke on the sidelines several plays later he was told, "Should have had another touchdown, Red. You didn't cut at the right time. . . ."

Grange returned in the third quarter to gain 85 more yards (13 of these on his fifth touchdown run) and throw a pass to a teammate for a sixth score. He also held for the kicker on all conversions. Illinois won the game 39 to 14 and Grange, playing 41 minutes, had carried 21 times for 402 yards and completed six passes for 64 more. After the game he left a victory party at his fraternity house to eat at a small restaurant in downtown Champaign and go to the movies.

Though he missed one game and part of another because of a shoulder injury that *annus mirabilis* of 1924, Grange's season statistics were 1,164 yards gained, 13 touchdowns scored, and 27 pass completions for 524 additional yards. Camp again selected him All-America. The sports writer Grantland Rice wrote a poem about his feats titled "The Galloping Ghost."

The Illinois team of 1925 was weakened by injuries, transfers, and graduation, and it lost three of its first four games. The fifth game on its schedule was against the pride of the Ivy League that year, the University of Pennsylvania, which was undefeated in its first five games of the season and had beaten both Yale and powerful Chicago.

It was Grange's first trip East and he was determined to do well; it irritated him that many Easterners felt his exploits were exaggerated or the result of luck. But a steady rain turned Philadelphia's Franklin Field into a bog of thick mud by the day of the game and not even his most faithful supporters expected Grange to gain much yardage in the sloppy footing.

Running in slick mud, playing with a weak team against a strong team, Grange had one of the best days of his college career, second only to his game against Michigan the previous year. He ran for 363 yards and scored touchdowns on off-tackle slants of 56 and 13 yards and on an end sweep for 20 yards, as Illinois beat Pennsylvania 24 to 2. On that dreary October 31st he silenced every skeptic.

His totals for the 1925 season were six touchdowns, 1,213 yards gained, and 15 completed passes for 119 yards. Ten days after his last collegiate game, No. 77 played in his first professional football game—against the wishes of his father and of his college coach. "Football isn't meant to be played for money," Zuppke told him. Charles C. Pyle was the person who persuaded Grange otherwise.

Forty-two years old, Charlie Pyle stood 6 feet 1 inch, weighed 190 pounds, wore pearl-buttoned spats over brilliantly shined shoes, carried a cane, had a small, dapper mustache, and sported a derby. As a young man he had been a boxer, then the impresario of a barnstorming basketball team, next of a small vaudeville company. Now he owned three movie houses: one in Kokomo, Indiana, two in Champaign. One night in November of 1925 he sent an usher to bring the 22-year-old Grange out of his seat to the owner's office in the Virginia Theater.

Many, many years later Grange looked back: "Charlie was the

most impressive man I ever met in my life," he recalled, "and I've met millions of people, Presidents and everything else."

Grange thought he was going to be given free tickets to the movies, as Illinois' football players often were. Instead, Pyle asked him, "Red, how'd you like to make a hundred thousand dollars?"

The month before, a film distributor, Frank Zambrino, had approached George Halas, owner, coach, general manager, and player of the Chicago Bears (the Decatur Staleys till 1921) and said a friend in Champaign was thinking of becoming Grange's manager. Would Halas be interested in having Grange play for the Bears? Foolish question, and Zambrino became the Halas-Pyle courier.

In response to Pyle's $100,000 question that night in the Virginia Theater, Grange replied, "I don't do those things," thinking Pyle had something illegal in mind. He was assured that this was not so, and the two came to a verbal understanding: For 40 percent of Grange's earnings, Pyle consented to manage his career.

Zambrino brought word of this agreement to Halas, and Pyle and Halas met secretly at the Morrison Hotel in Chicago. Halas, too, was impressed. The man who can justly be called the father of the National Football League said of that first meeting, "Pyle had been around. I was just a country boy."

Halas had in mind Grange joining the Bears after Illinois' season-ending game and playing in the Bears' final two NFL games. Agreed, responded Pyle, and then proceeded to outline his own plan: After the Bears' last game the Bears would go east and, after Christmas, south to Florida and then work their way across the country to California and up the Pacific Coast, playing exhibition games in major cities along the way.

Halas was astounded at the scope of the plan. He asked who would make arrangements. Pyle said he would.

Halas had no free cash for an advance (NFL teams were stumbling to bankruptcy, their crowds ranging from 2,000 to 5,000 usually, compared to 50,000 and 60,000 for major college-game crowds). He proposed a two-to-one split of earnings from the tour. Agreed, said Pyle.

Halas began to grow slightly uneasy. The bargaining was proceeding too smoothly. "All right," he said, "it is agreed the Bears will get two-thirds, and—"

"Oh, no, George, Grange and I will get two-thirds. . . ."

And so negotiations began that continued for the next 26 hours. Finally, on November 10th, a 50-50 agreement was signed. ("We were also allowed to bear all the expenses," Halas remembered.)

On the Saturday before Thanksgiving, in his last game for Illinois, Grange ran for 192 yards, threw a pass for a touchdown, and intercepted a pass to save a 13 to 7 Illinois victory over Ohio State before a crowd of 85,000 at Columbus.

At the team's hotel after the game, Grange put on a black wig to cover his red hair and took the fire escape out of the hotel. At the Columbus RR station he boarded the midnight train to Chicago, where he checked into the Belmont Hotel under an assumed name. The next day he met Pyle and Halas at the Morrison and signed a contract formally naming Pyle as his manager. Then both signed with the Bears. (Because of protests by collegiate forces, this early signing by Grange subsequently led to an NFL resolution prohibiting its teams from inducing college students to play for them until their class graduated.)

Reporters were called in and it was announced that Red Grange would play in the last two Bears' games and the team would than go on a coast-to-coast tour. Grange was asked why he was turning pro. Two agents sent to sign Grange by Tim Mara, owner of the fast-failing New York Giants, looked on ruefully as Grange responded: "I am going into professional football to make money. . . . It seems to me to be the same thing as playing professional baseball. I have to get money now because people will forget all about me in a few years. . . ."

On Thanksgiving Day Grange played for the Bears for the first time—before a capacity crowd of 36,000 in Wrigley Field. In 23 attempts, the opposing Chicago Cardinals kicker, Paddy Driscoll, punted away from Grange 23 times and the game ended in a scoreless tie. Three days later 28,000 fans came out to Wrigley in heavy snow to watch Grange run for 140 yards and the Bears beat the Columbus Tigers. Then the entire Bear team of 16 players plus Grange and player/owner/coach Halas set off on C. C. Pyle's grand cross-country tour.

They played 17 games in the next 47 days, with crowds of 73,000 in New York City (making up Mara's losses for the entire 1925 season) and 75,000 in Los Angeles. It was tramp-on-the-injured and hurdle-the-dead football and Grange was slugged, kicked, and piled-on, partly because the other players were getting, on average, $50 to $150 a game and Grange and his manager were getting 50 percent of the Bears' share of the gate.

In New York City Pyle promoted endorsements for his client: Red Grange helmets and caps ($2,500), sweaters ($13,000), candy bars, ginger ale ($5,000), dolls with red hair ($10,000), shoes ($5,000), and even Red Grange sausage sandwiches and yeast foam malted milk. Pyle wrested $10,000 from a cigarette maker for Red's endorsement, which went: "I don't smoke but my best friend smokes. . . ." He signed Grange to a movie contract for $50,000 and $5,000 a week ("One Minute to Play," 1926, followed by "Racing Romeo," 1927, and "The Galloping Ghost," 1929). C. C. Pyle became known to the world as Cash and Carry Pyle, aka Cold Cash Pyle.

Reporters began to write the occasional unkind story about Grange's commercialization of his sports fame. Babe Ruth, baseball's

Sultan of Swat, visited Grange at New York's Astor Hotel. "Keed, I'll give you a little bit of advice," the Babe said. "Don't believe anything they write about you, good or bad. Two, get the dough while the getting is good, but don't break your heart trying to get it. And don't pick up too many checks!"

In Washington, D.C., on December 8, Illinois Senator McKinley sent a limousine to take Grange and Halas to the White House to meet President Coolidge. The senator made introductions. "Mr. President, this is Red Grange, who plays with the Bears."

The President shook Grange's hand and said, "Nice to meet you, young man. I've always liked animal acts."

In mid-tour Grange summed up his professional initiation: "I look for professional football to be the football of the future. . . . But, professional or amateur, I have had all the football I want. I'd sooner be back on my ice wagon. . . . The human frame can't stand 30 games in 12 weeks but I've got to go through with it because it will mean my financial independence. Being famous is bunk. I've never felt worse. . . . I'll never marry unless I find someone far more sensible than the flappers who flock around. I'll never be a millionaire. I'm glad I turned pro, but I'll be glad to quit."

Twice during the tour Pyle gave Grange checks for $50,000. At the close of the tour he gave him a receipts-and-royalties check for another $100,000. In seven weeks Grange had become rich—that is, for just a country boy ice man from Wheaton, Illinois.

Dion O'Banion

"HE'S IRISH, HIT HIM AGAIN!"

Dion O'Banion's hands were seldom idle, but that didn't mean the Devil couldn't find work for them. The leader of the North Side bootlegging mob moonlighted as a circulation slugger for Hearst's *Herald and Examiner*, which had its plant about a mile from the offices of the Chicago Typographical Union in the Postal Telegraph Building—where about 3:15 the morning of June 1, 1921, a policeman found him and three companions with the combination knob of the union's safe, which held $35,000, already sledged off.

O'Banion turned at a noise the policeman made, his cocked pistol at the ready, then let the hammer down. "Don't shoot," he said. "We give up." He and his associates were put under arrest. Money in the quartet's possession, burned and ragged around the edges, was presumed to have been taken earlier from the safe blown at Joseph Klein's Feed Store at 525 West 35th Street.

The arresting officer got a $25-a-month raise for his enterprise. Six months later, for theirs, the four errant safecrackers were acquitted of charges of possession of burglary tools, whereupon they, the judge, the prosecutor, defense counsel, and some members of the jury went to celebrate at the Bella Napoli.

On the stand O'Banion's testimony was:

"We had all met at about three o'clock in the morning in the all-night Raklios restaurant there on the corner. We were having hot chocolate and chocolate eclairs. We heard a lot of racket, could have been an explosion in the union office in the Postal Telegraph Building. So we climbed the fire escape to see what it was all about.

"Whoever was blowing the safe must have heard us coming. They got away. We stepped off the fire escape through the window and were just looking at the safe when the policeman came in. I always carry a gun in the course of my work. At first I thought it might have been the thieves coming back. But when I saw it was a policeman, I put my gun down and we gave ourselves up. Like good citizens."

161

This explanation and much money given to judge, prosecutor, and jurymen, won the acquittal, after which O'Banion gave the reason for his uncharacteristic failure to use his pistol in the early morning: "I was just about to shoot that yokel cop when I remembered the Ox had a pint bottle of nitroglycerine in his pocket. One shot in that room would have blown the whole south end of the Loop to Kingdom Come." He knew whereof he spoke, once having blown away the entire wall of a building while leaving the safe itself unharmed.

Deanie was born July 8, 1892, in Aurora, 25 miles southwest of Chicago's Loop. His mother died when he was six and when he was nine his father moved the family to the edge of Chicago's Little Hell, which, as we know, had earlier been the Irish shantytown Kilgubbin. He peddled papers, picked pockets, snatched purses, got hit by a streetcar (leaving him with a shortened left leg and a limp), jackrolled drunks, and became a singing waiter at a very rough joint, McGovern's Liberty Inn at Clark and Erie. He joined the Market Street Gang which terrorized residents of the 42nd and 43rd Wards before World War I, took up burgling, in 1909 went to work for the *Tribune* beating up newsstand vendors who refused to sell the *Trib*, later switching allegiance to the *Herald and Examiner*. (There he worked as a slugger and killer for Moses Annenberg, father of Walter Annenberg, publisher of *TV Guide, Seventeen*, and *Racing Form*, and later U.S. Ambassador to England; circumstances, or perhaps wealth, alter cases.) He was a crack shot and ambidextrous and had three pockets tailored into his suits for his pistols, one right-front pants, one left armpit suit jacket, and one center-front of pants.

In 1909 he served three months in the House of Correction for burglary, in 1911 another three months for assault with a blackjack. Except for these two small blemishes, and even though police estimates of men he'd personally killed ranged from 25 to 63, his record was otherwise clean—that is, he was able to buy his way out of all his other mischance with the law.

It helped greatly that he controlled the votes in the Gold Coast's 42nd and 43rd wards. Floaters, repeaters, ballot-box theft, and intimidation by slugging, shooting, and kidnaping were the means. "I always deliver my borough per requirements," was his boast. Because he did, politicians and judges listened to him. For example, his second-in-command, Hymie Weiss, was up before Judge Robert E. Crowe in January of 1920 charged with larceny. After hearing the case the jurist in avuncular voice told the defendant:

> "There is not enough evidence here to convict, I am sorry to say. I have heard of you, young man. The police tell me you are in all kinds of mischief and just laugh at the law. I warn you to straighten up. Society will not stand for this sort of thing. If you ever come before me again,

162

and there is enough evidence to convict, I'll give you the limit. I hope it never happens. Now think of your mother and try to do better."

Judicial prudence deterred Judge Crowe from mentioning that only the night before the defendant and O'Banion had been to see him at his home to plan election-day mayhem. (Crowe went on to become State's Attorney.)

If O'Banion had not succeeded so well in his endeavors, he could be dismissed as just another low-level Chicago hoodlum, but he did succeed and with an Out-of-my-way! elan that appealed to native Chicagoans. He's a rascal, all right, our Deanie is, but he's *our* rascal, not some damn foreigner, by God! At least he can speak English! "Who'll carry the Forty-second and Forty-third?" they'd ask, grinning; and answer, "O'Banion in his pistol pockets!"

In 1922, his Lake Shore bootlegging territory well established and grossing $2 million a year, he bought a half-interest in Schofield's, a florist shop on North State across from Holy Name Cathedral. He was an excellent arranger of floral designs and relished the work, coming to the shop at 9:00, leaving at 6:00. Three clerks at Schofield phones handled orders for O'Banion alcohol. He had a high-domed, blue-eyed, surface-innocent face, with a smile at his lips whether he had a florist's shears or a pistol in his hand. He and all members of his gang dressed in businessmen's suits and often wore tuxedos in the evening when they went on the town.

Two weeks before Prohibition he undertook Chicago's first hijacking. ("Hi, Jack," you call to the trucker; he stops and you climb in behind the wheel. You are a modern highwayman. It helps to be showing a revolver.) On the morning of December 30, 1919, he was walking in the Loop on Wells south of Randolph when he was brought to a halt by a long, loaded flatbed truck blocking the sidewalk. A congregation of pedestrians was gathered there, waiting for the truck to clear, the street being full of snow and slush. O'Banion lifted the flatbed's tarpaulin; the cargo was case after case of Grommes & Ullrich whiskey.

He signaled to the driver who leaned out the cab window the better to hear, upon which O'Banion circled the driver's neck with his left arm and slugged him with his right fist in which he held a roll of coins. He pulled the groggy driver from the cab, propped him against a building, climbed behind the wheel and drove out the alley, heading for the garage of Samuel J. "Nails" Morton (Marcovitz) on Maxwell Street. (Morton's garage specialized in the disguise and resale of stolen cars.) The day before the last New Year's Eve before Prohibition, the selling was easy. In 20 minutes by telephone the entire load was placed with saloonkeepers, much of it to O'Banion's one-time place of employment, McGovern's Liberty Inn. The truck was sold to a Peoria brewery.

O'Banion paid for information. "I'm in the market for tips on alcohol and booze. I pay 10 percent of whatever I can sell it for. Nobody who tips me off ever gets implicated." This he told strangers on being introduced to them. Newspaper reporters got 15 percent and a couple of pints for tips.

He did not drink himself. As well as being a killer he was a sadistic practical joker (pack clay into a shotgun's barrel, hand it to someone to fire). He was unpredictable and spontaneous, quick to react. One morning in November 1922 he was ordering breakfast with "Dapper Dan" McCarthy in the Sherman House coffee shop. (McCarthy, a mob member, had taken over Chicago's plumbers' union by the expedient of killing its incumbent head, shooting him dead at the Auto Inn.) An excited nearby speakeasy owner came into the coffee shop and to their table to tell O'Banion a trucker was just setting out to deliver a load of bonded to West Side drugstores, having stopped for an eye-opener before starting his rounds.

O'Banion and McCarthy told the waitress to hold their food. They intercepted the truck at Randolph and Canal as it slowed for a stop sign. They brandished their revolvers and ordered the driver to get out and leave. Then O'Banion parked the truck a block away and he and McCarthy returned to the Sherman House. "My coffee was still hot, but I had the girl bring me another order of wheatcakes," O'Banion said. After breakfast he returned to the truck and drove it to Morton's garage where Morton paid him $22,500 cash for the prize: 225 24-pint cases of aged, uncut, pre-WWI, 100-proof whiskey.

Morton had been awarded the Croix de Guerre in WWI, arriving in France a private in the U.S. Army, leaving as a First Lieutenant. He was a true momser—a tough chancer open to any worthwhile proposition. Another member of O'Banion's command, "Three-Gun Louie" Alterie, owned a 3,000-acre ranch in Colorado and Morton had there grown fond of horseback riding. One day while cantering along a bridle path with Mr. and Mrs. O'Banion in Chicago's Lincoln Park, his horse threw him and kicked him to death.

Morton, who was known to have committed half a dozen murders, was buried with full military honors, the rites attended by gangland and political luminaries and 5,000 West Side Jews, including rabbis. Six limousines carried the flowers. While still a very young man Morton had organized a defense league to drive Irish and Polish Jew-baiters from the West Side, and his community showed its appreciation.

After Morton's funeral, Alterie stole the guilty horse from its Lincoln Riding Academy stable, and shot it. Then he called the Academy's owner. "We taught that horse of yours a lesson," he said. "If you want the saddle, go get it."

Alterie began in crime with Terry Druggan as a jewel thief. He sometimes wore a ten-gallon hat and had survived a Western-style shoot-out (over a blonde) in the Auto Inn. He had founded Chicago's Theater and Building Janitors' Union, charging broompushers $10 a month to belong. But he got their wages doubled. His preferred hair color in women was blonde. Discovering a lady friend with whom he was ranch-bound was bleached, he threw her off the train.

The mainstays of O'Banion's command, however, were Hymie Weiss (real name Earl Wojciechowski), George "Bugs" Moran, and Vincent "The Schemer" Drucci. Weiss was six years younger than O'Banion and brainy as well as vicious. (It was Weiss who gave Steve Wisniewski Prohibition's first one-way ride.) His early criminal acts were burglaries. It was thought by police that Weiss was able at times to curb his leader's impetuosity, but only at times, this partly because he himself was highly volatile. He once sued arresting U.S. marshals for the theft of his silk shirts. His eyes burned with a feverish intensity. He did not look to be a calming influence.

Bugs Moran was from Minnesota, his parents Polish and Irish. (He married a full-blooded Sioux.) As a teenager he kidnapped delivery-wagon horses and held them for ransom. From this he graduated to the more mature and responsible acts of robbery, burglary, and safecracking, going to prison first for two years then for almost five before he was 30. He was usually stolid and dependable but had a violent temper (would go "bugs" with rage)—as well as a wry sense of humor. Brought before a judge who asked him, "Don't you like me, Moran?" he replied with a smile, "I like you, Your Honor, but I am suspicious of you."

Drucci began as a looter of telephone coin boxes. He was known as The Schemer for the elaborate, complicated, and impractical plans he concocted to rob banks or kidnap wealthy pillars of the community, but he was also known as "The Shooting Fool." He had once vaulted his car over the gap of an opening bridge to escape pursuing police. Like Weiss and Moran, he had been with O'Banion since his youth.

The North Side higher echelon was deeply loyal to their chief. In their histories and ways they were probably no more eccentric than he was, but on average they seemed distinctly more individualistic than their Italian counterparts, somehow more colorful.

Walking on Madison Street with Weiss the night of January 20, 1924, O'Banion saw the prizefight referee Davey "Yiddles" Miller and his brother Max emerge from the LaSalle Theatre with the rest of the audience from the comedy *Give and Take*. Surrounded by hundreds of witnesses, O'Banion shot Yiddles in the stomach, then shot at Max but the bullet glanced off the younger brother's belt buckle. O'Banion was arrested but both brothers declined to press charges. "I'm sorry it happened," O'Banion declared. "It was just a piece of hot-headed foolishness."

. . . Except that the brothers were two of four West Side Millers who dealt in extortion, gambling, and bootlegging, and who had then recently made threats to take over O'Banion's 15 percent of Cicero's profitable Ship, a gambling house O'Banion owned jointly with Torrio and Capone.

The night before he shot up the Miller brothers O'Banion with others had stolen $1 million worth of whiskey and grain alcohol from the Sibley Warehouse Storage Company at 1530 South Sangamon. In a few very active hours they replaced 1,750 barrels of alcohol with 1,750 barrels of water. (Earlier, the O'Banion gang was suspected of the $1.5 million burglary of the Werner Brothers Warehouse, and with a $2 million mail robbery at Chicago's Union Station.) O'Banion used the proceeds from the Sibley coup to buy into the Cragin distillery, the biggest in the Midwest, at 1833 North Laramie. Using the same counterfeiter who forged the bills of sale and warehouse receipts for him for the Sibley job, he had a bogus certified check made for $41,000 and used this to pay a debt. The joke did not sit well with the debtee, and as the year proceeded Deanie's behavior became even more erratic.

Five days after shooting the Millers, he, Weiss, and Dapper Dan were curbed by two policemen on the Near South Side. In the back seat of the car the trio was holding captive two truckdrivers whose shipments of 251 cases of Haviland rye the three had appropriated. The police took them to the detective bureau, where they were booked. The next day they were released on bail. Three months later—about the time Johnny Torrio returned to Chicago from Italy where he had left his mother to live out her life in a palatial seaside villa—a federal grand jury indicted O'Banion, Weiss, and McCarthy for hijacking, trial set for July 7. On May 30, O'Banion was indicted for the Sibley Warehouse robbery and the robberies of two others, Harder and Mayer Brothers, trial set for November.

When Torrio left for Europe Cicero was safe enough as a place to hang his hat. Headquarters had been established on the entire steel-shuttered second floor of the three-story Hawthorne Inn Hotel and the allotment of beer territories had been formalized. While Torrio was in Europe, Al Capone gained him the keys to the city. For this deed Torrio gave him a 50 percent share of the take in Cicero. Just five years before, Capone had been a $35-a-week bouncer at the Four Deuces. Now he was a full partner with Johnny Papa.

Joseph Z. Klenha had been bipartisan Mayor of Cicero since 1917 but for the April 1, 1924, election Cicero Democrats proposed a separate ticket—a reform ticket pledged to enforce the law. Ciceronians, with their small, neat houses and scrubby but well-kept lawns, were not taking kindly to the invasion of their quiet town by Chicago gangsters. Republican boss man Eddie Vogel asked Capone for help. Capone sent in 200 thugs, including a contingent of 20 experienced O'Banion election terrorists.

The night before the election the Democratic candidate for town clerk was beaten up and his office wrecked as a warning to would-be Democratic voters. Election day a dozen Capone limousines cruised the streets, stopping at polling places, where defiant voters were slugged and their ballots taken from them, other voters were intimidated into the Republican column, unsympathetic poll watchers and judges were kidnapped and taken into Chicago for the day, opposition campaign workers were shot or had their throats slashed, and police observers were blackjacked.

Responding to desperate pleas for armed aid, Mayor Dever of Chicago had a judge he trusted—not Cook County Sheriff Hoffman—deputize 70 Chicago patrolmen and detectives and sent them into the besieged town, but they did not arrive until late afternoon. Toward dusk, one detective squad car came upon Frank Capone, Al's brother, their cousin Charles Fischetti, and a hoodlum named David Hedlin outside a polling place. Frank Capone took aim as a detective stepped out of the car but was killed by blasts from two shotguns. Hedlin escaped into the night. Fischetti was captured in an adjoining field, then released. Klenha and his slate won and Cicero belonged to Torrio and Capone lock, stock, and beer buyers.

One month later the Hawthorne Smoke Shop, a gambling resort, opened for business several doors down from operations headquarters in the Hawthorne Hotel. Soon thereafter there were 150 Torrio-Capone gambling dens in Cicero, each selling beer and whiskey as well, running full-tilt 24 hours a day. True to Torrio's word, he opened no brothels in Cicero, but its streetwalkers and call-flat chippies paid tribute to his collectors.

The nearby small town of Forest View adjoining Stickney did get a brothel. Founded in 1924 by WWI veterans, Forest View (pop. 300) was dedicated "to our soldier dead so as to perpetuate their deeds of hero-ism and sacrifice." Within a few months of its incorporation, the mayor of the village approved the construction of a small hotel and social club by Al and Ralph Capone. (Al had brought brothers and cousins from New York to Chicago to work for him.) The Capones came recom-mended by Forest View's chief of police. (It later came to light that the chief was an ex-con pardoned by Gov. Small.) "I did not know just who the Capones were," the mayor recalled.

When the syndicate's gunners and harlots arrived, the mayor ordered his police chief to show them the road. When Ralph heard of this he threatened to throw the mayor into the canal. The mayor thought he was joking. The next morning, at 4:00 A.M., two Capone strongarms took the mayor from his bed and out of his home to the village hall where seven more thugs waited. "They beat me over the head with the butts of their guns and though I was streaming with blood and dazed from pain they kicked me over the floor." He begged for his life and it was granted him provided he move out of town immediately. Another 20 villagers were beaten and driven out of Forest View.

At the next election all successful candidates were Capone-sponsored. Forest View became known as "Caponeville," and Capone was popular with most of the small population that remained. He bought groceries for the poor, saw to the care of orphans, and paid many residents $500 a week from 1924 into the Depression for the use of their garages to house stills.

The town's 60-girl brothel was Torrio's largest. It was officially designated The Maple Inn but was better known as The Stockade because it was used as an ammunition and weapons storehouse and as a hideout. The Stockade's female attractions grossed $15,000 a week. (The combined annual gross of Torrio brothels now exceeded $10,000,000.) The huge stone-and-wood structure was honeycombed with secret chambers and hideaways and had one large hidden room in which the girls gathered when raids took place.

The afternoon of May 8, 1924, Jake Guzik stumbled into the Four Deuces, blood on his face and terror in his eyes. Joseph Howard, a small-time hood, had amused himself by taunting and slapping the short, fat bookkeeper and boasting of how easy it was to hijack Torrio trucks. . . . Of loud "hard" guys like Howard the Italians had a derisive and contemptuous phrase: "*Che malandrino*"—"What a tough one."

About six-thirty Al Capone entered the saloon in which Howard was drinking and boasting, about half a block from the Deuces. He ignored Howard's condescendingly friendly greeting, grabbed him by the shoulder, and with a snarl demanded to know why he had hit Guzik. "Aw, g'wan back to your girls, you dago pimp," was the gist of Howard's reply. Capone took his revolver from his pocket and put the barrel against Howard's cheek, under his eye, and sent six slugs, one after another, into Howard's skull. A clear sign of disapproval.

The bartender and two patrons were present at the murder and were questioned by the police. The next morning the *Tribune* published Capone's photo over a garbled cutline: "Tony (Scarface) Capone, also known as Al Brown, who killed Joe Howard. . . ." Capone had left Chicago the night before.

As a reward for the use of his mobsters in the capture of Cicero, O'Banion initially got a thank-you but when he protested that this was not enough Torrio allotted him beer distribution rights to a large section of Cicero, rights worth about $20,000 a month. It was Johnny Torrio's philosophy that there was always enough to go around, so long as he got the lion's share. And that peace was better than contention.

O'Banion persuaded half a hundred saloonkeepers from the South and West sides to move their businesses into his section of Cicero and soon he quintupled his revenues there—in doing so draining off some of that of the Torrio and Capone interests. He was offered a percentage of the syndicate's brothel earnings in Stickney in exchange for a cut of the new Cicero beer business but he rejected the offer indignantly.

He complained to Torrio that the Genna brothers had begun to infringe on his territorial rights on the North Shore, selling their bad booze there for half and a third of what he sold his quality Canadian import whiskey. He told Torrio to keep the Gennas out of the North Side or he would see to it himself. Torrio answered reasonably enough that no one could tell the Gennas what to do except Mike Merlo, head of the Unione Siciliana, and sometimes not even him.

O'Banion hijacked a $30,000 shipment of Genna whiskey. The six Gennas met in family council and voted unanimously to kill him, but Mike Merlo vetoed their decision. Merlo (who was dying of cancer), like Torrio, believed that negotiations solved problems best, not open warfare. Moreover, he apparently liked O'Banion, who considered him a friend (his only Sicilian friend).

And then O'Banion came to Torrio with a surprising offer: He had decided to retire and move West and would sell out his bootlegging interests. He had money in the bank (estimates were more than $1 million) and word had reached him of the Gennas' vote. It was no longer worth the strife. He would sell Torrio his interest in the North Side's Sieben Brewery—which he, Torrio, Capone, and Stenson owned in partnership—for half a million dollars and pack it in.

Torrio accepted the offer at once and paid him immediately, no doubt pleased and relieved that he would no longer have to deal with this troublesome Irish cock-of-the-walk. As one last favor, O'Banion asked Torrio to be present at the next—his last—shipment: a gesture of good will. Because Capone was in hiding and could not be sent, Torrio agreed to be there.

At 5:00 in the morning of May 19, 1924, under the watchful eyes of two precinct policemen, 13 trucks were taking on beer from the Sieben Brewery in the 1400 block of North Larrabee when squads of Chicago police led by Chief Collins swarmed over the premises. The police confiscated roughly 130,000 gallons of beer and arrested 31 bootleggers, including Johnny Torrio and Dion O'Banion, and took them to federal authorities—not to State's Attorney Crowe. In the brewery yard Chief Collins ripped the badges from the two precinct officers who had been standing watch and sent them to jail.

O'Banion seemed almost elated by the arrests. Whistling and laughing he sent out for breakfast for the crowd in the holding tank, his treat. This was his first Prohibition offense and would bring only a fine.

Johnny Torrio was quiet, almost sullen. From a roll of bills he paid his own $7,500 bail and left the Federal Building. His erstwhile partner, Irish eyes twinkling, watched him go. This was Torrio's second Prohibition arrest (for the first the year before he had been fined $2,000) and if he were convicted, it meant jail.

On June 11, a month and a few days after killing Joe Howard, Al Capone reappeared in Chicago and presented himself to the Cottage Grove precinct commander. "I hear the police were looking for me," he said, "and I was curious to know what it was for." He was taken to State's Attorney Crowe's young assistant, William H. McSwiggin, for questioning. He said he had been out of town the day of the Howard killing. When the three witnesses from the saloon were brought in to identify him they agreed that Capone was not the man they'd seen. Howard's death was recorded as "murder by person unknown."

In the meantime, from one of his police informants, Torrio confirmed what he had suspected when he was arrested at Sieben's Brewery: O'Banion knew well in advance there would be a raid by the police on Sieben's on May 19th; he even knew the hour it would take place. And knowing this he had made sure Torrio would be there. And now word was reaching Torrio that O'Banion was bragging about the set-up. Still, Johnny Torrio bided his time.

On July 7, O'Banion, Weiss, and Dapper Dan McCarthy went on trial for stealing the two truckloads of Haviland rye. On the witness stand the drivers appeared confused and could remember nothing ("Chicago amnesia," O'Banion termed it) and after 36 ballots the jury remained hung, 10 to 2. One of the ten, an elderly farmer, went to his knees and prayed the two holdouts would vote for conviction but each had already pocketed $25,000 in cash money. The case was dismissed.

His good name restored, O'Banion with his wife Viola left for a vacation in Colorado at a lodge south of Denver. He liked the Western outdoor life so much that he sponsored a rodeo, spending freely to make it a success, and bought a ranch, paying cash for 2,700 acres. He had found his Land of Cockaigne. Yet according to local police he also bought "enough guns to outfit a Mexican army," returning with them and his wife to Chicago on October 20.

Fearful that he might defect to the Republicans in the soon-due election, Chicago Democrats gave him a testimonial dinner November 1st in the Webster Hotel at 2150 North Lincoln Park. Besides Democratic politicians from the Lake Shore wards and the guest of honor's gang lieutenants, Mayor Dever's Commissioner of Public Works and his Chief of Detectives were in attendance. O'Banion was presented with a $1,500 platinum watch amid widespread camaraderie and conviviality. The next day Mayor Dever called in his Commissioner of Public Works and asked him what in the hell he thought he was doing. The Commissioner resigned. The Chief of Detectives claimed he had been told it was a dinner for someone else and when he recognized the O'Banion crew "I knew I had been framed, and withdrew almost at once."

On November 3, O'Banion and Weiss and Schemer Drucci attended the weekly split-the-profits session at the Ship. Capone said that the previous week Angelo Genna had lost $30,000 at the Ship's tables, some of it in IOUs. He proposed that as a professional courtesy they destroy the markers, O'Banion's response was to pick up a telephone, call Angelo, and demand payment within one week.

Back at Schofield's Weiss urged moderation. He suggested that his leader treat the Gennas with less severity. "Ah, to hell with them Sicilians," O'Banion replied, a remark that then circulated in the underworld, angering continental Italians as well as the Sicilians. Torrio and Capone met with the Gennas. O'Banion had mulcted Torrio of half a million dollars, mocked him, and put him in jeopardy of serving time. The vote was unanimous for death.

On November 4, O'Banion and his thugs toured the Lake Shore polling places. The $1,500 platinum watch given him by hopeful Democrats adorned his wrist as he asked the voters, judges, and clerks to let "the Republicans get a fair shake this time instead of all you people giving all the edge to the Democrats." Leaving one or two of his men behind at each polling place he would then adjourn to the nearest speakeasy, where he first bought drinks for everyone, then usually shot the doorknobs off the toilet doors to get the drinkers' attention, and said, "We're going to have a Republican victory celebration tonight. Anybody who votes Democratic ain't going to be there—or anywhere else!" Election day's tally was 98 percent Republican in the 42nd Ward.

Four days later on Saturday November 8, peace-loving Mike Merlo, head of Chicago's Unione Siciliana, died. Torrio ordered $10,000 worth of flowers from Schofield's florist shop; Capone, $8,000 worth. On Sunday Jim Genna picked up a $750 wreath at the Schofield shop and that night, after O'Banion had left, Frankie Yale—national head of the Unione—called and placed an order for $2,000 worth of flowers.

About 11:30 Monday morning Dion O'Banion was in the workroom at the back of the florist shop. The janitor was sweeping up in the showroom. Three men entered from the street, the front door's tinkler announcing their arrival. O'Banion came out into the showroom, a pair of clipping shears in his left hand. He extended his right hand in greeting as the janitor headed for the back of the shop. "Hello, boys," O'Banion said, "are you from Mike Merlo's?"

The man in the center clasped Deanie's right hand and held it in a firm grip as the men on either side of him began firing—two shots in the chest, two in the throat, a fifth smashing into the jaw. O'Banion fell to the floor against a showcase and in a moment more the janitor heard a sixth shot. It stained Deanie's cheek with powder burns.

171

The killers ran from the shop and down State Street to the corner of Superior where they got into a dark blue Jewett, its motor running, and sped off as six other cars pulled away from curbs and stopped crosswise on State and Superior, blocking traffic until the blue car turned south on Dearborn. Then, at the beep of a horn, the six cars turned into their proper lanes and moved off.

Mike Merlo's funeral was held on Friday, 20,000 mourners in attendance at Mount Carmel Cemetery. Merlo's 266-car cortege extended a mile behind the hearse. Mayor Dever, Police Chief Collins, and State's Attorney Crowe were among the honorary pallbearers.

Dion O'Banion's funeral was held the next day, 20,000 men, women, and children in attendance at the Mount Carmel gravesite. O'Banion's cortege stretched for two miles. More Irish could afford motorcars.

Capone sent a basket of roses, the card from "Al Brown," and both he and Torrio attended O'Banion's wake. After Deanie was laid to rest, Three-Gun Louie Alterie said, "If I knew who killed Dion, I would shoot it out with the killers before the sun rose. . . . I'll go with a smile because I'll know that two or three of them will go with me."

Four days after O'Banion's funeral the police picked up Frankie Yale at the LaSalle Street Station as he was about to board a train for New York. Yale explained that he had come to Chicago to attend Mike Merlo's funeral and also a dinner given him by his old friend Diamond Joe Esposito. And at the very time O'Banion was killed, he said, he was having lunch with Samoots Amatuna in the Palmer House. Waiter Nick Delassandro confirmed this alibi and Frankie Yale was permitted to return to New York.

The other two killers of O'Banion were Albert Anselmi and John Scalisi. Mike Genna drove the blue getaway car. Jim Genna had cased the shop's layout on Sunday. It was probably Yale who delivered the coup de grace that burned the flesh of Deanie's cheek. The *colpo di grazia* was an old Sicilian custom.

ARRIVEDERCI

God gives the man He hates what that man most desires.

By 1924 the Terrible Gennas had the tenement stills of almost 2,000 Italian-American families contributing to their $2 million net from the plant and warehouse at 1022 West Taylor (assets valued at $5 million), and were the wealthiest—therefore the most powerful—family in Little Sicily. On the death of Mike Merlo they moved swiftly to install "Bloody" Angelo as president of Chicago's Unione Siciliana, and as swiftly got national head Frankie Yale to endorse him. Johnny Torrio and Al Capone would have much preferred one of their own as president, though most of the residents of Little Italy liked and certainly respected the Terrible Gennas. In addition to providing them a good income from alky cooking, the Gennas were thoughtful neighbors. There were many occasions like the one where a woman whose family lived on Taylor Street was ill; the Gennas put up a street barricade at each end of the block in which she lived and until she recovered no noisy traffic passed the house, a matter of months.

After the Merlo and O'Banion funerals, Johnny Torrio and his wife went on an extended vacation trip: Hot Springs, New Orleans, St. Petersburg, Palm Beach, Havana, and the Bahamas. It has been speculated that he was fleeing North Sider vengeance, but it may have been simply that at middle age he felt like relaxing with his wife (though, admittedly, his moves were seldom simple). Capone had proven capable while the Torrios were in Europe, even if the young thug's temperament still had its raw edges and he sometimes proved green in judgment. But a struggle with the Weiss-led O'Banion forces seemed certain, and hunting and killing were done best by young men.

On January 12, Capone's limousine was cut off by a sedan and riddled with pistol and shotgun slugs. The chauffeur was wounded but the car's two occupants dove to the floor and escaped injury. Al himself had not been a passenger but the attempt prompted him to order an armored

Cadillac from General Motors with bullet-proof windows, weight seven tons, cost $30,000. (A conventional Cadillac went two tons and $2,000.)

Capone celebrated his 26th birthday on January 17, the same day that John Torrio pled guilty to the Sieben Brewery charges. On the 20th, given a few days to settle his affairs before going to jail, Johnny The Fox celebrated his 43rd birthday. Four days after his 43rd, he and Anna left their apartment at 7011 South Clyde about 11:30 and were driven into the Loop where Torrio met with Michael Hinky Dink Kenna at the latter's cigar store, then accompanied Anna on a shopping tour of department stores.

They returned to their apartment building in Jackson Park a little after 4:00. Anna took some parcels from the back seat of the Lincoln and walked to the front door, turning to push the door open with her hip.

She saw her husband at the rear door of the car loading his arms with packages. And then she saw a grey Cadillac—no license plates, backseat window curtains drawn—pull parallel to the Lincoln. Two men leapt from the Cadillac, one running to the rear of the Lincoln, the other to the front, and both began firing through the car. The Lincoln's windshield shattered and the chauffeur was hit in the knee.

Torrio dropped his packages and started for the apartment's front door but was caught in a cross-fire. He was hit in the arm by a .45 slug, then with shotgun blasts that tore into his jaw and his throat and blasted into his chest and belly and dropped him to the concrete walk. From the front of the Lincoln the gunman advanced on him, leaned down, and held his .45 to John's temple. When the trigger was pulled there was a harmless click.

A woman in an apartment across the street was at her window, transfixed as two men fired shots at her neighbor, the quiet Mr. Langley who, gossip had it, was in finance on LaSalle Street. The man standing over him was trying to put something into his gun. Poor Mr. Langley was trying to crawl toward the door of his apartment house.

Just then a laundry delivery van turned onto Clyde. As it did, the Cadillac's driver—Schemer Drucci—sounded the Cadillac's horn and instantly the shotgunner, Hymie Weiss, and the .45-holder, Bugs Moran, turned and ran to the car. The trio roared away, turning east toward Stony Island, then north, content in the knowledge they had partially avenged their beloved Deanie.

Anna Torrio ran to her husband, who lay bleeding and crumpled on the walk. She pulled him into the apartment's vestibule. Across the street the woman at the window shook herself and went to the phone to call the Woodlawn police station. Soon an ambulance came and took the badly shot-up Torrio to Jackson Park Hospital. The wounded chauffeur drove to a drugstore and phoned Cicero.

When Capone arrived at the hospital he was in a state of near panic. "Did they get Johnny?" Told of the seriousness of his chief's wounds he repeated over and over, "That gang did it! That gang did it!"

Fearing gangrene, Torrio asked the doctors to cauterize his wounds. After surgery, Torrio had four of Capone's men stand guard in his third-floor room. Two policemen were already on duty there, more outside. Capone took a room at one side of Torrio's, Anna a room on the other side. When the police questioned Torrio he answered, "I know who they are. It's my business."

Earlier at the hospital, when Mrs. Torrio had reason to believe she would soon be a widow, Patricia Dougherty of the *Herald-Examiner* spoke to her.

Anna Torrio was an attractive, slim, auburn-haired 35-year-old woman. She looked directly into Miss Dougherty's eyes. (Dougherty described Anna Torrio's eyes as green-gold.) Twisting her platinum wedding ring on her finger, Anna Torrio said,

"I know you are a reporter. And I know what you people are saying about my husband.

"You think you know him . . . but you don't. I'll tell you about him. He's a wonderful man. Thoughtful, considerate. Our married life has been 12 years of unbroken happiness. He has given me kindness, devotion, love—everything a good man can give a woman.

"Look what he did for his mother! Just last year he took her back to her birthplace in Italy. She left there a poor peasant. She came back the richest woman in the village. A fine home, servants, money—he's given her everything. He's always been that way. He's taken care of her since he was a small boy."

"I understand," Dougherty said. "But I was wondering about Capone. I saw him there. Isn't it true that your husband and Capone are good friends?"

"They are business associates. That's all. I never met Capone before tonight. He has never been to our home. Johnny has many business associates. But he has never asked me to meet them. They have never set foot in our house."

She stood up. "I have no more to say. Thank you for listening."

The 17-year-old son of a neighborhood janitor had watched the shooting. When he was shown a police mug shot of Moran he identified him as one of the two gunmen. Brought face-to-face with Moran he said, "You're the man."

Moran said, "You're off base, kid."

"I saw you shoot that man," the boy responded, and repeated his identification a third time.

But Anna Torrio said, "No, that's not one of them," and when the police took Moran to her husband's bedside he said, "No use bringing anyone here. I won't rap them." No indictments were brought in the

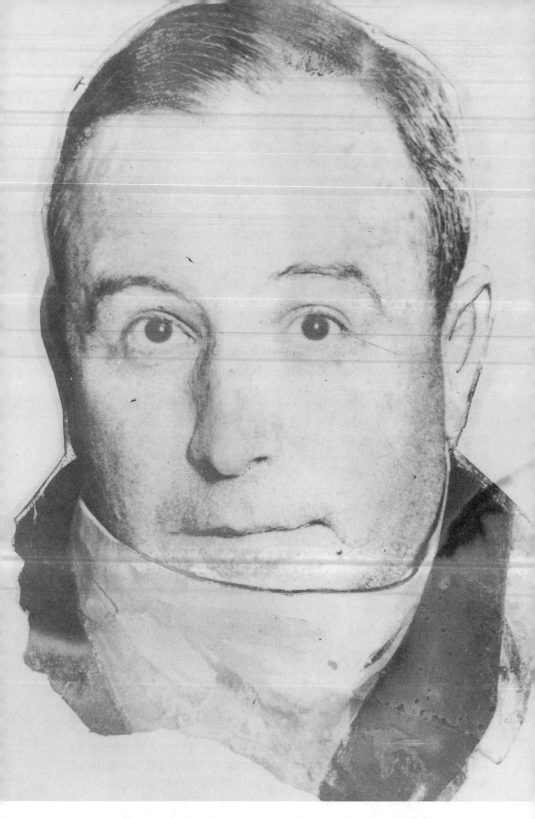

Johnny Torrio, bandaged after assassination attempt

attempted murder.

His first several days in the hospital Torrio ran a high fever from his neck wound, which became infected. Then he began to recover and two weeks after he entered the hospital Capone took him out via a back fire escape.

At his sentencing, Torrio paid a $5,000 fine and was given nine months in jail (max would have been five years). He was taken to the Lake County Jail in Waukegan where the sheriff let him furnish his cell with throw rugs, a radio, a gramophone, wall pictures, and a brass bed with comfortable mattress. The sheriff put bullet-proof steel-mesh blinds on the cell's windows, and permitted his prisoner to hold business conferences with Capone, Guzik, and others in his cell and on the sheriff's front porch. Torrio hired deputies as his personal guards and took most of his meals at the sheriff's home, Anna frequently joining him.

(In Cook County, Torrio's earliest bootlegging allies, Terry Druggan and Frankie Lake, serving sentences of one year for contempt of court, came and went as they pleased. Druggan spent most of his evenings with his wife in their Gold Coast apartment, Lake with his mistress in hers on North State Parkway. Druggan and Lake played golf, shopped, dined in Loop restaurants, attended the theater, and went to nightclubs. Their jail terms did not interfere with the normal course of their lives; they had spent $20,000 to ensure this. When a reporter from the *American* stumbled onto the arrangement and exposed it, Cook County Sheriff Peter Hoffman was fined $2,500 and given 30 days of his own.)

The Torrio syndicate had leased an office for "A. Brown, M.D." at 2146 South Michigan Avenue in Chicago, a block from the Four Deuces. (In his first year or so in Chicago, Capone's underworld nickname was "Scarface Al Brown.") Behind the doctor's waiting room was the workplace of Jake "Greasy Thumb" Guzik and his clerical and accounting staff, as well as row upon row of neatly labeled medicine bottles. The bottles contained samples of Dr. Brown's liquors. Volume retailers could, if they wished, have these samples analyzed to verify quality before placing orders.

Guzik kept at least six kinds of vital information in this office, ledgers listing (1) individuals, hotels, and restaurants buying wholesale; (2) Chicago speakeasies; (3) suppliers and routes from Canada and the Caribbean; (4) corporate structure of breweries owned or controlled; (5) bordello and gambling resort locations and income; and (6) politicians, police, and Prohibition agents on regular payoff schedules. In early April Mayor Dever ordered a surprise raid on Dr. Brown's office. Miraculously the raid was kept a secret until made and in the course of it Guzik's ledgers were seized. The Mayor was jubilant. "We've got the goods now!" he rejoiced.

Before anyone could study the ledgers' incriminating lists, however, high police officials and Assistant State's Attorney William McSwiggin conferred and decided it would be illegal to go public with them—the raiders had forgotten to get a search warrant. When a municipal judge then impounded the records the federal District Attorney told the judge that if necessary the government would seize them. The next day, without notifying the federal DA, the judge held a quiet hearing, at the conclusion of which he returned the records to Al Capone's lawyer. . . . Disaster judicially averted.

Bloody Angelo Genna, proud new president of the Unione Siciliana and happy new bridegroom (married four months to pretty Lucille Spignola of a prominent Sicilian family), set off in his $6,000 roadster to drive to Oak Park where he intended to pay for a new house for himself and his bride. A sedan with four men in it came up close behind his roadster. Angelo put his foot to the pedal and pulled out his gun. He was up to 60 mph and firing back at the pursuing sedan when he attempted a sharp turn off Ogden. His car swerved out of control and crashed into a lamp post. As he sat there stunned, the sedan pulled alongside and stopped. The men in it began pumping shotgun slugs into Angelo, one of which shattered his spine. He was taken to a hospital, where he died after his bride came to him but before his brothers could get there. Angelo's murder took place on the morning of May 25, 1925.

The morning of June 13, Chicago police found Bugs Moran's abandoned Hupmobile, its body riddled with bullet holes and its upholstery slightly bloodstained. They located Moran at his ease in his home. He told them his car had been stolen.

Earlier that morning Mike "The Devil" Genna, Albert Anselmi, John Scalisi, and a driver had fought a brief, indecisive, running battle with Moran and Schemer Drucci. Drucci had been slightly wounded but he and Moran escaped.

While Moran was being questioned at his home, Genna, Anselmi, and Scalisi were searching for their quarry on Western Avenue. When their car almost hit another, Detective Michael J. Conway in an approaching squad car recognized Mike Genna and said, "Hoodlums—let's get after them."

The squad car made a sweeping U-turn and took off in pursuit, its gong clanging. The chase reached 70 mph before the fleeing car swerved to avoid another collision, spun twice, jumped the curb and came to a halt at a lamp post at 59th Street.

Genna, Anselmi, and Scalisi jumped out and barricaded themselves behind their car, weapons in hand. Their driver ran. The police car stopped a few feet away. Detective Conway and three fellow officers got out and Conway stepped forward. "Why all the speed when we were giving you the gong?" he called.

178

The next moment he and detectives Charles B. Walsh and Harold F. Olson were cut down by a shotgun fusillade. Detective William Sweeney emptied his gun at the trio behind the gangsters' car. They turned and ran. Sweeney snatched two guns dropped by his brother officers and pursued, chasing the trio into an alley, firing as he ran.

Scalisi and Anselmi turned into a passage between two houses. Mike Genna stopped, turned, and leveled his shotgun at Sweeney 30 feet away. The trigger fell on an empty shell and Sweeney's answering shot hit Genna in the leg. Mike the Devil smashed a basement window with his shotgun and dived in. Two policemen had jumped off a streetcar and joined Sweeney, together with a third, retired policeman whose wife had called him to the chase. They burst open the locked basement door and found Genna on the dirt floor, blood spurting from a leg artery. He fired once at them with his revolver before being hauled out.

He was dying when hoisted onto a stretcher from Bridewell Hospital but managed to kick a stretcher-bearer in the face and say, "Take that, you dirty son-of-a-bitch!" before he fell back and died.

Anselmi and Scalisi ran on across vacant lots—their flight excitedly watched by householders standing on their back porches—and into a dry goods store where they tried to buy caps to disguise themselves but the proprietor was suspicious and wouldn't sell to them. They ran out of the store and leaped onto a northbound streetcar on Western. A West Englewood Station flivver patrol car overtook the streetcar and they were arrested. "We're just looking for work," Anselmi protested. "You know where there's jobs?"

Detectives Olson and Walsh died almost on admittance to German Deaconess' Hospital. Detective Conway gradually recovered in St. Bernard's. The identity of the murderers seemed clear-cut enough—there had been scores of onlookers—but it would be two years before guilt or innocence was determined in court.

Tony The Gentleman Genna took a phone call on July 8 from Antonio The Cavalier Spano, who asked to be met that night at the corner of Grand Avenue and Curtis Street where The Cavalier said he would give Tony important information. Spano had worked and killed for the Gennas but was now bootlegging in Chicago Heights, Torrio-Capone territory. In fear of his life after Angelo's and Mike's murders, Tony Genna had remained locked in his mistress's hotel suite for weeks, refusing to attend family meetings and sending his mistress, Gladys Bagwell, out only for absolute necessities. But Spano had hinted that Scalisi and Anselmi had gone over to Capone and said he knew more of value.

That night Tony The Gentleman Genna drove to Grand and Curtis. (When you hunt, let the game come to you—but The Gentleman had never had a gangster's mentality.) Spano was in the doorway of a grocery store used by the Gennas as a front for other activities. Tony parked his car, donned his dark glasses, and went to meet The Cavalier. Tony put out his hand, Spano took it—and held it: "Mister Genna, my fren'." Scalisi and Anselmi came up behind Tony Genna and emptied their .38s into his back.

Tony was taken to County Hospital, where Gladys, a Baptist minister's daughter from Chester, Illinois, begged him to tell her who had shot him. "*Il Cavaliere*," he finally breathed, and died. The police canvassed Little Italy for a man with the last name "Cavallero," but found no such man.

The Gennas' chief contact with politicians and their police fixer, Samoots Amatuna, had seized control of the Unione Siciliana as soon as Bloody Angelo was buried, forestalling Capone's choice again. Samoots did it by walking into the Unione's offices accompanied by two gunmen and declaring himself president. After Mike The Devil and Tony The Gentleman were also killed, Sam and Pete Genna left Chicago and went into hiding. The chief Genna, Jim, had returned to Sicily, where Marsala police arrested him on an old jewel robbery charge. He spent the next two years in prison. The Terrible Gennas were no more.

Not unmindful of the ongoing bloodshed in Chicago—quite probably having initiated much of it—Johnny Torrio gave his own situation careful thought over the long afternoons and evenings he and Anna spent rocking easily on the sheriff's front porch. He was 43 years old and had a personal fortune of roughly $25 million deposited in eastern U.S. and European banks. The Genna deaths were only a prelude, that he *knew*. Weiss and Moran would not give up trying to exact full revenge, and there would be other battles to be fought until, finally, someone subjugated or destroyed all the others.

He came to a decision much like the one he had made 17 years before when he sold out his James Street properties in Brooklyn because of the carnage he foresaw impending there. Johnny Torrio believed in the Sicilian proverb: The man who plays alone never loses.

His protegé Capone brought his lawyers to Waukegan and with his own lawyers Johnny Torrio met with Al and transferred all his Chicago properties to Capone. The sale price was thought to be a payment in the millions of dollars plus 25 percent of syndicate profits for the next ten years.

When he was released from jail in the fall of 1925 three cars of Capone gunmen escorted him and his wife through Chicago to Gary, Indiana, where the Torrios took a train to New York City, where they took a luxury liner to Naples. Al Capone, at 26 years of age, was the boss, Chicago's king of vice. Torrio's reign had lasted from May 11, 1920, the day of Colosimo's murder, to January 24, 1925, the day of the attempt on his own life—4 years, 8 months, 13 days.

THE PRIVILEGED

In 1904 the 38-year-old widow Anita McCormick Blaine, daughter to the reaper dynast Cyrus McCormick, had financed the establishment of the Francis W. Parker School on Chicago's Near North Side. In 1906 she became assistant principal of the school. By the mid-Twenties she had given $3 million to the Parker School; before that, $1.5 million to its predecessor, the Chicago Institute. In 1905 the mayor appointed her to the Chicago Board of Education; she served through mid-1908. She was also involved with the Board of Associated Charities, the Audubon Society, the Consumers League, a new Chicago art league, Jane Addams' Hull House, the Chicago Playground Association, tenement work with the City Homes Association, teaching classes at the Home for Self-Supporting Women, teaching Presbyterian Sunday School, and taking fencing lessons with her sister-in-law, Edith Rockefeller McCormick.

Anita and her son Emmons relaxed at their private wilderness estate on Upper St. Regis Lake in the Adirondacks. When they and guests left commodious cabins to rough it, servants accompanied them bearing canoes, blankets, provisions, and chilled champagne.

Wherever she traveled, Anita took at least two servants with her and a secretary. By the mid-Twenties she was employing 11 secretaries. Despite continuous efforts to organize her activities, her affairs were usually in vast disorder. Filing systems were set up, then ignored, though she never threw anything away. Schedules were drawn, then lost. If margins on a letter were the least bit crooked, she returned it for retyping, then often let it linger on her desk for weeks before signing it. Household bills went unpaid because overlooked; appointments were missed because forgotten. She delegated no task, and at home and in her office she was mired in the trivial.

Anita McCormick Blaine asked herself, "Why should I . . . have the privilege of doing and having whatever I please, while so many who could do more than I, could make use of it?" She dreamed of "a state of

181

affairs where all paid of their own rightly earned product, in full and just proportion, into a treasury so filled to cover all of the common benefits needed by the community, to be disbursed by responsible agents for the public good."

In 1899 Anita had filed a schedule of her personal property at the office of the Cook County Assessor in the amount of $1,005,063, the largest individual schedule ever filed in Chicago. Mother Nettie, inspired by her daughter's example, filed an equally realistic schedule of her own, this at a time when the much more substantial personal property of traction magnate Charles T. Yerkes, for example, was assessed for tax purposes at $7,000, that of Marshall Field at $20,480, that of P. D. Armour at $5,090.

Brother Cyrus pointed out to Anita and their mother that they had by their actions jeopardized all other major stockholders in the McCormick reaper company, all of whom believed the personal property tax to be robbery to begin with. (In 1906 the Square Deal Tax League presented evidence that reaper company stockholders in Cook County were cheating the county out of taxes on $150 million worth of property annually. . . . No action was taken.)

Anita's father had founded McCormick Theological Seminary to spread the Presbyterian gospel but Anita withdrew from the rest of the family in its continuing support. "I had long felt a difficulty about the Presbyterian Church," she wrote. Her feeling was that grace had to be earned through "struggle, effort, fight," that strength was "not through swaddling clothes."

Sister Virginia McCormick required the constant supervision of a keeper and companion, Anita's mother was becoming a deaf hysteric, and by 1906 her younger brother Stanley was plunging into psychosis. Having been taught that non-marital sex of any kind was the equivalent of depravity, Stanley rigged a harness for his ankles and wrists while he attended Princeton so that he could not touch himself in his sleep. After his graduation from Princeton, Stanley lived at home with mother Nettie. She took him with her on a tour of Europe and the Middle East, hid his books and gave him religious tracts to read, criticized his friends and spending of money, and lied to him that she had a heart condition his behavior aggravated. Over his mother's strenuous objections he stayed on in Paris to study art when she returned to Chicago. Within a week he was seduced; six months later he was back in Chicago working at the reaper company.

He continued to live with his mother at the Rush Street mansion. On his mother's orders, the door to his room was left open at all times and a maid had instructions to telephone him and order him home if he stayed out late.

Proclaiming that the money made on McCormick reapers belonged to the workers, Stanley bought a ranch in New Mexico that he helped manage on a co-op basis. In 1903, after quarreling with the cowhands over what he considered their ingratitude, Stanley returned to the East, met Katherine Dexter of Boston, and married her in Geneva, Switzerland, in 1904. They returned to Chicago in July 1905, the marriage unconsummated. Stanley gave up his job at the reaper company and moved with his wife to Washington, D.C.

Anita was comforting him one afternoon when he turned on her, accusing her of wasting her time on schools and of smothering her son Em as their mother had smothered him. Brother and sister had never quarreled before. In tears, Anita urged him to see a doctor. He said he preferred to study fencing.

At a party in 1906 he stopped immobile on the dance floor and had to be led home. A dog looked back at him from his mirror, then nothing looked back at him. He bought eight different weights of underwear to be worn at different temperatures, attacked his dentist, began eating like a dog, begged to be killed, struck his nurses and asked them to show him their private parts. Stanley was removed to an estate in southern California, the one he had helped plan for his sister Virginia's care years before.

Handsome brother Cyrus, seven years older than Anita (15 years older than Stanley), grew a dark beard and mustache like his father and managed the reaper works. In 1902 with J. P. Morgan assistance he merged the McCormick company with five other agricultural implement firms, one of them its chief competitor, to form International Harvester. A loan of $4.5 million from John D. Rockefeller, the world's richest man (Standard Oil) enabled the McCormicks to hold more than 50 percent of the merged stock.

Brother Harold—13 years younger than Cyrus—married his childhood friend, Edith Rockefeller, daughter of John D., a few months after he graduated from Princeton with brother Stanley. Where his sister Anita dressed sloppily in clothes 20 years out of style, Harold was a fashion plate. Where his sister spent her quixotic energies on good works, Harold spent his on having fun—after first fathering four children and working as an executive for the harvester company for a quarter century. Harold liked fine clothes, airplanes, whistling, and—after Edith left him—he cultivated a liking for beautiful women.

His wife Edith was not a beauty; she resembled her father. She and Harold lived in Chicago at 1000 Lake Shore Drive, the heart of the Gold Coast, in a grey stone, turreted castle set behind a block-long, high iron fence. The castle's regular staff numbered 24. Menus for every meal were printed in French, at formal dinners place cards were engraved in gold and a footman stood behind each chair, and at large formal dinners the uppercrust dined from a thousand-piece service Napoleon had given his sister that contained 700 pounds of precious metals.

Edith—Mrs. Harold Fowler McCormick (who came to supplant Mrs. Potter Palmer as Chicago society's grande dame)—had beaucoup jewelry. She and husband Harold were patrons of the opera and other operagoers were treated to glimpses of her collection; for example, a $1 million necklace with 10 large diamonds spaced on a rope of 1,657 small diamonds, or her $2 million necklace with 23 large pearls and 21 large and 100 smaller diamonds. Edith knew the history of every stone she owned (some had been Catherine of Russia's) and what had been paid for it.

In 1911, in an effort to close the rift in their marriage, Edith and Harold built a 44-room Lake Forest mansion (it had 12 master bedrooms identical in every way, even to furnishings). They—or she—called it "Villa Turicum," but they never lived in it. The housewarming was called off without explanation and barrels of fine china stood unpacked in the villa gathering dust for 30 years alongside expensive period furniture. In 1913, Edith left Chicago for Switzerland to study "synthetic psychology" with Karl Gustav Jung.

In 1915, Emile Ammann took leave from the Swiss Army, neutral in WWI, and became Edith's chauffeur in Zurich. Initially he thought of her as the "Standard Oil Princess," and then, "to be quite honest," he said in his memoirs, "I considered her to be completely crazy." Ammann worked days, evenings, and weekends. In the less than two years he drove for her, he wore out a Renault, a Fiat, a Lorraine, a Rolls Royce, and a Delage.

> She had the most beautiful and expensive clothes sent out from Wiesbaden and Paris. . . . She wore the dresses four or five times. Then into the closet with them, where over 200 dresses, shoes, and hats were piled up. . . . And that at a time when millions of people were going to bed hungry or dying in the trenches.

Mornings, Ammann would drive her to Kusnacht for her hour with Dr. Jung but she often walked back to her hotel in Zurich, with Ammann following in the car at 4 mph. One day her walk was overtaken by a rainstorm.

> She turned around, looked angrily at me and placed her finger on her lips. That was my signal that she did not want a ride. . . . Slowly the cloudburst became more and more intense. The gutters swelled to brooks and lakes. . . . I could see her hat melting down. How the light, drenched dress clung to her like a bathing suit. . . ! How Madame began to shiver and shake, but with what imperturbability she strode through puddles. . . !

Madame vouchsafed something of an explanation to her chauffeur: "Today I forgot my umbrella, which usually I never leave behind. Logic told me that the most important thing was to walk back to the hotel. That I ended up in a cloudburst is regrettable. But you're not supposed to . . . you may not change your habits. What could have been the deeper motive for my forgetting?"

Ammann recalled that he almost answered, "Insanity," but those believers who wish to delve deeper will want to know that the forgotten umbrella (which had a massive gold handle) was a souvenir of Edith's idol, the handsome chief conductor and director of the Chicago Opera Association, maestro Cleofonte Campanini, who now and again visited her in Zurich. Make of *that* what you will! . . . As for Ammann: "I am convinced that Professor Freud . . . would make the sign of the cross if he had experienced the assault on his theory as I experienced it."

Edith founded a psychoanalytic club/clinic in Zurich to which many came seeking her help. To all she gave analysis, to some more. One apt pupil, a musician, came away with title to a villa in Zurich's best quarter. Another remembered by Ammann was

> . . . a man of 25, the Austrian Krenn. . . . Since he did not have any visible means of support and thus as a foreigner was threatened with deportation, he turned . . . to Mrs. Rockefeller who began immediately to analyze him. His expectations were fully met, for after a month of daily instruction, for which he no doubt showed a remarkable ability, Mrs. Rockefeller enabled him to purchase Swiss citizenship, thereby removing the threat of deportation. . . .
>
> Any way you look at it, he was an exceptionally avid pupil who in a flash won the affection and trust of his instructor. In the beginning he took three hours a week; later he came every day, then two or three times a day. Finally, he had only an hour a day that lasted "from morning until midnight."

And sometimes much later than midnight. Edith also, in February 1918, began giving the language teacher James Joyce 1,000 francs a month to aid him in his literary labors (*Ulysses*, at the time), unaccountably cutting off these funds in October 1919.

Meanwhile, back at the castle, a restive Harold met the aspiring Polish opera singer Ganna Walska after she called him at his New York hotel. Twice widowed, Ganna had had her operatic debut in 1917 and it had likewise been unfortunate: she was nearly hissed from the stage and at the second performance was the target of eggs and vegetables. But her large eyes were dark and fetching, her nose pure Grecian, and her skin a bewitching white. Harold brought her to a high society luncheon where her charms dazzled the men but seemed to have the opposite effect on the women, especially when she confided that every man she had ever met proposed to her the second time he saw her. "Yes," remarked a thirtyish Chicago belle, "but she doesn't say what they propose."

Harold journeyed to Zurich to see Edith on a marital matter, leaving Ganna behind in Paris to await the outcome. When Edith reluctantly agreed to a divorce, Harold hurried to wire the news to his one true love but was handed a telegram from her informing him that she had that day married playboy and carpet tycoon Alexander Smith Cochran, "the world's richest bachelor." A distraught Harold sped to Paris, took a room in the honeymooners' hotel, and phoned Ganna at 7:00 in the morning. She invited him to the Cochran suite for coffee.

While the bridegroom slept in the adjoining bedroom, Harold demanded that Ganna leave her hours-old husband and marry him. She said she'd think about it.

Perhaps if Alexander Cochran had not been quite the insensitive brute he was, Ganna would have remained his wife. But not only did he at breakfast—taken not long after a crestfallen Harold departed their suite—flaunt his mastery of the material world by announcing he was giving her a house on the Rue de Lebeck for her very own and $100,000 a year as "pin money," he went so far as to ask her to go to Cartier's and select anything she saw and wanted there as a wedding present. His final crudeness was to go hunting without her and, by way of requital, force her "to accept a sable coat worth a million francs and so big, so heavy it made me look old and fat; [and he] reserved an entire floor at the Carlton Hotel in Cannes and sent me there alone with half a dozen servants to enjoy the grand season on the Riviera."

Determined to soothe her bruised sensibilities, Harold sponsored her in the title role of Leoncavallo's *Zaza* with the Chicago Opera Company. Rehearsals did not go well and when at the final, dress rehearsal the conductor asked Ganna to "sing for me once with full voice, so that I may modulate my orchestra according to your powers," the soprano was aghast. "But, Maestro," she cried, "didn't you know? It's what I've been doing since we started to rehearse."

Zaza was cancelled, the prima donna blaming this disappointment to followers of her career on her Philistine of a husband, Cochran. She divulged that he demanded she cancel her appearance because he had learned that *Zaza* contained long stage kisses and that many of the singers were scantily costumed.

The mismatched couple divorced—Ganna receiving $200,000, a Rolls Royce, her house on the Rue de Lebeck, a chateau, jewels, and the despised sable coat—and she and Harold McCormick were free at last to marry. For his fiancee's birthday, Harold demonstrated his own gauge of the artistic soul by sending her one of every kind of agricultural machine made by International Harvester. Happily, she was not offended when there appeared on the lawn of her chateau near Versailles—"to my great surprise . . . . a whole regiment of robot soldiers."

Before the wedding took place, however, Harold quit as president of Harvester (at the board's request) and submitted to precautionary surgery. In Switzerland, visiting his wife Edith and their children, he had heard of Dr. Serge Voronoff's work on the rejuvenation of human males by transplanting to them the thyroid glands of monkeys. In Chicago, Dr. Victor D. Lespinasse, the dean of U.S. gland transplantation—indeed, he had coined the saying "A man is as old as his glands"—took scalpel to Harold on June 12, 1922. Dr. Voronoff had told Harold that at 51 he was too old for monkey glands but that a younger human male's would accomplish the desired objective. A quatrain became briefly popular throughout the United States:

> Under the spreading chestnut tree,
> The village smithy stands;
> The smith a gloomy man is he;
> McCormick has his glands.

Harold and Ganna were wedlocked in Paris in August. Ganna wrote her new sister-in-law Anita McCormick Blaine:

> People made about me quite wrong impression, and they imagine that I am foolish, vane, consited personne who imagines that she can sing because she is pretty and through her husband's money tries to push herself. As a matter of fact I am entirely, not consited, but wrongly or rightly, (to be seen some day!) quite sure that something is in me and that I should deliver a message and leave something behind me as an example. I want other people to know that Harold did not marry a foolish woman, but a person who wants to give at cost of terrible suffering and undiscrable misery.

To the new man and wife the ever-tolerant Anita replied: "You had to find it. It was there to find. It was yours. It is all one road—the seeing, the findings, the attaining, the giving, the sharing."

Alas, the road diverged after two years' travel (during which time mother Nettie died, leaving an estate of $12 million; she had given away $8 million in the last 34 years of her life). They came to a fork in the road and took it.

What caused the seemingly destined-to-be-eternal union of Harold and Ganna to sunder? The brute grossness of men, wouldn't you know it. According to Ganna, Harold was "insatiable in his search for the realization of the physical demands—insatiable because they were unattainable for him anymore." (An aspersion on the skills of Dr. Lespinasse, perhaps?) She, conversely, was "an idealist who was able to put so much value on the richness of his soul that she would not even imagine the possibility of his preferring to seek further for a gross and limited pleasure, rather than being satisfied with the divine companionship of the spiritual love she was willing to share with him."

187

In the divorce settlement, Ganna's disillusionment was somewhat eased by a portion of Harold's richness of purse: $6 million, a fourth of his fortune.

But woe unto you that are rich! for ye have received your consolation. Each of Harold's three surviving children married someone at least 20 years older. As a teenager, Mathilde had married her 40-year-old Swiss riding instructor; Harold's son Fowler married "Fifi" Stillman, the divorced mother of his Princeton roommate; and Harold's daughter Muriel married Major Hubbard, a near-invalid of World War I, who lasted connubially five years before cashing in. By then an alcoholic, Muriel insisted that the major's dog march in the major's funeral procession, upsetting her brother Fowler, who called her "mentally unbalanced."

Edith Rockefeller McCormick returned to Chicago in 1921 thinking to reassume her place as head of the city's haut monde, and bringing with her Zurich star pupil Edward Krenn. The young architect took rooms at the Drake Hotel, diagonally across the street from Edith's castle. Every afternoon at one o'clock he appeared at her door in spats and the striped trousers of one of his 200 suits and carrying a nosegay for Edith. The two had luncheon, then language lessons. At four o'clock, tea, then to the movies (car, chauffeur, and footman waiting at the curb) or the theater, the symphony, or the opera. Since before 1910 the McCormicks had made up the opera's annual deficit—it was owing to Edith and Harold that Chicago so much as had a civic opera company—and Edith's taste in music was excellent, her experience wide, and she knew the good from the inferior (as her love-deafened ex-husband had not). Krenn once responded to a husband's complaint that his wife had a box for them on Mondays with: "Ayeeh! You should complain about Mondays—*I've* got to go to the opera every single night!"

Edith believed in reincarnation (she had been an Egyptian queen in a previous life), once paid $25,000 for a horoscope, and felt she had a rare talent for business. She bought 1,500 acres south of Kenosha, Wisconsin, at over $1,000 an acre and with Krenn and his Austrian school classmate, Edward Dato, planned a model city for millionaires to be called Edithton. She lavished $4 million on landscaping and a yacht harbor but the Crash of 1929 obliterated Edithton since it badly damaged her portfolio of stocks. In Highland Park on Chicago's North Shore Krenn, Dato, and Edith did manage to build several modest homes and had curb and gutter poured for a larger development but that never got beyond the cement work.

With her fortune dissipated, she asked for help. Her brother, John D., Jr., assumed her debts and moved her out of the castle into the Drake Hotel. Almost 60 years old, abandoned by husband and children, tolerated by Chicago society but regarded as an oddity and object of pity, she was next beset with a painful, lingering cancer that she tried to cure with psychiatric self-analysis. She had made new friends since her return to the city because she had retained her interest in psychiatry and developed interests in poetry and philosophy ("My object in the world is to think new thoughts"), but the only person at her bedside in her last hours was Harold, who came from California to be with her. Every year on her birthday since their divorce he had sent her a single rose. It was only after her death that he learned, from a former servant, that his lonely, wisp-haired ex-wife had kept a room ready for him in the castle, hoping he might one day return to her.

After his divorce from Ganna in 1931 (six years after they separated), Harold danced attendance on the movie actress Pola Negri, and then on the Baroness Violet Beatrice Wenner, who was good enough to accompany him on the harp when, as he occasionally did (once over radio's airwaves), he gave his whistling recitals. In 1938 he married his nurse, 30 years younger than himself. He died three years later, the same year his older sister Virginia, who had been confined under care for almost 60 years, also died. She had become a plump, child-like old lady who cried a lot. "I love to think what I will tell Jesus when I see him," she declared not long before her death.

Stanley McCormick languished "timid, introverted, masochistic," and watched over in California for 40 years. The outlay for his care reached $250,000 a year by 1943. His condition was diagnosed as "malignant compulsion neurosis." His wife Katherine, who spent brief periods with him off and on throughout his confinement, was diagnosed by the same psychiatrist who diagnosed Stanley as "dominating, aggressive, impulsive and sadistic"—in other words, the couple matched perfectly. When he died in 1947 Stanley's $33.5 million estate went to his widow Katherine.

Anita McCormick Blaine spent these years working for and promoting her causes and trying to mediate family disputes, and failing to meet the normal, everyday obligations of living, such as paying bills, answering mail, keeping appointments, being on time, or following up on requests or promises. Her son Em graduated from Harvard and in 1916 completed graduate work in engineering at MIT. At age 26 he became the proprietor of the Milford Meadows Farm in Wisconsin, which he and his mother owned. The next year he married Eleanor Gooding, the daughter of a New Hampshire Unitarian minister. Rejected by the Army because of a doubtful adolescent medical history, he went to work as a clerk for the American Shipbuilding Company in Philadelphia, his way of helping in the war effort.

The shipyard was located on dismal Hog Island, formerly a swamp. In October 1918 a pregnant Eleanor wired her mother-in-law that Em had a cold and possibly a light case of influenza. Influenza was epidemic in Philadelphia at that time; 40 percent of its physicians, for example, had been stricken. Anita took a train to her son and managed to find four nurses for him but he developed pneumonia and six days after her arrival he died. She took her daughter-in-law back to Chicago with her and a month later Eleanor presented her with a granddaughter, Nancy. On Em's death, Eleanor had been left $1 million, with another $1 million in trust for his child.

Anita became interested in psychic phenomena, hoping her father, husband, or son would speak to her from the great beyond. In November of 1921 voices of the war dead commanded her to attend a disarmament conference in Washington, D.C., to deliver the message: "The only work the conference has to do is find God. God is everywhere." She spent seven days in Washington trying at high levels of government but failing to get permission to address the conferees.

She became obsessed with the idea of taking her granddaughter from Eleanor and raising the infant herself—though Eleanor and her daughter Nancy lived only 45 minutes away in Winnetka. Rebuffed, Anita persuaded her daughter-in-law to adopt a "companion" for Nancy. The boy was given the name John Blaine. Curiously, he was never legally adopted.

In 1927 Eleanor married a captain from WWI, Clark Lawrence, who gave up a small architectural practice in Florida so that Anita could establish him in Chicago with a gift of $75,000. When the Crash occurred, "Larry" took a premature retirement. He liked to be among the rich and was a fine horseman and he became master of the Longmeadows Hounds in Illinois. The adopted companion for Nancy, John, was a reckless, rebellious boy and Larry was a poor stepfather to him and to Nancy. He was given the rank of colonel in WWII but his service was cut short by a mental breakdown. Anita bought him and Eleanor and their children an historic estate, "Castle Hill," in Virginia on 1,180 acres, and paid all their bills thereafter. Larry liked to be addressed as "Colonel." And just because he took Anita's financial aid did not mean he approved of all of her causes or the people she associated with. He personally, himself, disliked Negroes and distrusted Jews.

Companion son John's first marriage broke up and by the time he was 40 he was a talented but unemployed pianist and on his way to becoming an alcoholic derelict. He visited Anita and spoke of his problems and his anger. She told him "one doesn't quarrel with one's life, one just handles it." He married a Chinese girl who had studied music in Paris and seven years later he was shot to death on a dark Harlem street.

Anita busied herself sending cables of admonition and advice to world leaders—Japanese Emperor Hirohito, Mahatma Gandhi, President Franklin D. Roosevelt, Benito Mussolini, Adolf Hitler. She went to Europe in 1937, aged 71, to get Sir Oliver Lodge's advice on spiritualistic research. She brought an English medium back to the States, gave her a secretary, and kept her in Chicago and Boston hotels for ten years, all expenses paid, but seldom saw her.

When the United States entered WWII in 1941 her cable traffic to world leaders increased. She sent flowers to army and navy bases at Easter in 1943, gave Madame Chiang Kai-shek $100,000 in IH stocks when China's dragon lady stopped over in Chicago. She distributed 150,000 free copies of her approval of the United Nations Charter. Here is part of her endorsement:

> Oh world of souls, look up! The next step is always higher than the last. The free world becomes a responsible world, the free press a responsible press. The free soul becomes a responsible soul and is his brother's keeper.

When Henry Agard Wallace was forced to resign from President Harry S Truman's cabinet in 1946 she sent Wallace a check for $10,000 because he had promised to "carry on the fight for peace." She had admired Wallace since 1940, when he was elected FDR's vice president, because he was a man, she believed, who "tells America to be good," while others "tell everyone else in the world to be good." In 1945 she wired all 96 U.S. senators to tell them that Wallace was "conservative, not radical. . . ." When in 1948 Wallace ran as the Progressive Party candidate for President, Anita was the party's largest single contributor—$800,000—for which her cousin Robert's *Tribune* ("The World's Greatest Newspaper") attacked her as a communist sympathizer.

In 1948, she established a $1 million trust fund for the Foundation for World Government, a hybrid creation of the jejune World Federalists and the Progressive Party.

Her last beneficiaries were the *Weekly National Guardian*, a new and strong voice of progressivism and dissent, and the liberal *Daily Compass*. She loaned the *Guardian* $200,000 and began contributing $5,000 a month to its support. Next, Henry Wallace led the editor of the *Compass* to her and he came away with $600,000 and the promise of $1 million more and a column of religious and philosophical quotations from Anita.

She had a probably unneeded operation in 1949, was returned to her home at 101 East Erie, and never after left it. Physically she was still able, if infirm, but the power of speech had deserted her and she had to be attended day and night. She died on Lincoln's birthday in 1954, 88 years old.

It is to the everlasting credit of this nation's overworked obituary writers that not a single one in giving their accounts of the lives and deaths of Chicago's many privileged McCormicks over the years ever succumbed to the temptation to cite Galatians 6:7.

191

Al Capone

CAPONE

At 26 Al Capone became the ruler of the $100-million-a-year criminal empire that Johnny Torrio had constructed. Capone's objective remained that of Torrio—out of syndication, total control. Capone's methods were both Torrio's and his own and his own were necessarily of the kind that had prompted Torrio to abdicate because he did not wish to put himself at such risk. Within the boundaries of metropolitan Chicago, Capone succeeded (as Torrio would have, had he stayed—and survived), though Capone was at last brought down by forces he could not deal with or kill or even, perhaps, fully comprehend. But who can look into the seeds of time?

Alphonsus James Capone was born on January 17, 1899, to 34-year-old Gabriele and 29-year-old Theresa (née Raiola) Capone, who had come to Brooklyn six years before from Castellammare di Stabia, 16 miles south of Naples on the bay. The rough, poor neighborhood Al was born into was close to the Brooklyn Navy Yard and predominantly Italian. The Capones already had three children—Vincenzo (James), Raffalo (Ralph), and Salvatore (Frank)—and were to have four more—Amadeo Ermini (John or Mimi), Umberto (Matt), Rosalia (Rose), and Mafalda (named after the Italian royal princess).

When Al was eight the family moved to South Brooklyn into what was also a poor and predominantly Italian neighborhood, one hard by the rough Irish section of Red Hook. They settled at 38 Garfield Place. Al attended Public School No. 133 until he was 14 and in sixth grade, when he slapped a teacher and quit after he was whipped for it.

He shined shoes, clerked in a candy store, set pins in a bowling alley, worked in a book bindery. He learned to shoot pool from his father—a barber with a weakness for alcohol—and became the neighborhood hustler. When he was 16 he went to work as a bartender and bouncer for Frankie Yale at Yale's Harvard Inn on the Coney Island waterfront. On summer Sundays half the arrests for drunkenness in NYC were made on Coney Island. Capone, almost six feet tall and heavy, with solid shoulders and large, meaty hands, was a tactful bouncer; that is, the drunks he threw out were not offended and came back to the Inn when less polluted. The youthful Capone also strong-armed for some of Yale's many other ventures: black-hand extortion, shylocking, protection for shopkeepers or street merchants, tribute from pimps and gamblers, and slugging during elections or strikes (for the highest bidder). Good with his fists, he perfected his pistol marksmanship on beer bottles in the basement of Brooklyn's Adonis Social Club.

When he was 18 he made an insulting remark to the sister of a patron at the Inn. The patron—Frank Galluccio—took a clasp knife to Al's face, leaving a 4-inch scar across the left cheek, a 2½-inch scar on the left jaw, and the same on the neck below the left ear. Sometimes Al explained that his scars came from a shrapnel wound received on the Western Front, where he had served with the "Lost Battalion" of the 77th Division in the Great War. He was never averse to an elaborate lie.

When he was 19 he lost his heart to a pretty Irish girl, Mary (Mae) Coughlin, two years older than himself, and they were married on December 30, 1918, eight days after their son, Albert Francis, was baptized. Despite simmering hostility between the Irish and Italians, such matches were not uncommon, because the Italian young men did not wait until their thirties or forties to forsake their mothers' cooking.

Though he was a suspect in two murders during his stint at the Harvard Inn, the only charge ever brought against Capone back then was for disorderly conduct, and that was dropped. Yale—14 years older, a graduate of the notorious Five Points gang, and national president of the Unione Siciliana—valued his young employee; sometimes, if they left the Inn very late in the morning, Al slept over at Yale's house. Besides the Inn and his extortion rackets, Yale owned a funeral parlor, distributed a line of cheap cigars (a "Frankie Yale" was synonymous with a bad smoke), dabbled in managing race horses and prize fighters and night clubs, and had his eyes on the Brooklyn docks and their cargo-laden piers, but there the Irish White Handers were already entrenched among the stevedores.

While out making collections for Frankie one day late in 1919, Capone stopped at a dockside bar for a drink. Arthur Finnegan also stepped in for a quick one. Finnegan was a White Hand gang member whose recreation was baiting and abusing Italians and he started in on Capone. Big Al beat him to a bloody pulp. At the hospital they thought Finnegan would die. He didn't, but Capone and Yale both knew the White Handers would mark a young dago with a scarred face. Yale called his friend and one-time partner, Johnny Torrio, in Chicago, and Al Capone, his wife Mae, and son Albert Francis entrained for the Windy City.

Al's first tasks for Torrio were the lowest—steering customers into the world's oldest libertine institutions, driving for Torrio, and bouncer and barkeep at the Four Deuces. In an unused store front of Torrio's building on Wabash, Capone set out an old piano and some junk furniture and had business cards printed for himself.

ALPHONSE CAPONE
Second Hand Furniture Dealer
2220 South Wabash Avenue

What did he sell? "Any old thing a man might want to lay on." When was he open? "We ain't open today."

Torrio was mildly impressed by this attempt at a respectable cover. He liked the young man, who brought with him high recommendations from Yale, and from another NY *compare*, Charlie Luciana, and he came to trust him. When Capone's son Albert was confirmed in 1920 Torrio sponsored "Sonny" and later that year gave him a $5,000 bond on his birthday, a gift repeated in following years. He also gave Al responsibility for the management of operations in Burnham.

On November 14, 1920, in Brooklyn, Gabriele Capone suffered a heart attack while watching a game of pool, and died, age 55. After his father's funeral, Al moved the Garfield Place Capones cross-country into a 15-room brick duplex at 7244 South Prairie, together with his own Mae and Sonny. The basement windows at 7244 had steel bars set so close that a bomb could not be thrown through them and the walls at ground level were reinforced concrete a foot thick.

The Al Capone family lived on the seven ground-floor rooms with Al's mother and two sisters. Al's brother Ralph and his wife and son and daughter lived in the eight rooms on the second floor. For a time in 1922 18-year-old brother Mimi also lived with Al at 7244, as did 14-year-old youngest brother Matt until Al sent him to a military school in Aurora, from there to Pennsylvania's Villanova University. Mafalda, the youngest sister, was sent to a private girls' school near the home. At Christmas Al would be limo-driven to the school where he distributed candy, fruits, a turkey, and a gift to every teacher and all of Mafalda's schoolmates.

The Italian saying "*Tratta con quelli che sono miglio de ti e fagli le spese*" means, roughly, "Associate with those better than you and pay full expenses." This was what Capone did working for Torrio, and he put the older man in his debt thereby. No task was so mean or bloody that Torrio could not safely give it to his lieutenant. He also came to know that Capone was loyal to him, a rare quality in their calling. The young man's attitude toward his chief was expressed in what he called him: Johnny Papa.

Capone learned fairly quickly, and what he learned were Torrio's methods, which ran counter to his own instincts and to his tendency to act in moments of blind rage. But, as he saw, Johnny Papa's methods worked: "We don't want any trouble" was usually more effective than a truculent "You asking for trouble?" The true Italian way—exemplified by Torrio's methods—was to avoid confrontations. A smile and a little quiet talk resolved most problems, although as Al observed in a later year, "You can get a lot more done with a kind word and a gun, than with a kind word alone."

Capone's temperament did not transform itself into that of a smooth diplomat all at once, if ever. Driving drunk east on Randolph in the early morning of August 30, 1922, a girl beside him and three men in the back seat, he sideswiped a parked taxi at Wabash. His companions discreetly left the scene but Al went to the cab's window waving a revolver. The cabbie was slumped stunned over the steering wheel. Capone began to berate and threaten him. The motorman of a passing streetcar jumped off and intervened. A police ambulance came clanging up and took the cab driver to a hospital, Al to jail. He was charged with driving while intoxicated, assault with an automobile, and carrying a concealed weapon. Diamond Joe Esposito came to the station and stood his bail.

The next day the *Tribune* carried the story on an inside page, identifying Capone as "Alfred Caponi" and quoting him as saying, "I'll fix this thing so easy you won't know how it's done." The case was never called.

In Cicero, where older brother Frank was killed in Capone's 1924 takeover (from Little Italy in New York to an appointment with death 29 years later in the streets of Cicero—on April Fools Day! who *can* look into the seeds of time, Salvatore?), Mayor Klenha tried to assert his independence. Al met him on the steps of Town Hall, slapped him down the steps and, with a Cicero policeman looking on, kicked him when he tried to get up. The Mayor reassessed his own importance. Yet it might have been a tempered response, for as Capone pointed out in speaking of another such incident (when he sent his men into the Cicero town council to physically break up its meeting because it was going to pass a measure hostile to his interests), "This way they learn their lesson and nobody gets really hurt."

What was not a tempered response was his shooting of Joe Howard in retaliation for Howard's roughing up of Jake Guzik. Sending six bullets into Howard's skull, however, proved to be a most wise rash act. After that murder, no mobster ever questioned Capone's loyalty to those who were loyal to him—even though he might punch them around a little, as he occasionally did, if they screwed up. "I'm with Capone," or ". . . the Outfit" became a declaration of pride.

196

Quiet and retiring when he arrived in Chicago, deferential to the capos such as Diamond Joe Esposito and certainly Johnny Papa, Capone grew self-assertive as his responsibilities and income increased, and he became, finally, loquacious. Unlike his mentor Torrio, he would answer questions put to him by reporters. When asked about his thoughts on the flower-shop killing of O'Banion, for instance, he responded at length—at the same time sending a clear warning to ambitious allies in the Chicago syndicate:

> "Deanie was all right, and he was getting along to begin with better than he had any right to expect. But like everyone else his head got away from his hat. Johnny Torrio had taught O'Banion all he knew and then O'Banion grabbed some of the best guys we had and decided to be the boss of the booze racket in Chicago. What a chance! O'Banion had a swell route to make it tough for us and he did. His job had been to smooth the coppers and we gave him a lot of authority with the booze and beer buyers. When he broke away, for a while it wasn't so good. He knew the ropes and got running us ragged. It was his funeral."

With Torrio serving his term in the Lake County Jail in Waukegan, Capone assumed full executive powers for day-to-day operations of the Outfit. He also saw to the last mopping up of the South Side O'Donnells and, probably, to the downfall of the Terrible Gennas, though Torrio may have guided him in this. No one ever identified the killers of Bloody Angelo (though police supposition was that they were Weiss, Drucci, and Moran), but it seems fairly certain that when Mike the Devil's ride was interrupted by a squad of detectives he was being taken to a place of execution by Scalise and Anselmi (who had surreptitiously gone over to Capone); and when The Cavalier delivered death from a doorway to Tony the Gentleman, The Cavalier was making his living as a bootlegger only by the sufferance of Capone.

Big Al the family man found time to apply for life insurance in 1925, giving his occupation as "Dealer in second-hand furniture." Half a dozen companies rejected the application. And he found time also to ask Bathhouse John Coughlin to call on him at the Metropole Hotel. The Bath's truncated grey eminence, Hinky Dink Kenna, had retired from the City Council—though he retained his powerful post in the Democratic Party as First Ward Committeeman—but Coughlin remained as the ward's elected representative.

"Alderman," Capone said, "you were a good pal of Big Jim's. You stood in with Torrio. Well, they're gone now and we're running things and we don't want trouble with you. Let it get around. I'm telling you because I like you."

The alderman left, as frightened as when he entered the suite but now immensely relieved as well. "My God," he told everyone who would listen "what could I say? Suppose he had said he was going to take over the organization? What could we do then? We're lucky to get as good a break as we did!"

In the Outfit-infested western suburbs, the better elements fought the good fight, spurred on by a young, crusading newspaper editor, Robert St. John. The Juvenile Protective association was able to get Stickney's Roamer Inn brothel padlocked, and when it was reopened the West Suburban Ministers' and Citizens' Association raided it and got it closed again.

St. John, 25 years old, was part-owner and editor of the *Cicero Tribune*, a weekly. The paper's front page regularly reported on vice activities in the west suburbs and St. John's editorials regularly excoriated the local politicians who made those activities possible. Through his Town Hall vassals and his mob sluggers, Capone brought pressure against merchants who advertised in the *Cicero Tribune*, but the paper did not go under.

When a new brothel opened near the Hawthorne Race Track in Cicero township, St. John dressed himself in shabby clothes and went there late one night to report:

> The place was a square, unpainted frame building two stories high and the size of a small armory. . . . To pass from the bar into the main building, it was necessary to go through a series of three doors only a foot or two apart. The first and third were hinged on the right; the middle one on the left. The bartender was the establishment's "spotter." He controlled all three doors with electric buttons. It was possible for him to allow a client to get through the first door and then lock all three electrically, thus imprisoning the visitor. The establishment's "bouncer" sat at a small table just inside the main building. The barman could communicate with him by house telephone. If a man marked for extermination were to be locked in the small corridor with the three doors, it was simple for the bouncer to fire a few bullets through the door on his side. Although the place had been open for business only about two weeks, the doors already looked like pieces of Swiss cheese and there were black stains on the floor and walls of the corridor.
>
> The ground floor of the main building was a single large room, its four walls lined with wooden benches. A client coming from the bar took a seat on a bench just to the left or right of the bar door.
>
> The procedure from then on was obvious at a glance. A girl wearing only the two most essential feminine garments would come down from upstairs, enter the large waiting room through a door in the far wall, make a slow circuit of the room, greeting anyone she already knew, and then would go back upstairs accompanied by the man who occupied the spot on the bench just to the left or right of the far door The man next to the place now vacated would move into it. This was a signal for all the other bench warmers to move a foot or two closer, ultimately leaving a vacancy by the bar door. The bouncer would then communicate by phone with the barman, who would press his electric

buttons and allow another client to enter.

Little conversation was taking place. Traffic moved rapidly. It took about half an hour to get from entrance to exit. In that time nearly 100 different girls would each have made two appearances. When a man had worked his way to a place by the exit door, he had the privilege of leaving with the next girl going upstairs or, if he had taken a fancy to some particular female employee during the half hour, he could wait for her. . . .

One paid the five-dollar fee just before going upstairs where there were at least 100 small rooms.

St. John stayed upstairs talking to different girls (paying $10 for each 15 minutes), until Ralph Capone arrived about 4:00 A.M., when he thought it best to leave, making his exit down a fire escape. His story filled an entire issue of the *Cicero Tribune* and led to formation of the Ministers' and Citizens' Association. Its representatives first called on local officials, then on Cook County Sheriff Hoffman and State's Attorney Crowe. Swift repressive legal measures were promised by all. When they were not taken, the Association created an action committee and gave it $1,000, no questions to be asked. The action committee got the money to Hymie Weiss and the O'Banions burned down the new brothel.

Three days later, about 8:30 in the morning, a black limo pulled to a stop beside St. John who was on his way to work. Four men got out of the car and three of them began to beat St. John with blackjacks, taking their orders from the fourth, Ralph Capone. A Cicero policeman stood at each corner of the block while the beating took place.

St. John was in the hospital a week. When he left, he found his bill had been paid by an unknown benefactor with a long scar on his cheek. St. John went to the Cicero police chief to swear out warrants against his assailants and was told to come back to Town Hall the next morning. When he did the chief took him to an empty room on the second floor and left him there.

Al Capone entered the room. He expressed his regrets for the beating; it had been a mistake: his brother and the three other men were returning home from an all-night party and were drunk. "I'm an all right guy," Capone said. "Sure I got a racket. So's everybody. Most guys hurt people. I don't hurt nobody. Only them that get in my way." He said he would especially never hurt a newspaperman: they gave his various enterprises too much free advertising for that. He took out a roll of bills and offered St. John $1,000 for the inconvenience. St. John walked out of the room. He slammed the door, which he later said he regretted doing.

Soon after this meeting, Capone bought out St. John's partners in the *Cicero Tribune*. The crusader no longer had a paper to write for. He left town for a career as an international correspondent and well-respected author of books.

About noon on Saturday May 16, 1925, the ministers'-citizens' vigilantes raided the Hawthorne Smoke Shop gambling resort in Cicero. Capone had spent a hard Friday night into Saturday morning checking on operations and carousing and he arrived from his quarters at the Hawthorne Inn sleep-tousled and wearing a suit coat pulled over silk pajamas. The gambling equipment had been loaded on trucks and a big insurance salesman from Berwyn, Chester Bragg, was guarding the door. Capone shoved against the door and growled, "Let me in. I am the owner of this place."

Inside, Capone confronted the leader of the raid, the Reverend Henry Hoover, a Congregational minister from Berwyn. "Why are you fellows picking on me?" he asked. He ordered his bookkeeper, Leslie Shumway, to take charge of the money and empty the safe. He asked Hoover, "Reverend, can't you and I get together—come to some under-standing? . . . If you will let up on me in Cicero, I'll withdraw from Stickney."

"Mr. Capone," Hoover replied, "the only understanding you and I can have is that you must obey the law or get out of the western suburbs."

The gambling operation was back in business by the middle of that same afternoon. Chester Bragg, the door guard, had his nose broken that afternoon and another of the raiders was also beaten up. A month later this second raider was shot, but after spending a month in the hospital, recovered. The vigilantes disbanded.

But pajama-clad, probably hung-over Al Capone had made an admission that afternoon of May 16 that he would come to regret: "I am the owner of this place."

When John Scalise and Albert Anselmi went on trial for the killing of Detective Olson—killed the day they were stopped while taking their countryman Mike Genna for a ride—their defense was financed by a fund of $100,000 to which most residents of Little Italy contributed, whether they wanted to or not. Raising of the fund was directed by Unione Siciliana president Samoots Amatuna.

The prosecution in the first Scalise-Anselmi trial—headed by State's Attorney Crowe himself—called eyewitnesses who testified to the shooting and identified the defendants as the killers. The young chief defense counsel, Michael J. Ahern, did not attempt to impeach this testimony. Instead, he presented an unusual principle of law for the jury to ponder: "If a policeman detains you," he stated, "even for a moment, against your will, and you kill him, you are not guilty of murder, but only manslaughter. If the policeman uses force of arms, you may kill him in self-defense and emerge from the law unscathed."

The jury brought in a verdict of manslaughter (though the judge in the trial had ruled they could not), specifying 14-year prison sentences. Scalise and Anselmi had still to be tried for the murder of Detective Walsh, and the defense-fund raisers set to work again, but this time without the direction of Samoots Amatuna. Two days before the first trial's verdict was in, the man who had seized the Unione Siciliana presidency coveted by Capone was having his hair cut in preparation for attending a performance of *Aida* that evening. Schemer Drucci and another gunman entered the barber shop, drew their guns, and shot him half a dozen times. He was 26 years old and had served as president not quite a year after succeeding Bloody Angelo. From his hospital bed Samoots tried to marry his childhood sweetheart, but unfortunately died halfway through the ceremony.

A cheese merchant and wholesale grocer became the new president of the Unione:

> Chicago owes much of its progress and its hope of future greatness to the intelligence and industry of its 200,000 Italians, whose rise in prestige and importance is one of the modern miracles of a great city.
>
> No people have achieved so much from such small beginnings, or given so much for what they received in the land of promise to which many of them came penniless. Each life story is a romance, an epic of human accomplishment.
>
> Antonio Lombardo is one of the most outstanding of these modern conquerors. . . . He was one of hundreds who cheered joyously, when, from the deck of the steamer, they saw the Statue of Liberty, and the skyline of New York, their first sight of the fabled land, America. With his fellow countrymen he suffered the hardships and indignities to which the United States subjects its prospective citizens at Ellis Island without complaint, for in his heart was a great hope and a great ambition.
>
> After he had landed he paid his railroad fare to Chicago, and came here with just $12 as his initial capital. . . . Mr. Lombardo, however, accepted the hardships as part of the game, and with confidence in his own ability and assurance of unlimited opportunities, began his career. . . . He became an importer and exporter. . . . Like most successful men, he has received much, but has given more to the community in which he lives. It is to such men that Chicago owes her greatness.

Thus, Tony Lombardo, new president of the Unione, as seen through the eyes of Tony Lombardo and recorded by the pen of Tony Lombardo on his accession to the presidency. Not incidentally, he was a good friend of Al Capone; was, in fact, Capone's advisor in matters of commerce. He also supplied sugar to alky cookers.

In late December Capone went to New York City with his wife

and son. Seven-year-old Albert Francis had a deep mastoid infection and Capone took him to a noted Manhattan specialist. The operation saved Sonny's life but left the boy partially deaf.

As Capone recounted what happened next, "It was Christmas Eve when my wife and I were sent home to get some sleep. We found her folks trimming the Christmas tree for her little nieces and nephews and it broke her up."

The next night, late, "A friend of mine dropped in and asked me to go around the corner to his place and have a glass of beer. My wife told me to go; it would do me good. And we were no sooner there than the door opens and six fellows come in and started shooting. My friend had put me on the spot. In the excitement two of them were killed and one of my fellows was shot in the leg. And I spend the Christmas holidays in jail."

This was, to be sure, not the whole story. For a number of years Frankie Yale had been trying to move out the last of the Irish White Handers who opposed him on the Brooklyn docks. By 1925 he had reduced their forces to a dozen or so. Early in December he learned from a turncoat in the gang that their leader, red-haired, by-now desperate Richard "Pegleg" Lonergan, planned to invade the party that Yale customarily threw on Christmas night in the Adonis Social Club, and kill the host. It may be that Yale asked Capone to come to New York to do a job for him—payback for Yale's usefulness in the matters of Colosimo and O'Banion—or it may be that Capone's presence in NYC for Sonny's operation gave Yale the idea to use his former bouncer. In any event, Capone agreed to Yale's counter-plan, which put at risk his own personal income of at least $10 million a year and his command of the largest bootlegging empire in the United States. . . . Sometimes you don't do what's best to do, you do what you do best.

Capone arrived at the club—in whose basement not too many years before he had sharpened his marksmanship—about midnight. Lonergan and his five gunmen arrived about three hours later. They saw the "MERRY CHRISTMAS AND HAPPY NEW YEAR" banner stretched along one wall, they saw a scattering of partygoers at tables, but few of them were Blackhanders and none of them was Frankie Yale, the party's host. Already quite drunk, the Irish thugs ordered drinks and stood at the bar bantering about "wops" and "dagos" and "guineas," hoping to provoke someone, anyone. When an Irish girl came in with an Italian escort, Pegleg Lonergan—killer of at least 20 men—drunkenly and loudly told her to get herself a "white man."

Capone sat quietly with his group, which included his Brooklyn bodyguard, Frank Galluccio, the man who years before had slashed his face; Al had chosen to forgive him. Then, suddenly, by prearrangement, the lights went off in the club. Shots crashed, women screamed, and tables and chairs were overturned as the Yule-season revelers scrambled for the front door.

When the lights went on again, Lonergan lay dead, a toothpick still between his lips. Beside him near the piano lay one of his gunmen, also dead. Another White Hander was curled dead in the street outside the club, another was found wounded and crawling on his hands and knees down Flushing Avenue. Two of the White Handers had escaped with their lives.

Police arrested the owners of the Adonis Social Club, their four employees, and a man identified by the *Brooklyn Eagle* as "Alphonso Capone, 'bouncer' of the club and an alleged former Chicago gunman." The *New York Times* spelled the name "Caponi" and identified him as the club's "doorman."

No one would testify to anything. The White Hander found crawling down Flushing Avenue maintained he had not been in the club at all; the bullets that hit him had been fired from a passing car. Charges were dropped. Capone and family returned to Chicago.

"Nothing causes a prince to be so much esteemed as great enterprises and giving proof of his prowess."—Niccolo Machiavelli.

Italian-American enterprises, Chicago

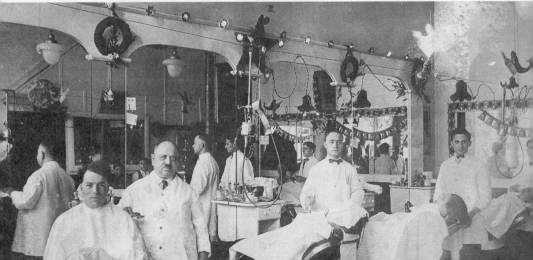

REASONABLE FELLOWS

In 1926 in the big wide world the escape artist and magician Harry Houdini died—unexpectedly. So did the "Great Lover," movie idol Rudolph Valentino (Rodolpho Guglielmi di Valentina d'Antonguolla). So did Orazio "The Scourge" Tropea—in Chicago; was killed, that's to say. Tropea possessed *il malocchio*—the evil eye—and with this occult power was usually able to terrorize his victims without resort to force. But not even il malocchio could save him when his fellow Sicilians discovered that as chief fund raiser for John Anselmi's and Albert Scalisi's second murder trial The Scourge was appropriating a goodly portion of the funds to himself.

So, too, did an assistant state's attorney die unexpectedly in Chicago—in the company of notorious gangsters, prompting a short-lived local burning question: "Who killed McSwiggin and why?" and so, too, did many more, many more, as relentlessly as the gold certificates piled higher in the desk drawers of Capone's office. Capone was a rabid gambler, and a loser at it, but not even his addiction to craps or thoroughbreds could much diminish the stacks of bills that came to him from his control of Chicago vice, gambling, and bootlegging.

John Anselmi and Albert Scalisi went on trial February 10 for the murder eight months before of Detective Walsh when they were pulled over while taking Mike Genna for a last ride. This time State's Attorney Crowe entrusted the prosecution to two assistants (one of them McSwiggin) who declared in their summation, "Either this is a hanging case or a case of justifiable homicide," options that, given the manslaughter verdict in the earlier trial for the death of Detective Olson, left the jury only the conclusion to which it came after three ballots: Not guilty. Detective Walsh's widow said, "My husband and his friend were killed by these men who now have a crowd waiting to shake their hands. I give up." At the champagne banquet for 100 that Capone gave to celebrate the acquittal, Scalisi and Anselmi were joined in their happy caperings by compare Giuseppi Giunta, a hoodlum known as "Hop Toad" because he loved to strut and cavort on the dance floor. The festivities climaxed with a mock gun battle, the celebrants popping champagne corks at each other instead of bullets.

Later that year the Illinois Supreme Court granted Anselmi and Scalisi a retrial for Detective Olson's killing (the jurists considered 14 years excessive for manslaughter) and in June of the next year they were acquitted and released from prison, their jury finding that, as their counsel maintained, they had only defended themselves against "unwarranted police aggression." Given their ultimate fate, the two killers would have been more comfortable serving time.

Frankie McErlane and his partners Polack Joe Saltis and John "Dingbat" Oberta, having cleaned out the South Side O'Donnells for Torrio and Big Al, had gone independent and were now making war on Ralph Sheldon's Ragen's Colts, long-time South Side allies of the Outfit. When McErlane began to use a Thompson submachine gun in his homicides, Capone ordered Tommy guns for his own troops. He also imported 15 Sicilians from New York City to bolster his forces and commissioned a favorite aide, Jack McGurn, to scout local, Chicago talent. McGurn recruited Tony Accardo, Felice DeLucia—later to be known as Paul "The Waiter" Ricca—Murray Humphreys, and Frankie Rio, among others, including at a later time Sam Giancana.

As events in the next several years were to prove, when Capone saw trouble approaching he readied his forces and then seized opportunity as it came, moving on what seemed in retrospect the basis of a long-term objective but as chance provided, but usually moving with violence rather than, as Torrio might have, diplomacy. He left it to the consequences of his actions to prove if he was right or not.

The West Side O'Donnells formed a loose alliance with McErlane, Saltis, and Oberta and began to encroach on Capone's Cicero beer territory. They even opened a book in Cicero, which was a clear instance of offense against the ruler. Capone may have felt not only this but also that if the O'Donnells continued unchecked the O'Banions would find encouragement and incentive for more inroads of their own to the north.

Twenty-five-year-old Bill McSwiggin had worked his way through De Paul University to a law degree and after he passed the bar he was hired by State's Attorney Crowe to exercise his legal skills on behalf of the citizens of Cook County. Honors-level grades and diligent precinct work for Crowe won McSwiggin the appointment, but he soon became locally famous for his adversarial talents as the "Hanging Prosecutor," obtaining seven death penalties from juries in eight months. None of these cases had gangster defendants.

On the evening of April 27, about 7:00, McSwiggin was with his parents at the dining room table of their home at 4946 West Washington

Boulevard when an old neighborhood pal, Tom "Red" Duffy, called for him. Duffy, a precinct captain, was a West Side O'Donnell beer-runner and gambler but the Irish stuck together in the neighborhood, no matter on which side of the law they stood. McSwiggin told his parents, with whom he lived (his father was a Chicago police sergeant), "We're going out to Cicero to drink a little good beer." (Ten days before, McSwiggin had gone out to Cicero to confer with Al Capone at the Hawthorne Inn. His father later claimed he knew what was discussed but said, "If I told, I'd blow the lid off Chicago.")

In the car waiting outside were Myles O'Donnell and another of McSwiggin's boyhood friends, Jim Doherty, the O'Donnells' ace gunman. McSwiggin had just the year before unsuccessfully prosecuted this pair for the gangland murder of Eddie Tancl and his bartender. Also in the back seat with Myles was his brother, Klondike, the leader of the West Siders. Duffy, the O'Donnells, and Doherty had spent the day as ballot watchers in the County Building for State's Attorney Crowe in a confirming recount of a Crowe victory in the April 13 primary election. As they left the building Klondike said, "We'll adjourn to Cicero and brace up on some good beer. I know it's good because I delivered it myself." A Capone stooge at the County Building overheard this boast and telephoned Capone at the Hawthorne Inn to report it. On their way to Cicero Duffy, Doherty, and the O'Donnells picked up McSwiggin.

Following the phone call from his informant, Capone gave his orders: A lead car would precede his sedan to ram any police flivvers encountered; two cars would follow his to block traffic at intersections if need be; a fifth car would stage an accident to halt traffic if his sedan was pursued.

After an hour of patient trailing from tavern to tavern, the 30-man Capone motorcade was a block from the O'Donnell car when it stopped in front of the Pony Inn, a saloon situated on an otherwise empty lot at 5613-15 Roosevelt Road. As McSwiggin, Doherty and Duffy got out of their car, Capone's flotilla approached slowly from the east on the darkening road and then Capone and three others in his sedan opened fire. Hit by five bullets, Duffy staggered from the parkway into the vacant lot. Doherty fell to the sidewalk with 16 bullets in his chest and legs, and McSwiggin stumbled to the Pony Inn's entrance before falling, 20 slugs in his back and neck. Myles and Klondike O'Donnell had gone to the car's floorboards as soon as the shooting began. When Capone's sedan roared away they got out of the car and dragged Doherty and McSwiggin into it.

A passing motorist saw Red Duffy propped against a tree and took him to a west suburban hospital. "Pretty cold-blooded to leave me lying there," Duffy said. He died early in the morning. Doherty and McSwiggin died on the drive to Klondike's house. The brothers carried

McSwiggin's body into the house and cut the identifying marks from his clothes and emptied his pockets. Then they drove his and Doherty's bodies to a prairie in Berwyn and dumped the boyhood pals there. They abandoned the car in Oak Park, five fedoras and McSwiggin's glasses inside, and were not seen again for a month. Capone went into hiding in Indiana for three months.

The bodies of McSwiggin and Doherty were found about 10:00 o'clock but it was midnight before a Chicago newspaper reporter recognized McSwiggin's as one of two newly arrived corpses. The morning headlines screamed shock and outrage. State's Attorney Crowe vowed that "It will be war to the hilt against these gangsters." He offered a reward of $5,000 of his own money for information leading to the arrest of the killers. The newspapers began their daily refrain: "Who killed McSwiggin and why?"

Crowe's detectives were told to arrest known gangsters on sight. The State's Attorney then had the Cook County sheriff deputize 100 Chicago detectives for duty; they were sent into the suburbs to raid speakeasies, brothels, gambling houses, and saloons, arrest girls, smash slots, roulette wheels, crap tables, beer barrels, cases of liquor—and Crowe himself led a raiding party into Capone's stronghold, Cicero. The Hawthorne Smoke Shop there was among the places raided. Along with other items seized in it, three ledgers were confiscated and taken to the State's Attorney's office. There they were tossed into a file cabinet in a storeroom and there they rested for four years. Then they were accidentally found by a U.S. Treasury agent and—linked with Capone's anger-prompted admission that "I am the owner of this place"—the existence of one of them came to prove much more than an embarrassment.

Most of the police agreed with McSwiggin's father: "Those shots were never meant for my boy," but the *Chicago Tribune* wanted to know who fired the shots. A week after the murders it reported angrily that "The police have no more actual evidence as to the motives of the shooting and the identity of the killer than they did when it happened." In response, Crowe issued a statement: "It has been established to the satisfaction of the state's attorney's office and the detective bureau that Capone in person led the slayers of McSwiggin. . . . It has also been found that Capone handled the machine gun, being compelled to this act in order to set an example of fearlessness to his less eager companions."

The deputized city detectives ransacked and partially destroyed 25 of Capone's suburban whorehouses, speaks, and gambling houses, including his largest brothel, the Stockade in Forest View—Caponeville. The night after the raid there, three carloads of citizen vigilantes burned the Stockade to the ground. Fire companies from Berwyn and other western suburbs came to the scene and wet down the roofs of nearby homes. Urged to save the Stockade, they said they couldn't spare the water.

Three grand juries investigated the murders but brought no indictments. Capone came out of hiding and surrendered himself to Crowe on July 28. The big man was voluble. He said he had fled Chicago because he feared police would shoot him on sight. "I've been convicted without a hearing of all the crimes on the calendar. But I'm innocent and it won't take long to prove it. I trust my attorneys to see that I'm treated like a human being and not pushed around by a lot of coppers with axes to grind."

Did he kill McSwiggin by mistake?

"Of course I didn't kill him. Why should I? I like the kid. Only the day before he was up to my place and when he went home I gave him a bottle of Scotch for his old man. . . ."

In the course of his ramblings he made a remark that put the matter into a different perspective. "I paid McSwiggin," he told reporters. "I paid him a lot and I got what I paid for."

At the Federal Building two days later he continued. "McSwiggin was my friend. Doherty and Duffy were my friends, too. I wasn't out to get them. Why, I used to lend Doherty money. Bighearted Al, I was just helping out a friend. . . ."

An assistant state's attorney withdrew the murder charge against him—"Subsequent investigation could not legally substantiate the information"—and the case was dismissed. McSwiggin's father said, "They pinned a medal on him and turned him loose." As a sergeant in the bureau of detectives, the father had his own underworld sources and he named the killers: Capone, his bodyguard Frank Rio, and gunmen Frank Diamond and Bob McCullough.

A fourth grand jury interrupted its deliberations to indict Joe Saltis, Dingbat Oberta, and Frank "Lefty" Koncil for the murder of John "Mitters" Foley, a Ragen's Colts' hoodlum, but could uncover no evidence sufficient to support an indictment in McSwiggin's murder. The judge presiding over a fifth grand jury said, "I believe I know who killed McSwiggin and Sergeant McSwiggin probably knows. But we need evidence." A sixth grand jury found no more than its five predecessors had and the investigation was finally closed; it could give no official answer to the question of who killed McSwiggin or why. Its four months of inquiry had cost Cook County taxpayers $200,000. The killing of McSwiggin may have been a mistake, but after it the West Side O'Donnells gave Capone no further trouble. And because of it State's Attorney Crowe had to abandon his plans for becoming the political boss of Cook County, plans he had set in motion with an eclipse of Big Bill Thompson's fortunes; the public felt that Crowe had whitewashed the investigation of the circumstances of his young assistant's death.

"They killed me, too," McSwiggin's father would say, "when they killed my boy." A story circulated that the broken-hearted father went to

Cicero and confronted Capone in the Hawthorne Inn and called him a murderer. Whereupon Capone drew his automatic and handed it to Sergeant McSwiggin, saying "If you think I did it, shoot me." A pretty story but security was too tight at the Inn for it to have happened.

Roger Touhy, a thriving independent bootlegger whose territory lay to the west and northwest of the city, heard a more likely tale in prison years later, after he was railroaded there by the Outfit. It seems two detectives walked Capone into a room in which Sergeant McSwiggin waited. They left Capone there with the understanding that the sergeant would kill him; self-defense would be the plea and all concerned were sure it would prevail.

". . . They walked Capone in. But at the last minute Sergeant McSwiggin lost his nerve. He was just too decent a guy to shoot a man, even Capone, in cold blood."

Two weeks after Capone's return to Chicago, his enemies Hymie Weiss and Schemer Drucci had an appointment to meet Morris Eller, a trustee of the Metropolitan sanitary District, and John Sbarbaro, an undertaker, and assistant state's attorney, and a gangland favorite (he had buried Dion O'Banion), in the new, 19-story Standard Oil Building at 910 South Michigan Avenue. As Weiss and Drucci approached the building's entrance four men ran toward them and began shooting. Drucci ducked behind a curbside mailbox, Weiss dove to the side walk, and they returned the fire. Windows were blown out and concrete chips flew from buildings; an office clerk was pinked in the leg. Both sides ran out of ammunition as a police patrol rattled up. The four gunmen turned and fled to their car parked across Michigan Avenue. Three of them made it and sped away; the fourth, a Capone gunman, was left behind. Weiss had found refuge in the lobby of the Standard Oil Building but Drucci tried to flee on the running board of a passing car and was collared by the police. He denied ever having seen the Capone gunman before. "It was a stickup, that's all," he said. "They were after my roll." Drucci was carrying $13,200 in cash.

Just five days later he and Weiss were driving south on Michigan Avenue when a car behind them pulled alongside and rammed theirs and shot out its windows. Firing back, Weiss and the Schemer jumped out of their car and ran into the lobby of the conveniently once-again-at-hand Standard Oil building as the attacking car drove away.

A week before the first Standard Oil Building shootout, the body of Capone's chauffeur, Tommy Ross, had been found burned with cigars and matches, trussed with wire, and shot five times in the head. The body had been weighted with bricks and dropped into a cistern. "They call me heartless, eh?" Capone said. "Ross was tortured to make him tell my business secrets. He knew nothing whatever about my affairs." . . . What he did know was Capone's daily routine.

A little after 1:00 P.M. on September 20, five weeks after the second attack on Weiss and Drucci, Capone was having a cup of after-lunch coffee with his bodyguard Frankie Rio at the rear of Cicero's Hawthorne Restaurant. Both men looked up quickly when they heard the staccato sound of a machine gun. The sound grew louder as what appeared to be a gong-clanging Chicago detective bureau's car sped past the restaurant's windows, then faded away. Capone stood and started toward the restaurant's double doors. Rio tackled him, knocking him to the floor. A block behind the lead car came ten others.

This 11-car caravan had traveled from the north side of Chicago to Cicero on Austin Boulevard, at the outer limits of Chicago. As it traveled south, Chicago police patrols brought their flivvers to a stop on side streets and watched it pass, knowing where it was going and what it intended. When it got to Cicero it turned east down Twenty-second Street, a wide boulevard centered on a double-tracked trolley line, and as it approached the 4800 block the lead car accelerated to 50 mph and began sounding a gong as a lone machine gunner in it began firing blanks, the feint that drew Capone toward the restaurant's doors.

Rio held his chief to the floor as the next ten cars, spaced at car lengths, slowed to 15 mph and opened fire with live ammunition. When the first of the ten cars came abreast of the Hawthorne Restaurant, the procession came to a stop, one by one, bumper to bumper, and its machine gunners opened fire into the Anton Hotel next to the Hawthorne Inn, into a barber shop, a deli, a laundry, and the Hawthorne Beauty Shop, but especially into the Hawthorne Restaurant and the lobby of Capone's headquarters, the Hawthorne Inn. Plaster and glass and splinters of paneling went flying, neat rows of bullet holes stitched themselves at waist level into walls.

When this firing ceased, a man in brown overalls got out of the next-to-last car and walked briskly to the door of the Inn, knelt there, and with his Thompson submachine gun began to spray the lobby, moving his gun's barrel methodically from left to right, right to left. Men with shotguns from the eleventh car stood on the sidewalk and kept watch over the kneeling gunner. When he finished he rose and went back to his car, the shotgunners to theirs, and at a signal of three honks of a car horn the caravan moved off toward Chicago's wind-blown streets.

Police estimated that at least 1,000 shells were fired. The side-walks had been crowded, the restaurant full, yet there were, surprisingly, few casualties. A man and his five-year-old son were grazed; his wife was shot in the arm but not seriously, though a shard of glass lodged in her eye; and a Capone mobster who lived in the Inn was nicked in the neck and shoulder. By coincidence he turned out to be the Capone gunman police had detained at the first Standard Oil Building shootout, the gunman Schemer Drucci had never seen before. Police took him to headquarters and brought in Weiss, Drucci, Moran, and Peter Gusenberg, one of three brothers who were O'Banions. (Earlier in the year the fanatical O'Banion Louis Alterie had been banished to his Colorado ranch by his fellow mobsters because of his increasingly erratic ways.) "Never seen them before," Capone's gunman said.

Speaking to reporters about the raid—dubbed "The Bootleg Battle of the Marne" by the newspapers—Capone said, "It has shown the authorities that I have no corner on the machine gun market. . . . Why, I'm still paying owners of automobiles parked in front for the damage done to their cars in that raid, and I am trying to save the eye of the poor innocent woman they wounded sitting in a car in front. I have paid all her expenses and the best doctors have been engaged to care for her." He also paid shopkeepers for damage done to their places of business. As one of his men said, "The Big Fellow never wants bystanders to get hurt."

The Big Fellow had Unione Siciliana president Lombardo call Weiss and arrange an October 4 meeting at the Sherman Hotel to discuss terms for peace. (In February the Unione's name had been officially changed to Italo-American National Union.) It was underworld lore that the only man Capone ever feared was the 28-year-old intense and deadly Hymie Weiss. Lombardo represented Capone at the meeting. He offered the O'Banions exclusive rights to the sale of beer in all of Chicago north of Madison Street. Weiss said that was not enough; his minimum price for peace was the bodies of Anselmi and Scalisi, Deanie's killers. Lombardo phoned Capone with these terms. "I wouldn't do that to a yellow dog," was the response and a coldly angry Weiss walked out of the meeting.

Weiss used the rooms above Schofield's at 738 North State—O'Banion's old florist shop—as his office. On October 8 a man calling himself Oscar Lundin moved into a second-floor front room at 740, next door north of Schofield's, and a woman signing herself Mrs. Thomas Schultz rented a third-floor room at 1 Superior Street, which intersected State just south of the florist shop. From her room, both the front and rear entrances of Schofield's could be seen. "Oscar Lundin" then mysteriously disappeared and his room was taken over by a man who wore a grey fedora and a grey overcoat and a man wearing a cap and a dark suit. "Mrs. Schultz" also vanished, her room taken by two men who were said to have the look of Sicilians; the identification assumed that ethnic origin can be ascertained by physiognomy, but it was probably correct.

Hymie Weiss spent most of October 11 in the Criminal Court Building where the jury was being chosen for the murder trial of Polack Joe Saltis and Lefty Frank Koncil. (Oberta had been granted a separate trial.) The word was that Weiss had $100,000 to spend for acquittal. He left the courtroom that afternoon with his driver, Sammy Peller, and a small-time bootlegger, Paddy Murray, to go to his office. They parked on Superior, as did the car containing Saltis' chief defense attorney, William W. O'Brien, and Benjamin Jacobs, a low-level pol in Morris Eller's 20th Ward and an investigator for O'Brien. The five men started across State and when they were almost at the curb in front of Schofield's, machine gun fire and shotgun blasts erupted from the second-floor window at 740. Paddy Murray fell instantly dead. Weiss staggered to the sidewalk with ten slugs in him. Hit four times, attorney O'Brien crawled into a stairwell. Peller, shot in the groin, and Jacobs, limping from a leg wound, lurched back toward Superior around the south corner of Holy Name Cathedral, which faced Schofield's. A machine gun fusillade followed them, chipping half the letters from the inscription on the cornerstone of the cathedral: "A.D. 1874—AT THE NAME OF JESUS EVERY KNEE SHOULD BOW—THOSE THAT ARE IN HEAVEN AND THOSE ON EARTH."

Weiss died at Henrotin Hospital. A complete list of the veniremen called for jury duty in the Saltis-Koncil trial was found in his pockets along with $5,200 in cash. In the second-floor room at 740 State police found 35 empty machine-gun cartridges, three empty shotgun shells, hundreds of cigarette butts around the chairs at the window, and a grey fedora with a label from a Cicero haberdashery near the Hawthorne Inn. Searching the neighborhood, they found a Tommy gun on top of a dog kennel a block to the south at 12 West Huron.

At the Hawthorne Inn Capone, in shirtsleeves and slippers, dispensed cigars and drinks to reporters and was regretful:

> "That was butchery. Hymie was a good kid. . . . When we were in business together in the old days, I got to know him well and used to go often to his room for a friendly visit. . . . Right after Torrio was shot—and Torrio knew who shot him—I had a talk with Weiss. 'What do you want to do, get yourself killed before you're thirty?' I said to him 'You'd better get some sense while a few of us are left alive.' . . . Who wants to be tagged around night and day by guards? I don't, for one. There was, and there is, plenty of business for us all and competition needn't be matter of murder, anyway. But Weiss couldn't be told anything. I suppose you couldn't have told him a week ago that he'd be dead today. There are some reasonable fellows in his outfit, and if they want peace, I'm for it now, as I have always been."

Chicago Police Chief Collins was not regretful. "I don't want to encourage the business," he said, "but if somebody has to be killed, it's a good thing the gangsters are murdering themselves off. It saves trouble for the police."

Weiss was buried out of Sbarbaro's funeral parlor. (Placards on cars in the cortege asked for votes for Sbarbaro, who was running for municipal judge.) Hymie was buried with his rosary and his automatic.

He left his heirs almost 1.5 million dollars.

A period of peace came about through a somewhat involved chain of events. In early May of 1924 Frankie McErlane—fat, pig-eyed Frankie McErlane—was drinking in a Crown Point, Indiana, bar. His drinking companions began to twit him that he was too drunk to shoot straight. Determined to prove them wrong, McErlane drew his gun and shot a man at the other end of the bar through the head. He fled to Illinois and because Governor Small was not one to quickly extradite an Illinois citizen he was not arrested until almost two years after the murder, and then he was held in an Illinois jail until August. (A year later an Indiana jury acquitted him after a witness was beaten to death with a hammer and surviving witnesses changed their testimony.)

But the incarceration of McErlane in the summer of 1926 meant that his partners Saltis and Oberta had to do their own killing. In August Saltis dispatched the Sheldon beer pusher, Mitters Foley, giving him two barrels in the chest as he lay sprawled on the pavement, having tripped trying to flee. Two witnesses saw him do it and placed his partner Oberta and his driver Koncil at the scene.

After Weiss was killed, Saltis began to sweat. He was probably safe in jail until he was acquitted—which he was fairly certain he would be given the arrangements that had been made—but once he was a free man again he would be subject to retribution from Capone now that his alliance with Weiss and the O'Banions had come into the open. He consulted his partner Oberta who went to see Maxie Eisen who was close to the O'Banions yet with enough distance to be on fairly good terms with Capone as well. Eisen, a fish and meat market racketeer who also collected protection from Chicago's pushcart peddlers and ragpickers, was well spoken of in the underworld as a crafty thinker. He met with Antonio Lombardo on October 16 with a proposal for a peace parley. The two men contacted the involved parties and a meeting was set for October 20 in the Sherman Hotel: principals only, no guns, no bodyguards.

A detective from the Chief of Police's office sat in on the meeting, which was chaired by Eisen, with Lombardo at his side. In attendance were some 30 high-up gangsters, chief among them Capone and Jake Guzik; Schemer Drucci and Bugs Moran; accountant and whoremaster Jack Zuta; Myles and Klondike O'Donnell; Ralph Sheldon, leader of Ragen's Colts; Roger Touhy, baron of the northwest suburbs: a board of millionaire directors.

Eisen, representing Saltis, McErlane, and Oberta, opened the meeting with "Let's give each other a break. We're a bunch of saps, killing each other this way and giving the cops a laugh." After this theme-setting opener, Capone and his program dominated the meeting. His five-point treaty was adopted without argument. Essentially it provided:

1) General amnesty; the past was to be considered over and done with.

2) Arbitration to be substituted for violence in settling disputes.

3) No more "ribbing," that is, one gang trying to get another in trouble with a third.

4) No more stealing customers; gangs would stay within their assigned territories. (These to be nearly those Torrio had established; thus, Capone came away with the lion's share.)

5) The head of each gang to punish violations committed by any member of his own gang.

The meeting closed in a spirit of good will, almost jubilation—though Bugs Moran had reservations—and adjourned to Diamond Joe Esposito's Bella Napoli Café for a feast and celebration. Much chianti was drunk, much grisly humor was displayed concerning torture, past killings and near-killings, many sentimental speeches were given.

Speaking to reporters later, Capone recalled that

"I told them we're making a shooting gallery out of a great business, and nobody's profiting by it. It's hard and dangerous work, aside from any hate at all, and when a fellow works hard at any line of business he wants to go home and forget it. He don't want to be afraid to sit near a window or open a door. . . .

"I wanted to stop all that because I couldn't stand hearing my little kid ask why I didn't stay home. I had been living at the Hawthorne Inn for 14 months. He's been sick for three years—mastoid infection and operations—and I've got to take care of him and his mother. If it wasn't for him, I'd have said 'To hell with you fellows. We'll shoot it out.' But I couldn't say that, knowing it might mean they'd bring me home some night punctured with machine gun fire. And I couldn't see why those fellows would want to die that way either."

In early November Saltis and Koncil were acquitted and the separate pending trial of Oberta was taken off the court calendar. "I expected a different verdict on the evidence presented," the judge said. But in the minds of 12 good men and true, guilt had not been established beyond a reasonable doubt, apparently.

Big Bill Thompson

ZENITH

After jumping ship from his 1923 voyage to search for the fabled tree-climbing fish (mudskippers—specimens of which Chicago's Field Museum had already had for some years), William Hale Thompson returned to Illinois where before too long the ex-mayor was deep-sixed, so to say, by his one-time devoted ally, Governor Len Small, because Thompson went to Springfield and challenged the governor publicly. It is always a mistake to use both feet to test the depth of unknown waters.

Shorn of his patronage and thus without a power base, Thompson entrained for Palm Beach to vacation and nurse his wounds. But shortly after he and his wife registered at their hotel, it burned down, and with it went their wardrobes and other belongings. Fortune was proving not just fickle, but downright malicious.

Once back in Chicago, Big Bill attempted to recoup politically by attempting an alliance with his old enemy, U.S. Senator Deneen, but was rebuffed. Next he approached his on-again, off-again supporter and present rival for leadership of Cook County Republicans, State's Attorney Robert E. Crowe, who consented only because he needed help with the ticket he was trying to put together—especially after his candidate for county treasurer, Sheriff Peter Hoffman, was caught coddling the gangsters Lake and Druggan. In a cold house, Thompson and Crowe each found a warm body—the other's.

Looking to the primary, Big Bill began making flamboyant speeches attacking his enemies. The appeal he most frequently voiced to the local electorate, however, was international—"America First! No World Court!" to which end he endorsed Frank L. Smith for U.S. Senator. Crowe was backing the incumbent, McKinley.

Thompson's long-ago Svengali, now bitter foe, the Poor Swede, Fred Lundin, ignored him until Big Bill's attention-getting tirades forced him to counterattack. Then, too, Governor Small had given Lundin the state patronage in Cook County and Small expected Lundin to do

217

something to protect him.

One week before the primary Thompson replied with what is conceded by political-science savants to be among all-time lows in 20th-century campaigning, his "Rat Show." He paused during a speech and two caged rats were brought on stage and placed on a table close to the podium. Pointing a quivering, accusing finger at one of them, Thompson addressed it as "Doc"—Dr. John Dill Robertson, a Lundin favorite. The other rodent turned out to be Lundin himself. Thompson told his appreciative listeners that he had started with six rats but Fred and Doc had eaten the smaller four.

"This one here on the left is Doc. I can tell him because he hadn't had a bath for 20 years until we washed him yesterday. But we did wash him and he doesn't smell like a billy goat any longer."

Next addressing the caged rodent on the right as "Fred" in equally plain-spoken terms, he concluded his tribute to Lundin: "I know that for many years you have been referred to as 'The Fox' in politics. But now I think this justifies my saying that your moniker ought not to be 'The Fox' but 'The Rat.' "

Two days later Thompson devoted most of a speech to attacking the King of England. Among many other crimes he found George V guilty of was the curse of Prohibition. "I shouldn't be surprised if the King had something to do with slipping over the Volstead Act on us so that all their distillers can make fortunes selling us bootleg liquor." He made a promise: "If George comes to Chicago, I'll punch him in the snoot."

His candidate Smith won in the primary by almost 200,000 votes. Then, within two weeks, one of State's Attorney Crowe's young assistants was murdered outside a Cicero saloon and Crowe had to try to find a half-way acceptable answer to the question, "Who killed McSwiggin and why?" or forfeit his bid for party leadership. As we know, he didn't find it. Pity, because by marriage he was allied with the Cuneos, a powerful Italian family in Chicago. Which could explain a few of his many nole prosequis.

The summer saw Senate hearings begin on the Smith-McKinley contest. Testimony taken from a sneering, tight-lipped Samuel Insull, the utilities and traction magnate, and from two other utilities executives who did business in Illinois, disclosed that Frank L. Smith, while chairman of the Illinois Commerce Commission, which regulated public utilities, had accepted $170,000 from them for his Senate campaign. (Ultimately, Smith was denied a Senate seat because taking such a huge sum from the utilities was deemed "contrary to sound public policy, harmful to the dignity and honor of the Senate," and "dangerous to the perpetuity of free government." Within just a few decades, of course, the Senate discovered that, quite to the contrary, what this country *needs* is the best Congress big money can buy. Participatory democracy it is called.)

Thompson sailed on. In mid-October he held a rally for himself at the Medinah Temple. After the audience of 5,000 was entertained by the Last of the Red-Hot Mommas, nightclub singer Sophie Tucker, and edified by fulsome tributes from Thompson's political cronies, it was addressed by Big Bill himself. Yes, he would agree to run for mayor again—provided that his friends were able to get 125,000 pledge cards signed for his candidacy. (Let the voice of the people be heard!)

At the Hotel Sherman in December he was presented with not 125,000, not 225,000, not 325,000, but 433,000 signed pledge cards. A supporter snatched the grey sombrero from Big Bill's head and flung it onto the pledge cards. "In behalf of the voters of Chicago," he cried exultantly, "I throw your hat into the ring!"

Thompson's platform had two major, and apparently equally important, planks: (1) getting rid of Mayor Dever's superintendent of schools, William McAndrew, whom Thompson had discovered to be King George's lackey, a "pro-British rat" who was "poisoning the wells of historical truth"; and (2) overturning Dever's reform policy, that is, Dever's attempts to enforce the Volstead Act.

It was about this time that Al Capone's interest in the forth-coming primary increased. He began to contribute heavily to Big Bill's campaign chest and from his suite in Chicago's Metropole Hotel his emissaries—Daniel Serritella, a First Ward politico, Morris Eller, 20th Ward boss, and Jack Zuta, whoremaster and accountant—wore a path to Thompson's headquarters in the Sherman.

In December, however, Capone's attention was diverted from the primary race when Polack Joe Saltis had a Sheldon beer runner killed. The period of peace had lasted 76 days—two and a half months. After Capone's orders for the retaliatory execution of Lefty Koncil and another Saltis henchman were carried out, Saltis gave no more trouble to the Outfit; he semi-retired to his lodge in Wisconsin.

The O'Banions, who had chafed under the pact's restraints, made a hostile move before the Saltis killings. Capone and Theodore "The Greek" Anton, owner of the restaurant above the Hawthorne Smoke Shop, used to like to sit in a back booth of the restaurant and schmooze. Anton often told the story of the bitter-cold winter night a newsboy came in and Capone called him over. "How many papers you got left, kid?" (Papers cost 2¢ each.) "About 50." Capone gave the boy $20 and told him, "Throw them on the floor and run along home to your mother."

Anton, who was going to retire, and Capone were enjoying each other's company in a back booth late the night of January 6, 1927. Anton was called to the front of his restaurant to deal with a customer. That was the last he was seen until his body was found in quicklime. It was said that when Capone realized Anton was not going to return that night, or any other, he sat on in their booth for an hour, sobbing.

Thompson had two opponents in the Republican primary race: Lundin's candidate, Doc Robertson, and Senator Deneen's candidate, Edward R. Litsinger, who attacked Big Bill on many fronts, one of them being the $2.7 million in fees paid by the city to real estate experts in 1920 during Thompson's administration. (On behalf of taxpayers, the *Chicago Tribune* was suing Thompson on that same score.)

Of Robertson, Thompson said, ". . . I'm not descending to personalities, but you should watch Doc Robertson eating in a restaurant—eggs in his whiskers, soup on his vest. It's enough to turn your stomach. . . ."

Of Litsinger, ". . . I'm not a mud-slinger, but the papers

have been saying things about me that I can't let pass. And Ed Litsinger's been making statements about me. I've told you and I tell you again that he's the biggest liar that ever was a candidate for mayor. And you know what else? He plays handball in the semi-nude! That's right, with only a little pair of pants on. I know one thing. You won't find Bill Thompson having his picture taken in the semi-nude. . . ."

This last avowal may have been due as much to the 245 paunchy pounds his once athletic frame now carried as to a sense of propriety. At any rate, Thompson's peculiar brand of rhetoric was approved of by Chicagoans; he defeated the nearest of his two opponents, Litsinger, by a margin of 180,000 votes, the largest ever in a Chicago mayoral Republican primary.

Running in the general election against reform incumbent Mayor Dever—"Dever and Decency"—Thompson made his first campaign speech in the Eighth Regiment Armory, drill hall for the city's black troops, before a cheering audience of 6,000 South Siders.

While Thompson had been on a pre-campaign vacation in Georgia, and after Dever's campaign manager had calculated that 45,000 of Thompson's primary votes were from the South Side, the police were sent to raid the South Side's Second and Third Wards. One thousand black gamblers, saloon and speakeasy keepers, and whores had been jailed over a weekend. Police also invaded private homes.

"We stand for America First! We stand for Old Glory!" Thompson told his Armory audience. Then, ". . . You have been patient as I asked you to be. You have accepted your persecution. When the time comes we'll show this Cossack mayor that he's up against a buzz saw and a buzz saw isn't any joke!"

He looked out at the crowd, waved his cigar and gave a conspiratorial grin.

"I don't say that these arrests wouldn't have taken place if I had been here. But I sent out word when I got back to get those star numbers and I notice that nobody has been arrested since. . . .

"Elect me and I'll turn the police from sneaking under the mattresses of your homes, looking for a little evidence of a minor infraction of the Volstead Act, to driving the crooks out."

Leaving the meeting he bent to embrace the nephew of one of his chief South Side backers. Dever's campaign manager immediately had tens of thousands of cartoon-flyers printed showing Thompson kissing black children under the question: "Do You Want Negroes or White Men to Run Chicago? Bye, Bye, Blackbirds!" The flyers were used by Dever's backers throughout the rest of the campaign.

Thompson exhorted his audiences to ". . . remember what George Washington said. He said, 'Keep out of foreign wars and make the King of England keep his nose out of our affairs!' "

A Dever advisor thought he knew why Thompson campaigned against a monarch who ruled from a throne four time zones distant from Chicago: "Some think it is due to a brainstorm, but we don't. We think it is because he hopes to win German and Irish and Polish votes and raise class distinctions in the minds of workingmen who he thinks hate the very mention of kings."

It was equally possible that, as a former speechwriter for Thompson charged, he was using leftovers. "I wrote those speeches when he was running for senator in 1918," said the former speechwriter. "Thompson didn't even know George Washington wrote a Farewell Address until I dug it up and brought it to him."

Poor Swede Lundin also claimed that Thompson's anti-royalty theme harked back to the 1918 senatorial campaign. According to Lundin, Thompson had back then asked Lundin what he meant by "America First!" Lundin answered by telling Thompson that the American people were supporting the rotten government of King Peter. "Who's King Peter?" Thompson asked. "He's the rotten monarch of Serbia." To which, Lundin claimed, Thompson responded by asking, "Fred, what is Serbia, or where is it?"

Dever asked his audiences to "Think of Chicago's future. Let the other fellow have the vaudeville and the clowning and the billingsgate. . . . Think of the best interests of our city and think upon matters of government." He posed rhetorical questions for his opponent: Hadn't Samuel Insull contributed to Thompson's campaign? Wasn't it true that Thompson was a "tool of the transit lines?" "Isn't it a fact that through your former corporation counsel, Samuel Ettleson, you were always in touch with the public utility companies?"

Thompson, who had accused Dever and Decency of running a racist campaign with its "Bye, Bye, Blackbirds" flyers (to which Dever responded, "I don't know what ails this man"), counterattacked by intensifying his vilification of Superintendent of Schools McAndrew and reaffirming his own, personal dedication to America's tradition of individual freedom and liberty by bellowing to cheering Chicago crowds, "I'm wetter than the middle of the Atlantic Ocean!"

A reporter capsuled the situation in Chicago with the observation that "Thompson's for America First and Capone's for America's Thirst."

The day before the election, one-time O'Banion stalwart Schemer Drucci pushed into a Dever alderman's office with several other hoodlums. Not finding the alderman, whom they'd hoped to kidnap and hold until after the election, they wrecked the premises. Detectives caught up with Drucci at the Hotel Bellaire. In a transfer to the Criminal Courts Building, Drucci and Detective Daniel Healy—who had once beaten up Polack Joe Saltis—got into a shoving match and Healy drew his gun, saying "You call me that again and I'll let you have it."

The scuffle continued inside the car, Drucci telling Healy, "You take your gun off me or I'll kick hell out of you." As Healy got out of the car when it stopped, Drucci yelled at him, "I'll fix you!" and lunged for Healy's gun. Healy shot the Schemer four times at point-blank range. Drucci died on the way to County Hospital.

"I don't know anything about anyone being murdered," the chief of detectives said. "I do know Drucci was killed trying to take a gun away from an officer. We're having a medal struck for Healy." (Drucci was given an elaborate funeral out of Sbarbaro's Funeral Home. Bugs Moran sent a modest wreath with a card that said: "Our pal." Moran was now the leader of the North Side remnants of O'Banion's forces.)

Capone let his stubble grow in mourning but shed no tears. A month before, Big Al had gone to Arkansas for a short vacation at Hot Springs. Parties unknown overtook his car and tried to kill him while he was crossing the mountains. Capone survived the attack by throwing himself out of his car and rolling down a slope to cover. Rumors had circulated that Schemer Drucci was one of the assailants.

The election on April 5 was peaceful, perhaps due to the calming influence of the 5,000 police who patrolled the streets and polling places—though their presence did not prevent Capone's gunmen from carrying out their Thompsonite duties at the polls. Big Bill's final margin of victory was 83,072 votes out of 993,616 cast—and there was wild rejoicing at the Sherman that night. "Tell 'em, cowboys, tell 'em!" Thompson bellowed through a megaphone. "I told you I'd ride 'em high and wide!"

Their hero had been vindicated, and some 1,500 of the most whiskey-laden celebrants left the Sherman and gathered at Belmont Harbor to the north, where the schooner that was the official clubhouse (and speakeasy) of Thompson's popular Fish Fans Club lay tied. Stomping and cheering, so many crowded onto the vessel that it quietly settled to the bottom, effectively disbanding for all time the Fish Fans Club, but happily without loss of a single life at sea. An omen perhaps. Perhaps a paradigm. . . . Or possibly nothing but an overburdened-by-drunks ship sinking in Belmont Harbor; not the first or the last.

The humorist and sage Will Rogers commented on the Chicago election: "They was trying to beat Bill with the better element vote. The trouble with Chicago is that there ain't much better element."

On Thompson's victory, Capone—who had anted up $260,000 for Big Bill's campaign—expanded from his single suite at the Metropole Hotel at 2300 South Michigan (where once Thompson and his pal Gene Pike had lived) to the occupancy of two entire floors and rooms on several others and moved his central command post from Cicero's Hawthorne Inn to the Metropole, using the Hawthorne thereafter only for meetings with politicians and police officials. A block from City Hall, at Clark and Madison, he established offices for his Cook County gambling network, Jake Guzik and Jimmy Mondi in charge. (Mont Tennes had retired from the gambling scene in 1923 under pressure from the Dever administration.) Forty percent of the gambling gross in Cook County was the Outfit's take in dives it did not itself operate.

Throughout most of the decade of the Roaring Twenties, the Outfit (two or three dozen men at the top, well less than a thousand below them) almost totally controlled the city of 3,000,000. The Outfit was able to do this because it paid the police and politicians and judges to do its bidding. Who pays well is served well. Dever's reform administration did not even hold the gangsters in check; two-thirds of his police force remained on Capone's payroll.

Hundreds and hundreds of thousands of lunch-pail workers—the "people"—got up at dawn, labored till dusk, nine to ten hours a day once they got to their place of work, half a day at least on Saturdays, and come payday pocketed 35 or 45 dollars (tops) and went home to their families just after the time most of the gangsters were going to work. And the city's merchants, bankers, industrialists, financiers—serious, honorable men of good character—for the most part looked on and what they saw was good in their eyes. Or at least tolerable. For long after other sins grow old, avarice remains young.

The Outfit's control emboldened other, lesser criminals. The incidence of bank robberies in Chicago, house burglaries, holdups, gem thefts (from wealthy women as well as stores), pickpocketing, other petty theft, con games, payroll robberies increased many times over in Chicago during the Twenties.

Herbert Asbury, the best chronicler of this and earlier crime times in Chicago, reported that "Chicago seemed to be filled with gangsters—

> gangsters slaughtering one another, . . .; gangsters being killed by the
> police, . . .; gangsters shooting up saloons for amusement; gangsters
> throwing bombs, called "pineapples"; gangsters improving their marks-

manship on machine-gun ranges in sparsely settled districts; gangsters speeding in big automobiles, ignoring traffic laws; gangsters strutting in the Loop, holstered pistols scarcely concealed; gangsters giving orders to the police, to judges, to prosecutors, all sworn to uphold the law; gangsters calling on their . . . protectors at City Hall and the County Court House; gangsters dining in expensive restaurants and cafes; tuxedoes gangsters at the opera and the theater, their mink-coated, Paris-gowned wives or sweethearts on their arms; gangsters entertaining politicians and city officials at "Belshazzar feasts," some of which cost twenty-five thousand dollars; gangsters giving parties at which the guests playfully doused each other with champagne at twenty dollars a bottle, popping a thousand corks in a single evening; gangsters armed with shotguns, rifles, and machine guns, convoying beer trucks; gangsters everywhere—except in jail. And all with huge bank-rolls; a gangster with less than five thousand dollars in his pocket was a rarity.

With Big Bill Thompson back in the saddle for a third term—a public servant freely elected by the people—the future for the Outfit promised to become even more lucrative.

Capone's six-room, fourth-floor living quarters suite (Nos. 409 and 410) at the Metropole cost him $18,000 a year. In his office there, seated in a throne-like chair before a mahogany desk with half a dozen phones on it and beneath the combined gazes from portraits on the walls of Washington, Lincoln, Big Bill Thompson, and a personally auto-graphed photo of Jack Dempsey, the 28-year-old Capone—"Mayor of Crook County"—ruled a bloody, all-encompassing empire of vice, gambling, bootlegging, and labor racketeering that grossed roughly $6 million a *week*. His personal net a year was nearly equal to what Chicagoans spent in total to maintain their entire police force, $15,000,000. Capone was paying them twice this much.

What cannot be cured must be endured, of course—but, as is also well known, women, wind, and luck soon change. The good time comes but once.

Thompson's point man in redeeming his campaign pledge to oust King George's lackey, Chicago Superintendent of Schools William McAndrew—a first-rate educator of high standards—was the businessman "Iron-Handed Jack" Coath, president of the Board of Education. A précis of Coath's view of the educational process was given by Iron-Handed Jack in a speech to almost 300 elementary school principals: ". . . Teaching is a business. You are salesmen. Your commodity is education. . . . You must remember that you are no more than a small cog in a great educational machine!" (Iron-Handed Jack was obviously no Francis Wayland Parker, nor even Anita McCormick Blaine in trousers.)

In August 1927 Coath brought charges against McAndrew, chiefly that of insubordination. It was also charged that McAndrew had recommended textbooks that contained pro-British propaganda; he had removed from classroom walls the patriotic picture "The Spirit of '76"; he had been party to a conspiracy to portray George Washington as "a rebel and a great disloyalist."

The board, six to five, voted to dismiss him. At the beginning of the hearing demanded by McAndrew's lawyer, a former Washington State Supreme Court justice testified he had noticed "a lack of patriotic verve" in the nation. He attributed this to British propaganda at Columbia, Princeton, and other eastern universities and at the American Library Association. McAndrew's lawyer asked that this testimony be stricken as irrelevant. Coath refused the request.

Next, former Congressman John J. Gorman, a practicing Anglophobe, reported that only one of the Chicago school system's history texts he'd investigated (at Coath's request) was of any worth. The rest were un-American. From his researches, he said, he had concluded "that the purification of our histories and the dissemination of American patriotism can be successfully attained only by the compilation of an entirely new history."

A former board president pointed out to Gorman and the board that many of the history texts Gorman found so reprehensible had been adopted during Big Bill's own second administration and the one text Gorman found satisfactory devoted only six pages to the American Revolution.

Undeterred, Gorman began to read selected passages from the offending texts to demonstrate their pro-British bias. Day after day he read. Finally, Board President Coath bestirred himself. "Something's gotta be done to pep up this trial," said Iron-Handed Jack. "I'm beginning to get tired of all this history-book stuff."

Gorman summed up: "Mayor Thompson's fight against these objectionable histories is the fight of a courageous American to restore love and admiration for those who established the Republic. . . . This is not a fight against England or her people. It is a fight for America."

The author of one of the texts Gorman attacked sued him for libel ("The last refuge of a coward," said Gorman). The same day the suit was filed Mayor Thompson told reporters he had been informed there were hundreds of books on the shelves of the Chicago Public Library that were subversive to American patriotism. He was appointing his good friend (and fellow yachtsman) "Sport" Herrmann to find those books.

Herrmann was the man for the job in spite of his reputation as an aging playboy-about-town. "There must be thousands of propaganda books in the library system" he declared. "I'll hunt them out and when I find them I'll burn them on the lake shore."

He was asked if he thought there was any objection to what he planned to do.

"Not a bit of it. The library's supported by public taxes and if this thing of undermining Americans isn't stopped, the country'll go to pieces, that's all!"

Mayors of Canadian and British towns wired Thompson asking him to send the undesirable volumes to their libraries. The grand dragon of the Illinois Ku Klux Klan endorsed Thompson's patriotic book-hunt and asked him to next go after Catholics and Jews.

Herrmann finally sequestered four public library books (all reputable, straightforward volumes of American history). How had he found these vile volumes?

"A fella tipped me off. I can't just remember who the guy was that told me about them but he said these are pretty bad. I haven't got time to read them myself."

The attack on the library's collection dwindled away to nothingness. Thompson took a trip East. In New York City he was asked about crime and killings in Chicago. "That's a lot of newspaper talk!" he responded. As the *Chicago Tribune* had commented editorially after his primary victory: "Thompson is a buffoon in a tommyrot factory but when his crowd gets loose in the City Hall, Chicago has more need of Marines than any Nicaraguan town." Throughout Europe Big Bill's regicidal book-hunt was viewed as laughable. And in their newspapers, other countries laughed—at Thompson and at Chicagoans. Newspapers and magazines in this country echoed their mirth, though with also a note of alarm and very nearly shame.

But in Chicago teacher after teacher took the stand as the hearing continued to testify to McAndrew's arrogance, domineering attitude, flippancy, insolence. Their union's leader had assailed him as a "stooge of the union League Club and the Chicago Association of Commerce." All this pleased Iron-Handed Jack. "It is one of the most gratifying spectacles in the history of my school board experience," he said, "and I thank God for the real, human, honest people in the Chicago public schools."

McAndrew asked that he be tried on the charge of insubordination and that all other issues be dismissed as irrelevant. Coath ignored this request and at last the hearing was adjourned. In March of the next year, the board, voting eight to two, fired McAndrew as superintendent. But Thompson could not savor his triumph. By that time Big Bill had other and far more pressing concerns.

McAndrew filed suits for $6,000 in back salary and $250,000 for libel. He dropped both suits the next year when a judge overturned the board's ruling, declaring that McAndrew had been neither insubordinate nor unpatriotic. McAndrew traveled, lectured. He did not dwell on his Chicago experience but he would occasionally relate an episode in Thompson's pro-America crusade. It seems that someone asked Big Bill if he opposed George III or George V. The mayor was stunned and barely able to croak a question in return: "What? Are there two of them?"

Thompson's buffoonery and demagoguery, his ignorance, his willing complicity with gangland so long as there was a quid pro quo, had its consequences, of course, in gangland's grip on the city. It had its consequences on an individual scale as well. For example, in the life of William McAndrew. Or that of Fred Mann.

Mann, genial owner of the Rainbow Gardens at 4836 North Clark, one of Chicago's largest night clubs, was a hero-worshipping supporter of Thompson. After Big Bill's election victory the new mayor-elect told Mann that he wanted to hold a victory banquet at the Rainbow. There were to be 3,000 guests, two orchestras, the finest food, the finest liquors. To Mann, it sounded like a wonderful tribute to a great mayor. Anything Big Bill Thompson wanted he, Mann, would provide.

The celebration was a success. At it, the mayor was presented with a Lincoln sports coupe. He exchanged this for a touring car and had the left side of the rear seat raised and a spotlight installed in the back cushion of the front seat. Now when he rode around his town of an evening, the car's top down, Thompson's torso and head were illuminated for all of Chicago to admire

The mayor had publicly thanked Mann for the splendid banquet but when after several weeks passed and Thompson made no move to pay the $10,000 the party cost, the night club owner sent him a bill. He heard nothing in reply.

Prohibition agents called on Mann, however. They had evidence of liquor law violations at the banquet. Facing prosecution, Mann tried to see the mayor. The mayor was busy.

A second-echelon gangster who had attended the banquet also called on Mann. He thought it would be a good idea if he and Mann became partners in the Rainbow Gardens, what did Fred think? Mann tried again to see the mayor at City Hall. Again he was turned away.

Mulling over his situation, considering its ramifications, Fred Mann took a stroll in beautiful Lincoln Park to consider his predicament further. There he shot and killed himself.

Jack Dempsey

SWAN SONGS

Jack Dempsey had fought hundreds of brawls and regular bouts on his way to the heavyweight title that he took from Jess Willard on July 4, 1919, but in the next seven years he defended his championship a scant six times.

. . . *versus Billy Miske*, September 6, 1920, 14 months after winning title: KO in three rounds, Dempsey. Miske was ill with kidney disease and needed a big payday, which Dempsey gave him at Benton Harbor, Michigan.

. . . *versus Bill Brennan*, December 14, 1920: Come-from-behind KO in 12 rounds, Dempsey. Brennan was far ahead in the 12th when Dempsey, in desperation, went to the body and knocked him out. Bout promoted by Tex Rickard in Madison Square Garden, NYC.

. . . *versus Georges Carpentier*, The Orchid Man, July 2, 1921: KO in four rounds, Dempsey. Promoter Rickard billed the fight as the Battle of the Century because it pitted war hero Carpentier, idolized in France and England, against the champion, who had been called a "slacker" because he was not in uniform for World War I, but the smaller Carpentier had no chance. Ex-Marine Gene Tunney, who had fought and won earlier on the prelim card, watched the fight closely, and said of Carpentier: "He should have boxed on the retreat." Bout held at Boyle's Thirty Acres on outskirts of Jersey City; official attendance, 80,183; gross, $1,789,238, more than twice as much as any previous fight, first million-dollar gate.

. . . *versus Tommy Gibbons*, July 4, 1923 (two years since previous title defense), decision in 15 rounds, Dempsey. Bout held in Shelby, Montana, promoted by local citizens who—obsessively, it seemed—wanted to put Shelby (pop. c. 1,000) "on the map" now that oil had been found nearby. Crowd of 7,202 paid to sit in 40,000-capacity arena.

Gibbons fought a shrewd if losing defensive battle but Doc

Kearns fought an even shrewder and winning financial battle, demanding and getting a guarantee of $300,000. The first $100,000 was paid on signing, early in May. The second installment, due June 15, was a day late and paid only after Shelby's mayor mortgaged his oil and cattle land and borrowed the rest from a Great Falls banker. (The mayor eventually lost $140,000 of his own money promoting the fight.)

The last $100,000 was due July 2 but the citizens of Shelby were tapped out. After a midnight conference with Shelbyites, Kearns agreed to take the last installment from gate receipts. After the fight he left town with $132,000 in two canvas sacks; for $500 he hired an engineer to hook his engine to a caboose and take him to Great Falls, 85 miles distant, where he spent the rest of the night in a cellar to safeguard the cash. The next day he left Montana, and within a month four Montana banks in and around Shelby closed their doors as a result of the fight's inroads on their funds. Gibbons received nothing for managing to stay on his feet for 15 rounds.

. . . *versus Luis Angel Firpo*, the Wild Bull of the Pampas, September 14, 1923: KO in two, Dempsey. Firpo, 6'3" and 220 pounds, had no training in proper ring moves, but when Dempsey rushed at him at the bell starting this second Battle of the Century, Firpo sidestepped his wild right and dropped him with a left uppercut. Dempsey went to his knees but was up immediately and dropped Firpo with a right to the jaw. Firpo regained his feet at the count of nine but was dropped again, got up again and he and Dempsey clinched. The referee ordered them to break and as Firpo stepped back Dempsey stepped forward and knocked him down again. Standing close to the fallen Firpo, Dempsey began punching as Firpo got his hands off the canvas and put him down again. Firpo tried to crawl away from his attacker but this time when he got up Dempsey was behind him and knocked him down again. Firpo got up swinging and knocked Dempsey down but Dempsey bounced up and hit Firpo with a right hand, putting him down again. Firpo got up and was knocked down once more.

Dempsey stepped over the fallen Wild Bull and stood in the near corner, sure the fight was over. But once more Firpo got to his feet and this time he threw a looping right which knocked Dempsey into the ropes, where Firpo hit him five times with right hands, the last blow knocking Dempsey head first backwards out of the ring. Two sportswriters pushed Dempsey off the press table back into the ring and upright at the count of nine and though Dempsey said he saw 20 Firpos in front of him, he managed to duck and bob his way to the bell ending the round. Kearns met him at center ring, led him back to his corner, and dumped a bucket of water on his head.

The fighters came out for the second round punching as they had in the first, Dempsey hitting Firpo as they broke from a clinch and at the next clinch throwing him to the canvas. Firpo got up and ran into a Dempsey left to the jaw and as he was falling was hit with a short right uppercut. He stayed down. Twelve knockdowns in three minutes and 57 seconds, probably the most ferocious action ever seen in a prize fight in such a short span.

Bout promoted by Tex Rickard, held in Madison Square Garden; official attendance, 88,228; gross, $1,188,603, second million-dollar gate. The next day Dempsey went to Rickard's office to collect his share of the purse—$550,000—since Kearns already owed him more than $150,000 and he didn't trust his big-spending manager not to borrow more from the Firpo proceeds. It was the first indication that the Doctor was no longer wholly trusted by Dempsey.

The year 1925 was the first year George Halas' Chicago Bears made a decent profit. They did it because of the drawing power of Harold "Red" Grange in their cross-country tour, and it was a hopeful George Halas who broached the subject of Grange's playing for the Bears again in 1926. Grange's manager, Charles C. ("Cash and Carry") Pyle agreed at once—in return for a one-third interest in the Bears (today worth at least $150 million) plus a whopping salary for The Wheaton Ice Man.

A stunned Halas declined and Pyle announced that he would then have to establish his own NFL team in New York City. It would be called the Yankees, play in Yankee Stadium, and have Red Grange in its backfield. The NFL refused to admit the Yankees, however, and Pyle was forced to found his own league, raiding NFL teams for players and coaches.

Pyle kept the new league barely alive through 1926, hurting NFL attendance in the meanwhile, but his league fell apart in 1927 and he was left with his lease on Yankee Stadium and with his client, Grange, but no team. The NFL—because of Grange's lure at the gate—permitted Pyle to pick up the dormant Brooklyn franchise and to play in NYC on Sundays when the Giants were away, in other NFL cities when the Giants were home.

Playing against the Bears in 1927 in Wrigley Field, Grange hurt his knee. "I had my cleat dug into the ground and it was a kind of wet day and somebody fell over my knee. It was nothing deliberate, just one of those things."

He was sidelined the rest of the 1927 season and all of 1928 and the injury finished him as a breakaway threat and broken-field runner. "I was just an ordinary back after that," he said, "the moves were gone forever. I wore a brace with steel hinges on both sides."

His earnings through those first three years as a pro—'25 through '27—closely approached a million dollars. "I thought I'd never play again. But George Halas talked to me about it. 'Why don't you get yourself up and in shape and give it a try again?' he asked. I decided I would and it worked out all right. . . . I worked on playing defense and that became a strong point with me."

He played for the Bears for six years after coming back from his injury in 1929. The first of the modern T-formation quarterbacks, the Bears' Carl Brumbaugh, recalled a game in 1930 when he sent Grange in motion and the linebacker followed him out. Brumbaugh handed off to Bronko Nagurski who went through the vacated linebacker's position for 45 yards. They tried it again but the linebacker stayed put this time so the next play Grange was sent in motion a third time, turned upfield all alone and Brumbaugh passed to him for a touchdown. This was the beginning of the development of the man-in-motion from the T that ultimately did away with the traditional seven-man defensive line.

Two years later, in the 1932 NFL championship game, the Bears were stopped on the Portsmouth 1-yard line after three Nagurski line smashes. Portsmouth's linemen massed at the goal waiting for Nagurski a last time. "Red went in motion," Nagurski explained. "The ball came to me. I took a step or two forward as though to begin the plunge everyone expected. The defenders converged . . . there was no way I could get through. I stopped. I moved back a couple of steps. Grange had gone around and was in the end zone. I threw him a short pass." Portsmouth's coach protested vehemently that Nagurski had not been five yards behind the line of scrimmage when he passed, as the rules then required, but the TD was allowed and the Bears won 9 to 0.

The game did more than bring the Bears the NFL championship. It also brought into focus the essential dullness of NFL games, and in 1933 the rules committee (Halas, president) met to open up the game by legalizing the forward pass if thrown anywhere behind the line of scrimmage. From the 1933 season on scoring increased in the NFL, as did attendance.

The next year the Bears met the Giants for the League championship at Wrigley Field before 26,000 fans, the largest football crowd there since Grange's pro debut nine years before. The lead changed hands six times and late in the game—Bears leading 23 to 21—a Giants' back broke through with only Grange between him and the goal line, with Mel Hein, the Giants' all-pro center trailing a stride or two behind. If Grange committed himself to a tackle, the back would lateral to Hein, who would go in for the winning touchdown. Grange went for the back but not with a diving tackle. He pinned the back's arms to his sides so he could not lateral and threw him down and the Bears had another NFL championship.

But football was not important to Grange anymore and for some time he had been talking retirement. He couldn't do the things he'd once been able to do, and practice was drudgery. In a 1934 exhibition against the Giants the Bears had the ball on their own 20. In the huddle Brumbaugh said, "I'm giving the ball to Red for the last time. Boys, let's give him some help. Red, when you reach the end zone, put the ball down between the posts and head for the bench." The stage was set for a touching, dramatic farewell.

Grange took Brumbaugh's handoff through a big hole and Bears' linemen knocked down the secondary. No. 77 had a clear field ahead to his last, twilight touchdown.

"My legs kept getting heavier and heavier," he said. "I was caught from behind on their 39 by a 230-pound tackle."

Grange left the ball on the 39 and walked to the sidelines to tell Halas it was his last year. . . . It wouldn't have ended that way if it had been a movie.

He stayed with the Bears three years more as an assistant coach, and for the next 30 years off and on was a radio and TV commentator on Bears' games. He managed a Hollywood night club, was a sales rep for a bottling company, and—like many retired sports figures—sold insurance for a time. He died in Florida in 1991, age 87. There are many who say that without the lure of his name and college reputation in the mid-'20s, the NFL would have no-gained to failure.

When he was not fighting in his years as champion, Jack Dempsey was still not far from the public's eye. On winning the title in 1919 he began traveling with a circus, boxing exhibitions. Later he and Kearns did the same on the vaudeville circuit. And by 1920 the Manassa Mauler was working fairly steadily making movies, both serials and features. The scripts presented him as a Horatio Alger hero, fighting to defend his own or someone else's honor. Of his acting he said, "When I started I was really bad and I never got any better."

In 1920 his ex-wife Maxine, whom he'd divorced in 1919, tried to blackmail him as a slacker and wife-beater, but her efforts failed. (Maxine died asleep in bed in a Juarez, Mexico, dance hall fire in 1924.)

In 1922 Jack and Doc Kearns traveled together to Europe. At a fancy dinner at Lord Northcliffe's London town house, Jack was asked to make an after-dinner speech to the assembled nobility and notables. He mumbled something about feeling like the Irishman who couldn't perform and then in his high-pitched voice said mock-seriously, "I can't sing, I can't dance, and I can't tell a story, but I will tell you what I'll do. I'll fight anybody in the house."

They went on to Paris, then to Berlin, Dempsey lionized wherever they stopped. When they returned home Dempsey was wearing a monocle, which Kearns correctly said made him "look like an ass."

In 1924 he moved from New York to Los Angeles, where he was making films. From his movie roles and stage appearances he earned about half a million dollars in 1924, roughly half of which went to Kearns. (In earlier years Kearns got two-thirds of all Dempsey's earnings.)

He wanted—counter to Kearns' stern warnings of the dangers involved—to find a woman to settle down with. (In at least one instance Kearns paid a woman to leave Dempsey when he got serious about her.) He said he was tired of one-night stands and 2 A.M. bargains. He found his woman in Estelle Taylor, a second-rate actress and well-worn Hollywood commodity. They were married February 7, 1925.

Estelle had a sharp tongue and strong opinions—and she disliked fighting and fighters—and she and Doc Kearns were enemies on first meeting. When she married Jack and then gave him his choice between her and Doc she precipitated a break between her husband and the man who for seven years had managed her husband's life in and out of the ring.

At Estelle's insistence, Jack had an operation to repair his broken nose (it had always been patched with putty for his movies) and after a high-spending trip to Europe (Estelle was a good spender), the Dempseys appeared together on the Broadway stage in *The Big Fight*. This melodrama lasted eight weeks and cost Dempsey $80,000.

By now Doc Kearns was filing lawsuits against Jack, who offered to keep Kearns as his manager but at 35 percent, not 50 percent. Kearns raged against Estelle and refused. Promoter Tex Rickard was impatient for Dempsey to defend his title and so Jack, on his own, agreed to meet Gene Tunney, a former light heavyweight champion now campaigning as a heavyweight. Tunney was a coldly scientific boxer.

By the time Dempsey and Tunney met, it had been three years since Dempsey's last title defense; Kearns had served him with seven harassing suits and injunctions; and the day of the fight Dempsey became ill with a sickness resembling ptomaine poisoning.

. . . *versus Gene Tunney*, September 23, 1926: decision in 10 rounds, Tunney. The champion was booed on being introduced in the ring before the fight began. Boxing on the retreat, Tunney won every round of this third Battle of the Century, which was fought in the rain. When the decision was announced a battered Dempsey had his second lead him across the ring to Tunney. He hugged Tunney and said, "All right, Gene. All right, good luck." The crowd cheered the ex-champion when he left the ring, surprising him. But of course Dempsey was a fighter, and Tunney was a boxer.

Bout held in Philadelphia's Sesquicentennial Stadium; largest paid attendance in history of boxing, 120,757; gross, $1,895,733, third million-dollar gate.

Dempsey did not believe a wife should see her husband fight so Estelle had not been in Philadelphia. She phoned him after listening to the fight on the radio and asked with concern, "What happened, Ginsberg?"

Dempsey's answer reduced the situation to its basics. "Honey," he said, "I just forgot to duck."

In the months following the Tunney fight Dempsey said he had retired. His wife didn't want him to continue, and, too, he had doubts about his ability to deliver as he had when he was younger. So he retired—but he kept training.

Babe Ruth, whom Dempsey had known since 1921, visited him in Los Angeles and tried to talk him out of retirement. Growing angry the Babe said, "Awright then, sit on your ass and feel sorry for yourself. You know, pal, it's guys like us who just can't back off from the spotlight. We're the ones who got to be at bat, trying for those frigging home runs until we grind ourselves into the ground. . . . Every time I walk up to home plate, I'm at zero. Zero. Know what that means? And here you are, walkin' sideways and bumping into yourself, for Chrissakes."

"Babe, I don't know if I've still got it, see?"

"Well, goddamn it, you won't know till you get out there and try."

Whatever his reasons—sheer love of fighting, possibly because his marriage was breaking up, more probably simply to prove something to himself—Dempsey changed his mind about retirement, and Rickard matched him with leading contender Jack Sharkey for a fight in Yankee Stadium July 21. Sharkey was confident he could knock Dempsey out and for six rounds it appeared he might. Then, in the seventh, with Dempsey hammering at his belt line, Sharkey grabbed his groin and turned his head to complain to the referee. He was hit with a left hook that traveled a foot and he went down for the full count. Paid attendance, 72,283; gross, $1,083, 529, fourth million-dollar gate, first in a non-title bout.

Rickard set September 22 as the date for the Tunney rematch, almost exactly a year since the first fight; place, Soldier Field, Chicago. When Tunney arrived in Chicago, he said, "I am here to train for a boxing contest, not a fight. I don't like fighting." His ring record proved Tunney was more than tough, but he was serious when he said he disliked fighting.

While training, Dempsey received about 5,000 fan letters a day, and his sparring sessions were watched by up to 8,000 fans a session—and Estelle was heading toward a nervous breakdown, her career in the movies at a dead end, her disgust with fighters and fighting greater than ever. She told Dempsey in Chicago that "If I weren't married to you, I'd have nothing to do with you."

It was rumored that Al Capone had bet heavily on Dempsey and that the fix was in. Dempsey wrote Capone a note asking him not to do anything that he, Dempsey, might regret. The next day Estelle received several hundred dollars worth of flowers at her Edgewater Beach Hotel suite, with an unsigned card that said: "To the Dempseys, in the name of sportsmanship."

Davey Yiddles Miller was assigned to referee the fight, the same Davey Miller shot by Dion O'Banion outside the LaSalle Theater almost four years before. The night preceding the match he was summoned from dinner and driven to the Metropole, where Capone got in the car, put his arm around Miller's shoulders, and told him he was betting $50,000 on Dempsey. "Dave," he said, "all I want you to do tomorrow night is give Dempsey an even break."

Minutes before the fight the next night the Illinois Boxing Commission substituted Dave Barry for Miller as referee. No reason was ever given for the substitution.

Estelle, who was under a nurse's care, locked herself in the bathroom for the first few rounds, refusing to listen to the fight on the radio. Tunney boxed with the same defensive strategy he had used so successfully in the first match, always moving to his left, away from Dempsey's left hook. He would hit Dempsey five or six times for each blow that Jack landed and he had Dempsey leaning against the ropes as early as the second round. By the sixth, Dempsey's right eye and ear were bleeding and his left eye was badly swollen.

A minute into the seventh round Dempsey hit Tunney with a long right and—finally—with a left hook—one of the blows catching Tunney in the throat—then a straight right, and another left hook as Tunney came off the ropes. As Tunney started to fall, Dempsey hit him with a left-right, left-right combination. With Tunney glassy-eyed and down—for the first time in his career—Dempsey stood in the corner a few feet from him.

The rules stipulated that he go to the furthest neutral corner, and referee Barry yelled at him to do that. "I'll stay here," Jack said. Barry grabbed him by the arm and shoved him to the furthest neutral corner. When Barry returned to Tunney, the timekeeper was calling out "five" but Barry began his count at "one" and Tunney got up at "nine." He had been down for at least a 14 count, some ringside reporters said 17—the famous Long Count (the term followed Barry as his nickname).

Tunney retreated and Dempsey chased him, but Dempsey was tired. He waved a glove at Tunney, as if asking him to stand and fight, but Tunney kept backpedaling. He lasted the round, and was Dempsey's master in the final three rounds, knocking him down for a one-count in the eighth. Gene Tunney was still champion, having decisively defeated Jack Dempsey in a bout that drew 104,943 spectators to Soldier Field and grossed $2,658,660, the first two-million-dollar gate.

At 32 Dempsey had fought his last championship fight. He declined Rickard's offer of a third match with Tunney and became a co-promoter with Rickard and then went on to other business ventures, most notably a Broadway restaurant.

In 1928 Estelle Taylor divorced him. Approached for an autograph after the divorce, she saw Jack's signature among the first few on the sheet handed her. She delivered her curtain line as she signed, observing, "This is the last time that son-of-a-bitch is on top of me."

Dempsey lived for a remarkable 55 years more after the Long Count, always popular, always friendly.

The sportswriter Paul Gallico remembered how it was after Tunney got up and Dempsey began to chase him—that over Dempsey's "swarthy, blue-jowled fighter's face there spread a look the memory of which will never leave me. . . . First it was the expression of self-realization of one who knows that his race is run, that he is old and that he is finished. And then through it and replacing it there appeared such a glance of bitter, biting contempt for his opponent that for a moment I felt ashamed for the man who was running away."

It will be recalled that in his match with Jack Sharkey—the hurdle to his rematch with Tunney—Dempsey knocked out Sharkey with a short left hook when Sharkey turned his head to complain to the referee about a low punch. The fairness of that left hook, delivered when it was, was heatedly debated at the time. In a later year, when asked his own opinion, Dempsey answered, "What was I going to do—write him a letter?"

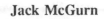
Jack McGurn

Jake Guzik

FOUR-SQUARE

Other cities in the United States did not experience so violent a disruption of civic order in their enforcement of Prohibition as did Chicago. (Though it must be said that most other cities did not like their beer as well.) Nor did the grip of the gangster in other cities ever reach the same extent and strength as in Chicago. By 1927, the Outfit—after Chicago's men of finance—was the single most powerful force in the city.

> Four-square . . . it stands, in physical fact a monument to trade, to the organized commercial spirit, to the power and progress of the age, to the strength and resource of individuality and force of character; spiritually, it stands as the index of a mind large enough to cope with these things, master them, absorb them and give them forth impressed with the stamp of large and forceful personality. . . .

Thus, Chicago's Outfit, a monument to the organized commercial spirit, and the index of a mind large enough to cope with these things and give them the stamp of large and forceful personality—that mind and personality, Al Capone's. (The words are architect Louis Sullivan's; he used them in tribute to a Chicago structure he much admired, the Marshall Field Warehouse and Wholesale Store by H. H. Richardson.)

Capone's chief lieutenants might have seemed a motley crew to manage such a vast enterprise as they did, but all could not only talk the talk, but walk the walk; that is, they were skilled at their jobs and, of equal importance, they were considered loyal.

Oldest in time of service to the syndicate was Jake Guzik, Capone's business manager, chief accountant, and record-keeper. Jake was the man for whom Joe Howard died with six of Big Al's slugs in his skull, a curse on his lips, and $17 in his pocket. Jake was called "Greasy Thumb" by reporters, a description he had inherited from his older brother, white-slaver Harry. (Old-timers in Wheaton say that Red Grange inherited "The Ice Man" from *his* older brother.)

Guzik came from a family of Chicago pimps and was himself first arrested as a panderer in 1912 at the age of 25, though he had been pimping since before his teens and owned several whorehouses before he was 20. In 1917 he was convicted of larceny and spent time in city jail. Caught again the next year, this time he shared his ill-got loot with his Democratic precinct captain and received only five days in the Bridewell and a $10 fine.

His pimping brought him into contact with Johnny Torrio, and with Torrio's backing and Colosimo's money and his own savings he bought a small brewery at 2340 South Wabash and from that time on his services—indeed, his life—were dedicated to Torrio, to Capone, to the Outfit. His older brother Harry worked for Torrio and Capone as one of their chief whoremasters, along with Mike "de Pike" Heitler. No, Reverend, those girls on the corner aren't gathered there to sing hymns.

The Outfit's treasurer was Frank "The Enforcer" Nitti (Francesco Raffele Nitto), born in Augori, Sicily, in 1889 and brought to the United States in 1892. He worked as a barber and was a fence for stolen goods before he became an Outfit gunman, eventually taking charge of its machine gunners, then its cash. He was a small, quiet, deliberate but forceful man, given to introspection. Ten years older than Capone, he was second-in-command to him.

Big Al's brother, Ralph "Bottles" Capone, was director of beer sales. When they first came to Chicago, his family lived with Al's at Al's Prairie Avenue home. Besides beer sales, Ralph also operated the Suburban Cigarette Service and the Waukesha Waters mineral water franchise to restaurants, hotels, and speakeasies, selling them ginger ale, fizz water, and other mix as well, checked on brothel receipts for Al, and on the side made book. The other Capone brothers worked for the Outfit off and on but never rose to positions equal in responsibility to that of Ralph or of Al's cousin, Charles Fischetti, who with Laurence "Dago" Mangano was in charge of beer distribution. Bert Delaney was supervisor of Outfit breweries. Joe Fusco, whose family name was on the Illinois charter of the Unione Siciliana (significant in the Sicilian Badlands), handled liquor sales and distribution.

Five-foot, 100-pound Louis "Diamond Lou" Cowan was the Outfit's bail bondsman. Since boyhood he had run a Cicero newsstand. Capone put half a million dollars worth of real estate in Cowan's name and this Cowan used as security as the courts required.

Every Outfit member carried a card with Cowan's name and a phone number on it. The phone was in a pay booth of a Cicero drugstore at 25th Street and 52nd Avenue. If a caller asked for Cowan, the druggist went to the door and waved to Louis at his newsstand to come and pick up the phone. Cowan had a limousine at the curb in which he would then speed to the police station the arrested caller had named.

240

Vincenzo Gibaldi was born in 1903 in Sicily and brought to the United States when he was a year old. In Brooklyn his father was murdered by mistake by Irish White Handers. (His father was a look-alike for a Frankie Yale gunman.) Vincent's father died with three nickels in his hand, payment for a shoeshine he was getting when he was shotgunned.

The widow married a grocer, Angelo DeMora, and the family moved to Chicago's Little Italy, where Vincent taught himself to shoot. The oldest of six children, he was a fast learner in school and good at sports, becoming the school's boxing champion even though often outweighed by 20 to 30 pounds. He joined an amateur athletic club, learned more of the rudiments, and began to score victories as a welterweight.

At 19 years of age he returned to Brooklyn, severely wounded the leader of the Irish White Handers and killed the two who had murdered his father. He left a nickel in the hands of each of them.

The next year his stepfather, who sold sugar to Little Italy's alky cookers, was found shot to death in front of his grocery store at 936 Vernon Park Place. Vincent was silent at the inquest until questioned.

Had he any suspicions as to who killed his stepfather?

"No."

Having become the head of the house, was he not fearful for his own life?

"I'm big enough," he said softly, "to take care of this case myself."

Vincent pomaded his curly black hair flat and parted it down the middle, wore shoulder-padded wide-checked suits, loud neckties, pointed patent-leather shoes (the Valentino look). He strummed a ukelele, frequented night clubs (not unusual for a gangster), and loved to dance. He cultivated the company of beautiful women, most of them blondes. Police attributed at least 15 murders to Vincent. He had taken the name "Jack McGurn" when he started to box professionally (only a few bouts) and it was as "Machine Gun" Jack McGurn that he was known in the Outfit, Al Capone's favorite gunman.

McGurn's closest friend, from whom he was nearly inseparable, was Michael Spranze (alias Kelly), a Capone bodyguard. Other bodyguards were the tough, sharp-shooting Phil D'Andrea, William "Three-Fingered" Jack White, Louis "Little New York" Campagna, Louis Consentino, "Big Mops" Volpe, who came to Capone from service with Diamond Joe Esposito, the ever-reliable Frankie Rio, Frank Milano, Frank Maritote (alias Diamond, husband of Capone's sister Rose), Jack Heinan (reputed to be more nerveless and tougher than McGurn), and Sam "Golf Bag" Hunt, who carried his shotgun in a golf bag. (One of Hunt's intended victims survived and was ever after referred to as "Hunt's hole in one.") The veteran Black Hander James Belcastro and Johnny Genaro and their bomber squads were available for explosions at two-timing breweries or speakeasies, and Ragen's Colts could be levied upon at any time for muscle, or Sicilian triggermen could be imported from other cities for special projects, or freelance mechanics could be hired for others. Bodyguard Phil D'Andrea was on the Chicago city payroll as a Municipal Court bailiff at $200 a month, and other Outfit gunmen carried cards bearing an official city stamp and the words: "To the Police Department—You will extend the courtesies of the department to the bearer." Most of the higher-ups in the organization had businesses of their own going for themselves—handbooks, call flats, gin flats, hotels, speaks—all of which contributed a sizable percentage of their gross to the Outfit's coffers.

Frankie Pope, "The Millionaire Newsboy," managed the Hawthorne Smoke Shop gambling operation in Cicero. He was responsible for day-to-day operations and in charge of off-track horse- and dog-racing betting, while Pete Penovich oversaw roulette, faro, poker, chuck-a-luck, craps, and other games of chance and supervised the ropers, friskers, door men, stick men, bankers, and shills. (Most of the table specialists were Irish.) Capone's collector from gambling houses the Outfit did not itself own was Hymie "Loud Mouth" Levine.

Johnny Patton, the "Boy Mayor of Burnham," who had brought the profits in suburban sin to Johnny Torrio's attention, continued to work closely with Capone, especially in the matter of arranging political fixes. Dennis "Duke" Cooney, a holdover from the Kenna era, was in overall charge of prostitution operations. He had the experience. For advice and counsel in matters of business and commerce, Al had Antonio Lombardo, his chosen head of the Unione Siciliana, and for advice and counsel in matters of general policy, strategy and tactics, he had long-distance access to Johnny Papa, more or less his *consigliere* after Torrio returned from Europe. *Venire a piu miti consigili* means "to become more reasonable." A consigliere is someone who provides an objective, reasonable, seasoned point of view of problems.

In 1925, released from the Waukegan jail and on his way to Europe, where he intended to stay for a while, Torrio met with an old acquaintance, the New York mobster Charlie "Lucky" Luciano (Salvatore Luciana). "Johnny was a guy who could always look around corners . . .," Luciano remembered:

> "When we met he told me he was gonna take a vacation in Italy; he'd gotten his naturalization papers, so he didn't have nothin' to worry about, and he had millions stashed away. He told me he wanted to talk over a plan. He thought booze was gonna become legal again and he wanted to become my agent in Europe, to start buyin' up legal options on the best Scotch to get ready for the end of the Volstead Act. This

was seven long years before Repeal, and it was almost impossible to believe. Here was a guy predictin' that my whole fuckin' business, and everybody else's for that matter, was gonna wind up in the shithouse."

(Torrio's scheme to buy up European Scotch in anticipation of Repeal was one that Joseph P. Kennedy, father of a U.S. President, acted upon to a considerable fortune—with the help of NY mobster Frank Costello.)

The day after his first meeting with Luciano, Torrio met with him again and Meyer Lansky, Frank Costello, and other high-level Rum Row runners and repeated his assessment of their situation. Most scoffed, except Lansky. He said, "The only way to get legitimate is to move in with the legitimate people." To which Torrio responded, "You've gotta get into the big politics. You can buy the top politicians the same way you bought the law." (Luciano was to take this advice and apply it with remarkable success in gaining political influence in NYC.)

When Torrio returned to the States some 2½ years later, after Mussolini's Fascist government labeled him an undesirable visitor (Il Duce was attempting to rid Italy of both the native Mafia and U.S. gangsters), Luciano welcomed him back and Torrio began to work closely with him and other top NYC mobsters. To the outside world Torrio represented himself as a "real estate agent." He and Anna had an apartment in White Plains. He had a small office in Brooklyn. And Johnny Papa remained in touch with Big Al; he had a percentage to protect.

The phones on Capone's mahogany desk at the Metropole also connected him to local politicians, police officials, and judges, with his lieutenants throughout the city and suburbs, and with mobsters in other U.S. cities—New York, St. Louis, Minneapolis-St. Paul, Philadelphia, Kansas City, Cleveland, Detroit, Des Moines, elsewhere—New England down the Atlantic Coast to Florida, Los Angeles, Canada, Mexico, the Gulf. He was in regular contact with Abe Bernstein's Purple Gang in Detroit, for instance. It supplied the Outfit with Old Log Cabin whiskey. This was re-sold to Bugs Moran for his North Side customers. When Moran was offered a steady supply of Canadian whiskey at a cheaper price, however, he abruptly discontinued his arrangement with the Outfit and Capone then arranged to sell his consignments of Old Log Cabin to Paul Morton, brother of the late, lamented equestrian, Nails.

But Moran's North Side customers preferred Old Log Cabin. Moran called Capone and told him he would like to be restored to the delivery schedule. Capone told him that was not possible, which rankled with Moran. The whiskey was there. He was willing to buy it again. Capone should sell it to him. Eventually trucks loaded with Old Log Cabin began to be hijacked.

The motto of William Hale Thompson's third administration was "Make Chicago Hum!" The mayor named Samuel Ettleson (Insull's lawyer) as his corporation counsel—again. He named Michael Hughes, State's Attorney Crowe's cousin, chief of police and charged him to rid the city of all crooks within 90 days. At a testimonial dinner for Hughes to celebrate his appointment, the new chief—who had once been chief of detectives—told the 2,500 guests that crime suppression would be his first priority, Prohibition enforcement his second.

To the post of city sealer, Thompson named Daniel Serritella, a First Ward America First Republican, once a newsboy and founder of the Chicago Newsboys' Union. It was not common knowledge that Serritella was Capone's messenger boy to Thompson. As city sealer, Serritella's official responsibility was to see that Chicago merchants gave their customers honest measure. (Is it necessary to record that four years later Serritella was indicted for conspiracy with city merchants to short-weight consumers? He was found guilty but the verdict was reversed on appeal.) In the state legislature at Springfield, Capone's interests were advanced by representative William V. Pacelli, later by Roland V. Libonati.

On April 28, two weeks after assuming command, Chief Hughes stated that "frightened by the police drive, the gunmen, bandits and other underworld characters are on the run already." Less than a month later the dead body of a well-dressed man was found at Des Plaines and Dekoven streets. The man had a $1,200 roll of hundred-dollar bills in a hip pocket, a loaded revolver in a shoulder holster, and a nickel in his right hand. His fingers had been folded over the coin.

On August 11 two more mystery bodies were found, on September 24 a fourth—all well-dressed, all with large bank rolls, all carrying an unfired gun, all clutching a nickel. It was finally established that the first victim came from NYC, the second and third from St. Louis, the fourth from Cleveland, and that all were professional killers, all were Sicilian, and all had come to Chicago to earn a $50,000 reward offered by Joseph Aiello to anyone who killed Al Capone.

Aiello had been a partner of Tony Lombardo in the produce business but quarreled with him when Lombardo became president of the Unione; Aiello felt the post should have been his. (Frankie Yale had wanted him to succeed Angelo Genna, or so Aiello thought.) Aiello lived in a regal three-story mansion north of the Loop in West Rogers Park. He and his brothers and their many cousins dealt in produce—including the ingredients for distilling alcohol—and owned a large commercial bakery. They also had gained control of the greater part of the Genna brothers' shattered kingdom of 2,500 alky-cookers.

After their out-of-town Mafioso killers were tipped to Capone by his city-wide network of informers (waiters, bartenders, bookies, newsboys, jitney drivers, police) and eliminated, the Aiellos offered the chef at Diamond Joe Esposito's Bella Napoli, Capone's favorite ristorante, $10,000 to put prussic acid in the Big Fellow's soup. The frightened chef told Capone, who reacted with disgust. "If I had known what I was stepping into in Chicago," he said, "I never would have left the Five Points outfit."

The Aiellos formed a coalition with Bugs Moran and what was left of the O'Banion gang and also with Billy Skidmore, a professional bondsman and gambler/politician, and Barney Bertsche, another gambler/politician, and Jack Zuta, who already had ties with Moran's North Siders. The objective was to depose Capone by killing him and to take over the Outfit.

But as in stalking a panther, you could never be sure who was after whom. In a six-week period beginning June 1 Capone's gunners killed six Aiello triggermen (inherited from the Gennas)—"Slayers not apprehended." An upset Police Chief Hughes mobilized volunteers from the department and gave them machine guns and passed down orders through his chief of detectives that they were to roam the city in armored cars and exterminate the gangs, a not entirely inappropriate response, though to kill suspected lawbreakers "without mercy. . . . Make them push up daisies. Shoot first and shoot to kill" were not commands ordinarily given to police officers by their superiors.

When not dealing with attempts on his life, Capone worked hard and efficiently at managing the business affairs of the empire, as Torrio had. But unlike Johnny Papa, Capone also took opportunities to relax. He was a very poor gambler but he loved to gamble. In his decisions as head of the Outfit, he had a gambler's luck, a sense of risk—almost instinctual—that told him when to bet, when to pass, not to force it but when to ride a winner. Not so with the dice or at the track.

At craps he rarely bet less than a thousand a roll, sometimes as much as $100,000. Coatless, vestless, collarless, he would sweat over the dice 12 and 16 hours at a stretch, always highrolling, always losing over the long run. He would bet $100,000 on the spin of a roulette wheel. At the race track he bet to win, seldom across the board. As happens, the other guy's hunches always won, not his own. He occasionally bet on fixed races himself, but usually passed on his insider's info to a deserving underling. His IOUs were good at any U.S. track. After a day at a New Orleans track he wrote a marker for half a million dollars. He calculated that in the four years he had been betting the horses in Chicago (it started with the Cicero takeover) he had lost roughly $10 million on them.

Because dog racing was so easy to fix he did not bet at his own Hawthorne Kennel Club in Cicero, a half-million-dollar plant with a stable of 400 greyhounds. A St. Louis lawyer, Edward O'Hare, held the rights to the mechanical rabbit the dogs chased and when he opened a track nearby the Outfit's Capone suggested they merge their interests and parimutuel booths. In time the Outfit had O'Hare managing dog tracks for it in Florida and Massachusetts as well as in Illinois. (Bugs Moran built a dog track in southern Illinois and one in Cicero. Capone had a county official have the roads leading to Moran's Cicero track torn up, and bombed the grandstand of the downstate track. Moran retaliated by setting a fire at the Hawthorne Kennel Club.)

When Capone traveled in the city, a scout car preceded his armored car, a touring car of bodyguards brought up the rear. At the theater or opera three boydguards sat behind him, three in front, two at each side, all in tuxedos. When he attended a baseball game or a fight he was always accompanied by at least a dozen gunmen.

He was lavish. After the second Dempsey-Tunney fight in Soldier Field, he threw a party for movie and theater stars, socialites, politicians, boxing celebrities, and mobsters that lasted three days and nights and consumed $50,000 worth of liquor (wholesale). Going into a fight he would pass out tickets to kids who had none. His shoeshine boy, "Shorty" Harris (4 feet, 2 inches tall, full-grown) got $20 a shine. He tipped newsboys $5 (a "fin"), hat-check girls $10 (a "sawbuck"), waiters $100 (a "C-note"). He gave jockey Joseph Ballero $500 the first time Ballero rode a winner on one of his thoroughbreds. (The horses were not registered under Capone's name.)

He went to central Illinois and hunted and fished among the backwater lakes scattered along the Illinois River, or at one of the 700 private hunting clubs in the area, one of which he was supposed to own. He had a lodge in Wisconsin and the Brooklyn boy fished there under the tutelage of Louis St. Germaine, the Northwoods' No. 1 guide. (Preparing a shore lunch for two mobsters on one outing, St. Germaine watched as the hoods mixed their martinis in the minnow pail—for laughs—then took the two tough guys to the local hospital to have their stomachs pumped when they got sick from their reaction to the lead lining of the pail.) Capone's lodge was near Couderay; he called it "The Hideout."

Jazz in the gin mills was big in Chicago. Jazz and the blues— Bessie Smith singing "Nobody in Town Can Bake a Jelly Roll Like Mine," Alberta Hunter singing "Loveless Love." *Pro*-fessor Tony Jackson and his bass were featured through the muggles smoke at the Pekin Inn. Jackson had worked in the Levee in bygone years at Pony Moore's and at the Everleigh Club. He still played and sang the old songs:

> I got an all-night trick agin,
> So keep a-knockin' but you can't come in.

Capone would enter a club with his bodyguards and the doors would be secured; no one could enter or leave while he was there (So keep a-knockin' but you can't come in). He would buy drinks for the house, have his bodyguards dispense hundred-dollar bills to the jazzmen and the waiters. Band members got $5 or $10 for each request they played and all the mobsters had their favorites. Capone would sit at a table, usually alone, sometimes with a woman, sipping a drink—the "amber"—and listen. Apparently as with opera, there was in jazz, too, and the blues, something that appealed to the outlaw Italian soul—the innermost core of the men with deadly cold eyes and a kernel of absolute, controlled hardness.

On the North Side in Uptown, at 4802 North Broadway, there was (still is, a remnant at least, and thus the oldest night club in Chicago) The Green Mill gardens. In the early days, when it was owned by the three Chamales brothers, silent movie actors from the nearby Essanay (Spoor and Anderson) Studios hitched their horses to an anachronistic post outside the Mill—stars such as Wallace Beery and Broncho Billy Anderson, one of the Studios' owners. (Charlie Chaplin made movies for Essanay; he didn't like Chicago's weather. Among the Studios' featured players were Ben Turpin, Fatty Arbuckle, Francis X. Bushman, Gloria Swanson, and Beverly—Beverly Hills—Bayne. Chicago had a thriving film industry before the movies went Hollywood.)

Among visitors and performers at the Green Mill were Mary Pickford, John Barrymore, Tom Mix, Al Jolson, Eddie Cantor, Sophie Tucker, Lillian Russell. The chorus line at the Mill numbered 50 girls and if the Chamales brothers liked a girl and she liked strawberries, say, and strawberries were out of season they chartered a plane to go to Florida and get the girl strawberries.

An emcee at the Green Mill fell in love with one of its chorus girls and when she threw him over he was desolate. One of his friends, wanting to comfort him or maybe to twist the knife a little—both of which friends will do—asked him, "I wonder who's kissing her now?" and the emcee went ahead and wrote that song and sang it at the Mill, his heart breaking all the while.

Joe E. Lewis came to work at the Green Mill in 1926 as a singer and comedian. He was very popular with the supper-club crowd. The owner, Danny Cohen, was paying him a hefty $650 a week. After a year the owner of the New Rendezvous Café near Clark and Diversey offered Lewis $1,000 a week to switch to his club. Danny Cohen took Machine Gun Jack McGurn aside and told him he could have a 25 percent interest in the Green Mill gardens if he would persuade Lewis to stay on.

McGurn told Lewis he'd be killed if he opened at the Rendezvous. Lewis laughed and promised McGurn a center table on opening night and hired a bodyguard who slept in the front room of his quarters at the Commonwealth Hotel.

For a week Lewis played to capacity at the Rendezvous. Then, on November 10, McGurn sent three hoods to the Commonwealth. First they took out the bodyguard, then Lewis, slashing his throat and vocal cords, cutting his tongue and jaw, and pistol whipping him, fracturing his skull. After a six-hour operation Lewis recovered but at first he could not recognize words and he had to learn to talk again. He was back on the Rendezvous stage in ten weeks to try a comeback but he could barely sing or talk and his following deserted him. For ten years he worked very little. He never did regain his ability to sing. Capone gave him $10,000 to help tide him over. "Why in hell didn't you come to me when you had your trouble?" Al asked. "I'd have straightened things out." Al was always very good at commiserating after the fact.

Police Chief Hughes' roaming killer squads did not accomplish anything noteworthy over the summer but on November 21, acting on a tip from a stool-pigeon, they raided a flat in an apartment building across the street from Antonio Lombardo's home in the 4000 block of West Washington Boulevard, north of Cicero. The flat was empty except for machine guns trained on Lombardo's front door. The stoolie had also given the police a 7002 North Western Avenue address, ten miles distant in Rogers Park. There they found dynamite and percussion caps and a receipt for a room in a hotel at 3142 North Ashland. At the hotel the officers surprised 23-year-old Angelo La Mantio, a Milwaukee gunman, Joseph Aiello, and two of Aiello's cousins.

The young La Mantio was a talker. He said he had been brought to Chicago to kill Al Capone and Tony Lombardo. He told the officers to go to room 302 of the Atlantic Hotel at 316 South Clark Street. There the police found rifles clamped to the windows aimed at the entrance of 311 South Clark, Hinky Dink Kenna's cigar store at which each day the Big Fellow stopped for cigars and a chat with the Little Fellow. (For never specified reasons, many a Loop bookmaker and businessman would pay political chief Kenna $100 or more for a five-cent cigar.)

La Mantio and Joseph Aiello were taken to the Detective Bureau. About half an hour after they were put in cells, a policeman glancing out of an upper-story window saw six taxis stop in the street and unload two dozen hard-looking men. Some of the men began walking up and down the sidewalk in front of the Bureau, some made for the alley which led to the building's back entrance. Three of the men approached the front entrance. The policeman called a fellow officer to the window. He recognized one of the three as Louis Little New York Campagna. "That," he said, "is the Capone crowd." The Bureau was surrounded by gangsters.

The police went to the entrance and brought in Campagna and the two men with him. The three mobsters were disarmed and put in a cell next to Aiello. A policeman who understood Italian was disguised as a prisoner and put into an opposite cell.

In Sicilian dialect Campagna told Aiello, "You're dead, friend, you're dead. You won't get up to the end of the street still walking."

Aiello begged. "Can't we settle this? Give me just 14 days—14 days—and I'll sell my stores, and house, everything and leave everything in your hands. Think of my wife and baby."

When he was released Aiello pleaded with the chief of detectives to provide him with an escort. Because he was leaving with his wife and baby, who had come with his lawyer to post bail, two policemen were assigned to see the family safely away in a taxi cab. Aiello left Chicago that night for Buffalo, New York. The next day's newspapers headlined the Outfit's siege of the Bureau: "GUNMEN DEFY POLICE! INVADE LAW'S STRONGHOLD!"

Aiello remained in Buffalo for the next year and some months more. . . . Power is holding someone's fear in the hollow of your hand.

In 1927 the Supreme Court handed down its decision in the case of a bootlegger, Manley Sullivan, who had not filed income tax returns on the grounds that income from illegal transactions was not taxable and that, even if it were, to file on it would be self-incriminatory under the Fifth Amendment. The Court found against Sullivan, giving Elmer L. Irey, chief of the Internal Revenue Bureau's Enforcement Branch, a weapon he could use against gangsters.

Some few years later, with the Bureau hard on his case and the country deep into a catastrophic Depression, Big Al permitted himself a moment of rueful reflection: "I've been made an issue, I guess," he said, "and I'm not complaining. But why don't they go after all these bankers who took the savings of thousands of poor people and lost them in bank failures? How about that? Isn't it a lot worse to take the last few dollars some small family has saved . . . than to sell a little beer, a little alky?"

Fear is power holding you in the hollow of its hand—like a nickel.

Diamond Joe Esposito dispensing cheer at one of his holiday dinners for children at the Bella Napoli

THE LAST GOOD YEAR

In 1928, the population of the United States of America was 120,000,000. In the main, the mood of the country was optimistic. On Wall Street, fortunes were being made. The year was the seventh straight the market went up. Nothing but blue skies from now on. Permanent prosperity.

On the occasion of the dedication of its new building (on the site of its old at Jackson and Federal), the Union League Club of Chicago published on May 21, 1926, a history of its first 47 years of accomplishment. Members in that time had numbered U.S. Senators, a Vice President, a Speaker of the House, a Chief Justice, and of course the leading financiers and merchants of the city, "men of character and serious purpose."

The dedicatory volume stressed that one of the Club's most important objectives was "To resist and expose corruption, . . . and to secure honesty and efficiency in the administration of national, state and municipal offices." So, in the mid-Twenties, with Chicago's streets and back alleys ablaze with gangland gunfire and its polity in a chaos of rigging and fixing and bribery, what was the proudest accomplishment of the Club in public affairs?

"There is probably no single feature of the Club's public work which better expresses its spirit and aims, or which has evoked a heartier support from the entire membership, than its celebration of the anniversary of Washington's birth."

Big Bill Thompson may at many times during his public career have seemed demented, but perhaps he knew exactly what he was doing when he keyed his mayoral campaigns to the defense of George Washington against the King of England.

A year after the Union League Club and its membership of Chicago's leading citizens congratulated itself, the city fathers welcomed

Mussolini's goodwill ambassador, Commander Francesco de Pinedo, and his hydroplane when they landed in Lake Michigan off Monroe at Grant Park. Leading citizens were in the official welcoming party, including, by special invitation, Al Capone. The police had expected demonstrations by the anti-*Fascisti* Sicilians of the city and hoped that Capone's presence would exert a calming influence.

Just half a year after this honor, Al Capone found to his surprise (especially considering his contributions to Thompson's third-term success) that his presence was no longer welcome in Chicago. The mayor had been bitten by the Presidential bug again and Capone was an embarrassment, a symbol of rampant lawlessness not only in the United States but even in countries that did not celebrate the anniversary of George Washington's birth. The pursuit of Aiello in the siege of the Detective Bureau was the Capone action that precipitated Thompson's order of exile.

On December 5 Capone held a press conference at the Metropole to announce that he was leaving for Florida.

"Let the worthy citizens of Chicago get their liquor the best way they can. I'm sick of the job. It's a thankless one and full of grief. . . .

"I violate the prohibition law, sure. Who doesn't? The only difference is I take more chances than the man who drinks a cocktail before dinner and a flock of highballs after it. But he's just as much a violator as I am.

"There's one thing worse than a crook and that's a crooked man in a big political job. A man who pretends he's enforcing the law and is really making dough out of somebody breaking it. A self-respecting hoodlum hasn't any use for that kind of fellow—he buys them like he'd buy any other article necessary to his trade, but he hates them in his heart. . . .

"I've been spending the best years of my life as a public benefactor. I've given people the light pleasures, shown them a good time. And all I get is abuse—the existence of a hunted man. I'm called a killer. . . . Public service is my motto. . . ."

He was asked what a gangster who killed another gangster in a mob war thought about.

"Well, maybe he thinks that the law of self-defense, the way God looks at it, is a little broader than the lawbooks have it. Maybe it means killing a man who'd kill you if he saw you first. Maybe it means killing a man in defense of your business—the way you make the money to take care of your wife and child. I think it does. You can't blame me for thinking there's worse fellows in the world than me."

He took two bodyguards with him but went to California, not Florida. En route he stopped in New Orleans but the local Mafia chief there sent men to meet his party at the train station who broke the fingers of his bodyguards.

He found he was not welcome in Los Angeles either. The police chief there said, "We have no room here for Capone or any other visiting gangsters . . ." and gave him 12 hours to leave the city.

He returned to Chicago but learned that a 24-hour police watch had been posted outside his Prairie Avenue home so that he could not visit his mother and wife and son without risking a scene. This time he did leave for Florida.

In 1928, the population of Illinois was 7,296,000. The population of Chicago was 3,157,400. The city easily led other cities of the nation in disorder, arrests for drunkenness, and municipal venality.

"If you stammer or stutter, Benjamin Bogue can cure you, just as he has cured hundreds of others of all ages."

In 1928, Bathhouse John Coughlin owned a thoroughbred, Roguish Eye, which had won three out of seven starts for the alderman. The Bath entered "The Eye," as he called him, in the Belmont Futurity (purse, $97,990), and though his horse went off at 15 to 1 against, it ran neck and neck with High Strung to a photo finish—but lost. The grief-stricken alderman obtained a photograph of the finish taken from an angle that showed Roguish Eye winning. He labeled the photo "Who Win?" and posted it in Hinky Dink's cigar store and printed his plaintive question on all his insurance business literature thereafter. (An historical note: Coughlin had been sponsored in his political career by "Chesterfield Joe" Mackin, early Democratic lord of the First Ward. Mackin introduced the free lunch to the world: At his saloon every man who bought a beer got a free oyster.)

"They Snickered When I Got Up to Speak—But from the First Word, I Held Them Spellbound."

In 1928, "Sonny Boy," "Lover Come Back to Me," "Button up Your Overcoat," "You're the Cream in My Coffee," and "I Can't Give You Anything But Love (Baby)" were the popular songs. In 1928, *Whoopee*, Charles MacArthur and Ben Hecht's *The Front Page*, Eugene O'Neill's *Strange Interlude*, Mae West in *Diamond Lil*, and the Marx Brothers in *Animal Crackers* were the hit plays on Broadway. Greta Garbo (with a Sarah Bernhardt hair-do) in *The Divine Woman*, Charlie Chaplin in the award-winning *The Circus*, Gloria Swanson with Lionel Barrymore in *Sadie Thompson*, and Janet Gaynor and Charles Farrell in *Seventh Heaven* (probably the most popular love story ever filmed) were the silent movie box office draws. The anti-war film *The Big Parade* (1925) was also still popular. (*All Quiet on the Western Front* was two years in the future.) Mickey Mouse made his debut in 1928 in *Steamboat Willie*, an animated cartoon with sound.

"The U.S. Government Job Is a Good Job, $1260 to $3400 a year—Steady Work—Vacation with full pay—Men-Women 18 to 55—Common education usually sufficient."

The national debt of the U.S. Government on June 30, 1928, was $17½ billion, a reduction of almost a billion from the previous year. There were 58,813 federal court convictions in Volstead Act cases in 1928, 15,793 persons receiving jail sentences totaling 5,631 years and fines aggregating $7,031,199. In addition to these federal cases, the 4,396 Civil Service employees and agents of the Bureau of Prohibition in the Department of the Treasury aided in 15,077 cases in state courts in which 9,025 convictions were obtained. A drop in the bucket, so to say.

Once again, as had happened a decade before, Big Bill Thompson's Presidential aspirations were quickly dashed by the (comparative) grasp on reality of his party's national leaders, and it was once more possible for Al Capone to frequent Chicago, even though no one had heard him renounce rampant lawlessness.

Capone had established a second home in Florida, first in a luxurious Miami Beach bungalow, then in a two-story neo-Spanish 14-room house on an estate on Palm Island. Before he could take possession of the estate, however, two of Thompson's political acolytes had their homes bombed in Chicago, the funeral parlor of John Sbarbaro (now a Municipal Court judge, thanks to Thompson) was bombed, and so also was the home of State's Attorney Crowe's brother-in-law and secretary, Lawrence Cuneo. Thompson was politically beleaguered and Capone made plans to return to the Toddling Town to protect his investment.

Bombs were exploding all over town, but Big Bill Thompson had made peace with Illinois Governor Len Small and, in return for control of all Park Board patronage, Big Bill promised his support to Small in the 1928 primary. Besides Small, Thompson worked industriously for the candidacies of Frank L. Smith for U.S. Senator (the same Smith the Senate had already rejected), and State's Attorney Crowe. Opposed to his chosen triumvirate were Louis L. Emerson ("Lop-Eared Lou," as Big Bill called him) for governor, Otis F. Glenn for senator, and Circuit Court judge John A. Swanson for state's attorney—all backed by Senator Deneen, Thompson's arch-foe in the Republican party.

Eight years before, the only winner against Thompson's slate of ward committeemen candidates had been Diamond Joe Esposito. Esposito's connection with Senator Deneen was his stamp of respectability, so when the senator asked him to run for ward committeeman again in the 1928 primary, Don Peppe agreed—with misgivings because he felt Thompson had become too strong to beat and his own ward had been split to blunt the Italian vote. The mayor of Little Italy was a somewhat strange ally for Deneen to be seeking, in any case, since Deneen was an avowed Dry and reformer and Diamond Joe had grown rich supplying sugar to alky cookers. (For his part, Esposito had always sought friends in every camp.)

For nearly 40 years political power in Little Italy had been in the capable, grasping, hands of Democratic alderman John Powers. Nine-teenth-ward Italians called him "Johnny DePow" or "Gianni Pauli." Esposito's political strength in the ward was, in a strange way, then, an anomaly, since he was Italian by birth, not Irish.

Finley Peter Dunne's Mr. Dooley remarked of alderman Powers that:

> I don't believe they was anny reason in Jawnny Powers' eddication f'r to think that he'd throw away money because iv his conscience throublin' him. The' place he lived in was the toughest on earth. They was hardly a house around that didn't shelter a man that was able to go out anny night with half a brick or the' end iv a bullyard cue an' arn his daily bread.

Mr. Dooley also observed that when Powers entered politics, for role models "he met a lot tht'd steal the whole West Side iv Chicago an' thin fix a gr-rand jury to get away with it."

Powers was first elected to the City Council in 1888 when the 19th ward was still Kilgubbin, and in a short time he became the leader of the council's Grey Wolves. For his individual labors with Billy Lorimer on behalf of traction magnate Charles T. Yerkes, he was known as "The Prince of Boodlers." He took this as a compliment. To Jane Addams of Hull House he was the Prince of Darkness. Nonetheless, Powers liked Addams, smoothed the way to city permits for her projects, and wanted to work with her. She would have no part of him.

As the Italians displaced the Irish in the 19th, Powers acquired the nickname "The Mourner" because he financed so many funerals of the poor, saving loved ones from the horror of burial by the county. At some of the many last rites he attended he kissed the dead twice—once in the home, then at the cemetery—as Italian ritual prescribed. He distributed turkeys to the poor at Thanksgiving—while garbage went uncollected in the streets—and dispensed other aldermanic favors throughout the year. One-third of his constituents were on the city payroll. The people of the 19th grew to depend upon him, which was fortunate since they had little other choice.

255

Beneath his anxious-to-please, yet dour exterior, Powers was an arrogant autocrat. He boasted that "I can buy the Italian vote with a glass of beer and a compliment." He had started his working life as a grocery clerk, then opened a grocery of his own, then a gambling den over a saloon. The latter combination profited mightily during the 1893 World's Fair, even after paying King Mike McDonald 65 percent of the take. It was behind Powers' saloon that work was begun on a modest telephone-line Loop tunnel from which—to the astonishment of most of Chicago—enough dirt was extracted to provide the fill for all of Grant Park. (The ordinance sanctioning the small tunnel had been covertly altered after passage to provide for a much larger underground excavation. Ninety years later this tunnel—12 feet wide, 14 feet high, and 60 miles in extent—cost Chicago citizens $2 billion in repair costs and loss of trade- and wage-time when in 1992 a pile-driver punched a hole into it near the Kinzie Bridge and a quarter million gallons of the Chicago River coursed through, flooding the Loop's southern business section and shutting it down for several weeks.)

Powers was first challenged by an Italian in the 19th ward in 1916 by Tony D'Andrea, scholar, linguist and wealthy lawyer—also an unfrocked priest and convicted counterfeiter who had served 13 months at Joliet before being pardoned by President Theodore Roosevelt at the urging of the husbands of Gold Coast ladies he had tutored in Italian. When his brother Joey was killed in a dispute over Union Station construction contracts, Tony succeeded him as president of the Sewer Diggers' and Tunnel Miners' Union (Diamond Joe Esposito his chief lieutenant). He later became president of the Macaroni Manufacturers' Association, then of the International Hod Carriers' Union (Diamond Joe here, too, his chief lieutenant), finally of the Unione Siciliana.

D'Andrea lost in 1916 but ran against Powers again in 1921. In this election a bomb was exploded on Powers' front porch, one at a D'Andrea rally and a third and fourth in D'Andrea's headquarters and at his home. In a close election, D'Andrea lost again and a month after the election a blast from a shotgun ended his life. Thirty murders were committed during the campaign but Angelo Genna was the only suspect brought to trial and he was acquitted.

Esposito's victory in 1920 as a representative of the anti-Thompson (thus "reform") wing of the Republican party had more than his bootlegging ties to its ironic aspect.

One evening in 1920 after a long day's campaigning against his Thompson-backed opponent, the veteran Powers' hack, Christopher Mamer, Don Peppino dismissed his bodyguards and stopped at a neigh-borhood saloon for a quiet glass of beer before going home. A Valley crazy, Pete D'Alessandro, known to all who feared him (including the police) as "Two-Gun Johnny," was terrorizing a patron who had made the mistake of stumbling against him.

Puffing on a Perfecto Garcia, Diamond Joe stood at the bar feeling comfortable in the shabby saloon, even nostalgic, but D'Alessandro's hectoring was beginning to irritate him. He was too old to listen long to such nonsense.

"*Cretino*!" Two-Gun shouted into the face of his hapless victim, "I am going to shoot out both of your eyes."

Diamond Joe stepped away from the bar toward the two men. He smiled. "*Calma, calma*," he said. "*Pace*."

D'Alessandro looked at this middleaged, portly figure with the diamonds on his belt buckle and spat toward the man's shoes.

The next moment D'Alessandro was sitting on the floor looking both damaged and surprised, the left side of his face red and beginning to swell.

The mayor of Little Italy adjusted his tie, tugged at his vest, and glanced down at D'Alessandro, shrugged, finished his beer and walked to the door of the saloon and out.

Throughout the following week his men repeatedly told him that Pete D'Alessandro was "looking for Esposito." On the Saturday before the election Two-Gun Johnny found him. His hand went inside his coat pocket as he stood facing Esposito.

"Yes," Esposito said, "take out your gun. I will stuff it up your ass. All the way up. Until you can fire from your big mouth."

D'Alessandro shook his head. "No," he said, and drew a handful of cigars from his coat. "For you, Don Peppino," he said. "Never has any man knocked me down. Because you have the courage, I wish to be your friend. Is there anything I can do to help in your election? *Anything*?"

On election day, April 19, Esposito was busy from early morning directing his forces. By evening he had begun to wonder why he had not crossed paths with Mamer's most active precinct captain. Nor had any of his men.

Big Bill Thompson's candidates captured 34 of the city's 35 wards—all but the 19th. There, Joseph Esposito received 1,410 votes for Republican committeeman, Christopher Mamer, 900. The celebration at Esposito's headquarters began a few hours after the polls closed. Resplendent in suit, vest, and silk scarf with diamond stickpin, the "moon," and flashing his big smile and his diamond ring, the "sun," Esposito greeted his well-wishers. Outside four bands played martial music as more than 3,000 supporters from the Valley—men, women, and children—cheered, "Diamond Joe is king! Long live the king!" over and over through the night. The King of the Valley.

Early the next morning Esposito went to his barbershop for a shave. Within minutes the shop was filled with his followers. "Upon my side," he told reporters, "it was the cleanest election—the cleanest political

257

fight ever made in the 19th. . . . But with the Mamer organization and the City Hall crowd it was another story. The police kidnapped my men, wherever they could be identified by a badge, to carry them away from the polling place. . . . So I told them to take off their badges." It was the speech of a victor who had triumphed as much by right as by might.

That same morning the wife of Mamer's missing precinct captain called the city Detective Bureau to report that her husband had not been home for two days and nights.

That afternoon Pete D'Alessandro came to Esposito's offices. When Diamond Joe mentioned the mysterious disappearance of his opponent's chief precinct captain, D'Alessandro winked. He put his palms on Esposito's desk and leaned forward. With pride in his voice he explained that—not having heard from his friend Don Peppino—he had devised a plan of his own. On election eve he had locked Mamer's best precinct captain in the basement of a saloon in the adjoining First Ward. "Now that you have won such a great victory, Don Peppino, I will let him go. He had these papers in his pockets. What are all these names, eh?"

As Esposito later explained, "That captain had the list of bogus names Thompson had put on the poll sheets. And all these names were supposed to have been voted by their repeaters. But I won because Two-Gun Johnny took their lists."

After the election, the mayor of Little Italy sent the mayor of Chicago an oil painting of a Neapolitan countryside as a token of his good will. The mayor of Chicago did not acknowledge the gift.

Politics was far from the whole of Esposito's life, however. He had his business interests to manage, of course—the supplying of alky cookers in Little Italy and Chicago Heights and Melrose Park—and his union responsibilities (he was on the executive board of the American Federation of Labor), and he had his diversions. "I love opera," he told a reporter. "My waiters, any barber along Halsted Street, he'll whistle you 'Lucia' or 'Pagliacci' and you'll find the gallery full of 19th-ward people every night when Mary Garden gives opera in Italian."

(One of his waiters was Felice DeLucia, a fugitive from Naples, where he had killed a man who slighted his sister. Felice served his two-year sentence and upon release killed the man who had testified against him. His mother had written Esposito asking for sanctuary for her son. DeLucia stayed in the Esposito home for half a year, then in a room adjoining Esposito's office above the Bella Napoli until he married. In Chicago he took the name "Paul Ricca" and became known as "The Waiter.")

Esposito's ristorante, the Bella Napoli, took much of his time but he gloried in playing host. Tony Mops Volpe was his manager (formerly his chauffeur) until regular customer Al Capone hired him away.

There was Esposito's $80,000 summer home on Bass Lake in Indiana, and his knockabout boat there, the *Olive Queen*, which he captained with reckless nautical ignorance. He often had long-term guests at his summer home, men from New York, say, who preferred the quiet of Indiana to the attentions of Manhattan police. Esposito also maintained a hideaway for mobsters in Terre Haute, 200 miles south of Chicago. Like Capone, he had connections in other parts of the country, his mainly in the Midwest, where he cultivated the highest state politicians. The Purple Gang of Detroit and mobsters in St. Louis and Cleveland had him on their payrolls.

His summer home sat on a peninsula and was modeled on an Italian villa. The water fountains on its grounds Diamond Joe built himself, working on his hands and knees with rocks and cement. At Bass Lake every Fourth of July he would give a day-long party for friends (among them Frank Nitti, Capone's second-in-command, and Frankie Rio, Capone's bodyguard, who had given the Espositos their family pet, an amiable German shepherd). The holiday began with a band playing the national anthem as the Stars and Stripes were raised, and ended with four or five hours of fireworks lasting till midnight. He had his daughter, Jeanette Frances, swimming across the lake by the time she was four (and taught her at an early age how to gamble and smoke cigars). And there at Bass Lake he kept his ready money hidden. The rest of his steadily accumulating fortune was deposited in out-of-state banks.

Meeting Esposito on Halsted Street one day, the West Side priest Father Francis X. Breen asked him outright when was the last time he had gone to church. The next Sunday Father Breen walked into church with Diamond Joe at his side, and from that Sunday on Don Peppino attended mass regularly. (He became good friends with Father Breen, gave his daughter the priest's name as her middle name.) The rest of Sundays he would spend with his family, usually in the backyard of their modest two-story frame house at 800 South Oakley Boulevard. The home was modest in obedience to the ancient admonition never to appear better off than your neighbors. (Nothing is sure in this world; evil may come from what appears to be good fortune.)

The buildings of Hull House stood next to the Bella Napoli and Jane Addams' settlement-house workers would sometimes congregate in front of the restaurant to sing. "Oh, my god!" Esposito would say when he heard their voices, "*ahmonamie*—here she comes again!" Addams refused to take money directly from Esposito; he had to send an emissary to put $1,000 into the Hull House donations box.

He was not always served well by his employees. He could only write his name in English (his wife Carmela taught him how) and one of his secretaries became an expert forger of this signature. The politician Roland Libonati cashed many checks for Esposito, taking 20 percent as his fee. Some of the checks returned to Esposito after cashing he said he did not remember signing. Libonati advised him to put a circle over the "i" instead of a simple dot, so he could authenticate his signature. When checks came back after that, Esposito would say, "I did sign them. You see my circle?" His secretary would nod knowingly.

He paid a percentage of Bella Napoli receipts, a strong-foot percentage, to a man high in the councils of the Unione Siciliana, Mike Merlo, a close friend. When Esposito told him he was a little short at the end of one month, his friend said he found that exceedingly strange since Esposito's head waiter had told him the restaurant had enjoyed a very good month. (If Esposito were holding out on him he would have to have him killed; both men knew this.)

It was Esposito's secretary who told him how to prove his honesty. Thus it was that the president of the Unione Siciliana was hidden behind the drapes of Esposito's office when the head waiter was summoned.

"What did we make last month?" Esposito asked. "Would you tell me?"

"You hardly made anything, Don Peppino. Lotsa customers but you give away more than you charge for. It's no way to do business."

"The reason I don't charge is I never know when I'll need a favor. One hand washes the other. Are you sure we had a bad month?"

"Yes."

On this the head of the Unione Siciliana stepped out from behind the drapes, badly frightening the waiter.

"Do you have the truth now?" Esposito asked.

"I will never not believe you," replied Merlo to his vindicated friend.

When Capone fell out with the Terrible Gennas, Esposito incurred the Big Fellow's displeasure by continuing to supply the Sicilians with sugar. But Esposito was not all that pleased with everything the younger man did, either. For example, he hated Capone's smoke houses, his four dens of joy on the South Side into each of which on a Friday night 30 to 40 men would disappear to emerge Monday morning pale and sickly. Esposito's disapproval of opium smoking was based on moral grounds; it robbed a man of his will.

In 1922 and 1926 he ran for county commissioner but was defeated both times. He could deliver the vote of the fierce-eyed men of the 19th who survived by dago guts and guile, but the well-spoken silk-stocking voters had no use for a man who talked such broken English. The rising young politician Roland Libonati told Esposito it would be better, perhaps, if he were to give Esposito's speeches to those audiences. "No," was the rejoinder, "isn't it better they know me?"

A heckler sent by Thompsonites taunted him by shouting "Don

Bizzaro!" as he spoke at one meeting. The heckler was referring to an earlier rally—Esposito's supporters scratching washboards and banging pot covers to attract a crowd—at which Don Peppe had released almost a thousand pigeons tagged with the Italian flag, his name on the flags, and when the pigeons flew out the flags all came off and the horde of pigeons panicked and shat upon the crowd below and the police came and threatened to arrest Esposito for creating a public nuisance.

When the heckler was shortly after wounded by gunfire Esposito was taken by the police to the hospital. "As he entered the room," an officer said, "he spoke several words sharply in Italian. Di Presio paled and then declared that Esposito was not his attacker."

An old score had been settled, though. The wounded heckler was Jacobus (now James) di Presio who, 40 years before, had cut Esposito in a scuffle outside the young boys' home village of Acerra.

Because he had not supported Thompson candidates, the Bella Napoli was raided by Prohibition agents in 1923 and then Jim Genna was sent by State's Attorney Crowe to reason with him when he scornfully refused a deal with City Hall. "I told them to go to hell. I am afraid of none of them. . . . Treat everybody right, everybody fair and square, that's always my rule."

He paid a $1,000 fine for Volstead Act violations and the Bella Napoli was padlocked for a year—but permitted by court order to open for the one night of December 22 so that he could give his annual Christmas dinner for hundreds of the ward's poorest children. At some of these dinners in the past, the Outfit's lawyers, Michael Ahern and Thomas Nash, had helped distribute the food baskets (each with a five-dollar bill in it) and toys and items of clothing the children took home with them. Esposito also distributed food baskets at Thanksgiving and Easter, 1,500 to 2,000 of them each holiday. Thirty men spent two weeks preparing the bushel baskets, a task his children were also required to help with. They didn't like the work but they liked it better than being made fun of by their playmates when their father was serenaded with the Italian national anthem by a 40-piece band on St. Joseph's Day. On that day every year Diamond Joe gave a grand festival-feast for the 19th. The Esposito children—and the maids—would run and hide when the band marched onto the Esposito front yard lawn and a laughing, affable Diamond Joe strode to his front porch to receive the accolades of his people.

While the Bella Napoli was shuttered, Esposito took his family across the Atlantic to Italy. (Frank Nitti and his wife stayed in the vacated house.) When the Espositos arrived in Acerra the piazza was crowded with villagers in their Sunday best. As a band began to play, the mayor of Acerra came forward to shake the hand of *Il Milionario*.

Esposito was led to the center of the square and there he pulled a cord that unveiled a 10-foot-high statue of himself, Acerra's most distinguished son. And then, before everyone sat down to eat and drink, the mayor presented Esposito with a testimonial bearing his photograph above intertwined U.S. and Italian flags. Inside, was a message of goodwill and an assurance of welcome upon his return to the United States signed by the governor of Illinois, Len Small, the mayor of Chicago, William Hale Thompson, and U.S. Senator Charles S. Deneen.

The Espositos stayed in Italy nine months and on their return to American shores Carmela fell to her knees and bent her head to kiss the ground. "I feel like that," Diamond Joe said, lifting his wife to her feet.

In 1925 Esposito was one of Illinois' 29 Coolidge Presidential electors. He had the photograph of himself with the President-elect hung in his office. It impressed his callers.

His people came to see him at Polk and Halsted on Saturdays. There he sat behind his desk in his office above the Bella Napoli, a stack of currency at his right hand, and dispensed help and cash and advice to the men and women who waited in a line that extended down the stairs onto the sidewalk.

His benefactions were not confined to the poor in his ward. In 1918 he brought a black Italian boy from Italy to Little Italy and supported him, even after his marriage to a Sicilian girl and the seven children who followed, to three of whom he became godfather. He paid for most of the training of a young Italian who went to Italy to study voice, and he put up the total capitalization for a young Italian manager at the Sawyer Biscuit Company to start his own biscuit company—Fred Salerno. These were only a few of his gifts. His instincts all his life were generous and giving. One of the lesser reasons he sought the hand of teen-aged Carmela Marchese was so that he might help her 16 brothers and sisters.

The women in Esposito's life were not merely diversions. He pursued them with an almost religious zeal. One of his chauffeurs, Joseph Varchetti, said that sometimes he would wait at the curb for two days for Dimey to return to his limo from a call on a lady friend. For a time, the wives of Little Italy were distracted beyond simple excitement by the ferocious intensity of Esposito's affair with the daughter of Bimbo, King of the Halsted Street Gypsies. None of his liaisons lasted, however, though one nearly did. It was with a woman rather high in the scale of Chicago society. (She suggested he tone down his wardrobe.) For a time he contemplated leaving Carmela but at the last moment decided he could not subject his children to such an upheaval. His three children were blood of his blood, flesh of his flesh, his true diamonds. Their welfare came before anything or anyone else.

And Carmela, his bird-in-a-gilded-cage bride ("You may think she's happy and free from care . . . , her beauty sold for an old man's gold"), where did she stand in his loyalties? . . . Perhaps it had been an unwise union, but there are those who maintain that that can be said as a general principle of any marriage. At the least, the Esposito house was divided. In retaliation for his affairs, Carmela would scissors his $200-$300 suits and his fine shirts into strips. His daughter would watch, in tears, and then her mother would beat her in exasperation. Once Carmela issued an ultimatum: Either her husband's adulteries ceased or she would not provide meals for him (a restaurant owner).

"No food?" was his response. "No cook? All right, we got some crackers?" These he dipped into soda and made a meal.

In the middle of the night she stole money from his wallet. Most of the time he was unaware of this but once she took $500 he'd just gotten as a payment that day and the payee was briefly in fearsome trouble.

Esposito had a violent temper when he was aroused—he nearly choked a guest to death in an argument over *bocce* at Bass Lake (his workers there let him win when they played)—but the sternest he could bring himself to be with his young wife was, "Do keep still. You talk like a clock." In a way, after his fashion—the old-country Italian fashion—he loved her. Sometimes to placate her he would give her diamonds. "You like?" he would say. "They please you?" And he had a standing order with DeCarl, the florist at Oakley and Taylor, for bouquets or baskets of flowers to be delivered to her every other day.

No, politics was far from the whole of life to Diamond Joe Esposito, but having a political office sometimes helped in influencing others, especially judges, and was, after all, *in fondo*, a prestigious calling. So when Senator Deneen asked him to run for ward committeeman the year of 19 and 28, he said yes, even though he felt he would lose. Capone would disapprove of his opposing Thompson's candidate, but Capone had disapproved when he ran in 1926, too, and who was Al Capone to tell him what to do? Towel boy at a whorehouse, wasn't he? The son of a Brooklyn drunkard who might not be alive today if he, Diamond Joe, had not helped that family to survive, just as he had helped the Gennas and many others to survive.

Besides, Senator Deneen had permitted him to give his youngest son his name and had come to his son's christening. A man must return favor for favor, or what was honor?

"SUCCESS—Will You Pay the Price?"

"I am like every other girl. My happiness means a home of my own, a successful husband, perhaps a circle of interesting friends—things that will be endangered by the disappointments and failure bound to be caused by your stammering. . . . But did you know that it could be cured?"

The outgoing 30th President of the United States, Calvin Coolidge, was born in Plymouth, Vermont, of English ancestry. The President-elect, Herbert Hoover, was born in West Branch, Iowa, of Quaker parents, and during the campaign promised that "Poverty will be banished from this nation."

An early mayor of Chicago (1858-59), John C. Haines, was called "Copper Stock" Haines because he speculated in copper. This led to the men in his police force being called "coppers."

In 1928, Thornton Wilder won the Pulitzer Prize for his novel *The Bridge of San Luis Rey*. The Norwegian Sigrid Undset was awarded the Nobel Prize in Literature. In China Generalissimo Chiang Kai-shek was consolidating his power. In Germany the President was World War I Field Marshal Paul von Hindenburg, whose term was scheduled to end in 1932. In the Kingdom of Italy the Fascist Premier Benito Mussolini was firmly in control, and in Russia the Secretary-General of the Central Committee of the Communist Party, Joseph Stalin, strengthened his position by banishing his chief rival, Leon Trotsky, from Moscow. In 1928 Freeman Godsen and Charles Correll brought their vaudeville blackface act to Chicago radio as "Amos 'n' Andy" and within a year the comedy was NBC's and the country's most popular radio show. Check and double-check.

"My voice, clear as a bell—strong, forceful, unfaltering—rang out through the hall as I hammered home each point of my message with telling strokes! I let myself go—soaring to a smashing finale. . . .
"When I finished, there was an instant of dead silence! And then it came—a deafening wave of applause rolling up from one hundred pairs of hands—spontaneous, excited, thrilling!"

Early in 1928, the Internal Revenue Bureau obtained indictments of Terry Druggan and Frankie Lake for evasion of income taxes. The Bureau's agents had been after Ralph Capone since 1926. Told he owed $4,065, Ralph failed to pay and in January 1927 the Bureau prepared to attach his property. Bottles then offered to settle for $1,000. (Ralph was making at least a million dollars a year at this time.) Treasury officials in Washington declined his offer and the Bureau's enforcement chief, Elmer L. Irey, assigned a special agent to Ralph's case. Later the next year, 1928, officials at the Bureau targeted his brother Al, as well, unbeknownst to either Capone.

The bird of time has but a little way
To fly—and lo! the bird is on the wing.

PERFIDIA

A month before the April 10, 1928, primary, Big Bill Thompson's America First candidates appeared sure, certain winners. As if to underscore the certainty of their triumph, on March 14 a Deneen candidate for reelection, Joseph Haas, the County Recorder, died and his 600 patronage jobs reverted to Thompson, who with Small and Crowe already controlled almost all city, county, and state jobs in Cook County.

Diamond Joe Esposito's annual Little Italy feast to celebrate St. Joseph's Day was given on Saturday, the 17th of March. St. Joseph's Day (nominally, Thursday) originated during a time of severe drought in Sicily. St. Joseph, beloved by Sicilians, was promised a feast to be shared by the needy if only he would intercede and bring the rains. So he did, and ever after Italians have kept the promise.

Diamond Joe had been giving his Festa San Giuseppe in Little Italy for 13 years. No cheese, no meat (it was Lent), but a groaning abundance of every other Italian food and wine, and one small dish of dry fava beans, an acerbic reminder of all that God had given the starving peasants centuries before.

Diamond Joe made a speech that morning as the crowd in his front yard pitched coins for the poor into the hammock-slung Italian flag stretched across his front porch. He deplored his own ignorance and said how sorry he was he had no education. But, he said, his boy Joseph was going to have all of the advantages he'd missed—all of his children were, and he hoped and was sure that all of the children in Little Italy would someday have those advantages, too.

The following Wednesday evening, as Esposito was about to leave the house, his wife detained him. He had been coming home more often the past year and, comparatively, there was peace in the household. (Some months before, Carmela had astonished him by giving him a new, $12,000 Cunningham car. "Where did the money come from?" was his first question. She confessed that little by little over the years she had stolen it from him.) Now Carmela said, "Gio?" She put her hands to his coat lapels. "Gio, I love you." She could not think why she was moved to tell him this now.

Ten days before, David "Cockeye Mulligan" Albin (whose lawyer, Joseph P. Savage, a boon companion of State's Attorney Crowe, was Esposito's opponent in the race) and Lawrence Dago Mangano, a Capone hood, had come to see Esposito. "You can't win," Albin said. "Why are you making us go to a lot of expense just to play it safe? Get out of the ward. It'll be healthier for you."

Esposito shrugged his shoulders. "I can't cross 'em," he said. "The senator and his associates have been my friends. I can't throw them down."

That Wednesday morning he had received a single-sentence telephone call: "Get out of town or get killed."

His friends—the "boys"—begged him to leave. "Go down to Bass Lake and raise chickens for a while."

"I can't," he told them. "Just today my boy Joseph was taken with scarlet fever. And I promised Senator Deneen I would run."

That night his 11-year-old daughter, Jeanette Frances, went to the silent movie *The Big Parade* with the Espositos' cook and his wife. On Jeanette's return, she was standing on the porch with her mother when they saw Diamond Joe approaching between his bodyguards, the Varchetti brothers. He had been at his headquarters, the Esposito National Republican Club, only a few blocks away. "Papa," Jeanette called to him when he was three houses from the porch.

"Stay there," he called back. "I'll be right there."

She saw a slow-moving car pull alongside the three walking men. "What'sa matter, fella?" she heard her father ask. "You gotta flat tire?"

She saw his bodyguards drop to the ground on either side of him as the shooting began, blast after blast from a shotgun, her father turning and turning in front of a dark, huge tree as the bursts ripped into his body, not falling till the car pulled away.

Carmela ran out to her husband. "Oh, is it you, Giuseppe?" she wailed. She bent over his body and heard his last words: "*Povra filia mia.*"

She threw herself to the ground beside him. "He was so good to the Italian people and this is what he got for it," she moaned. "I'll *kill!*" she shrieked. "I'll kill them for this!"

Diamond Joe, the Mayor of Little Italy, King of the Valley, was 56 years old when he was murdered. (For God's sake, let us sit upon the ground and tell sad stories of the death of kings.) He had lived 21 years beyond the length of life he could have expected had he not as a young, lustful guappo left his village of Acerra for the golden opportunities in the land of pane e lavoro. He was killed, it is noted, after the filing date had passed for a candidate to replace him.

In the days before the ceremonies of high requiem mass at Holy Family church, thousands of men and women of Little Italy filed through the Esposito home to pay their last respects. Through unseasonable snow, sleet, and rain 8,000 men, women, and children attended the funeral mass, including Senator Deneen, many other high-ranking politicians, and judges and lawyers, among the last the Outfit's, the partners Thomas Nash and Michael Ahern. After the church rites a cortege of 300 automobiles drove slowly through Esposito's kingdom and past the Bella Napoli, according to Italian tradition, and then to Mount Carmel Cemetery. The 31-year-old widow had almost to be carried from the graveside.

A newspaper reporter claimed he found a man standing in the rain after the funeral, "a little man wearing a black Italian society band [who] hunched his shabby coat collar up around his neck. 'The world, too,' he said, shrugging, 'is weep for Joe.' "

The night of the day Esposito was buried a bomb loaded with dynamite wrecked the front of Senator Deneen's home on the South Side and another bomb was tossed onto Judge Swanson's driveway, exploding seconds before Crowe's opponent, turning into his driveway, would have passed over it. These were the 60th and 61st bombings of a campaign that had come to be called "The Pineapple Primary." A newspaper columnist wrote:

> The rockets' red glare, the bombs bursting in air
> Gave proof through the night that Chicago's still there.

State's Attorney Crowe issued a statement claiming that leaders of the Deneen forces, knowing they were defeated, had bombed their own homes "to discredit Mayor Thompson and myself." Mayor Thompson quickly agreed that this was what most assuredly had happened.

Chicagoans were first dumbfounded by this explanation, then outraged. Crowe's cynical bluster proved a gigantic blunder. The revulsion was city-wide.

On April 6 the Chicago Crime Commission, which had been pro-Crowe, published an open letter "To the Voters of Cook County" stating that Crowe was "inefficient and unworthy" and recommending "that he be defeated. . . ."

On Easter Sunday, the Catholic, Protestant, and Jewish clergy of Chicago spoke almost as one to their congregations, denouncing Thompson's rule and his slate of candidates. Thompson issued a threat: "If Deneen's candidate, Swanson, wins in this election," he vowed, "I will resign."

On election day the Outfit—generaled by Capone himself—did its work. Ballot boxes were stuffed before the polls opened; the names of fictitious and unregistered voters were inserted into the lists to be voted by repeaters (who voted as many as 100 times under different names at the same precinct), floaters (transported from poll to poll), and mattress voters (vagrants); unfriendly election officials were intimidated or kidnapped; friendly election officials destroyed opposing ballots or disqualified them by double-marking them, or falsified their place's tallies—all of these activities with the complicity of the police assigned to poll-watching. A black candidate, Octavius C. Granady, running against a Thompson candidate, was shot and killed in the streets after he voted. (Four policemen and three gangsters were later adjudged not guilty of Granady's murder.)

In addition to the Outfit's strong-arm help, Thompson's slate had 100,000 patronage employees ostensibly behind it—and yet on April 10 his slate (in a voter turnout twice what was expected) was smashed. Governor Small lost to Deneen's man by 439,792 votes; Thompson's America First Smith lost to Deneen's man by 243,477; and State's Attorney Crowe lost to Judge Swanson by 201,227. Thompson himself was defeated for Republican committeeman in his own 46th ward.

The election left Thompson's political machine and career in shambles. Reminded by reporters he had said he would resign if Crowe lost, he snapped back, "Well, now I'm saying definitely that I'm not getting out!" His only apparent concession to the voice of the people was to replace his ineffectual Chief of Police Hughes with Deputy Chief William F. Russell, whose past record promised no better.

Capone met with the widow Esposito, at her insistence. Her husband's body had been torn by 58 slugs. She and her daughter had seen the faces of the killers and knew them. She wanted to know why her husband was killed.

"It was a mistake," Capone told her. "It wasn't supposed to happen," his customary explanation to the victimized, and one he apparently thought consoled them.

"I don't want my husband in the ground," Carmela said. "I want him buried in a mausoleum."

Capone called in his assistants. They protested that the widow had enough money of her own to pay for a mausoleum. Capone told them to ante up—$30,000; he did not permit them to talk it over. "It is what I want," he said. In return, he took Diamond Joe's eight-carat ring (the "sun") from the widow. No one was ever arrested for Esposito's murder.

Don Peppe's estate was expected to come to about $4 million. The widow knew of a pillow-case a third full of diamonds, and there were the out-of-state bank accounts, the money hidden at Bass Lake, much else. When the estate was finally probated it totaled slightly more than $26,000.

Many years later, in 1993 (aged 96), the beautiful 16-year-old bride Carmela said of her husband: "He was a great man and a bad man, but more great than bad." The truth was that her husband was killed because he couldn't not keep his word.

On June 20, 1928, Chicago Mayor William Hale Thompson and six of his political associates were found guilty of having entered into a conspiracy to defraud the city of $2,245,604 in real estate expert fees to finance Thompson's political machine and for their private benefit. The finding in the Circuit Court was the culmination of a taxpayers' suit instituted in 1921 by the *Chicago Tribune*; the defendants were ordered to make complete restitution.

Like most politicians (and businessmen and gangsters), Big Bill Thompson liked money very much: It didn't have to be fed; it didn't take up much room; and if you dropped it, it didn't break. He had never dreamed that once you had it in your pocket you might have to give it back.

Coupled with his devastating primary reverses, the Circuit Court decision destroyed Big Bill. "They've ruined me!" he shrieked. "The sons of bitches are going to take everything I've got!" His drinking had always been close to or just past the limit. Now, bleary-eyed, red-faced, wet-lipped, he was never without a highball in his hand. He hurled insults at long-gone enemies, called old friends by the wrong names, blubbered, drooled, wailed, and moaned. Associates took him to a woods-shrouded estate in the Eagle River country of Wisconsin.

In the summer (peak beer season) of 1927 the Outfit's supply of suds failed to meet demand and Capone had bought 500 barrels from Roger Touhy, the bootleg and slot machine baron of northwest Cook County. He even got a discount to $37.50 a barrel because of his quantity order. A few days later he asked for 300 more. The day before payment came due, he called Touhy. "Fifty of those barrels were leakers," he said. "I'll pay you for 750, okay?"

Touhy laughed. He knew that his cooperage's barrels did not leak.

Capone paid for 800 barrels—$30,000 cash—and in a week called wanting 500 more, but Touhy this time said no, though he could have supplied them. Capone knew this, and marked it.

Touhy and his partner, Matt Kolb, supplied beer to a territory that stretched from the city line west to Elgin and from North Avenue to the Lake County line. Touhy also had 225 slot machines in choice locations. His was a rich barony and of course Capone had eyes for it. While he was in Chicago after the 1928 primary he sent Frankie Rio and Willie Heeney to see Touhy and tell him the Outfit would like to open the northwest suburbs to brothels, high-stakes gambling, alky stills, and punch-boards. A solemn-faced Heeney told Touhy that "Al says this is virgin territory out here for whorehouses."

Touhy put on a show for Rio and Heeney—tough talk, prop guns, fake phone calls, big, tough-looking ex-cops tromping in and out of his office. . . . A stand-off.

Next, Capone sent Louis Little New York Campagna and Machine Gun Jack McGurn. Touhy put on another tough-guy show and the Outfit's two top gunmen left, puzzled and wary. Their boss coveted the territory for bootlegging, but. . . .

By 1928 bootlegging accounted for only about 35 percent of the Outfit's revenues—gambling, prostitution, and labor racketeering the rest. As any prudent businessman would—given Johnny Pappa's prediction of the end of Prohibition—Capone had hedged the future by diversifying, especially very heavily into labor racketeering. He was interested only in the money to be made from employee-employer relations. As the Five Pointers from which he came had, he worked the side of the street that paid most—or both sides, if it came to that. What he hoped to have by the time Prohibition ended was control—through unions—of the liquor traffic. This meant owning the teamsters, bartenders, waiters and waitresses, cooks and bakers, and musicians and performers. Meanwhile, his personal view was that unions should be declared illegal, since they prevented their members from selling their services to the highest bidder, a violation of one of the mainstays of the free enterprise system in which he so strongly believed.

The unions the Outfit controlled negotiated benefits and higher wages for the rank and file, true. As Capone said, "The workers will always vote for . . . the guy who promises them the most in the way of more pork chops." But, as he added, "As long as their take-home pay is higher this year than it was last year they don't care how much you take from them in the way of dues." Or initiation fees, or special assessments.

On the other side, as *their* tribute to the Outfit, employers paid generously for sweetheart labor contracts and dearly to avoid strikes.

Mobsters had been taking over unions since Colosimo's time, most notably among them, Dago Mike Carozzo. As a grinning, curly-headed shoeshine boy of 14 (born in Montaguto, Italy, 1895) Carozzo had come to the favorable attention of Big Jim Colosimo. He was first given a job as a white wing street sweeper, then as a First Ward precinct captain, and then recommended to the spell-binding Big Tim Murphy, who ruled half a dozen Chicago unions. When in 1916 Murphy needed a new president of the street sweepers' union, he had Carozzo elected. Reporting to Colosimo's right-hand man, Johnny Torrio, and schooled in union management by Diamond Joe Esposito, Carozzo soon ran the Street Laborers Union and the City Street Repairers Union, as well.

In 1920, with Murphy, Vincenzo "Sunny Jim" Cosmano, and James Vinci, the 25-year-old Carozzo assisted in the murder of Maurice

"Mossy" Enright, business agent of the Garbage Handlers Union. The victim, a Max Annenberg *Tribune* circulation slugger with Frankie McErlane, Hymie Weiss, and Dion O'Banion a decade before, had been giving Murphy trouble over control of the Gas Workers Union. Enright's was the first from-an-auto murder in Chicago. Vinci, the driver, unaccountably suffered an attack of remorse and confessed to the police, naming names and witnesses. Thus, witnesses had to be eliminated. At the trial, Murphy, Cosmano, and Carozzo went free: no witnesses; Vinci was sentenced to 14 years: he had confessed.

Carozzo helped his rank and file. In 1925, for example, with a week-long strike, he won the white wings a 50-cent-a-day raise, the street repairmen a dollar-a-day raise, and the garbage dump foremen an increase from $165 to $200 a month. He also helped himself to a large salary increase as head of their unions.

By 1928 Carozzo controlled 23 Chicago unions—and with them all the public paving projects in the city, at 5 percent of all contracts from the private contractors. (When Dago Mike died in 1940 the price of paving in Chicago dropped a dollar a square yard.)

On the death of Diamond Joe Esposito, Carozzo took over his Hod Carriers International Union and his seat on the executive board of the AFL.

James "Red" Barker, a proficient gunman, was Capone's resident expert in unions. He subscribed to all the local and national union publications and by one means or another obtained union financial statements. When his researches discovered a union with a particularly healthy balance sheet, he informed Capone—who had his operatives, Murray "The Camel" Humphreys and "Three-Finger Jack" White, orchestrate the appropriate moves for a takeover.

White was a veteran of the newspaper circulation wars and a sometime safecracker. Humphreys, a glib and wisecracking Welshman and petty thief, went to work for Capone after being brought before him accused of hijacking an Outfit beer truck. His exculpatory spiel so impressed the Big Fellow that Capone hired him on. By the mid-Twenties Humphreys, now a top-rank man in the Outfit (and now also a jewel thief, kidnapper, and contract killer), "owned" 61 labor unions, these in addition to Carozzo's 23.

Takeover was usually accomplished by summoning a union leader to Capone's office, where in a warm but businesslike manner Capone would offer to come in as a partner, 50-50. It was explained that the Outfit would see to the doubling of union membership, and therefore the union leader's income would not suffer. The offer was, of course, a command, whether made in Capone's office or by Humphreys or White as messengers. A saying became current in Chicago: When the Outfit wants in, you might as well give it to them. (This saying's truth marches

271

on.) After the Outfit had clearly established its methods and seriousness, most union skates went along. Those who didn't, as Capone explained, ". . . you take them in the alley. When they get out of the hospital if they still want to squawk, you get rid of them." On takeover, the Outfit acquired the union treasury and transferred all but a token sum of the union's bank accounts to its own.

In late 1927 Morris Becker, the owner of 10 cleaning shops on the South and North sides, was approached by a representative of the Master Cleaners and Dyers Association—a price-fixing group of employers who controlled the industry's two labor unions—and told he would have to raise his prices. Becker, who had been setting his own prices for 42 years, refused. A bomb was exploded in his plant. He was then asked for a $5,000 donation to the Association. When he refused this, his plant was struck. Becker went to the state's attorney, who had him tell his story to a grand jury. The 15 members of the Master Cleaners Association were indicted, but at their trial all 15 were acquitted. (Did their lawyers know the law? No, but they knew the judge.)

When he left the courtroom Becker telephoned Al Capone and the next day met with him and Jake Guzik, Louis Cowan, and Abraham Teitelbaum, Capone's personal lawyer. Humphreys and Barker were present at the meeting. In a few weeks Becker called a press conference. He announced that he was "paying Al Capone $25,000 for the use of his name. I have no need of the police, of the courts, of the law. . . . With Al Capone as my partner I have the best protection in the world."

From that time on, Becker had no trouble with the Association. A lawyer for the Master Cleaners did call on Capone, but was greeted with, "Get the hell out of my office. You try to monkey with my business and I'll toss you out of the window." Becker was to say of the arrangement, "Al Capone was scrupulous in living up to his bargain. . . . If I had it to do over again, I would never ask for a more honest partner in any business."

Red Barker reported that one of the unions controlled by the Master Cleaners Association had $300,000 in its treasury. After digesting this news, Capone told Humphreys, "Nobody ought to keep a sum like that in a bank, just drawing interest. Let's put it to work in the American way."

In a short time, after threatening phone calls made at midnight, an arm-breaking, and a number of bombings, Humphreys took over the Master Cleaners Association and its two unions. (Humphreys had once run a cleaning and dyeing shop. He was known to make jokes about "laundering" money and about people being "taken to the cleaners"—fair samples of his wit.)

Another employer who called on Capone's labor-relations expertise was Colonel Robert R. McCormick, publisher of the *Chicago*

Tribune. Max Annenberg, the World's Greatest Newspaper's circulation director, invited Capone to the Tribune Tower, where he asked him to use his influence to prevent a strike threatened by the *Trib*'s drivers union. Capone said he would see to it and Annenberg then brought in McCormick. The Colonel thanked Capone and said, "You know, you're famous, like Babe Ruth. We can't help printing things about you, but I will see that the *Tribune* gives you a square deal."

While he was in Chicago, Capone moved his headquarters from the Metropole across the street to three floors of the 10-story, 400-room Lexington Hotel at 23rd Street and Michigan Avenue, a block away. He sent to Italy for laborers to build a network of secret escape tunnels connecting the Lexington's basement with adjoining buildings, then shipped the workers back to Italy when their task was finished. On one of his floors he installed a kitchen that was presided over by his personal chef, Provino Mosca, whose duties included sampling each dish and wine before it was served.

As in the Metropole, mobster women were allotted rooms at the Lexington. Capone's inamorata was a teenage blonde Greek girl he had taken out of one of his brothels. Capone liked young women, 13 or 14 if possible. This one consulted Capone's physician (a partner in the Cicero dog track) when a vaginal lesion began to bother her. It proved to be caused by syphilis. Capone refused to take a Wassermann test for the Old Ral himself because, as he said, he felt fine.

In Chicago on the evening of June 26, 1928, a black sedan turned into Kolmar Avenue in West Rogers Park. Ahead stood the mansion of Joseph Aiello, who was in hiding in New York but one of whose neighbors was Big Tim Murphy. After serving five of six years in Leavenworth given him by Judge Kenesaw Mountain Landis for a 1921 mail-car robbery, Big Tim had tried without success to get back into labor racketeering. One of his bids was for the Cleaners and Dyers Union, but there he ran into opposition from the Outfit's Murray Humphreys.

The bell rang at Big Tim's brick bungalow, he went to the door, opened it and stepped out, and was killed instantly by a Capone gunman shooting from the black sedan.

(One of Murphy's proteges was the young John Oberta, nicknamed "Dingbat," after a comic-strip character. When Oberta, a gunman for Polack Joe Saltis, ran for political office, Murphy would speak on his behalf at rallies. Because there were many Irish voters in Oberta's back-of-the-yards district, Murphy suggested that the lad apostrophize his Polish name. Thereafter, John's posters read "O'Berta." At Big Tim's funeral, Oberta's eyes and those of Big Tim's bedimpled widow Flo met across the deceased's grave—with the result that the two mourners were married 10 months later.)

At the time of Murphy's funeral, Capone was conferring at his

Palm Island estate with Chicago associates. (Big Al was personally supervising $100,000 worth of additions to his villa: the largest private swimming pool in Florida, a bathhouse, a boathouse, a new dock, new garages, rock gardens, and fountains.) The men with Big Al—Jake Guzik, Charlie Fischetti, Chicago City Sealer Daniel Serritella, Machine Gun Jack McGurn, Albert Anselmi, and John Scalisi—all realized there were problems attendant to any business grossing $6 million a week, but they also knew that their job was to solve those problems. For more than a year now the Outfit's shipments of high-proof, high-grade liquor from Rum Row had been getting hijacked in the East. Frankie Yale was being paid to prevent just this, and he was not doing it. The year before, Capone had sent a man to NYC to scout the possibility of double-dealing. The man was killed, but not before confirming the suspicion.

His Palm Island visitors left their leader to return to Chicago on June 28 but McGurn, Anselmi, and Scalisi got off the train in Knoxville, Tennessee, and purchased a black Nash sedan to continue on their own journey. Ten years after leaving Brooklyn and the employ of Frankie Yale, Al Capone had decided it was time to pay his apprenticeship dues in full.

On the quiet Sunday afternoon of July 1, Frankie Yale was drinking in his Sunrise Café at 65th Street and 14th Avenue. About 3:00 P.M. a phone call summoned him home. His Lincoln sedan, its bullet-proof windows rolled down to let in the summer's air, was overtaken by a black Nash sedan on 44th Street in Brooklyn's residential Homewood section and he was killed by one of the hundred bullets that pierced his body, his Lincoln sedan leaping the curb and sidewalk to deposit his corpse in the midst of a Sunday afternoon lawn party. His slaying marked the first use of a machine gun in NYC gang warfare. (Oddly enough, *two* Mrs. Yales appeared at the funeral.)

Nine weeks later, in Chicago on Friday afternoon, September 7, Antonio Lombardo, Capone's handpicked head of the Unione Siciliana, left the Unione's offices at 8 South Dearborn, two blocks from City Hall, with two bodyguards. The sidewalks were thronged with office workers and shoppers on their way to streetcar stops or commuter-train stations or to speakeasies or restaurants, the streets were bumper-to-bumper with automobiles. A block from the intersection of State and Madison—known in 1928 as the world's busiest corner—two men came up quickly behind Lombardo and at close range pumped two dum-dum bullets into his head, two more into the spine of one of his bodyguards, and ran off. The second bodyguard gave chase but was stopped and held by a policeman who thought he was one of the killers.

Hundreds of pedestrians had witnessed the shooting. The only place more public in which to have held an execution would have been a window at Marshall Field's. But no one was ever arrested for

Lombardo's murder. It was speculated that the killers had been sent by Joseph Aiello, resuming his pursuit of the Unione presidency, or that they were Sicilians from New York avenging Frankie Yale's death—or that Lombardo was slain by the two factions working together.

The next day, on September 8, feast day of Our Lady of Loretto, the biggest festival in Little Italy, the beginning of a week of celebration and worship, Father Louis Giambastiani put up a notice on the door or the church of San Filippo Benizi. In Italian the notice read:

> Brothers! For the honor you owe to God, for the respect of your American country and humanity—pray that this ferocious manslaughter, which disgraces the Italian name before the civilized world, may come to an end.

The church of San Filippo Benizi stood on a corner at the intersection of Oak and Cambridge, "Death Corner"—and also the corner where young friends from St. Phillip's parochial school and the Edward Jenner public school gathered at the lunch hour on school days. The week following Lombardo's assassination, attendance at the two schools was down by 600 pupils. Nearly a thousand families had fled their tenements to go into hiding in Wisconsin and Michigan small towns. And for some reason, all the butcher shops of Little Hell were closed.

Lombardo's funeral was suitably elaborate, befitting his standing in the community. His body was placed in a mausoleum at Mount Carmel Cemetery. An unshaven Capone attended the ceremony and then arranged for his friend Pasqualino "Patsy" Lolordo to succeed Lombardo as Unione president, once again thwarting Joseph Aiello's ambitions.

Lolordo assumed the presidency on September 14. That same week Capone's gunmen wounded Aiello's brother and in running battles that followed killed four Aiello followers, losing two men themselves.

On January 8, 1929, Pasqualino Lolordo and his wife, Aleina, were returning to their Northwest Side apartment on the third floor at 1921 West North Avenue from an afternoon of shopping. Two men Mrs. Lolordo said she did not know met them at their door and went upstairs with them, staying half an hour, talking with Pasqualino while Mrs. Lolordo ironed clothes in the kitchen.

Five minutes after the first two men left, three other men knocked at the apartment's door and were admitted, Pasqualino greeting them with hearty cordiality. Mrs. Lolordo and her maid prepared a platter of sandwiches and pastries and brought the food to the men in the living room. Pasqualino brought out a decanter of bourbon, four bottles of wine, and a box of cigars and closed the door to the living room.

Down the hallway, in the kitchen, Mrs. Lolordo could hear the men's voices growing louder as they talked and, apparently, as the spirits flowed. An hour passed, the sound of the voices growing louder still and frequently mingled with laughter. Then Mrs. Lolordo heard someone shout, "Here's to Pasqualino!" and then she heard gun shots.

As Mrs. Lolordo reached the living room, the door opened and the three visitors shoved past her and hurried down the stairs. Her husband lay dead, killed by 11 .38 caliber bullets. There was a .38 six feet from his body—one hand still holding his wine glass—and the police found another .38 on the stairs.

"Poor Patsy!" Capone said sorrowfully when told of the killing, one that would not have taken place, he knew, had he not elevated his friend to the Unione presidency.

Mrs. Lolordo was of no help to the police in their investigation, which eventually proved fruitless. Initially there was a report that from a photograph she had identified Joey Aiello as one of the three visitors, but the police denied this. They said she would only tell them that the three men were not Italian, which seemed to point to Bugs Moran's North Siders, who were known allies of Aiello. But it may have been that Mrs. Lolordo was not telling the truth, that she had indeed recognized the men but, of course, knew that silence was expected of her. Both her husband and Joey Aiello were once business associates of the murdered Antonio Lombardo, which could have accounted for Pasqualino's cordiality to his visitors when they arrived at the apartment door. That is, if Joey Aiello were back in town. Perhaps Pasqualino envisioned a reconciliation with his old compare, Joey, an end to the killing. *Il caso*—it happens. But it didn't.

Whether it was the Aiellos or the North Siders—or the two factions working in tandem—Capone knew that both would have to be dealt with. They were becoming major irritants. Meanwhile, at the urging of his most favored Sicilian killers, Anselmi and Scalisi, he installed Lolordo's lieutenant, 26-year-old Joseph Hop Toad Giunta, as Patsy's successor to the Unione presidency, a post that every Sicilian male seemed to want but which none were holding for very long.

SATCHMO

Prohibition did have a saving grace: It is fair to say that without it, jazz might have vanished. As a distinct, exceedingly bold and vital art form, "jass" survived and was elaborated, expanded, and more or less formalized in Chicago's South Side mob-run joints in the 1920s. Inside those all-night clubs, early giants of the revolutionary "hot" music broke the boundaries of the established musical order, and thereby incidentally also challenged the social hierarchy that the old harmonic structures implicitly supported. Audiences, black and white, went wild, literally, to the hard-driving and exotic beat of jass, while America's guardians of morality looked on in horror and disgust. But "jazz," as it was renamed to sanitize its brothel-slang denotation (said to have had 22nd St. Chicago origins), became a Roaring Twenties rage—and the Roaring Twenties also became the Jazz Age.

Jazz got started way down yonder in New Orleans, a city of almost as great antiquity as any on the continent. The trading village at the mouth of the Mississippi, founded in 1718 by French Caribbeans, was already a cosmopolitan city when it was ceded to the United States as part of the Louisiana Purchase in 1803. The southern outpost became an oasis of enlightenment for political and cultural dissidents. More, it specialized in the satisfaction of libertine appetites.

From the beginning, the powerful Mississippi brought wealth and commerce south from all points north, as well as exposure to every form of American music. The beat of all those sounds simmered in the city's swampland and traveled deep into the recesses of its underground social life. New Orleans celebrated itself around the calendar, and in some parts of the city around the clock. After the Civil War and the arrival of railroads, when its Gilded Age slipped into senility and the city began to reek of a growing decadence, the sound remained, making newer forms

---

This chapter was written by R. Craig Sautter.

of music possible and hard times a little bit easier.

One of the French government's legacies to the Crescent City was prostitution as a municipal institution. The French royal house had originally shipped willing—and unwilling—ladies of leisure across the ocean with the noble intention of providing wives to the colonists. Instead, a trade in flesh burgeoned. By the turn of the 20th century, whorehouses were scattered in nearly every neighborhood of New Orleans, and patronizing them was as natural an act as carrying a pistol in your boot or a bylow knife in your belt.

To control the spread of the trade, the city council passed a law in 1899 confining prostitution to one area, thereafter called "Storyville," after the law's author, Joseph Story. Soon Storyville was the city's biggest attraction, 24 hours a day, seven days a week. It featured street after street with inviting dens of iniquity that took from hard-working men only everything they had in their pockets in exchange for a phantasmagoria of carnal pleasures.

And the whole district moved and swayed to New Orleans' versions of slow drag blues, popular tunes, and ragtime, played by white, Creole, and black musicians who made a modest living pouring out their mix of songs into the sultry New Orleans nights. The musicians blew away on cornets, trombone, and clarinets, and beat their pianos, drums, guitars, bass, and banjos with a gusto that bordered on abandon. They took pride in their craft and sustenance from their art—and, after all, playing music all night easily beat hauling crates all day on the levees.

Storyville was segregated white. Next to it thrived a black red-light district sometimes called "Black Storyville," although black women and musicians worked both sections. Most New Orleans Afro-Americans (the term of the time) and Creoles toiled under strictly enforced Jim Crow restrictions dating from the 1870s, even though the city was thoroughly intermixed by several centuries of the races living and laying side by side. The black district of Storyville ran between Perdido and Gravier, and Locust and Franklin streets, uptown from the more ornate Creole French Quarter, which was called downtown. The red-light district of the black Third Ward was shabby, depressing, and dangerous. Slavery was still practiced: 12-year-old girls of all three races were sold at auction, while the poorest crib girls sold themselves in slow times for as little as a dime.

The red-light district of the black ghetto was interspersed with honky tonks and rough-and-tumble dance halls such as Funky Butt Hall where Buddy Bolden, who founded the first-ever jass band, nightly blew his horn to produce an exhilarating and soaring sound whose pace was said to burn the night with its brilliance. Bolden's cornet playing was to influence a generation of younger players, most of whom would further improvise on his innovations up north.

One of the ragtag youngsters running the streets of Black Story-ville was known as "Little Louis." He had a special affinity for the music that poured out of honky tonks like Funky Butt's, or Joe Segretta's, or Kid Brown's, or Spano's. The streets of the Third Ward were his home, and its music was in his blood.

Little Louis was the son of May Ann Miles, at one time a "hostess" in the red-light district, and Willie Armstrong, a roaming womanizer who deserted Mayann (as she was called) before Louis' birth. Louis Armstrong claimed he was born on the Fourth of July, 1900. In reality, as a boy, he had no reason to celebrate his birthday and no holidays to commemorate; all his days were equally harsh.

He was born in James Alley, in a section known as the "Battle-field" because, as Louis later said,

> ". . . the toughest characters in town used to live there, and would shoot and fight so much. In that one block between Gravier and Perdido Streets more people were crowded than you ever saw in your life. There were church people, gamblers, hustlers, cheap pimps, thieves, prostitutes and lots of children. There were bars, honky-tonks and saloons, and lots of women walking the streets for tricks to take them to their 'pads,' as they called their rooms."

After living the first years of his life with his grandmother, Josephine Armstrong, the boy was taken by his mother to live with her in a shanty at 1233 Perdido Street (today, the site of Louisiana's Supreme Court Building). Mayann went to work "for some white folks on Canal Street," cleaning house and doing laundry. Her short and outwardly shy little boy had a huge smile and a taste for the exotic life that he gained running barefooted and tattered on errands for the girls and their pimps. He was almost always hungry as a child; his lifelong appetite became renowned. And he never gave up the habits such as playing craps that he acquired at an early age. Even at the height of his career he would go uptown to NYC's Harlem to shoot dice on the sidewalks.

But another hunger was supremely fed. Music permeated the streets of the red-light district, played by house combos, and he listened to them all. He also loved to follow behind the marching brass bands like Bunk Johnson's "Original Superior Orchestra" and Joe Oliver's "Onward Brass Band" when the lodges and social clubs, such as the "Zulu Aid Pleasure and Social Club," celebrated Mardi Gras or led a funeral procession. (One day he would play in the Onward Brass Band himself and later still become "King of the Zulus.") Louis claimed that while still a child he heard the legendary Bolden play his blazing horn at Funky Butt Hall. But by 1907 Bolden was locked in an insane asylum, long before the record companies would come looking for the original generation of jazzmen.

The youngster formed a vocal quartet and they sang on the streets for small change, but he didn't learn to play cornet until he was consigned to the Colored Waif's Home at age 12. He was sent to this home in the honeysuckled countryside for shooting off Mayann's .38 in the street on New Year's Eve. Because he was from the Battlefield, the Home's music director expected the worst from him, but after a few weeks of good behavior, he was put in the brass band, under the direction of Peter Davis. Armstrong later remembered that

> "The little brass band was very good, and Mr. Davis made the boys play a little of every kind of music. I had never tried to play the cornet before, but while listening to the band every day, I remembered Joe Oliver, Bolden, and Bunk Johnson. And I had an awful urge to learn the cornet."

He quickly picked up the rudiments of the instrument and began to master the architecture of melody and rhythm, and to learn a repertory of brass band songs and popular melodies such as "At the Animals' Ball."

"Mutt" Carey, a trumpeter, recalled that "In New Orleans all the boys came up the hard way. The musicianship was a little poor. You see, the average boy tried to learn by himself because there were either no teachers, or they couldn't afford music lessons." In legal custody, Armstrong had the benefit of strict, if elementary, music instruction and a discipline he never would have found on the streets. That made his three-year stay ultimately rewarding to him, despite the loss of his freedom.

When he was released back onto the streets he was nearly 15 years old, and sought to make his living through the thing he now loved most, music. The honky tonks hired three- or four-piece bands with piano, brass, and strings, usually guitars. Now as an energetic teenager, Armstrong showed a determined streak that enabled him to make a living delivering coal all day under the hot Louisiana sun, while all night he hung around the honky-tonk bandstands hoping for a chance to fill a vacancy and strut his stuff.

Still lean and growing, he went around to the different tonks borrowing other musician's cornets, learning to play the blues, practicing phrases and melodies, repeating them time and time again in simple sequences. He could pick up any tune by ear, and by the time he borrowed $10 to buy his own horn, he was getting noticed. Band leader and trombonist Edward "Kid" Ory, who later was featured in Armstrong's own "Hot Five" in the mid-1920s, reported that on one occasion in Lincoln Park, "Louis came up and played 'Ole Miss' and the blues and everyone in the park went wild over this boy in knee trousers who could play so great." The pioneer jazz critic and historian Otis Ferguson told of when the New Orleans bands "used to hunt each other up in the streets, to out-blast, out-think, out-improvise the opposition.

There is a story, probably with some basis of fact, of the time two bands came together in New Orleans for a bucking contest, one of them eager for battle in the knowledge that it held the big buck of the trumpet players, Herry Renée, and that the other was a weak outfit. Of how the first band started riding away to glory, and then there popped out from under the tarpaulin of the second wagon, where they had hidden him, a kid with dynamite in his heart. Of how the kid was Louis Armstrong and how Louis pointed his horn to the housetops and blasted chorus for chorus, until it was dark and the other man was cut to the ground and ready to retreat. Of how then the men of Louis Armstrong's following quickly hooked their wagon onto the wagon of the retreating band, so it couldn't get away from them, and followed it through the town, with his horn raised in the air and in triumph.

Louis started working regularly in Henry Matranga's tonk for a buck a night. Tips brought in more. But he kept his day jobs, which now also included milk delivery, at least until the day the War to End All Wars ended. As he pointed out, the slogan back then was "Work or Fight."

The ambitious but still withdrawn youngster started frequenting the tonks where Joe Oliver, one of the Crescent City's top cornets, was dazzling crowds with his rich tone and theatrical tricks. Oliver was born in 1874 on a Louisiana plantation and was taken to New Orleans as a youngster, where he was raised by an affluent Jewish family. Few of the early jazzmen were ever as poor as Little Louis. Oliver had come up in Kid Ory's band, joining after the pioneering Creole cornetist Freddie Keppard, founder of the "Original Creole Orchestra," left town. Louis' smile got to Oliver, who let the young man carry his instrument case and run errands for his wife and himself. In return, Oliver gave Armstrong playing time, musical tips, and even one of his old cornets. When Oliver went north, he recommended Armstrong as his successor. As Armstrong remembered:

"Kid Ory had some of the finest gigs, especially for the rich white folks. Whenever we'd play a swell place, such as the Country Club, we would get more money and during the intermissions the people giving the dance would see that the band had a big delicious meal, the same as they ate."

Occasionally, he also got to play Pete Lala's in white Storyville.

Quickly the fluid and flamboyant music coming from the horn of the otherwise retiring Armstrong earned the respect of other musicians and eventually he played in some of the best halls of the city. He also started his own group with drummer Joe Lindsey to get other dates, including street parades. Even white bands were playing the new music.

281

Louis was among the freest, most graceful of the hot players, having none of the reluctance of some of the older players to leave rigid structures and patterns behind. At the same time, he was learning how to be a professional and disciplined member of a band with set routines and antics. Seemingly freeform, the New Orleans sound was tightly produced by an ensemble acting as one unit.

Then on November 12, 1917, the U.S. Department of the Navy, overreaching its authority, ordered Storyville and the red-light district of the Third Ward shut down. Over the vociferous protests of city leaders, the feds acted against the notorious quarters with the same puritanical zeal that would fuel their attack on demon rum the next decade. The Navy's claim was that it was protecting U.S. servicemen who would otherwise squander their meager paychecks on cheap wine and wild women, and bring back the gleet and Old Ral to their ships.

The federal action meant that most of the flashy, homegrown, ragtime, jazz bands had fewer places to play. And without Storyville or the black honky tonks, there were no all-night spots for large crowds to congregate to urge the jazzmen on, no places for the players to invent and perfect their musical idiom, no places to play their heartbreaking and gleeful masterpieces in the making, no places anywhere for the hot new music to ignite the loins of wild dancers and slick prancers.

No one knew it at the time, but America almost lost its most original art form when the New Orleans musicians were deprived of their livelihood. Had there been no Volstead Act, the jazzmen could have been forced into menial Jim Crow jobs to pay their rent and feed their families. It would be mob-run, Prohibition Chicago that saved a generation of New Orleans musical innovators and gave them a second stage to blow their horns from and perfect their discoveries.

In 1915, when Little Louis was still in the Colored Waif's Home, trombonist Tom Brown took a "jass" band to Chicago and raised a stir in the press and on the dance floor. Keppard, who had been crowned as Bolden's successor, disappeared from New Orleans in 1911, but later resurfaced in Chicago. Nick LaRocca led the "Original Dixieland Jazz Band" north, the group that cut the first jazz records in 1917 for Victor. To everyone's surprise, they sold millions. (LaRocca became the stylistic model for white Twenties' sensation Leon "Bix" Beiderbecke.) George Brunies and his white "New Orleans Rhythm Kings" (NORK) hit Chicago in the early 1920s. Even as these bands were creating a mass audience for jazz, young Louis Armstrong was one of its rising stars back in the New Orleans tonks.

When "King" Oliver left for Chicago in 1918, Armstrong was too uncertain of himself to make the long trip north yet. He was still learning his horn in his hometown and having a ball "throwing down the coal," as he would say. He continued playing off and on with Ory's band until

1919 when the group splintered. Ory went to California to seek relief for a lung condition and there gained a national following with his radio broadcasts of traditional jazz from Los Angeles.

When Storyville closed, some of the New Orleans jazzmen were able to find work on the riverboats of the Mississippi where they learned anew that the great river ran as far north as it surged south. After all, for three bitter centuries, runaway slaves and ex-slaves had followed the mighty river's banks north in search of freedom. The Streckfus riverboats that plied the Mississippi out of St. Louis featured black musicians and stopped at every port from New Orleans to Davenport, Iowa (Beiderbecke's hometown). Fate Marable, a pianist and band leader, was hired to put together a riverboat ensemble to play jazz along with popular dance tunes. He chose clarinetist Johnny and drummer "Baby" Dodds, Johnny St. Cyr on banjo, and "Pops" Foster on bass. The youngest member of the 12-piece orchestra Marable selected was Louis Armstrong, now known as "Kid Louis."

On the riverboat *Sydney*, Armstrong acquired further professional polish and was exposed to more musical variety. He worked on his ability to read music; he also remembered almost everything he heard, reintegrating it into phrases for his own solos. Many musicians called the riverboat jobs "going to school." One story Armstrong told shows how deprived he was of general knowledge of the world beyond the Third Ward: When the *Sydney* first reached St. Louis, Armstrong asked Marable if the tall buildings they saw were "colleges."

Knowing music was something else. On sultry summer nights the boats floated on a golden flow of hot lava licks pouring from the gold-tinted rims of the jazzmen's soul-ignited saxophones, cornets, and trombones, and from their sweet clarinets and persistent drums came a river of music on fire with discoveries of riffs too beautiful to forget and almost too powerful to recapture.

By then, the first World War's black migration had already become a flood upstream to St. Louis and Chicago. Those who couldn't take the fancy riverboats north hitchhiked or rode the train on a more direct route to the Promised Land in their "flight out of Egypt." Millions of ex-sharecroppers and vanquished freedmen fled the unrepentant Southland in search of a better life. In 1910, Chicago was home to only 44,000 Afro-Americans. By 1920, after WWI had drawn so many north for factory and steel-foundry jobs, Chicago's black population had expanded to more than 100,000; by 1930, to 233,000. Chicago was the first American black Mecca. Even after its vicious 1919 race riots Chicago was felt to be the place to go by blacks because "the worst place up there is better than the best place down here."

By 1921, when Armstrong played his last notes on the river, he had become a consummate professional musician, ready for a big city and the opportunities that awaited his talents. For a while he ended up in Storyville. He married a prostitute, Daisy Parker, a fiery personality who was the first of his four wives. She was known to attack Armstrong with fists, razors, and bricks when her jealousy was aroused. In part to get away from her, Armstrong quickly accepted when King Oliver in 1922 sent an invitation to join him on Chicago's South State Street. By this time, King Oliver's "Creole Jazz Band" was considered the best in Chicago, which meant in the world. As Otis Ferguson wrote:

> Chicago in the early and middle twenties was the place for a man to learn music. . . . And from then till now, there has been nothing to add to the elements present in those days. . . . But if you had it to do all over, you would do very well to be a kid with an instrument, learning it and trotting around to hear other people playing it, in the streets of Chicago during the years between 1922 and 1928. You could go wherever or do whatever you wanted after that, but you would have had the advantage of more natural education available in one place than you will find in many a day's journey over history and the map.

The jazzmen were welcome up north because the passage of the 18th Amendment had put big money into Chicago's speakeasies, clubs and dance halls, and the Outfit knew that it was easiest to keep customers drinking when they were dancing themselves into dizzy stupors to hypnotic drums or wailing trumpets or skydiving slide trombones. The musicians and the thrill-seeking crowds who came to hear them expected constant innovation, and got it. They knew that each and every night the music changed from what it had been, changed even with each and every set, liberated sounds feverishly unfolding and growing, with new arrangements, new improvisations, new acrobatics, new ornaments, grace notes, transitional passages. Each version of even the instant classics sometimes changed as fast as it could be learned and rearranged. The Chicago speaks and clubs vibrated to the freedom of these unrestrained and pristine sounds, to accompanying cries of sexual emancipation, to hollers of unrestrained ecstasy and booze-inspired joy.

When Louis stepped off the Illinois Central train at Union station, neither Oliver nor any of his sidemen were there to greet him. He had missed his originally scheduled train to play in a last funeral march and grab some extra coins. He later admitted that he was so disheartened he almost turned around and took the next train back south. He arrived in Chicago wearing old-fashioned shoes and clothes that he would soon shed for a bow tie and tuxedo, the uniform that made the jazzmen the envy and pride of Chicago's black population. He recalled that "The King was already at work. . . .I took a cab and went directly to the Gardens." The Lincoln Gardens Café at 459 East 31st Street was a large dance hall that catered to blacks but where white musicians crowded in after their own gigs to listen to the King swing. A huge crystal ball hung from the ceiling and a baby spot on it sent slivers of light shimmering across the dance floor. When Lil Hardin, Oliver's stunning pianist, first saw the newest Southern transplant, she was appalled:

> "Everything that he had on was too small for him. His atrocious tie was dangling down over his protruding stomach and to top it off, he had a hairdo that called for bangs, and I do mean bangs. Bangs that jutted over his forehead like a frayed canopy. All the musicians called him Little Louis, and he weighed 226 pounds."

Armstrong moved into a South Side rooming house with the luxury of his own private bath, something not even to be thought of in the red-light district of New Orleans. He ate his meals with Oliver and his wife. He was dazzled by the city's size and relieved by its relative racial freedom (although Chicago was as segregated as New Orleans, with blacks excluded from most white clubs and stores in the Loop and elsewhere—except, in the clubs, as performers). Armstrong felt at home playing with Oliver again, and his musicianship had grown impressively since the King last heard him. Still, it was Oliver's band and Louis never crossed him by out-shining the boss—"cutting" him—even on their always thrilling "breaks."

Music in New Orleans had revolved around joyous creative occasions. But Chicago had a harder edge and music was just one strand of the vast gangland commercial network that existed for the sole purpose of making money for the mob. In New Orleans, jazz was part of the open social life of the city. In Chicago, it was just another Outfit commodity. But it also became an underground narcotic as powerfully intoxicating as the illegal rum and gin the Outfit dispensed. Its seeming illicitness gave jazz an added attractiveness to many blacks and whites because they felt they lived only on the fringes of society anyway.

Armstrong loved the "Stroll" on South State Street in Chicago's black Second Ward. The street never slept. The Outfit's notorious Pekin Inn or Pekin Temple of Music at State and 27th Street opened at 1 A.M. and closed at dawn. The 1,200-seat music hall served whites and blacks of the "sporting fraternity." The Sunset Café was located at 35th and Calumet, the Dreamland Café at 3520 South State. The Plantation Café at 338 East 35th was a "black and tan" club run by the Outfit. The Elite No. 2 Café was at 3030 South State, the Elite No. 1 at 3445 South State, and the Deluxe Café at 3503 South State. Other joints lined 35th between State and Calumet. Vaudeville shows played at the Richelieu and the Deluxe. In 1927 the Savoy Ballroom opened at 47th and South Parkway. And there were more, many more, at least 100 in all.

Pianist Earl Hines, who later in the decade became Armstrong's partner on stage and in two failed clubs, and who was Al Capone's favorite piano player, described 35th Street off State as

> ". . . a bad street. It was lit up at night like Paris, and there were some
> of the most dangerous people in the world on it. That's why Jelly Roll
> Morton carried his pistol and was so loud-mouthed. You had to act bad,
> whether you were bad or not. Somebody was always getting hurt and
> you had to have a certain amount of courage to work in those clubs."

Inside the clubs the music steamed all night and the air grew thick with
smoke and hemp. Armstrong himself was a joyous consumer of marijuana
(which wasn't made illegal until 1937). Anything went; according to one
upset observer, "many of the dancers could be seen fornicating while
standing up, swaying slowly to the music, the girls' dresses pulled up."

The mind and the muscle and the moneymaker behind all this, Al
Capone, appreciated jazz, although sentimental tunes were his favorites.
But jazz was the sound that kept his customers hepped up and drinking,
and it also may have seemed to him to have conveyed the frenzy of his
time, his position, his city, his rise to power. The trumpeter "Doc"
Cheatham recalled that Capone "had nice cabarets and after-hours joints
all over the place. Everywhere there was space, he rented it, had music
in there and kept bringing in musicians from New Orleans." According
to Earl Hines, the Big Fellow "liked to come into a club with his henchmen, order all the doors closed, and have the band play his requests. He
was free with $100 tips." The band leader usually got $1,000 on these
occasions. Eddie Condon said one gangster told him that he liked jazz
because, unlike the sentimental favorites, "It's got guts and it don't make
you slobber."

But playing for the mob carried its dangers. One night an Outfit
limo carried Bing Crosby, Eddie Condon, and Bix—who were passengers
by command—to the Greyhound Inn in Cicero. Someone in the audience
there wouldn't quiet down so Bix told him to cool it. He complied. Later
the trio learned that the unruly patron was Ralph Bottles Capone. (And
there is an ugly story, not necessarily apocryphal, of what another
insulted gangster did to Beiderbecke with a coke bottle by way of a
lesson in manners.) Another time, "Muggsy" Spanier was blowing away
on his cornet when two mobsters were gunned down in front of the
bandstand. Jim Lannigan was wailing on bass at the Friars' Inn at Van
Buren and Wabash when one of Capone's boys pulled out his pistol and
blew off the back of the bass. Later he handed Lannigan a handful of
$100s, apologizing by saying, "I dunno. Something came over me. I
couldn't resist it." The musicians never left their instruments in a place
overnight for fear it would be bombed or burned out by morning.

Mezz Mezzrow, a clarinetist and good friend of Armstrong's,
described Capone as "sharp, young and ready in those days, with a couple
of trigger men always trailing along at his elbows. He was friendly

enough, and that was how I wanted him to keep feeling." But Mezzrow didn't like the mob. He called them

> a race of gangsters running amuck, a hundred million blowtops born with ice-cubes for hearts and the appetites of a cannibal. Nobody was safe in this funky jungle. It was all one great underworld, and they'd put their dirty grabbers on the one good thing left on earth, our music, and sucked it down into the mud with them.

Pianist Art Hodes said of the gangsters: "You observed and you kept your mouth shut and minded your business. And they left you alone, if you did that, because you were an employee."

In 1923, the King Oliver band first went into the recording studio for the Gennett Record Company (Richmond, IN), six years after the first jazz record was released by the Original Dixieland Jazz Band. In the interim the "Louisiana Five" had cut 40 sides in 1918-19. In 1921, Kid Ory put out his "Sunshine" sides. But Oliver showed exactly why he was called "King" and what the real up-tempo New Orleans ensemble was all about. Later that year the band also cut sides in Chicago for OKeh, Columbia, and Paramount. Performers on these lively records included Oliver, Armstrong, Lil Hardin, Honoré Dutrey on trombone, and Baby Dodds on drums, plus Johnny Dodds on clarinet, and Johnny St. Cyr on banjo on various takes. Armstrong played second cornet in all these sessions, willingly staying in the shadow of Oliver. He only soloed on four Oliver sides; these were "Chimes Blues," "Froggie Moore," and two versions of "Riverside Blues," showing some of his rhythmic virtuosity with irregular accents, dynamic changes, unevenly divided beats, skips and bounces of swing, and a rich, round sound. Armstrong frequently harmonized with Oliver as well. The recordings did not soar to the top of the sales charts as had those of other jazz bands before them—but they were received like sacred testaments by other musicians. In his "Origins of Jazz" Otis Ferguson summarized what Armstrong and Oliver had done:

> [They] were gradually teaching how the field could be widened musically without the loss of the first excitement, how the strident note could be deepened into a note of power. And their message, if you could put it into words, ran somewhat like this: "Play hard, blow even louder; but relax, take it easy, let the music do it." Those open tones and that echo of the blues were coming up the river just like southern airs in the spring, but not softly, because there was a bonfire under them. They were no breeze, but a hot wind.

When Armstrong met her, Lil Hardin was a pretty, talented, young girl. She had been born in Memphis in 1898 and educated in Fisk's college of music. Her mother regarded blues as nothing but "wurthless immoral music, played by wurthless, immoral loafers expressin' their vulgar minds with vulgar music." Somehow Lil broke loose; it helped that her cousin played blues guitar. She left Fisk after two years there, arriving in Chicago in 1918 and worked as a piano demonstrator of tunes, but soon jumped to Oliver's band as its pianist. By the time Louis arrived on the scene, she wore a mink and drove a big black roadster, demonstrating how far Chicago could be from any plantation. It took a little dressing him up and slimming him down, but Lil did it and then fell in love with Armstrong. "He didn't believe in himself to begin with," she said. But tested by competitors, he blew away all challengers, with the exception of the King, whom he always idolized. Two years after Armstrong came north, and after both of their divorces came through, Louis and Lil married.

She took charge of his career. That meant breaking away from Oliver. Louis fussed and fought against the move, but by that time it was obvious that he needed more room to exhibit his extraordinary talents. He played Dreamland with its glass floor along with his friend Earl Hines, but the gig was only temporary. He got a call from New York City, where they had heard the Dixieland sound on phonographs but no one there seemed to know how to play real jazz. It would be Armstrong's job to show them.

In 1924, Fletcher Henderson, about to move his band from the Cotton Club in Harlem down to Roseland north of Times Square, needed a cornetist and contacted Armstrong, whom he had seen as a talented teen in New Orleans and heard on Oliver's recordings. With Lil's encouragement, they left Chicago to set the Empire City a-talkin'. At the time, New York had at least 2,500 speakeasies, cabarets, and clubs, and 238 dance halls. The finest of the dance halls was the still-segregated Roseland. Henderson was recording, too. Louis got to New York in time to participate in an October 24, 1924, date. Within weeks, his superior talent and special knowledge of the New Orleans sound made him the band's top player and a sensation to watch. In addition to Roseland, the band played for black audiences all over Harlem. After a few months, however, Lil's mother became ill, so Lil returned to Chicago. Louis worked on his instrument and took his act into the studio with Henderson, soaring on solos in "Shanghai Shuffle," "Bye, Bye," "Sugarfoot Stomp," "Go Long, Mule." And he began doing impressive side work on recordings by classic blues singers Bessie Smith, Ma Rainey, Trixie Smith, and Clara Smith. His work on "St. Louis Blues" with Bessie is counted among the greatest blues collaborations ever. One night at Roseland, Louis not only played, but sang choruses of "Everybody Loves My Baby, But My Baby Don't Love Nobody But Me," and his gravelly voice made an instant hit with the crowd. From that point on, Armstrong began to think of himself as an entertainer capable of doing the whole show, emceeing and all.

But Lil pressured him to return to her in Chicago where the music was still far in advance of that of the New Yorkers. Besides, he was dissatisfied with some of Henderson's men:

> "When them cats commenced getting careless with their music, fooling around all night, I was dragged, man. They started goofing and drinking and didn't care. I was always very serious about my music, so I went back to Chicago."

In late autumn 1925 he returned to play Dreamland on the Stroll with Lil for $75 a week, and stayed in the Windy City until spring 1929.

Within a week of his return, he was back in the studio ready to lay down the cuts for OKeh that would define him to the world beyond the cabarets, sides that are now acknowledged to be some of the most exciting, most awe-inspiring jazz ever recorded. The records were released under the name "Louis Armstrong and His Hot Five." The musicians received $50 per session; Armstrong said they saw the dates as "just another gig." Historically, they became much, much more. The initial group included Lil, Johnny St. Cyr, Kid Ory, and Johnny Dodds, with later variations bringing in bluesman Lonnie Johnson on guitar, Earl Hines, and others. In the first sessions, the ensemble retained the original New Orleans format, with Louis working as lead cornet of an energetic and balanced ensemble.

But gradually, as the sessions continued over the next few years under various names such as "Louis Armstrong and His Hot Seven," and "Louis Armstrong and His Savoy Ballroom Five," Armstrong took over, relegating the band to a backup role for the genius of his horn, improvising and fronting in ways that opened up jazz to its modern incarnations. His range and inventiveness, his dazzling high notes, raspy voice, breathed fire and blazed with beauty. In all, Armstrong cut 60 titles in the format and almost every one of them showed him at work as a constant and brilliant inventor of phrases and intricate architectures, playing with a total sense of rhythm and rearranged melody that was daring, intricate, emotional, and unpredictable. His tone alone was incomparable. Out of those sessions came songs whose titles became successive national best sellers, with hyped-up names such as "Heebie Jeebies," "Cornet Chop Suey," "Skid-Dat-De-Dat," "Jazz Lips," "Hotter Than That," "Muggles," a code word for marijuana (whose use as an intoxicant, along with ether, had increased with Prohibition), "Melancholy," and the elegiac "St. James Infirmary." The stirringly elegant and sad "West End Blues," a classic that expressed Armstrong's feelings over the death of his mother (in her 40s), is considered his greatest piece from this period. Musicians everywhere were flabbergasted at the musical splendor of the recordings, and the public swarmed the stores for them. If Oliver was still King, then Armstrong had ascended a step above the throne. These sessions also produced wildly popular cuts such as "Musk-rat Ramble," written by Ory, "Potato Head Blues," "Savoy Blues," and the comic "Big Butter and Egg Man."

A dozen years later Ferguson attempted a one-paragraph summation of Armstrong's accomplishment during this period:

> This isn't the place for an appreciation of Louis Armstrong's amazing range and power, of the constant play of a musical imagination that could throw out enough careless phrases any night in the week to provide an orchestra arranger with material for a month's work. This is just the place where we say that Louis, as the flower of his field in music, had a vast influence all down the line, inspiring musicians by his example and bringing audiences to their feet yelling. From his entrance into the field as a star performer, people learned that jazz could swing—not with its former choppy drive, but with a new sort of continuous power, like waves on the beach. And from this time, the harsh musical outline of jazz began to fill out with warmth and color.

In the winter of 1926, Armstrong worked in Erskine Tate's orchestra at the Vendome, a theater for black audiences at 3145 South State, playing two shows an evening. It was here that he acquired the nickname "Satchmo," after a vaudevillesque turn he performed as "Reverend Satchelmouth" scolding a sinful Wicked City congregation. And somewhere along the line he traded his cornet for a longer, more powerful trumpet. Later in 1926 he starred at the Sunset, a stylish cabaret with a floor show, as the featured artist in the Carroll Dickerson band and then in his own "Stompers." The Sunset was often filled with rich, white patrons from Chicago's North Side. Other musicians were frequently in the crowd, including such future big names as Benny Goodman, Jimmy Dorsey, and teenagers from the Austin High Gang that included Frank Teschmacher, Dave North, Dave Tough, Muggsy Spanier, Jimmy and Dick MacPartland, and Bud Freeman, and others such as Eddie Condon and Gene Krupa also came for their lessons. One night King Oliver sat in and dueled Armstrong in "125 Choruses of Tiger Rag." According to cornetist Wild Bill Davison, "people went insane. They threw their clothes on the floor. It was the most exciting thing I ever heard in my life."

Armstrong, now a mature and handsome young man, was a hero in the black community. He was spending big on the folks around him, driving a Hupmobile Eight, hitting all the clubs when he was free. He and Lil moved into a house at 421 East 44th Street. They kept a summer place on Lake Michigan. But Lil's firm control over his behavior led to many quarrels and by 1928 he began to stray, dating Alpha Smith, future wife number three. (That marriage lasted until 1940.) But under the veneer of his laughing vaudeville act, Armstrong was still a shy and lonely man, with few close friends. His music conveyed that and the depth and range of his other emotions as well, and often carried a deep sense of sadness—in other words, an authentic blues spirit.

In 1928 the lights dimmed on Chicago's wild cabaret show. Political setbacks ganged up on Mayor Big Bill Thompson and his slate was defeated in the Republican primary, a signal for the morality crowd to turn its attention to the clubs and theaters, locking their doors and harassing their bars. As with Storyville's close, many musicians were suddenly without jobs—a year before the rest of the nation found itself in the same situation. The jazz pioneers who had worn tuxedos to work were forced into menial jobs. Kid Ory ran a chicken farm; Sidney Bechet became a tailor; Baby Dodds drove a taxi. King Oliver, Armstrong's guiding light, eventually died of cerebral hemorrhage in 1938 in Savannah, Georgia, his musical career over as a result of bad health and a damaged mouth. His last job was cleaning up a pool hall for loose change; in his rented room, they found $1.60.

So in 1929 Armstrong led a procession of cars with members of the Dickerson band cross-country to NYC, where there was still entertaining to do for a star as big as he had become. The great New Orleans-Chicago jazz years had ended; the Thirties and Forties would be the decades of the big dance bands. Chicago had been a hospitable host to classical jazz, giving it a critical forum and an economic foundation. But each wave of migratory blacks continued to bring new and original blues and jazz players to the city. In the 1940s, Muddy Waters came straight off a Mississippi Delta plantation to the South Side, electrified his blues guitar, and plugged in the foundation for rock and roll. A few years earlier, in 1936, the mysterious blues legend Robert Johnson, who was later—at age 23—murdered by a jealous lover, hitchhiked day and night with guitarist Johnny Shines to Chicago. He stayed just 24 hours, just long enough to leave behind his signature, today's blues anthem, "Sweet Home Chicago."

Despite the Depression, Armstrong's records continued to sell as many as 100,000 copies each. But now a matured and confident Armstrong was ready to perform as the total showman, and become belovedly known to the whole world as "Satchmo," playing his horn and jiving on stage for an international audience of kings and queens and jazz fans the world over.

In the early Thirties a young and worshipful Lionel Hampton had asked Armstrong, "Mr. Armstrong, just what is jazz?" To which Armstrong responded, "If you don't know what it is, don't mess with it." Louis Armstrong knew what it was, right from the git-go.

St. Valentine's Day's victims

THE FIRST REALLY BAD YEAR

Back in 1924, before the Outfit's conquest of Cicero was complete, a broken-nosed ex-lightweight (who had killed a man in the ring with one punch), Eddie Tancl, had a big following among voters in the town. He owned a saloon on the corner of 48th and Ogden Avenues, and he disapproved of the agreement his political pal, Eddie Vogel, had made with Johnny Torrio—slots for Vogel, gambling and bootlegging for Torrio. When Tancl's beer supplier, the West Side O'Donnells, delivered needled beer to him (near beer with alcohol added), Tancl said that from then on he would be buying his beer wherever he chose—which of course ran counter to Torrio's master plan for a bootlegging syndicate.

Tancl was told to get back in line or get out. "Try and put me out," he challenged Torrio's messenger. "I was in Cicero long before youse guys come."

Not long after, on a Sunday morning, Myles O'Donnell and Jim Doherty of the West Side O'Donnells swayed into the Hawthorne Park Café after Saturday night on the town and ordered drinks and breakfast. Tancl, his wife, his head bartender, Leo Klimas, and his star entertainer, Mayme McClain, were sitting at another, close-by table.

O'Donnell and Doherty ate and drank their breakfast and when their waiter, Martin Simet, presented them their bill for $5.50, they complained loudly and profanely that they were being overcharged. O'Donnell stood up and just as he threw a punch at Simet, Tancl grabbed his arm. O'Donnell shoved Tancl and both men drew their guns and fired, shooting each other in the chest. At this, Doherty pulled out his gun and began firing wildly. The waiter Simet and the bartender Klimas grappled for Doherty's gun and Klimas was shot and killed.

O'Donnell and Tancl continued firing at each other until their guns were empty. O'Donnell, hit by four bullets, staggered to the door of the café and went out, followed by Doherty, who was also wounded, and the two stumbled off in opposite directions.

The badly wounded Tancl got another gun from behind his bar and limped after O'Donnell, firing as he went. He overtook O'Donnell after a two-block, slow-motion pursuit, but only because O'Donnell collapsed.

By then, however, Tancl's gun was empty. He threw it at O'Donnell's head and collapsed beside him. An out-of-breath Simet arrived and Tancl gasped to his waiter, "Get him, he got me," and died. Simet jumped up and down on O'Donnell, kicking him repeatedly in the head, until a police ambulance arrived and stopped his assault.

A Sunday-morning murderous gunfight, savage, bloody, drunken, cruel, and senseless, but human. That is, men against men, face-to-face, each of the duelists having approximately the same chances of survival. Humanized—if the word is permitted—by anger, rage, and passion. That was in 1924.

Five years later, on the cold morning of February 14, 1929, St. Valentine's Day, about 10:30, five men—three of them wearing police uniforms—got out of a black Cadillac sedan that had been modified to resemble a police car and walked toward the entrance of the SMC Cartage Company building at 2122 North Clark, the office, garage, and warehouse of Bugs Moran's North Siders. Inside the garage were six members of Moran's gang and an optometrist who got a thrill out of hanging out with gangsters.

When the five men left the garage minutes later, everyone inside lay dead or dying on the concrete floor. The St. Valentine's Day Massacre was a cold-blooded, grisly, efficient execution; no passion entered into it. Thinking they were being routinely rousted by three policemen, the seven men had lined up tamely facing an inside brick wall and then been cut down by tommyguns, and shotgunned.

The massacre has been described by many writers for both print and screen. Typical of the overheated approach most often employed is this description from inside the garage, giving the reaction of Highball, an Alsatian dog owned by one of the victims:

> Highball had gone berserk, fiercely yelping and howling at the onset of the carnage. The dog ripped and tore at the leash that held him to the truck axle. One of the killers turned to the animal, remarking: "We oughta give it to him, too."
>
> McGurn kept staring down at the dead, fascinated by his own slaughter. "Naw, I like dogs," he said.

This from the typewriter of a prolific, much-remaindered Chicago writer of true crime who was born five years after the event he dramatizes with such teeth-gnashing suppressed emotion. No one in that garage who walked out of it ever talked about what happened; not for publication, at least. And since Highball gave no depositions, we must conclude the account is fictional.

The wordsmith quoted—like most of his confreres—confidently identifies the killers. To this date, about 25 different gangsters have been positively identified as one of the five men (some say six) who walked into the SMC building on St. Valentine's day.

For sure we know only that Machine Gun Jack McGurn's closest Outfit friend, the gunman Michael Spranze (aka Kelly) observed a ritual for many years each St. Valentine's Day after 1929. About 10:00 in the morning he would gather newspapers and magazines, fix some sandwiches for himself, take some soft drinks, and lock himself in his bedroom until the day had passed.

Killed that icy morning were the thrill-seeking optometrist, Reinhold H. Schwimmer, 29, who had met Bugs Moran in the Parkway Hotel at 2100 Lincoln Park West where both lived; Adam Heyer, 41, who had served time for embezzlement and was Moran's accountant; James Clark (born Kachelleck), 39, also an ex-con; Johnnie May, 40, a safecracker on Moran's payroll as a truck and auto mechanic (he was also Highball's owner); Al Weinshank, 36, a North Side speakeasy owner and labor racketeer (who had been organizing an association to oppose Murray Humphreys' Master Cleaners); and the gunmen Pete Gusenberg, 36, and his brother, Frank, 40, who had some months before trapped Jack McGurn in a telephone booth and shotgunned him so thoroughly that major surgery was required. The brothers were thought to have been Pasqualino Lolordo's killers.

The six mobsters were waiting for a whiskey shipment that was to be delivered at 10:30 and for Bugs Moran, their leader, who would have the cash to pay for it. The killers entered when they did because apparently their lookouts (in rented rooms across the street) mistook Al Weinshank for Moran, the bullseye of Capone's target. Moran was late, and approaching the garage, when he saw three policemen get out of the black sedan. He departed.

Sergeant Thomas J. Loftus of the Hudson Avenue station was the first police officer on the scene. One of the seven victims was still alive. Here is part of Loftus' report from the police files:

> I said to Frank Gusenberg, "Do you know me, Frank?" He said, "Yes, you are Tom Loftus." I said, "Who did it?" or "What happened?" He said, "I won't talk." I said, "You are in bad shape." He said, "For God's sake, get me to a hospital."
>
> I told him I wanted him to explain the shooting, and he said, "I refuse to talk." I told him the wagon was on the way to take him to a hospital.

At the hospital Gusenberg again refused to talk. Sergeant Loftus asked him if three of the killers wore police uniforms. Gusenberg's answer was yes and at 1:30 P.M. he died.

Most crime writers paint dramatic word pictures of Frank Gusenberg's death-bed dialogue with a certain Detective Sergeant Clarence Sweeney, who, after the massacre, alleged he was a schoolboy chum of the Gusenberg brothers. Here again from the pop crime writer quoted earlier:

> Gusenberg lingered for 90 minutes, talking with his friend Sergeant Sweeney, remembering what he could of the day's traumatic moments, drifting in and out of a coma, complaining that the day was darkening too soon. "I'm cold, Sweeney, awful cold. Pull the covers up over me."
> "Want a preacher, Frank?" Sweeney asked quietly.
> Gusenberg's lips barely twitched. "No."
> He was dead.

This account is suitably poignant, but lacks credibility, since Sergeant Sweeney was not at the hospital. Officers Loftus and James Mikes were the only policemen at Gusenberg's bedside. While there is nowhere a mention of Sergeant Sweeney in the official police reports, as late as 1959 Sweeney was still giving interviews about his vigil at the hospital bedside and, by then, had promoted himself to first on the scene at the garage, as well. A marvelous gift of gab.

The next day the police brought in Moran for questioning. Moran had taken to referring to Capone as the "Beast." He had told an interviewer,

> "The Beast uses his muscle men to peddle rot-gut alcohol and green beer. I'm a legitimate salesman of good beer and pure whiskey. He trusts nobody and suspects everybody. He always has guards. I travel around with a couple of pals. The Behemoth can't sleep nights. If you ask me, he's on the dope. Me, I don't even need an aspirin."

Moran had been regularly hijacking the Outfit's shipments of Old Log Cabin liquor, and of course was an avowed confederate of Joey Aiello—"Any enemy of the Beast is my pal," Moran had said. But the gangless leader had lost some of his bravado. "Only Capone kills like that," he told the police.

In their editorial columns, newspapers throughout the country expressed shock and outrage. "Crimes like this," said a writer in the *New York Sun*, "constitute the underworld's supreme defiance of society." The citizenry of Chicago (with its City Council, Association of Commerce, and State's Attorney's office) was angered, embarrassed, and aroused by this latest bloody blotch on its reputation, and posted $100,000 in reward money for the arrest and conviction of the killers. State's Attorney John Swanson ordered all speakeasies, gambling parlors, and brothels closed in Cook County. Many were. For a time. For a short time there was little action in the city.

On February 27, with a warrant based on eyewitness testimony, the police arrested Jack McGurn at the Hotel Stevens, where he was found in the company of a young lady, Louise Rolfe. The blonde and fetching Miss Rolfe told the arresting officer that she and Jack had occupied the suite for almost a month. Asked if they were married, she replied shyly, "Not yet." As bond for himself, McGurn posted the deed to a $1 million South Side hotel he owned.

Then, on the basis of a loose association of recent tommygun purchases in Chicago and their probable ultimate owners, the police arrested John Scalisi and Hop Toad Giunta, the head of the Unione Siciliana. Giunta was released for lack of evidence but Scalisi had to post $50,000 bail when witnesses placed him in the black Cadillac of death.

The State's Attorney's office added three more names to the list of alleged assassins: Joseph Lolordo, brother of the murdered Pasqualino, who would have had revenge as his motive, and two members of the Egan's Rats gang of St. Louis, the theory being that unknown outsiders would have been imported to pose as policemen.

Before a grand jury, McGurn testified that he had not left Miss Rolfe's side from nine in the evening of February 13 till three in the afternoon of February 14. A demure Miss Rolfe volunteered that "When you're with Jack, you're never bored."

The state's attorney indicted McGurn for perjury and there was talk of Mann Act violations, but McGurn then married his "Blonde Alibi" and, of course, wives do not have to testify against their husbands.

The investigation into the seven murders in the SMC building was at last dropped, without results. (As matters developed, Scalisi would not have been able to come to trial anyway.) Ten months after the massacre, tommyguns were found that proved to be among the weapons used for the killings. Further ballistics testing showed that the same weapons were used in the earlier, 1928 slaying of Frankie Yale in NYC. Nothing came of this discovery.

At the time of the massacre, Al Capone had been living and partying at his Palm Island villa, and at the exact hour of the killings he was in Miami in the office of the Dade County solicitor being interviewed—at the covert request of federal agents—about his sources of income.

Before the 1928 elections, 76-year-old Frank Loesch, a railroad lawyer and president of the Chicago Crime Commission, a private organization of citizens concerned to publicize the sorry state of their crime-ridden city in hopes of mobilizing public sentiment for action, had reluctantly called on Capone at his sixth-floor business suite in the Lexington to ask for a favor. "I told Capone I wanted him to keep his damned hands off the election," Loesch recalled. "He said he would not interfere. He kept his word. There was not one act of violence. It was the squarest and most successful election day in 40 years." (In contrast to that spring's Pineapple Primary, in which the Outfit had something at stake.) During their face-to-face, Capone said to Loesch, "I'll have the cops send out squad cars the night before election. They'll throw the punks into the cooler and keep 'em there until the voting's over." Loesch might have thought he was talking to a Chicago police chief.

The election swept Republican Herbert Hoover in as President, defeating the "wet" and Catholic Democratic candidate, Al Smith. A deputation of Chicago civic leaders, despairing of any action by city or state officials, called on the President-elect to ask him to intervene with federal enforcement officers. The notoriety of the Outfit's control of Chicago was stigmatizing the city and could, possibly, have adverse effects on their businesses.

Bootlegging and income-tax evasion seemed the likely chinks in mobster armor. Capone, for example, had never filed an income tax return. Shortly after his inaugural, President Hoover was exercising after breakfast, as was his habit, with his Secretary of the Treasury, Andrew Mellon. "Have you got that fellow Capone yet?" the President asked, throwing the medicine ball at Mellon. The Secretary of the Treasury shook his head no and heaved the ball back to his chief. "Remember," the President grunted, "I want that man Capone in jail!"

Though he was not aware of this exchange, and might have discounted it if he had been, the Big Fellow had been put on the spot; it was only a question of time before he answered for it. You could bribe precinct captains, mayors, and governors, but not the real rulers of America. Their agents, too, the bureaucrats of Washington, D.C., were in most instances unimpeachable. Represented at the highest levels of government by corporation lawyers, investment bankers, executives of the country's railroads, steel companies, oil firms, industrial combines—men who moved freely between their private offices and public posts—the real rulers of America saw to it that when necessary even the President bent to their collective will.

In his twilight years (in conversation with writer Stephen Longstreet), Theodore Dreiser reminisced about what he knew of the real rulers of late 19th-century Chicago. After speaking of the town's dives and saloons, its thieves and pimps, its crooked politicians, Dreiser summed up:

> "But what they all worked for really were the true rulers of the town; all nearly snow-white pure, with big mansions, fancy carriages, and the best horses. Also pious words of advice, they being churchgoers, and splendid social creatures—but close to the dirty money. The rents from the whorehouses, and stealing of the streetcar routes and El trains, shady deals in gas and waterworks stocks; the banks they owned that

took the notes of the pork packers, the packinghouses, the big department stores; all that was part of the whole pattern of Chicago—from top to bottom—a gaudy circus, beginning with the two-bit whore in an alley crib."

The true rulers of America in 1929 were not much different from the true rulers of Chicago 40 years before, just immensely more powerful. Mellon, for example, was a billionaire and had been Treasury Secretary since 1921.

Unaware that his ticket had been written and only waited to be punched, Capone went about the taking care of business. Whether he was in his Miami office or the Lexington in Chicago, his phones were always busy. Administrating the Chicago liquor and beer trade, its gambling, its vice, its labor racketeering, maintaining nationwide contacts with other mobsters, was a task requiring constant, daily attention. And outside the ordinary traffic of business there were always other matters of concern— Joey Aiello, for instance, who had indeed returned to Chicago—and ongoing matters of lesser concern, but important—the need, for example, to constantly expand, to eliminate competitors, to dominate the territory—an eight-county territory.

After McGurn and Campagna had visited Roger Touhy in his Northwest stronghold and been put off, Touhy went to the local police chiefs. He told them he wanted to stay in business but that

"If the Capone mob gets into your towns, there will be no law left. The mobsters will be killing each other on your streets. You'll have a cathouse in every block. I'm trying to bring up two sons out here in a decent way, and you law enforcement people have families, too. We must protect ourselves."

The word was passed through the suburbs, and when Capone's men tried to install punchboards in Touhy's domain, the merchants refused to take them. Touhy had 10 fermenting plants in the northwest suburbs. And to ensure that his barrels were leak-proof he had set up his own cooperage in Schiller Park. At the peak of the season he and his partner were selling 1,000 barrels a week at $55 a barrel. He and his partner, Matt Kolb, had also placed 225 slot machines in choice locations. They got 60 percent of the take. Touhy's split on the slots alone came to $4,500 a week. Whenever Capone thought of the Touhy territory west to Elgin and north into Lake County, his eyes gleamed. No sum was too large, no sum too small to covet.

He sent Frankie Rio, Frank Diamond, and Sam Golf Bag Hunt to call on Roger at Touhy's roadhouse, The Arch, in Schiller Park, to persuade him to be more reasonable. After Touhy's by-now standard tough-guy performance, an unimpressed Frankie Rio—who was hard to impress—asked, "You got a big organization, huh, Rog?"

Touhy's reply was given casually: "There are 200 guys out here from every penitentiary in the United States and from Canada. Say!—we're having a big party tonight. . . . Why don't you come out and bring Al and some of the other boys?"

That night The Arch was raided by six squads of Chicago police and two deputy sheriffs from southern Cook County. To their surprise, the raiders found The Arch closed.

For nearly the past decade Al Capone could have surveyed a map of the sprawling metropolitan area of Chicago and said of the city, in the 2,000-year-old words of his countryman Gaius Julius Caesar, "*Veni, vidi, vici*"—I came, I saw, I conquered. But Roger Touhy, the tough little mick to the northwest, was giving the conqueror unlooked-for trouble. The man was obviously a *demente* to go up against the Outfit. He was playing a game too big to buck. Didn't he know that?

As for Joey Aiello—another *pazzo*! His offer of $50,000 to the man who killed Capone was still on the table. It was rumored that he had even made overtures to gunmen in the Outfit itself. Hop Toad Giunta had elevated John Scalisi and Albert Anselmi to his chief lieutenants in the Unione, and after the St. Valentine's Day killings it was reported that Scalisi had said of himself, "I am the big shot now." There was even talk that the three Sicilians—Giunta, Scalisi, and Anselmi—were plotting to wrest bootlegging and labor racketeering from the Outfit and set up as independents with Aiello.

At first, Capone had difficulty believing such talk. His enemies knew he was not alone. He had 50 to 60 of the toughest, most murderous gunmen in Chicago at his instant command. He was guarded 24 out of 24 by half a dozen of the most trusted of these men. And hadn't he refused to give up Anselmi and Scalisi to Hymie Weiss? The two Sicilians were his chosen assassins, his "Homicide Squad," they were called. They would never betray him. And yet now there was a report that Scalisi had sat down with Aiello in a Waukegan restaurant. Unbelievable!. . . . And yet, in these matters, as in political contests or love affairs—or knife fights—the first rule is that there are no rules. So. . . .

Early in May Frankie Rio and Capone met for dinner with Anselmi and Scalisi at the Hawthorne Inn. Midway through the meal, Capone and Rio began to quarrel and finally the squat Rio stood up and slapped his 6-foot, 255-pound, scar-faced boss and walked out of the restaurant.

The next day the Homicide Squad came to Rio with sympathy and an interesting proposal. For the next three days Scalisi, Anselmi, Giunta, and Rio met together in secret and planned how *la belva*—the wild beast—would be disposed of and what they and Joey Aiello would then do. . . . After which, Rio made his report to Capone.

On May 7, a dozen of the Outfit's top echelon traveled to the

Plantation, a posh carpet (as opposed to sawdust) joint outside of Hammond, Indiana. At the rear of the casino was a private, soundproofed room in which the mobsters assembled. The occasion was a banquet given in general celebration of the Outfit's success and power, but also in specific testimonial to the valued services of John Scalisi, Albert Anselmi, and Joseph Giunta.

After a long and heavy Italian meal interrupted by many toasts, and after coffee and brandy had been brought to the table, the Big Fellow stood, apparently to propose another toast. But when silence fell he turned and went to the cloakroom, emerging with an Indian club (by some accounts, a baseball bat) in each hand, and then, his face coloring to an angry, almost purplish red by the time his work was finished, one by one he beat the three honorees to death. Like Ferrante, King of Naples, 500 years before, he had invited traitors to a banquet table set in their honor and there dispatched them.

The story went the rounds that when he was finally finished clubbing his helpless victims, his fury spent, he began to speak about loyalty and treachery and what happened to "double-crossing yellow bastards" but was interrupted by Jake Guzik pulling at his sleeve. "Okay, Al," Guzik said, "that's enough. You made your point."

The bodies were found by Hammond policemen the next morning near a road beside Wolf Lake, Indiana. Giunta's was put to rest in Mount Carmel Cemetery. The bodies of Anselmi and Scalisi were returned to Sicily.

A week later Capone and Guzik, with Frank Nitti, Frankie Rio, Joe Saltis, Frankie McErlane and two dozen other Chicago mobsters were in Atlantic City attending a conference of the reigning U.S. hoodlums. Besides Chicago's delegation, there were contingents led by Charles "King" Solomon, who ruled much of New England from Boston; Max "Boo-Boo" Hoff, Waxey Gordon, "Nig" Rosen, Sam Lazar, and Charles Schwartz from Philadelphia; Moe Dalitz, Lou Rothkopf, and Charles Polizzi from Cleveland; Abe Bernstein, head of the Purple Gang, from Detroit; John Lazia for Boss Tom Pendergast of Kansas City; Abner "Longy" Zwillman and Willie Moretti from New York's Nassau County and northern New Jersey; Albert Anastasia, Vince Mangano, and Frank Scalise from Brooklyn; and Lucky Luciano, Meyer Lansky, Frank Costello, Louis "Lepke" Buchalter, Joe Adonis, Frank Erickson, "Dutch" Schultz, and Johnny Torrio from New York City, and representatives from St. Louis, New Orleans, and Florida.

Enoch "Nucky" Johnson, Atlantic City's boss and ruler of the South Jersey coast, was in charge of arrangements. He and Capone almost came to blows the first day when most of the gangsters and their guests (wives and non-spouse female guests were given fur capes by Nucky) were refused rooms at the exclusive (white Protestants only) Breakers

301

Hotel where Johnson had made reservations for them under Anglo-Saxon aliases.

A conclave of top mobsters from six states had been held five months earlier in Cleveland, but that was restricted to Sicilians. Patsy Lolordo and Hop Toad Giunta had represented the Outfit at that meeting. In Atlantic City there were many ethnic origins and creeds represented, as well as girls for those who didn't bring one. There was food, wine, liquor, and day-long discussions. Much of the most serious business was transacted between principals as they strolled barefooted—socks and shoes in hand, pants legs rolled up to their knees—on the beach past the end of the Boardwalk, where they couldn't be overheard by their roller-chair pushers.

The chief mobsters stepped off the end of the Boardwalk to stroll along the Atlantic shore toward the adjoining suburb of Chelsea and back, and on these promenades in the course of three days it was agreed that they would thereafter cooperate in bidding for liquor from abroad, thus lowering prices and establishing the beginnings of a national monopoly in liquor, with decisions to be made by mobs from the entire country participating as equals.

Putting nationwide gambling on such a footing was more difficult, and so the matter was postponed. Each delegate was jealous of his local power in gambling and did not want to give it up to a cartel.

On one of his own Boardwalk strolls, Capone encountered Moses Annenberg, who had left Chicago years before. Annenberg had directed Hearst's *American* and *Examiner* circulation sluggers in Chicago (as the brother he despised, Max, had for McCormick's *Tribune*), and he owned the General News Bureau (bought from gambling czar Mont Tennes) and the *Daily Racing Form*. He and Capone talked over the possibility of setting up a nationwide system for laying off bets. Frank Erickson of NYC was commissioned to work out the details with Moe.

The end of Prohibition was accepted as inevitable and there was much talk of how to go legitimate when that time came. The mobsters felt they were the logical parties to import, brew, distill, distribute, and sell booze legally, since that trade—illegally—was the bedrock of their empires. They already had the personnel and experience.

The year before, after discussions with Johnny Torrio on his return from Italy, Lucky Luciano had formed the "Big Seven" or "Seven Group," a cooperative, more or less, of bootleggers to ensure supply and to give protection from outsiders to those in the group. The seven were: Lansky and Ben "Bugsy" Siegel; Joe Adonis; Zwillman and Moretti; Rosen, Gordon, and "Bitsy" Bitz from Philadelphia; King Solomon of Boston; Luciano himself; and elder statesman and "real estate agent" Torrio. By the time of the Atlantic City meeting in 1929, the Seven Group had made alliances with 22 different mobs from Maine to Florida and west to the Mississippi. Luciano's NYC headquarters was the clearinghouse for the group, Vito Genovese its coordinator. This network became the structural underpinnings on which the nationwide cartel anticipating Repeal was built.

A document was drawn up that provided for a united front against outsiders; for fixed territories or spheres of influence; and for arbitration of internal disputes by a national commission chaired by Johnny Torrio. Past aggressions were to be cancelled and forgotten. Smaller mobs were to disband and their members were to accept the authority of the largest mob in their territory. (In Chicago, what was left of Moran's North Side gang was to merge with the Outfit.)

The acceptance of the document's provisions, as acknowledged by the signatures to it of all the top mobsters there, marked the formal beginning of organized crime in the United States, an achievement that can be credited mainly to the business-wise mind and organizational savvy of Johnny Torrio.

One other significant decision was made: Al Capone would have to give himself up so as to placate and soothe public opinion. The outcry and outrage that had resulted from the spectacular bloodletting in Chicago was bad for business nationwide.

Torrio took on the assignment of telling Al. The suggestion was met with angry refusal. Frank Nitti wanted Capone to stall, then leave the conference. Jake Guzik was indignant. Torrio asked to be heard out. He told his protege that a vacation in jail would provide much-needed rest—he knew this from personal experience. He told Capone that with his money he would be treated as an honored guest, not as a common criminal; that he would be safe from attack in jail; and that he would be able to run the Outfit almost as well from jail as he could have from Chicago or Miami; that it wouldn't be for long, in any case. In the end, the reassuring words of Johnny Papa prevailed.

Capone and Frankie Rio arrived in Philadelphia by car the afternoon of May 16. They went to a movie, *Voice of the City*, a detective film co-billed with the on-stage appearance of Fred Waring's orchestra, the Pennsylvanians. Leaving the movie house at 8:15 they were arrested in the lobby by two detectives to whom they surrendered their snub-nosed .38s. They were in a two-man lineup (attended by all the police in the station) at 9:30 the next morning; indicted at 10:25; tried at 11:30; entered a guilty plea at 15 minutes past noon; and sentenced at 10 minutes to 1:00—from arrest to incarceration in just 16 hours and 35 minutes. Except for the length of their sentence, Boo-Boo Hoff, gang boss of Philadelphia, had arranged matters as only a good and gracious host would. And perhaps the sentence was no surprise to him, or to any other mobster besides Capone and Rio who had been in Atlantic City.

For carrying concealed deadly weapons, Capone and his

bodyguard were given the maximum: a year in jail (10 months with good behavior). Usually the offence drew only a fine, at the most 90 days. "It's the breaks, kid," Capone said to a bailiff as he was led away, "it's the breaks."

The night before his speedy trial, Capone had been given an opportunity to exercise his considerable gifts as a *commediante*—a performer who orchestrates his own image, varying his personality and message to suit the situation and the audience (serious and stern, even forbidding when necessary; courtly and charming, even flirtatious at other times—with the opposite sex, say). From midnight to 2:00 P.M. he chatted with Philadelphia Director of Public Safety, Lemuel B. Schofield. Asked about his involvement with the Chicago rackets, Capone told Schofield:

> "During the last two years I've been trying to get out. But once in the racket you're always in it, it seems. The parasites trail you, begging for favors and for money, and you can never get away from them, no matter where you go.
>
> "I have a wife and an eleven-year-old boy I idolize, and a beautiful home at Palm Island, Florida. If I could go there and forget it all I would be the happiest man in the world. I want peace and I'm willing to live and let live. I'm tired of gang murders and gang shootings.
>
> "With the idea in mind of making peace among the gangsters in Chicago I spent the week in Atlantic City, and I have the word of each of the men participating that there shall be no more shootings.
>
> ". . . We talked over our troubles for three days. We all agreed at the end of that time to sign on the dotted line to bury the past and forget warfare in the future for the general good of all concerned."

Schofield asked him how he felt he had fared in his profession. "I'm satisfied," was the answer—

> but it's an awful life to live. You fear death every moment, and, worse than death, you fear the rats of the game, who would run around and tell the police if you didn't constantly satisfy them with money and favors. I never was able to leave my home without my bodyguard, Rio. He lives with me and has gone with me constantly during the last two years. . . .
>
> "I'm like any other man. I've been in this racket long enough to realize that a man in my game must take the breaks, the fortunes of war. Three of my friends were killed in the last two weeks in Chicago. That certainly is not conducive to peace of mind. I haven't had peace of mind in years. . . ."

The three friends referred to—Scalisi, Anselmi, Giunta—he had, of course, with his own hands delivered to everlasting peace of mind.

"What are you doing now?" Philadelphia's Director of Public Safety asked.

Capone looked at his listener. "I'm retired," he said, "and living on my money." His face bespoke sincerity.

After the interview, Director Schofield's opinion was that the Big Fellow "talked throughout as a serious man talking of a responsible matter."

The prisoners were taken to the county prison, Holmesburg, in northeast Philadelphia. This not proving exactly to Capone's taste, in August he was transferred to the Eastern State Penitentiary just north of downtown Philadelphia. His cell at Eastern had a rug on its floor, a desk, a bookcase, pictures on the wall, a dresser, a smoking stand, a floor-model radio, and two cots (one for his embezzler cellmate) He was allowed unlimited visitors and mail and use of the warden's telephone. His brother Ralph, Jake Guzik, Mike Carozzo, and Frank Nitti visited him regularly. In Chicago, everything cleared through Nitti, who was made responsible for maintaining the Outfit's internal discipline.

While he was in prison, Capone had his tonsils removed by Dr. Herbert M. Goddard. Of his patient, Goddard said: "I cannot believe all they say of him. I have never seen a prisoner so kind, so cheery and accomodating. . . . He would have made good anywhere at anything. He is an ideal prisoner. You can't tell me he is all bad."

On the night of October 8 the ideal prisoner's brother, Ralph, decked out in a tuxedo, was approaching his front-row seat at a Chicago prize fight, but Bottles was arrested before he could sit down. Seven indictments were returned against him: six of failing to pay taxes and one of cheating the U.S. government. If Ralph, a millionaire, had paid the $4,065 he was told he owed, plus $1,000 in additional interest and penalties, his case would have been closed the year before. But Ralph Capone felt the $1,000 additional was unfair.

On October 24, after eight straight years of going only up, the U.S. stock market suffered "the most disastrous decline in the biggest and broadest market of history," according to the *New York Times*. That was Black Thursday, but it was only prelude. Four days later the market took another plunge and on Tuesday, the 29th, the loss of value of stocks on the New York Stock Exchange was more than twice the value of all the currency then in circulation in the United States of America.

The bottom had fallen out. The bubble had burst. The party was over. The Age of Permanent Prosperity had ended with a Crash and the Great Depression lurched onstage to take up residence. A goodly number of bankrupted speculators in NYC and Chicago high-dived from tall buildings. Unemployment began to rise. The man on the street—the common man—scratched his head and began to worry in earnest. A ticker-tape parade looks a great deal different to the white wing street sweepers than it did to the people who rode in the cars up front.

A reckless gambler at almost anything, Al Capone had shunned the market. "It's a racket," he said. "Those stock market guys are crooked."

While in prison, Capone made himself available to reporters. During one of his many interviews, which ranged over a wide spectrum of topics, from his weight to his charities to Napoleon ("he got the swelled head"), the former steerer for the Four Deuce's fourth-floor palace of fleshly pleasures declared, "The trouble with women today is their excitement over too many things outside the home. A woman's home and her children are her real happiness. If she would stay there, the world would have less to worry about the modern woman."

Also while in prison, Capone conferred with Lawrence P. Mattingly, Johnny Torrio's high-priced Washington tax attorney. Capone had gotten the word he was under investigation by the Internal Revenue Bureau. Since the government's policy was to avoid prosecution if a citizen came forward before legal action began, Mattingly advised him to seek a settlement. Capone retained Mattingly to represent him.

Advertisements—Miscellaneous.

POWER

It was probably the cigar that put the perpetual sneer on his lips, as if his estimate of others was extremely low and his face reflected that contempt. He grew a mustache to try to disguise the expression.

Samuel Insull, Jr., was born in London in 1859, the son of a Congregationalist preacher and temperance crusader. At 14 he left school to become an office boy. He taught himself shorthand and accounting, but at 19 was discharged from his job because his employer found a doting father who was willing to *pay* for the privilege of having his son keep the accounts that Samuel Insull, Jr., had been keeping for over four years for a weekly wage of five shillings ($1.25). "My experience is that the greatest aid in the efficiency of labor is a long line of men waiting at the gate," Insull was to observe many years later.

He found his next employment as the secretary of Thomas Edison's English agent and in 1881—at the age of 21—came to the United States as Edison's personal secretary. He was soon managing the 33-year-old Edison's business affairs; he held Edison's power of attorney, signed his checks, worked day and night. But in 1892, when the eastern Edison companies were merged by the elder J. P. Morgan to create General Electric, he accepted the presidency of Chicago Edison, one of Chicago's 40 power companies, and came west. The directors of Chicago Edison had asked him to recommend the best available man for the job; he determined that that man was himself.

(To purchase stock in the company as a bona fide of his good intent and to establish stature in the LaSalle Street financial community, he was forced to borrow $250,000 from Marshall Field. This galled him, and he repaid the debt at the first opportunity.)

In Chicago he continued to work day and night, pioneering in the use of ever-larger transmission coverage. By 1907 he had formed Commonwealth Edison out of Chicago's many electricity suppliers; by 1911, Public Service Company of Northern Illinois out of another 80 firms.

"Very early I discovered," he said, "that the first essential, as in other public utility business, was that it should be operated as a monopoly."

In 1912 Insull created Middle West Utilities, a holding company. Its capitalization was typical of his financing methods. Twelve million dollars' worth of common and preferred was issued, roughly half of which was "water," that is, stock unsecured by assets. As his self-conferred reward, he received, gratis, $5 million worth of stock—or more, depending upon how the complicated transaction was entered on the books. (It will be recalled that Insull was a self-taught accountant.)

It was also in 1912 that his 11-year-old son contracted scarlet fever, with complications. His wife—a successful actress he had married and taken from the stage in 1899; she was known as the "Pocket Venus"— nursed the boy back to health herself, daily scrubbing the sick room from wall to wall and keeping a constant, lonely vigil while her husband devoted his time and energies to business. When after five months Insull finally re-entered the house, his wife's bedroom door was closed to him, as it would remain from that time on. She was 43; he was 52.

By 1917 Middle West was operating in 11 states, and within another decade Insull's companies were supplying power in 32 of the 48 states of the Union and Canada. He also owned Commonwealth Edison's best customer, Chicago Elevated Railways, as well as Chicago's three electric railroads (he was now a traction as well as a utility magnate), and People's Gas, Light, and Coke Company. He was Charles T. Yerkes on a grander scale.

The Insulls lived in a Gold Coast apartment at 1100 Lake Shore Drive, had a 30-room Italian villa country estate, Hawthorn Farm (4,300 acres), near Libertyville in the Skokie Valley north of Chicago, a home in England, and Samuel Insull had a private aerie ("Insull's Throne") all his own atop the $20 million Chicago Civic Opera House, an Insull-built 42-story office building with a huge, ground-level auditorium on the Chicago River. Foreign governments decorated him, American universities awarded him honorary degrees, newspaper editorialists applauded his endeavors.

Toward his employees he practiced a paternalistic benevolence—and fired them if they neglected to greet him with "Good morning, Mr. Insull." He dictated terms to politicians, labor leaders, and bankers, buying their obedience or coercing it. His own chief counsel's law partner, Samuel Ettelson, was Chicago's Corporation Counsel and the guiding intelligence behind the city's blustering mayor, Big Bill Thompson. With $250,000 or so in 1926 Insull supported a man for senator the senate wouldn't seat. Of Mayor Thompson, who supported his projects, he said, ". . . you are a veritable reincarnation of Abraham Lincoln, a Father Abraham come to earth again." His lodestar was greed.

His public relations staff, headed by the publicist who at his instructions during World War I had spurred on U.S. intervention in England's behalf, projected an image of Insull corporate beneficence—the lowest rates to consumers, the highest returns to investors—which the public embraced wholeheartedly. By the end of the Twenties, a million people owned shares in Insull companies, the vast majority of them small investors, many of them Insull employees and customers and their neighbors and friends in Chicago and the Midwest. ("You are always thinking of the money angle," Thomas Edison had told his young secretary.)

By 1929 Insull was on the board of 85 corporations, the chairman of 65, the president of 11. He controlled a $4-billion empire. In 1929 he founded Insull Utility Investments out of two holding companies purchased in the East—where he came face to face with Morgan interests. (The $10 million of his own securities that he exchanged for Insull Utility Investments quickly soared to a market value of $143 million.)

It has been estimated that shortly before the crash in 1929, Insull company securities were increasing in value at a round-the-clock rate of $7,000 a minute. In just 50 days before the Crash, they appreciated more than half a billion dollars, and Insull's own wealth rose to a reported $170 million. But within three years he and his companies were mired deep in the Great Depression.

The precipitous descent in Insull's personal fortunes began in 1931 when he bought out Cleveland financier Cyrus Eaton's interest in Insull properties to forestall Eaton's sale of them to Wall Street. This cost Insull $56 million, $40 million of which he had to borrow, half of this from New York bankers.

Shortly before he bought out Eaton, in a speech to members of the Chicago Stock Exchange, he had railed against Wall Street financiers and their domination of U.S. economic life. From the beginning he had detested Eastern bankers. They, in turn, took note of his autocratic distrust and arrogance.

And then the market in Insull securities broke, helped to its quick and disastrous conclusion by House of Morgan manipulators on the Exchange and rumors of Insull's incapacity (he was 72 and, as always, overworking). By the middle of December of 1931, to keep his superpower ship afloat, Insull had pledged as collateral all of the securities he owned or controlled.

Early in April of 1932 he went to New York to discuss ways of refinancing a routine $10 million Middle West Utilities note due in June. After two afternoons of conferences, Owen D. Young, the chairman of General Electric, broke the news to him: New York bankers would put up no more money. "Does this mean a receivership?" Insull asked.

It did, and Insull was at that instant "too broke to go bankrupt," as one New York banker phrased it. His fall took with him, of course, the million or so investors who had placed their faith—and savings—in his omnipotence. Chicagoans alone lost at least $2 billion. Bank after bank failed in the city because of Insull's ruin.

It required an entire day of dictating and signatures to resign all of his corporate offices, and then he fled to Canada. Then to Paris, then Italy, and finally to Greece, which had no extradition treaty with the United States—an important consideration, since a Cook County grand jury had been asked to indict him for embezzlement and larceny. In Greece, as the novelist John Dos Passos reported, "He was the toast of the Athenians; Mme. Kouryoumdjouglou the vivacious wife of a Bagdad datemerchant devoted herself to his comfort."

He stayed in Greece 19 months before being driven out to Turkey, where he was arrested and returned to the United States. There, he spent a night in the Cook County Jail when his attorney was unable to immediately raise his bail. Some Chicagoans professed to feel sorry for him because he was being treated "as if he were a common criminal."

In October of 1934 he went on trial on a federal indictment for use of the mails to defraud the small investors who at his urging had entrusted their savings to his management. It had been discovered that, under the Insull system of keeping accounts, expenses were entered on his companies' books as assets—which meant that half the income reported year after year by a company such as Middle West Utilities, for example, was fictitious. Insull took the stand, recounted his humble London beginnings, wept, admitted that he might—yes, he might—have made a $10 million error in his accounts, but swore it was an honest mistake.

The jury voted acquittal.

In the spring of 1935 he was acquitted of the charge of embezzlement, and three months later the trial judge on the last of his federal indictments instructed the jury to bring in a verdict of not guilty.

Three years later, at the age of 79, he was felled by a heart attack in a Paris subway. His pockets held only a handkerchief monogrammed "SI" and seven francs, seven centimes (85¢). He left his heirs $10,000 in cash and $14 million in debts.

He had never liked newspaper reporters or photographers. "I'll see you get fired!" he had once yelled at a photographer who annoyed him. . . . Back in those days of his glory a reporter had asked him his greatest ambition. "To hand down my name as clean as I received it," was his answer.

A SOLDIER DEAD

For the mash, buy the best barley, corn, rice, and hops you can; add brewer's yeast and water; heat; let the wort ferment a dozen days; mellow it out at 30° Fahrenheit; carbonate it as you keg it, and you have beer. . . . *Good* beer if you start with good water. Roger Touhy brewed good beer.

Born in 1898, raised poor, the son of a Chicago policeman, Touhy married his Chicago sweetheart, a wee Irish lass, in 1922. He had an auto and truck sales and repair garage on North Avenue bought with money made wildcatting Oklahoma oil leases after he got out of WWI's U.S. Navy.

Finding himself unable to peddle two of six trucks he'd gotten at a bargain, Touhy struck a sideline deal to haul beer to saloonkeepers he knew, using the leftover trucks as carriers. In 1926 he moved his family to the suburb of Des Plaines, 15 miles northwest of the Loop.

Fat Matt Kolb, a Republican politico and a minor power in the Outfit before he left it because of its unpredictable violence, had a saloon on California Avenue not far from Touhy's garage. Kolb, still a boot-legger, offered to make Touhy his partner. Roger was netting $50,000 a year from his garage, but he knew where the real fookin' money was.

Kolb's beer was inferior. Not just bad, but "nasty bad," according to Touhy, so Touhy asked a City of Chicago chemist how to make good beer. "Good water" was the answer.

The best water the City chemist could find for him was from an artesian well in Roselle, seven or eight miles from Touhy's home. Touhy built his first wort plant there, eventually added nine more in the northwest suburbs.

The main attraction of Touhy's operation for Al Capone, how-ever, was not that Touhy's beer was good but that it was plentiful. When in September 1929 a 26-year-old Prohibition agent, Eliot Ness, was authorized to form a special task force to harass Capone's operations, he

311

was at first considered a joke. The men on his team were known as the "Untouchables" because, unlike most other Prohibition agents, they could not be corrupted. Months before Capone was released from his Philadelphia jail cell, the Ness team had become a major nuisance as it seized a few of the Outfit's trucks and closed some of its distilleries and breweries. Touhy's ten wort plants might become necessary suppliers to Chicago's demand.

From Philadelphia, on the warden's phone, Capone gave the order. After all, the Atlantic City agreement provided that smaller gangs were to be absorbed, didn't it? He sent his master persuader, Murray The Camel Humphreys together with James "Red" Fawcett to reason once more with the tough little Irisher. The Outfit's two hard guys arrived at The Arch in Schiller Park in a 16-cylinder limousine. Humphreys made the pitch: If Touhy would go with him to meet with Frank Nitti in Cicero, Nitti would explain the nature of the Outfit's proposition. Humphreys was sure that after listening to Nitti expound the benefits of partnership Roger would want to come in with them.

According to Touhy's account, the phone rang just then, a call from a Capone thug who owed him. "Don't go to Cicero," the caller said. "Don't do it. You won't come back if you do."

Thus forewarned (if a warning was necessary), Touhy told Humphreys that if Nitti wanted to see him, he should come out to Schiller Park, safe conduct guaranteed. As he spoke, he stroked the barrel of a shotgun hanging on the wall of his office. It was an ornamental wall-hanger piece, but Humphreys didn't know this.

Humphreys tried a different tack. "You know, Touhy," he said, "we can take care of you any time we want to."

Touhy shrugged. Humphreys' hand trembled when he lifted his wine glass. Humphreys was mean enough; he just wasn't tough enough. Suddenly, unaccountably, he blurted out, "Touhy, I've got a swell car parked outside. If you drive me back inside the city limits, I'll give you the car. I want to get home alive."

His partner, Fawcett, stared at him, dumbfounded.

The two men left but Fawcett came back inside The Arch alone. "Listen, Touhy," he said, "for $5,000 I'll kill that sonofabitch Humphreys on the way to the city and for another five grand I'll go to Cicero and knock off Nitti, too."

Touhy declined the generous, good-hearted offer.

Humphreys did not forget the encounter; he marked it. If it happens, mark it—don't forget it.

Since October of 1928, and now and again before that (as part of the investigation of Ralph Capone), Elmer L. Irey, Director of the Treasury's Enforcement Branch's Special Intelligence Unit, had had agents looking into the business affairs of Al Capone. When Treasury

Secretary Mellon, via the Commissioner of Internal Revenue, passed on President Hoover's directive to get Capone, Irey assigned the aggressive and tenacious Frank J. Wilson to lead an Al Capone investigation team. Irey had a high opinion of agent Wilson: "He fears nothing that walks; he will sit quietly looking at books 18 hours a day, 7 days a week, forever, if he wants to find something in those books."

Wilson set up a one-room office in Chicago's Federal Court Building and he and his small staff went to work combing old records seized in long-forgotten raids, and prowling Cicero and Chicago looking for merchants who might have dealt with Capone. Since the standard income tax deduction was $5,000, their first task was to find evidence that Capone's net expenditures in any one year exceeded that figure. Their second task was somehow to establish Capone's net worth, immense for all to see, but difficult to prove.

Their quarry was released from Eastern State Penitentiary on March 16, 1930, a day early to thwart a clamoring press corps. He returned to Chicago, sweet home Chicago, where he immediately got drunk and stayed drunk for four days. This release-celebration carouse showed a great deal of trust in his companions. (Heavy drinking was unusual in top-ranking Outfit gangsters. Frank Nitti—who took only an occasional glass of wine himself—frowned on it. Men not of the Outfit but owned by it—labor skates, business men—were ordered by Nitti not to drink at all if they showed a tendency to drink overmuch; 12 steps in Chicago in the twenties frequently led to a ditch.)

A government wiretap on Ralph Capone's phone furnished this message to Bottles: "We're up in Room 718 at the Western and Al is really getting out of hand. He's in terrible shape. Will you come up? You're the only one who can handle him when he gets like this. . . ."

"I'll be up a little later," was Ralph's reply. "Just take care of him the best you can right now."

The wiretap also provided this later exchange:

"Where's Al? I've been looking all over for him, and nobody seems to know where he is."

"I don't know where he is either, Jake. I haven't heard a word from him since he got out."

"Jesus, Ralph, this makes it very bad for me. I'm supposed to have my finger on these things. It makes it very embarrassing with my paper. Now get this, I want you to call me the minute you hear from him. Tell him I want to see him right away."

The caller was Jake Lingle, a reporter for the *Chicago Tribune*. An hour later he called again. "Listen, you guys aren't giving me the run-around, are you? Just remember, I wouldn't do that if I was you."

Tough talk to Al Capone's brother, but Alfred "Jake" Lingle

could apparently get away with it: He was Chicago's ace crime reporter. In his years at the *Tribune*, Lingle had worked on several thousand stories but not once had he typed the customary "–30–" (used by telegraphers to signify "Good night, no more") at the end of any of them because he'd never actually written a line. Lingle worked outside the office and often phoned his reports to the *Trib*, when he didn't make them in person. Lingle was valued by his editors because he seemed to know everyone in Chicago's underworld and on its police force. He was, in fact, a close personal friend of Police Chief Russell.

On the fifth day of his return to his home grounds, refreshed by a massage and a hearty breakfast, Al Capone emerged from Cicero's Western Hotel (with one hand bandaged) to spend the next three days absorbing bad news detailed for him by his accountant, Jake Guzik. Brothel by brothel, casino by casino, speak by speak Guzik showed how the Depression was affecting the Outfit's enterprises. Revenues were down—drastically—but overhead—chiefly payoffs to police and politicians—remained at its pre-Crash level, that is, high. It was decided as a first economizing step that payments to the lower levels of the police force would be reduced.

Meanwhile, Eliot Ness's special force continued its depredations, closing more of the Outfit's breweries. Ness's men were also taking mobsters into custody, which meant bail bond fees were mounting. All this with income down.

One of the other attractions of Roger Touhy's operation—besides its ten breweries—was that it was sweetly low cost. Whenever there was a job opening for a driver or in one of his breweries or the cooperage, Touhy hired away a highway patrolman or local policeman; $100 a week was three to four times what they were making. They provided instant fix for the price of labor only. Nor did Touhy have to make the costly payoffs that Chicago cops and politicians and judges demanded. A ham, a turkey, $20 at Christmas was enough for most of the smalltowners in his territory. He kept higherups happy with larger gifts, usually of good beer by the barrel or the case. (He set up a bottling plant especially for that purpose—750 cases a week of the very best.)

Each summer, for example, a politician such as Anton Cermak, chairman of the Cook County Board of Commissioners—a power outside Chicago, where Touhy's trucks rolled—would hold a huge Forest Preserve picnic for his supporters. For this, Cermak got 100 barrels of free beer, cost to Touhy less than $500. (Cermak had the beer sold at the picnics for a buck a mug.)

Capone sent a man whose name, as Touhy remembered it, was Tom Summers, a Capone recruit from NYC, to see the beer baron of the Northwest. Touhy listened to Summers deliver the standard partnership-in-girls, -gambling, -stills, virgin territory sales pitch and said he'd think about it. Then he introduced Summers to two out-of-town friends of his own, after speaking to them in private. He told Summers his friends would take him to Cicero, "show you the sights."

In Cicero, Touhy's friends got Capone's messenger drunk. The three men ended up at the Cotton Club, a highly profitable nightclub that Capone had remodeled at a cost of $40,000 and given to his brother Ralph to run.

Spurred on by his by-now bosom buddies, a drunken Summers picked a fight with Ralph Capone, not knowing who Bottles was. Touhy's friends helped Summers beat up Ralph, and then they took Bottles' gun from him. When two men in the club attempted to come to Ralph's aid, they got the same treatment from Touhy's friends. Then, at his request, a gleeful Summers was driven to Al Capone's hotel and deposited there.

The next afternoon Capone called Touhy. "Rog, who were those two guys with Summers at the Cotton Club last night? . . . Very tough, I hear. I won't hurt them, but I want them to return a couple of guns. It's very important."

Touhy said that he thought the two men were New York pals of Summers. He said he'd keep his eyes open.

Every few days Capone called again to say he had to have the guns that were taken from the two men in the Cotton Club. Touhy said he wished he could help.

As it happened, before Capone's first phone call his NYC messenger, Summers, was beaten to death, his body thrown into the Chicago River, on Capone's orders. The guns Capone wanted returned belonged to Prohibition agents—the two men who had tried to come to his brother's rescue. If the guns were not returned, the feds were going to padlock the Cotton Club—which they did.

Capone marked it—and Matt Kolb vanished. Two days after Kolb's disappearance, Big Al called Touhy. He was apologetic. "Rog," he said, "some people have got Matt." Capone explained it would take $50,000 in fives, tens, and twenties to free Kolb and that, yes, he would be willing to act as intermediary.

Touhy took the large bundle of bills, wrapped in a newspaper, downtown, and rode the elevator up to Capone's floor. Humphreys and Red Fawcett were there and five or six other hoodlums, oiling their .38s.

Touhy went into Capone's office and dropped the bundle on his desk. Capone tore off the newspaper wrapping. "Rog," he said, "I want you to know I had nothing to do with this. I like Matt. I'm trying to help him."

When Touhy picked up Kolb, the short, 220-pound victim was quite cheerful. "Now, Roger, my lad," he said, "I know I was careless in getting kidnapped and I'm sorry. Don't scold me." Touhy was still so angry he couldn't trust himself to speak.

The Internal Revenue Bureau (IRB) had announced on March 22 that five grand jury indictments for income tax evasion had been brought against Frank Nitti. The next day, Capone's tax attorney, Lawrence Mattingly, wrote the head of the IRB office in Chicago asking that he "examine Mr. Capone and his records the same as you would any other delinquent taxpayer with the view of satisfying your office as to his liability." Mattingly and his client were assigned an interview date of April 17.

Counsel Mattingly was proceeding on the assumption that the government wanted, as it had in similar cases in the past, to settle Capone's delinquency without going to court. In this he was mistaken. Later in the year, Jake Guzik was also indicted for income tax evasion.

To start Capone's interview, the head of the IRB office told him that "any statements which are made here, which could be used against you, would probably be used." Mattingly responded that "Insofar as Mr. Capone can answer any questions without admitting his liability to criminal action, he is here to cooperate with you. . . . Our action is without prejudice. . ."—that is, did not waive his client's rights. But by remaining to be questioned after the warning given him, Capone had (ipso facto) waived his rights.

"How long have you enjoyed a large income?" he was asked.

For his interview Big Al had dressed in a dark blue double-breasted serge suit, blue necktie with large white polka dots, blue silk socks with white clocks, black sports shoes with white tips. He wore a ring set with an 11.5 carat diamond ($50,000 value), a gold-and-diamond-studded watch, and a belt with a bejeweled buckle. A linen handkerchief protruded four crisp, white points above the upper pocket of his suit coat.

"I never had much of an income, a large income," he replied.

Responding to further questioning, he said he kept no records, had no checking accounts, no stocks and bonds, no interest in horse or dog racing except as a bettor, and the only property interest he had was mortgaged.

"What did you do with your money? Carry it on your person?"

"Carried it on my person," Capone affirmed.

When the stenographer was dismissed, Capone offered agent Wilson a Corona cigar.

"I don't smoke," said Wilson, who chain-smoked nickel cigars. He asked Capone if his wife or relatives kept safe deposit boxes and, getting no answer, inquired as to the source of the money wired to Capone in Florida.

"Somebody's trying to push me around," Capone said, for the first time appearing unsettled. "But I'll take care of myself. . . . How's *your* wife, Wilson?" As he got up to leave he said, "Mr. Wilson, you be sure to take care of yourself."

Ralph Capone was tried the same week. On the stand he admitted that he was related to Al Capone but confessed he did not know how his brother made his money. He showed emotion only twice during his trial, once when his hat was stolen and then on being sentenced to three years in prison and fined $10,000. "I don't understand this at all," he said. His lawyers prepared to appeal.

IRB agent Wilson and his staff had systematically sifted thousands of sheets of seized records, bank balance slips, bail bonds, interview transcripts, memos, correspondence, reports, but could not find enough evidence tying Al Capone to Outfit profits to make a case. Ending a workday at 1:00 A.M. one hot mid-summer night, Wilson accidentally locked a file cabinet to which he was returning records. He had no key with him but remembered a storeroom down the hall, empty except for a single filing cabinet. He went to the room and pulled open one of the cabinet's drawers, intending to leave the records there. At the back of the drawer was a package wrapped in brown paper. He tore off the wrapping; inside were three bound black ledgers with red corners. Wilson glanced through one of the ledgers: nothing. He looked into the second and stopped at a page of columns headed "BIRD CAGE," "21," "CRAPS," "FARO," "ROULETTE," and "HORSE BETS." The ledger detailed for 1924-26 a gambling operation with a $30,000 daily take, an 18-month net of more than half a million dollars. A balance for December 2 (a Tuesday), 1924, was parceled out like this:

Town	$6,537.42 (paid)
Ralph	1,634.35
Pete	1,634.35
Frank	5,720,22
J. & A.	5,720.22 (paid)
Lou	5,720.22
D.	5,720.22

Wilson took "Town" to mean payments to municipal officials. At the top of one page was the notation: "Frank paid $17,500 for Al." There were other payments to "Al" noted throughout.

Early the next morning Wilson took the ledger to the state's attorney's office. There it was identified as an item seized in State's Attorney Crowe's raid on the Hawthorne Smoke Shop in Cicero following McSwiggin's murder in 1926. Now all Wilson had to do was find out who had made the entries.

The get-Capone group included an undercover agent, Michael Malone, brought on at the request of agent Wilson, who in 1965 wrote of Malone:

I thought then, and still think, [he] was the greatest natural undercover worker the Service has ever had. Five feet, eight inches tall, a barrelchested, powerful two hundred pounds, with jet black hair, sharp brown eyes underscored with heavy dark circles and a brilliant, friendly smile, Mike could easily pass for Italian, Jew, Greek or whomever the occasion demanded. He was actually "black Irish" from Jersey City.

Malone's only child, a daughter, had been killed at the age of three by a truck; he and his wife drifted apart; Malone went into undercover work for the U.S. government.

For his Chicago assignment, Malone registered at the Lexington Hotel as "Michael Lepito" and was given room 724, which happened to be next door to that of Phil D'Andrea, a Capone bodyguard.

Malone-Lepito spent his time sitting in the lobby, a newspaper in his lap. He wrote letters to himself as Lepito and mailed them to friends in the East, who mailed them back to him at the Lexington. He was encouraged to find that his letters were being opened, and that his room had been searched.

One afternoon one of Jack McGurn's close buddies, Michael Spranze, asked him, "What's your line?"

"What's yours?" was Malone's response.

"I work around here."

"My line is keeping quiet."

Spranze smiled. "Where you from?" he asked.

"Originally I'm from Brooklyn. I came out here from Philadelphia."

Spranze nodded and walked away. In a few days he invited Malone to sit in at a mobsters' card game. In a few weeks—asking no questions but answering the odd question about Brooklyn or Philadelphia, and letting it become known he was in hiding from the law—he was on speaking terms with most of the Outfit's Lexington Hotel contingent.

One evening a slightly drunken mobster chided him on how loosely the Philadelphia mob was run compared to Chicago's tight discipline. He praised Capone as a right guy and Frank Nitti as deserving of his nickname:

"Somebody gets out of line, Al tells the Enforcer. The next thing you know, a couple of guys get off a train from Detroit or New York or St. Louis, and the Enforcer tells them who has to go. The guys do the job and go home. When the guys from out of town louse up a job and only 'hurt' somebody, the Enforcer don't fool around. He has one of his own guys get the two guys who blew the job. That's why very few fellas get 'hurt' around here. They get killed."

His listener's sharp brown eyes betrayed no emotion.

Early in June Malone passed on to Wilson a rumor that Frankie

318

Pope, manager of the Hawthorne Smoke Shop, had quarreled with Capone over money and might be feeling talkative. Wilson approached Pope but got nothing except a hint that Jake Lingle knew more about the workings of the mob than any other reporter in Chicago. Wilson went to see the *Tribune*'s publisher, Colonel McCormick, and arranged to meet with Lingle the morning of June 10.

Lingle was unable to keep the appointment. The day before, about 1:15 in the afternoon, he walked into the underpass at East Randolph Street and North Michigan Avenue that led to "Illinois Central Suburban Trains." The tunnel was crowded with pedestrians and Lingle was reading the *Daily Racing Form* as he walked. He took no notice of the man who approached him from behind—and who then pressed a .38 against his neck and fired.

Lingle pitched forward, instantly dead, his cigar clenched between his teeth.

The mob taboo against killing a poor but honest newspaper reporter was nearly as strong as that against killing a brave and honest police officer. Either action brought on too much heat. The day after Lingle's murder Colonel McCormick's *Chicago Tribune* carried this story:

> Alfred J. Lingle, better known in his world of newspaper work as Jake Lingle, and for the last 18 years a reporter on the *Tribune*, was shot to death yesterday in the Illinois Central subway at the east side of Michigan boulevard, at Randolph street.
>
> The *Tribune* offers $25,000 as a reward for information which will lead to the conviction of the slayer or slayers.
>
> An additional reward of $5,000 was announced by the *Chicago Evening Post*, making a total of $30,000.

The next day the total reached $55,000 when the *Chicago Herald & Examiner* posted $25,000. The *Tribune*'s lead editorial that day bristled with righteous but controlled anger for all of Chicago to ponder, especially its gangsters:

> Alfred J. Lingle, a reporter for the *Tribune*, was murdered Monday afternoon. . . .
>
> The meaning of this murder is plain. It was committed in reprisal and in an attempt at intimidation. Mr. Lingle was a police reporter and an exceptionally well informed one. His personal friendships included the highest police officials and the contacts of his work had made him familiar to most of the big and little fellows of gangland. What made him valuable to his newspaper marked him as dangerous to the killers.
>
> It was very foolish ever to think that assassination would be confined to the gangs which have fought each other for the profits of crime in Chicago. The immunity from punishment after gang murders

319

would be assumed to cover the committing of others. Citizens who interfered with the criminals were no better protected than the gangmen who fought each other for the revenue from liquor selling, coercion of labor and trade, brothel house keeping and gambling.

. . . To the list of Colosimo, O'Banion, the Gennas, Murphy, Weiss, Lombardo, Esposito, the seven who were killed in the St. Valentine's day massacre, the name is added of a man whose business was to expose the work of the killers.

The *Tribune* accepts this challenge. It is war. There will be casualties, but that is to be expected, it being war. . . . The challenge of crime to the community must be accepted. It has been given with bravado. It is accepted. . . .

The closing rhetoric of this acceptance of crime's challenge sounds very much that of the *Tribune*'s publisher—his pledge to a gallant soldier of the ranks fallen in battle. In the Forties, Colonel McCormick, who had served with General "Black Jack" Pershing in pursuit of Pancho Villa along the Mexican border and on his staff in WWI, regularly gave a talk on WGN, his radio station—the same talk every three or four months—that ended: "March on, then, First Division! March over the sunny hills of France; march thru the flaming towns of Picardy, up the shell-swept slopes of Lorraine, thru the gas-filled forest of Argonne—on to everlasting glory."

McCormick took an indignantly personal interest in seeing that his reporter's killer was brought before the bar of justice (Though initially he mistook Lingle for some other reporter on his staff.) He demanded a special prosecutor for the case's grand jury and got him: his own lawyer. In the Colonel's view, Jake Lingle's killer had attacked not only the sunny hills of the World's Greatest Newspaper but, also, that holiest of holies, a Free Press.

The martyred Lingle's friendship with Police Chief Russell went back to 1910, when Russell was a beat patrolman. The two men played golf together, dined with mutual friends often, went to the theater together. Lingle sometimes drove the chief's official car, used his racetrack pass.

Lingle gambled heavily on the horses. Flush one day, broke the next, he carried a "Philadelphia bankroll." (If you have only $50, say, change $40 of it into singles and wrap them with the remaining ten-dollar bill.) When he was flush, however, he carried thousands in cash on his person.

Lingle met Al Capone in 1920 when Capone—then called Al Brown or, sometimes, "Snorky"—was still a lowly steerer and blood-action handyman at Johnny Torrio's Four Deuces. In 1921 Lingle took an expensive vacation in Cuba. He explained to fellow reporters that his father had left him a $50,000 bequest. When Lingle's will was probated, however, the bequest turned out to have been for only $500. The fine

Italian hand of Johnny Torrio might be inferred.

At the time of his death, Lingle had his own chauffeur-driven Lincoln, lived at the upper-scale Stevens Hotel, wintered in Cuba or Miami, frequently with Capone. The diamond-studded belt buckle he wore had been given him by the Big Fellow. In addition to a West Side house in which his wife and two children lived, he owned an $18,000 summer home in Indiana.

In the 30 months preceding his death on June 9, 1930, he had deposited $63,900 in cash at Lake Shore Trust and Savings. Three months before his death he paid insurance premiums for a policy on $12,000 worth of jewelry. Many businessmen and aldermen—even the city's Corporation Counsel, Samuel Ettelson—had loaned him large sums.

As these facts developed day by day, the Colonel must have been deeply puzzled; he had been told he was paying his ace reporter $65 a week.

More of Lingle's activities came to light. For years he had been repeatedly sought out by police officers for help in getting promotions, by businessmen for aid in obtaining political favors, and by gangsters for protection from the police. Shortly before he died he had said to a reporter friend, "You know, I fixed the price of beer in this town."

He had an ulcer and he had four brokerage accounts in his name. If he had cashed in his securities at the peak of the bull market in September 1929, he would have made a profit of $85,000. The Crash cost him that and $75,000 more.

He had a fifth account in partnership with Police Chief Russell. (In this joint account the two lost $50,850.) When the partnership became known, Police Chief Russell resigned and there was a short-lived movement to force the absent—recuperating in the north woods—Mayor Thompson to resign, also. Russell had become chief at the *Tribune*'s behest. The trade-off had been that the $2,450,000 judgment against Mayor Thompson would be stayed, which it was, also at the *Tribune*'s behest. Russell was replaced by John H. Alcock.

At last the mortified—shell-shocked—Colonel capitulated. On June 30 a long *Tribune* editorial read, in part:

> When Alfred Lingle was murdered the motive seemed to be apparent . . . a murder to prevent a disclosure and to give warning against attempts at others. . . .
>
> Alfred Lingle now takes a different character, one in which he was unknown to the management of the *Tribune* when he was alive. He is dead and cannot defend himself, but many facts now revealed must be accepted as eloquent against him. . . . The reasonable appearance against Lingle now is that he was accepted in the world of politics and crime for something undreamed of in his office, and that he used this in undertakings which made him money and brought him to his death. . . .

There are weak men on other newspapers and in other professions, in positions of trust and responsibility greater than that of Alfred Lingle. The *Tribune*, although naturally disturbed by the discovery that this reporter was engaged in practices contrary to the code of its honest reporters and abhorred by the policy of this newspaper, does not find that the main objectives of the inquiry have been much altered. . . .

. . . That he is not a soldier dead in the discharge of duty is unfortunate considering that he is dead. It is of no consequence to an inquiry determined to discover why he was killed, by whom killed and with what attendant circumstances. *Tribune* readers may be assured that their newspaper has no intention of concealing the least fact of this murder and its consequences and meanings. The purpose is to catch the murderers. . . .

The nonsense of the sentence "That he is not a soldier dead in the discharge of duty is unfortunate considering that he is dead" also sounds very much that of the *Tribune*'s publisher, but it was now clear that Lingle's death ranked as a personal affront to the Colonel. He demanded action, and new Police Chief Alcock's force tried to comply. Hundreds of suspects were picked up, questioned—then released. The Colonel seethed.

One theory held that Lingle had, inadvertently, no doubt, double-crossed Capone by advising him that dog track racing would not be ruled illegal in Illinois. When it was, the Outfit lost half a million dollars. Another was that Lingle had done the same to the Zuta-Moran North Siders. Another was that his horseracing losses had put him irremediably in debt to the Outfit—$100,000 worth.

The most tenable theory was that Lingle, hard-pressed by his stock market losses, had gotten desperately greedy. When Jack Zuta and his partners were ready to reopen their luxurious gambling casino, the Sheridan Wave Tournament Club (621 Waveland), closed by the police after the St. Valentine's Day massacre, and invitations had gone out for June 9, Lingle demanded $15,000 or 50 percent of net for protection. (His usual cut was said to have been 10 percent.) When Zuta refused to pay so much, Lingle told him, "If this joint is opened up, you'll see more squad cars in front ready to raid it than you ever saw in your life before." So Jack Zuta, bookkeeper and North Side whoremaster, had Lingle killed on the day of the night the Sheridan Wave was to open.

Capone spent much of June in Florida, where the good burghers of Miami attended parties given by him to court their good will. Capone's fame—his notoriety—was at its peak. In Indiana a Charlestown racetrack crowd cheered him when he appeared with his bodyguards. At the Washington Park racetrack in Homewood the band played "It's a Lonesome Town When You're Not Around" as he took his seat, and then fans rushed to get his autograph. At Wrigley Field, Cub fans cheered him and at Northwestern's Dyche Stadium a Boy Scout troop cried "Yea-a-a Al!"

when he appeared. (He had bought their tickets.) His usual acknowledgment of these public tributes was to raise clasped hands above his head.

He had been named "Public Enemy Number One" by the Chicago Crime Commission but this distinction only increased the adulation. He was the most publicized gangster in the land and acclaim, of a sort, for his achievements spread worldwide. Fred D. Pasley's *Al Capone: The Biography of a Self-Made Man* was a 1930's bestseller, and was banned in London. A melodrama about him, *On the Spot*, played on London and Broadway stages. Ben Hecht wrote the script for a movie about him, *Scarface*. Edward G. Robinson played him in the movie *Little Caesar* in 1930; James Cagney, in 1931 in *Public Enemy*. In Berlin an aging Hungarian claimed he was Capone's father and would "box his ears for all his machine-guns if I get hold of him." A Vienna newspaper declared him the "real" mayor of Chicago. (And in Copenhagen police confiscated 400 slot machines placed there by his representatives.) A Paris newspaper sent its crime expert to interview him: "And the man of 50 corpses, always smiling, gave me his hand, fine and very white."

But back in Capone's hometown, Colonel McCormick's newspaper was demanding that Lingle's killer be apprehended. Worse, illicit traffic in the city had come to a standstill. Jake Guzik was heard on a tapped telephone wire telling one of his pay-off men, "We just ain't makin' any dough and if we ain't got it, we can't pay it."

Jack Zuta was picked up by police for questioning. The underworld knew Zuta to be too soft to stand up under pressure. When Zuta was released on bail he begged the police to escort him to safety. A lieutenant going off duty said he would drive him to the Lake Street El Station, a mile and a half north.

Six blocks from their destination, in the heart of the Loop, a blue sedan drew alongside and its driver and two passengers—one of them standing on the sedan's running board—opened fire with revolvers. (A streetcar motorman was killed by a stray bullet.) The lieutenant screeched to a stop, Zuta tumbled out and fled, and the lieutenant roared off in pursuit of the blue sedan. When he began to close on it, the sedan suddenly disappeared in a dense cloud of black smoke that covered State Street from curb to curb. A new tactic had been added to gang warfare: oil pumped into the intake manifold.

Capone returned to Chicago at the end of July to meet with a representative of the special prosecutor, for whose services the *Tribune* was paying. "I can't stand the gaff of these raids and pinches," he told him. He said he would produce Lingle's killer, but when he asked if a dead body would be sufficient, he was told that a corpse would not satisfy the Colonel.

Later, at the Lexington Hotel, IRB undercover agent Malone overheard Capone tell Jake Guzik he was not going to deliver the actual killer, but somehow he would satisfy the Colonel.

Many of the details of Jake Lingle's double life were first revealed in the St. Louis *Post-Dispatch* by its reporter John T. Rogers. They were furnished to Rogers by IRB agent Wilson, who several years before had helped Rogers win a Pulitzer Prize by supplying him with information for stories exposing a corrupt federal judge. In St. Louis, over lunch, Rogers introduced agent Wilson to Edward O'Hare, the lawyer who ran the Outfit's dog racing tracks. O'Hare had a 12-year-old son, "Butch," whose ambition was to attend the U.S. Naval Academy. "If I never do another thing in my life," O'Hare told Wilson, "I'm going to see that that kid's wish to get into Annapolis is granted."

Within a week of the lunch meeting O'Hare volunteered to be an informant for Wilson. The lunch had been his means of looking Wilson over. O'Hare wanted to break from the Outfit. If he could become legitimate, and had helped the government, he felt his son would stand a better chance of being appointed to the Academy.

Agent Wilson and his staff spent week after week gathering handwriting samples of known Chicago hoodlums from voting registers, savings accounts, police court records, bail bond certificates, auto license applications, trying to find a script that matched that in the Hawthorne Smoke Shop ledger Wilson had found. At last a deposit slip signature from a small bank in Cicero showed the man: Leslie Adelbert Shumway. But Shumway could not be found.

Jack Zuta had fled north to a summer resort on the shores of Upper Nemahbin Lake near Delafield, Wisconsin, 25 miles west of Milwaukee. On July 31, as he was feeding nickels into the electric player piano in the resort's pavilion where 20 couples were dancing, five men entered in single file carrying a tommygun, sawed-off shotguns, and revolvers. When Zuta saw them his face drained of color and he fell to the floor. He was picked up, carried to a chair in front of the piano and propped in it. The piano was playing "It May Be Good for You, but It's So Bad for Me." The five men put 16 bullets into Jack Zuta.

The slain man had kept records of his activities in safe deposit boxes: cancelled checks to judges, state senators, police officers, gang figures, city officials; letters from suburban police chiefs, at least 50 Chicago office holders—what might be expected, though not—possibly—that of payments to Richard J. Williams, police sergeant and chief aide to Frank J. Loesch, president of the Chicago Crime Commission. The recipient of the biggest payoffs was Roger Touhy's partner, Matt Kolb, the political fixer in north and northwest Cook County—until Bill Russell became Chicago's police chief, when payments to Kolb ceased. Jake Lingle had taken over.

("The five men put 16 bullets into Jack Zuta" does not express the grisly horror of the act. Nor does "A street-car motorman was killed by a stray bullet." Words on a page too often distance reality. They become commonplace. Ideally, there would be a smear of blood on every page on which the murder of a man is recounted—but even that would quickly become routine. Perhaps to begin approximating the brute meaning of every killing mentioned in these pages [forgetting the tears shed by wife, mother, children] the opposite page should be smeared with blood and a shred of brain or human gristle or a length of stinking gut. Imagine that and magnify it a hundred-fold for every death. Or see Jack Zuta's head jolted back and spraying blood as the first of the 16 slugs takes him in his mouth. There was no romance in mob warfare, only life's red blood, torn flesh, and death.)

Chicago's municipal government machinery was breaking down. The city was spending $23 million more in 1930 than it might expect from taxes and 1,500 employees were dropped from the public payrolls. Pay days were suspended for the remaining teachers, police, and firemen. The mayor's whereabouts was usually in doubt. Samuel Ettelson, Chicago Corporation Counsel, was in effect the mayor of Chicago. At new Police Chief Alcock's first press conference he began, "This afternoon I found Mayor Thompson—"

"By God, you are a detective!" a reporter shouted.

Hundreds of thousands of Chicagoans were jobless or on short hours. Thousands were homeless. Married couples and their children moved in with their elders. In a huge building on Chicago's South Side Capone instituted Chicago's first soup kitchen. "FREE FOOD FOR THE WORKLESS" the sign read, and 20,000 meals a week were dispensed: beef stew, chili con carne, thick rye bread, coffee, hot chocolate. "Good old Al," men said, standing in line, their bellies growling with hunger. The kitchen was open seven days a week from 6:00 in the morning till 10:00 at night. Naturally, merchants were assessed for contributions. For Thanksgiving Day Capone sent 5,000 turkeys to the kitchen. (One truck with a 1,000-bird cargo was hijacked.) At Christmas the Big Fellow sponsored a festa for the poor of Little Italy. An old woman knelt in front of him and kissed his hand, his fine and very white hand.

On September 20 his tax attorney, Lawrence P. Mattingly, still proceeding on the assumption that the government would prefer to avoid court, sent the Chicago IRB office a letter "Re Alphonse Capone." Mattingly's experience was that the government would settle on the basis of the figures he provided.

> Prior to the latter part of the year 1925 he was employed at a salary which at no time exceeded $75.00 per week. . . .
>
> Taxpayer became active and a principal with three associates at about the end of the year 1925. Because of the fact that he had no capital to invest in their various undertakings, his participation during the entire year 1926 and a greater part of the year 1927 was limited.

325

During the years 1928 and 1929, the profits of the organization of which he was a member were divided as follows: one-third to a group of regular employees and one-sixth each to the taxpayer and three associates. . . .

. . . I am of the opinion that his taxable income for the years 1926 and 1927 might be fairly fixed and not to exceed $26,000 and $40,000, respectively, and for the years 1928 and 1929, not to exceed $100,000 per year.

Government agent Wilson now had Capone's attorney's statement for the share-out of Outfit income as well as a written admission of tax delinquency. He knew Capone's share was at least twice that stated, and his income immensely larger but the letter was at least a starting point. What he did not have, however, was Leslie Shumway, the bookkeeper who kept the Hawthorne Smoke Shop ledger. Without him, he could not prove income from the Smoke Shop which, while only a small part of the Outfit's revenue-generating enterprises, was still enough to make a case.

On the evening of October 23, Joey Aiello—president of the Unione Siciliana since Hop Toad Giunta's bludgeoning—was cut down by more than 200 machine gun bullets. His killers were directed, in Chicago, by the Sicilian Al Mineo, head of a New York Family. The murder was a by-blow of the Castellammarese War then raging in NYC, but Chicago police were not aware of this and so of course attributed the killing to Capone mobsters. No charges were ever brought against anyone in Aiello's death.

On November 18, Jake Guzik was convicted of income tax evasion and sentenced to a fine of $17,500 and five years and one day in prison. Frank Nitti next, on December 20, pled guilty to tax evasion. His sentence was a fine of $10,000 and 18 months to be served in Leavenworth Penitentiary.

On December 21 Chicago detectives arrested Leo Vincent Brothers, a St. Louis gunman, at the Lake Crest Drive Apartments and charged him with the murder of Alfred J. Lingle. The *Tribune*'s editorial writers were exultant. Writers at other Chicago newspapers expressed skepticism that Lingle's true killer had been found.

On February 31, 1931, acting on a tip from Edward O'Hare, IRB agent Frank Wilson found Leslie Adelbert Shumway working at the Biscayne Kennel Club dog-racing track in Miami, Florida. Wilson gave Shumway two choices: (1) he could cooperate with the government, or (2) Wilson would have a deputy sheriff publicly and noisily serve him with a subpoena—and Capone would then know Shumway had been found and had to be silenced.

HUNGER

In 1894 when the 1,600 starving, discharged workers of George M. Pullman's works and model town appealed for help to Illinois Governor John Peter Altgeld—the infamous, un-American radical who had pardoned the three men in the Haymarket case—the governor asked Pullman to, at the least, exhibit some humanity.

Pullman refused. He said to do so would put his company in a bad light.

Altgeld replied to Pullman at the dynast's palatial Eastern retreat: "I cannot enter into a discussion with you as to the merits of the controversy between you and your former workmen. I assume that even if they are wrong and had been foolish, you would not be willing to see them perish. . . ."

Pullman—urged on by his company's largest stockholder, Marshall Field—declared himself willing, yes, to let his discharged workers and their families perish; it would be a salutary lesson to those who remained.

About this time, the English reformer and journalist, William T. Stead, gathering information for his book *If Christ Came to Chicago!* gave a talk to a group of Chicago clubwomen. "Who are the most disreputable women in Chicago?" Stead asked, and answered: "They are those who have been dowered by society and Providence with all the gifts and all the opportunities; who have wealth and who have leisure, who have all the talents, and who live entirely self-indulgent lives, caring only for themselves. . . . Those women . . . are more disreputable in the eyes of God and man than the worst harlot on Fourth Avenue." Many of the Gold Coast clubwomen in his audience were offended by Stead's observations.

And also about this same time the young economist Thorstein Veblen, an instructor at the University of Chicago, was working on his classic *Theory of the Leisure Class*, in which he purported to show that the families and heirs of the dynasts of the country (families such as

Chicago's McCormicks, Armours, Fields) led sybaritic, wastrel lives conspicuously consuming, not for enjoyment but to demonstrate their absolute power (through their wealth).

In January of 1895 Governor Altgeld told the Illinois legislature that

> "At present the status seems to be this: Combinations by capital against the public and against labor have succeeded, no matter by what means, and the men who accomplished it are now patriots; while combinations among laborers for self-protection have failed, and the men who advocate it are enemies of society. . . ."

When the U.S. Supreme Court, in a decision written by Chief Justice Melville W. Fuller (a member of the Union League Club of Chicago and earlier in his career a lawyer for Marshall Field) declared the income tax law of 1894 unconstitutional, Altgeld commented that "The Supreme Court has come to the rescue [of] the Standard Oil kings, the Wall Street people, as well as the rich mugwumps." The passage of the income tax had embittered them, he said; now they were "again happy. But the great business and producing classes do not share their joy. . . . Their burden is made a little heavier and the whip has made a new welt on their backs, but what of it? In fact, what are they for, if not to bear burdens and to be lashed?"

A corrective to such renegade views was that of George F. Baer, an Eastern railroad president, in his reply to a worker who in 1902 asked him to end a strike. "The rights and interests of the laboring man," Baer wrote, "will be protected and cared for, not by the labor agitators but by the Christian men to whom God in his infinite wisdom has given the control of the property interests of the country, and upon the successful management of which so much depends."

The successful management of the country's property interests had led, somehow, to nationwide money panics and depressed economic conditions and widespread unemployment in 1829, 1837, 1857, 1873, 1882, 1893, 1900, and would again in 1907 and 1913 (and roughly every seven or eight years thereafter, with mini-slumps along the way; this is the timetable U.S. monopoly capitalism works to, apparently—though the country's openly criminal syndicates seem to have discovered a formula that avoids such major disruptions). As we learned earlier, in the harsh winter of 1893-94 Chicago saloonkeepers fed 60,000 out-of-work men a day by setting out their establishments' free lunch even for those who couldn't afford a nickel beer as entry. Hinky Dink Kenna alone was feeding more than a thousand men a day in his saloons; 2,000 homeless slept nightly in the corridors of City Hall.

But by 30 years later, just before the *Great* Depression, all that was in the Inland Empire's past and forgotten. In the good times on the eve of the Great Depression, a new Ford automobile cost less than $500, a gallon of gas was 15 cents. A hot dog was a nickel; so was an ice cream cone. A three-bedroom house sold for $2,500 to $3,000.

But on that eve, in the year 1929, the average income of a household was only about $1,300. Though the year marked the end of a 10-year period of great national prosperity, more than 25 percent of all U.S. families that year had household incomes of less than $1,000; 42 percent less than $1,500; 71 percent (20,000,000 U.S. families) less than $2,500.

The United States was a land of bread and work in 1929 but for 55 hours or more a week the wages were not high—for most of its families. The wealth of the country in 1929 was concentrated in the hands of the privileged (by definition). Only 600,000 families—a scant 2.3 percent of the population—had household incomes higher than $10,000 a year. And an even scantier number, less than 300,000 families—1 percent of all the households in the United States—held a full 43 percent of the nation's entire wealth in their possession.

Then came the Great Depression. By 1931 4.5 million men were out of work. By the next year the total of unemployed had tripled, to 13.5 million. (The highest previous total of U.S. unemployed—excluding 1931— was 4 million in 1919.)

Economics is called the "dismal science" because its lab work is done with columns of figures (and also, perhaps, because it fails the test of a science). Statistics aside, economics may, as Sartre noted, "be reduced to the necessity of eating." That, of course, was what the labor agitation at the Pullman works was all about in the late 19th century: Getting paid enough for your labor to feed your family. Money, or the lack of it, determines everything, it seems.

"Statistics make unemployment abstract and not too uncomfortable. The human being is different. To be hungry is different than to count the hungry," wrote the peerless Midwest recorder, Meridel Le Sueur, in 1934.

We know about the millions upon millions of Depression-beset men—the "breadwinners" of their families—who could not find work to buy bread. In 1977 Le Sueur recalled her memories of the women of the time:

> During the Depression, as now, women and girls poured into the cities from the farms and ruined villages, looking for work. You never saw them on the soup lines. The city had no way to deal with the hungry women. There was no relief, no food program. You lost your job and in a week you were on the street. There was no severance pay, no unemployment insurance, no social security.
>
> You couldn't get a quarter or a meal for your body. Women were raped, beaten, died terrible deaths in abortion mills or from self-

abortions, were buried without names, in paupers' graves. Some merely quietly starved to death.

They were picked up on streets by police dragnets, sent to women's prisons, asylums. They were often sterilized. . . .

Many disappeared, took to the road, went east or west, were lost in the underground war against women. You cannot find or claim them, or recognize them to even say their names. They are outside the economy, the statistics. You cannot even claim the bodies.

More than half a million Chicagoans were jobless by the spring of 1931. (Only a million had jobs.) At Christmas a *Tribune* reporter found a woman with small children whose entire food supply for her family was "one loaf of bread, one pound of beans, and a small square of bacon." Her husband had purchased these rations by selling his overcoat for 30 cents. Thousands of "Hooverville" inhabitants were living off what they could find to eat at city dumps. (Hoovervilles were packing box, old car body, tin and tar paper hovels put together for shelter on vacant lots.) The Chicago Urban League reported that "2,000 homeless, decrepit, shivering and starving men" had lived 20 feet below the Michigan Avenue Bridge the previous winter. By September of 1931 hundreds of women were sleeping in Grant and Lincoln parks. As Le Sueur wrote of other starving women:

> A woman will shut herself up in a room until it is taken away from her, and eat a cracker a day and be as quiet as a mouse, so there are no social statistics concerning her.
>
> I don't know why it is, but a woman will do this unless she has dependents, will go for weeks verging on starvation, crawling in some hole, going through the streets ashamed, sitting in libraries, parks, going for days without speaking to a living soul like some exiled beast, keeping the runs mended in her stockings, shut up in terror in her own misery, until she becomes too super-sensitive and timid to even ask for a job.

By 1932, 100,000 Chicago families were on relief, and months of joblessness had lengthened into years of joblessness for hundreds of thousands. Al Capone's soup kitchens were feeding thousands of hungry Chicagoans every day. To get on the relief rolls ($23 a month for families) the jobless had first to sell all of their possessions. Men who had jobs walked to work because they couldn't afford seven cents for streetcar fare, cardboard lining their shoes because they couldn't afford to repair the worn-out soles.

And the women? Le Sueur tells of sitting in the city's free employment bureau:

> So we sit in this room like cattle, waiting for a nonexistent job, willing to work to the farthest atom of energy, unable to work, unable to get

330

food and lodging, unable to bear children—here we must sit in this shame looking at the floor, worse than beasts at a slaughter.

It is appalling to think that these women sitting so listless in the room may work as hard as it is possible for a human being to work, may labor night and day, . . . wash streetcars from midnight to dawn and offices in the early evening, scrub for 14 and 15 hours a day, sleep only 5 hours or so, do this their whole lives, and never earn one day of security, having always before them the pit of the future. The endless labor, the bending back, the water-soaked hands, earning never more than a week's wages, never having in their hands more life than that.

Thus the life of those who have not privilege, the short and simple annals of the poor, who are not only with us always, but in over-whelming numbers, good times and bad. As Le Sueur concluded, "It's not the suffering of birth, death, love that the young reject, but the suffering of endless labor without dream, eating the spare bread in bitterness, being a slave without the security of a slave."

In the late 1870s the great American novelist Henry James took time from his fiction to reflect on what he had seen and felt in his travels in Europe and America. He came to the conclusion that

toil and privation, hunger and sorrow, and sordid effort are the portion of the mass of mankind. . . . character consists simply in the slightly different costume in which labour and want present themselves. . . . I know that . . . half the time we are acclaiming the fine quality of the Italian smile the creature . . . may be in a sullen frenzy of impatience and pain.

Yes, agreed. So we go on with pick and shovel, till the work is done and we lay it down gladly. . . . Brother, can you spare a dime?

Al Capone

Capone flanked by his lawyers Ahern (left) and Fink

NADIR

A woman born to leisure, luxury, travel, and an acquaintance with the arts, Eleanor "Cissy" Patterson—Colonel Robert "Bertie" McCormick's cousin—was executive editor of the Hearst-owned Washington *Herald* (a newspaper she subsequently bought for herself) when in January 1931 she called at 93 Palm Island. "Come in," said Miami's most famous resident. "Let me show you around."

> He has the neck and shoulders of a wrestler. One of those prodigious Italians, thick-chested, close to six feet tall. The muscles of his arms stretched the sleeves of his light brown suit so that it seemed to be cut too small for him.
> Once I looked *at* his eyes. Ice-gray, ice-cold eyes. You can't anymore look *into* the eyes of Capone than you can look into the eyes of a tiger. . . .

His hands also fascinated her. "Enormous, powerful enough to tackle—well, almost anything, although superficially soft from lack of exposure, and highly manicured." But the eyes seemed to her his most seductive quality and she returned to them:

> Capone's eyes are "dime novel" gangster's eyes. Ice-gray. Ice-cold. I could feel their menace. The stirring of the tiger. For just a second I went a little sick. I had to fight the impulse to jump up and run blindly away.
> "Tell me, Mr. Capone," I ventured presently, feeling somewhat refreshed after the lemonade we had consumed, "what do you think about Prohibition? Do you think it will ever be done away with?" I asked.
> "Yes, I do, and I'm all for that time to come. Prohibition has made nothing but trouble—trouble for all of us. Worst thing ever hit the country. If I say I give it no more than another five years, then I'm right, you bet. It's like this. I don't interfere with big business. None of those big business guys can say that I ever took a single dollar from them. I only want to do business, you understand, with my own class.

I don't interfere with their racket. Why can't they leave my racket alone? Get me? But there they are—always after me, trying to frame me. They got me framed in Chicago now. If I don't answer this framed income tax charge, they're going to try and trump up a charge of vagrancy against me. It ain't fair."

The fascinated multimillionaire editor finally took her leave, a responsive chord obviously having been struck deep within her, despite the difference in class between her and Al Capone.

"Well, goodbye, Mr. Capone." I shook hands with him. "Good luck to you," I called as the motor started, and I meant it sincerely.

It has been said many times, with truth, that women have a special kind of sympathy for gangsters. If you don't understand why, consult Dr. Freud.

Without recourse to Dr. Freud, Cissy Patterson had come perilously close to telling her readers exactly how her own very special kind of sympathy for gangsters expressed itself.

Not long after Cissy Patterson's reportorial call, Capone invited Roger Touhy, who was in Florida vacationing with his family, to visit him at his Palm Island estate and fish from the Capone yacht. Touhy declined. He fished with his Irish labor leader friends instead. When Touhy returned to Chicago, his partner Matt Kolb told him that the Outfit had shaken them down for $25,000.

The Big Fellow appeared in Chicago on February 25 to answer a federal contempt charge for failure to appear before a grand jury investigating bootlegging two years before. He waived jury trial and Judge James H. Wilkerson found him guilty and sentenced him to six months in county jail. Capone remained free on $5,000 bail.

A federal grand jury, meeting in secret (although Capone knew of it), indicted him on March 13 for attempting to evade and defeat an income tax of $32,489 in 1924 on income of $123,103. The jury beat the six-year statute of limitations on tax offenses by two days. U.S. Attorney George E. Q. Johnson asked that the jury withhold its verdict until it completed its investigation for the years 1925-29.

The grand jury had heard testimony from Leslie Shumway. After IRB agent Frank Wilson offered Shumway his deadly Hobson's choice in Miami, Shumway gave a deposition: "Orders and directives relating to my work were issued to me by Frank Pope and Pete Penovich . . . the only other person whom I recognized as an owner of the business was Mr. Alphonse Capone."

Leo Brothers' trial for first-degree homicide in the death of *Chicago Tribune* reporter Jake Lingle began on March 16 and lasted till April 2. The jury deliberated 27 hours and found Brothers guilty. But instead of asking the death penalty, they imposed the minimum sentence of 14 years, commutable for good behavior in eight.

The Colonel was at last satisfied. Reporters from other Chicago newspapers, however, and even the police felt there was much room to doubt that Brothers was the killer: no motive was given; no gang connections, if any, were established; and the minimum sentence imposed by the jury for first-degree murder was quite unusual. As Brothers said, "I can do that standing on my head." But blind Justice had spoken and a Free Press was avenged.

An election for mayor was held in Chicago on April 7. Republican William Hale Thompson lost to Democrat Anton Cermak by almost 200,000 votes. On the morning after Cermak's victory, the *Tribune* published an editorial with which probably few elsewhere in the country would have disagreed, though 475,613 Chicago voters had the day before:

> For Chicago, Thompson has meant filth, corruption, obscenity, idiocy and bankruptcy. He has given the city an international reputation for moronic buffoonery, barbaric crime, triumphant hoodlumism, unchecked graft, and a dejected citizenship. He nearly ruined the property and completely destroyed the pride of the city. He made Chicago a byword of the collapse of American civilization. In his attempt to continue this he excelled himself as a liar and defamer of character. He's out.
>
> He is not only out, but he is dishonored. He is deserted by his friends. He is permanently marked by the evidences of his character and conduct. His health is impaired by his ways of life and he leaves office and goes from the city the most discredited man who ever held place in it.

In late May Capone played host at Chicago's Congress Hotel to a national crime convention. The guest list was equivalent to that in Atlantic City in 1929, but the purpose of this meeting was to affirm Salvatore Maranzano as victor in the Castellammarese War and his supremacy on the national scene. Capone—a non-Sicilian—was confirmed as head of the Chicago Family. Big Al was an extravagant host, providing all accommodations, food, drink, and women, and providing them lavishly. Maranzano gave a speech praising Alfonso, as he referred to Capone, who gave an equally glowing speech in praise of Maranzano, to whom he had already given a diamond-studded watch. (Three months later, Maranzano was dead, killed by assassins in the hire of Lucky Luciano. Charlie Lucky dispatched a man to Chicago to justify to Capone the necessity of killing Maranzano but by then Capone had little time to worry about the politics of NYC and national crime—even though his name had headed the dead Maranzano's list of rival mobsters to be eliminated.)

Since his youth, Roger Touhy had known the Irish labor leaders in Chicago. When he finished eighth grade he went to work as a Western

Union messenger, then as a telegrapher—and union organizer. When the Outfit moved against unions, many of the labor leaders bought homes in Touhy's northwest suburban territory, bringing their bodyguards with them. In 1929 Capone had sent Marcus "Studdy" Looney, an Outfit pimp promoted to labor muscle, to offer Touhy a cut of the Outfit's labor racketeering income if he would doublecross his friends. Touhy politely refused. Then he told his labor friends what had transpired, and wound up safeguarding their emergency bankroll—hundreds of thousands in cash. Another affront to the Outfit. There were rumors that his house would be bombed.

By 1931 the Touhy problem was being handled by Murray Humphreys, who that spring sent two men to grab Touhy's sons as they left school. By luck, the boys got away when they saw their mother's car and ran to it. The kidnapers had to return to their auto and U-turn to pursue Clara Touhy and did not overtake her and her children before they reached home. Mother and sons were unaware of the attempt but half a dozen teachers had seen it and were crying hysterically on the school grounds when Roger Touhy arrived there after one of them called him. Touhy—who since the April elections had a new and powerful ally in Chicago: Mayor Cermak—put on more bodyguards.

In anticipation of Repeal, Capone instructed Humphreys to gain entry for the Outfit into the retail dairy business. "You gotta have a product that everybody needs every day," Capone explained.

> "The workingman laps up half a dozen bottles of beer on Saturday night and that's it for a week. But with milk! Every family every day wants it on the table. Do you guys know there's a bigger markup in fresh milk than there is in alcohol? We've been in the wrong racket right along."

Humphreys began by attempting to persuade officials of Teamsters Local 753 of the Milk Wagon Drivers Union to guarantee the Outfit freedom from labor trouble. He also wanted them to buy into the Outfit's projected new business, which was to be called Meadowmoor Dairies. But Local 753 officials did not want to become Outfit partners.

On June 5 the federal grand jury indicated Capone on 22 more counts, these for evading a tax of $182,591 on income for 1925-29 of $915,558. Penalties added $164,445 to the tax due. The prosecutors did not contend they had given the true measure of Capone's income—only that which they intended to prove. A week later the jury returned a third indictment, this one against Capone and 68 members of the Outfit, charging them with 5,000 separate offenses of conspiring to violate the Volstead Act, some of this information developed by Eliot Ness. Capone remained free on $50,000 bail.

A story circulated that through a businessman friend of Elmer

Irey Capone had offered the Internal Revenue Bureau chieftain $1.5 million if Capone were pardoned. Another that Capone had imported five NYC killers to murder the Chicago IRB agents but that Johnny Torrio called them off. Torrio was in Chicago to attend the trial, at which he might be brought to the stand as a witness. He was also there to pay Capone's legal bills with cash so that the government could not impound those sums if paid by Al Capone. Another story that went the rounds was that Capone had offered the government $4 million to settle but was refused. Another that he had offered to give evidence against other defendants in return for a light sentence for himself.

What happened was that Capone's lawyer, Michael Ahern, met with the federal prosecutor, U.S. District Attorney George E. Q. Johnson, to plea bargain. On the one hand, the government had yet to lose a major tax evasion case. On the other, there was the question of whether or not the court would admit as evidence the Mattingly letter, which gave the government its starting point for Capone's income. There was also the notorious unreliability of juries, especially Chicago juries. And there was pressure on Johnson to obtain a Capone conviction before President Hoover ran for a second term.

Johnson told Ahern that in the past when he had made a sentence recommendation the courts had always followed it. A deal was struck: a sentence of only two and a half years plus a financial settlement in exchange for a guilty plea. The feds would have their conviction and Capone would do time, but not much.

On June 16 Capone pled guilty on all counts. His maximum possible theoretical sentence was 34 years in prison and $90,000 in fines. But as Ahern remarked in court, no tax evasion guilty plea had ever received more than 18 months in prison. And word was already out on the street that Al would be sitting for only two and a half years.

At the sentencing hearing on July 30 District Attorney Johnson told Judge Wilkerson that the recommendation for leniency had been approved by the Attorney General, the head of the IRB Intelligence Unit, and an Assistant Secretary of the Treasury.

To everyone's surprise, Judge Wilkerson replied angrily that

> "A plea of guilty is a full admission of guilt. The power of compromise is not vested in this court, but is conferred by Congress on other governmental offices. The court may require the production of evidence. If the defendant asks leniency by throwing himself on the mercy of the court, he must be prepared to answer all proper questions put to him by the court. . . ."

"We thought," Ahern said, mindful that an important part of his agreement with Johnson was that his client would not have to answer questions, "that the recommendation would be approved by the court. We believed that the department would have the power to compromise both the criminal and civil liability, that it constituted an inducement for the defendant to enter the plea we made. . . ."

"Certainly it is an unheard of thing in court proceedings," Judge Wilkerson responded, "that anybody, even the court itself, could bind the court as to the judgement which is to be made by the court. The court will listen to recommendations of the District Attorney, but the defendant cannot think that the court is bound to enter judgement according to those recommendations." And then he added ominously, "The defendant must understand that the punishment has not been decided before the close of the hearing. I must have it understood that there can be no bargaining in the Federal Court."

A previously confident Capone appeared slightly flummoxed as his counsel stood and withdrew his plea of guilty. Judge Wilkerson ruled that the 5,000 Volstead Act conspiracy charges could not be substantiated but that the defendant must stand trial for the income-tax evasion charges. Trial was scheduled for October 6.

In late August Capone gave an interview to a high-society reporter for *Liberty* magazine, Cornelius Vanderbilt, Jr. The interview was titled "How Al Capone Would Run This Country," and per *Liberty*'s custom its reading time was given: 15 minutes, 45 seconds.

> "Seems as if I'm responsible for every crime that takes place in this country. You'd think I had unlimited power and a swell pocketbook. Well, I guess I got the power all right; but the bank book suffers from these hard times as much as anyone else's.
>
> "My pay roll is about as big as it ever was, but the profits have done their share of dwindling. Say, you'd be surprised if you knew some of the fellas I've got to take care of."

He explained to Vanderbilt how he kept the Outfit running efficiently:

> "People who respect nothing dread *fear*. It is upon *fear*, therefore, that I have built up my organization. But understand me correctly, please. Those who work *with* me are afraid of nothing. Those who work *for* me are kept faithful, not so much because of their pay as because they know what might be done with them if they broke faith.
>
> "The United States government shakes a very wobbly stick at the lawbreaker and tells him he'll go to prison if he beats the law. Lawbreakers laugh and get good lawyers. A few of the less well-to-do take the rap. . . . On the other hand, do you know of any of your friends who'd go into fits of merriment if they feared being taken for a ride?"

He enlarged on the causes of the Depression:

"The world has been capitalized on paper. Every time a fellow had a new idea, they'd increase the capital stock—give themselves so much cash and their stockholders so much paper The rich got richer; the stockholders speculated with the paper. Someone found out it paid to keep a rumor factory going. Someone else interested women in gambling on the big board. The world was wild. . . .

"Why, down in Florida, the year I lived there, a shady newspaper publisher's friend was running a bank. He had unloaded a lot of worthless securities upon unsuspecting people. One day his bank went flooey. I was just thanking the powers that be that he'd got what was coming to him when I learned of another business trick that would make safe-cracking look like miniature golf.

"The crooked publisher and the banker were urging bankrupt depositors who were being paid 30 cents on the dollar to put their money in another friend's bank. Many did so; and just about 60 days later that bank collapsed like a house of cards too.

"Do you think those bankers went to jail? No, sir. They're among Florida's most representative citizens. They're just as bad as the crooked politicians! I ought to know about them. I've been feeding and clothing them long enough. I never knew until I got into this racket how many crooks there were dressed in expensive clothes and talking with affected accents."

Finally, he gave his slightly garbled version of what had happened to him in court on July 30:

"Why, when I was held the other day for evasion of federal taxes I nearly got myself into a fine pickle. Certain officials wished to make a bargain with me. If I'd plead guilty and go to jail for two and a half years, they'd dismiss the charges they had against me. A pretty penny had to be paid, but I thought that that was better than the strain of a long-winded trial. A day or so before the bargain was to be struck, though, I learned that someone was going to go to the appellate court and that there'd be a fly in the ointment and they'd have me in Leavenworth for ten and a half years. So I decided I could be just as foxy, and we entered a plea of not guilty, and when the case comes up we'll see what we will see.

"A little while ago in one of the Chicago newspapers it said that a local millionaire manufacturer had been found to be some $55,000 in arrears with his personal-property tax. A day later it was printed that this had been printed in error, and that the situation had been satisfactorily cleaned up. . . .

"Graft is a byword in American life today. It is law where no other law is obeyed. It is undermining this country. The honest lawmakers of any city can be counted on your fingers. I could count Chicago's on one hand!

"Virtue, honor, truth, and the law have all vanished from our life. We are smart-Alecky. We like to be able to 'get away with' things. And if we can't make a living at some honest profession, we're going to make one anyway."

He expressed the view that "When the prohibition law is repealed there'll be less desire for birth control. Without birth control America can become as stalwart as Italy. With an American Mussolini she could conquer the world."

As Vanderbilt departed Capone remarked that "The home is our most important ally. . . . The stronger we can keep our home lives, the stronger we can keep our nation," adding that he had fed 350,000 people a day in Chicago. "This winter it's going to be worse. . . . We've got to battle to keep free."

On September 23, two weeks before the trial was to begin, Edward O'Hare telephoned IRB agent Wilson and told him that the Outfit had secured a copy of the jury panel list for Capone's trial and that mobsters were calling on each person on the list, a bribe in one hand, a gun in the other. Wilson took the information to Elmer Irey and U.S. District Attorney Johnson and the three men called on Judge Wilkerson.

"Bring your case into court as planned, gentlemen," the jurist said. "Leave the rest to me."

When the trial opened in the soot-covered Federal Court Building on October 6, Judge Wilkerson told the bailiff to take his 60-member panel of prospective jurors to the courtroom of Judge John P. Barnes, who also had a trial commencing that morning, and exchange it with that of Judge Barnes. Capone did not stir on his chair, but his features darkened. He was flanked by his lawyers: Michael Ahern, the Outfit's long-time criminal counsel, and Albert Fink, expert as a trial lawyer. His bodyguard, Phil D'Andrea, sat behind him, steely-eyed. (D'Andrea had succeeded Joey Aiello as president of the Unione Siciliana.)

Ten of the 12 middle-aged and elderly men finally selected for the jury from the new panel came from small towns, one from Waukegan, one from Chicago. Ahern stated he preferred a more cosmopolitan jury. Wilkerson overruled him.

The prosecution began by establishing that Capone had filed no tax returns for the years 1924-29. Then Chester Bragg, the ministers'-citizens'-vigilantes' door guard during their 1925 raid on the Hawthorne Smoke Shop testified that Capone had said to him, "I am the owner of this place." He further testified that when he left the Smoke Shop "I was set upon by about a thousand hoodlums. I was slugged over one eye. My nose was broken with a blackjack. One of my eyes was blackened—maybe two eyes and I had to be taken to a doctor in Berwyn."

Next, with Capone glaring at him, a nervous Leslie Shumway identified the cash ledger Wilson had found and tabulated the profits of the Smoke Shop from it for the jury: $587,721 for 18 months of 1924-26.

The next day the opposing lawyers duelled over whether or not the letter to the Chicago IRB office from Lawrence Mattingly, Capone's tax attorney, was admissible. "A lawyer cannot confess for his client,"

Fink said. "When my client conferred power of attorney in this case to enable him to keep out of the penitentiary, it did not imply the power or authority to make statements that may get him into the penitentiary."

"It might have that effect ultimately," mused Judge Wilkerson aloud. The judge permitted the letter to be entered as evidence, giving the government its base for Capone's assets and income.

That night at the Lexington, as Capone was being measured by a tailor for two lightweight suits, his ever-loyal bodyguard Frankie Rio said to him, "You don't need to be ordering fancy duds. You're going to prison. Why don't you have a suit made with stripes on it?"

"The hell I am!" Capone said. He retained his faith in the U.S. legal system, in his lawyers, and in the large fees he was paying them.

On the fourth day of the trial IRB undercover agent Malone emerged from his identity as "Lepito" to give evidence. During the trial Edward G. Robinson and Beatrice Lillie sat in on part of the proceedings, causing the expected stir among other spectators. On being introduced to Capone, Lillie was struck dumb with stage fright. Each morning as Capone—resplendent each day in a different suit—alighted from his car he gave a $5 bill to the unemployed man selling apples at the curb.

The prosecution established that Capone had received more than $110,000 in Western Union money orders while in Florida. When the manager of the Western Union office in the Lexington Hotel took the stand, however, he could not remember who had sent the money orders—though before the trial he had given agent Wilson the sender's name. Wilson confronted him during a recess. "What can you expect," the manager said, "when one of Capone's hoodlums sits there with his hand on his gun?" He was referring to Phil D'Andrea.

The next morning D'Andrea was arrested and relieved of his concealed weapon, a .38 revolver. He was cited for contempt of court and sentenced by Wilkerson to six months in a federal prison.

For the next two days a succession of witnesses described Capone's extravagant spending habits: 20 suits and a dozen topcoats, cost $3,600; 22 beaded handbags, $495; 30 diamond-studded belt buckles, $8,190 (Frankie Yale had died wearing one of these; so had Jake Lingle); shirts at $22 and $30 each; custom-made shirts with reinforced pistol pockets at $135; ties, $4 each; handkerchiefs, $2.75 each; silk underwear, $12 a pair; a $39,000 telephone bill over a 4-year period (10 months of which was spent in jail in Philadelphia); improvements on the Miami estate, $50,000; $12,000 for a gold-plated dinner service; $26,000 for furnishings. His meat bill in Miami ran from $200 to $250 a week. In 1925 he contributed $58,000 to the police widows' and orphans' fund; in 1926, $15,000 to the Catholic Church.

The contractor who had built the dock and boathouse for the Palm Island estate said,

"I saw money wrappers marked $1,000 lying around the house. A couple of handfuls, I guess. There was enough money in a cupboard to choke an ox. Mrs. Capone got $250 out of these to pay me a bill. She paid me in $50 bills, and the roll was about as thick as your wrist."

The former manager of the Metropole Hotel said Capone's banquet tab the night of the Dempsey-Tunney fight was $3,000. The cashier at the Metropole said that Capone paid his bills from 1925-28 for rooms there in cash, sometimes with denominations as large as $500.

Fink objected. "I thought the government had to prove his income," he said, "not his outgo."

"It would appear," answered the judge, "what you pay out is at least a circumstance to show that you got something in." Since the prosecution's case was circumstantial, this comment did not harm their case; to legal minds, however, it might appear puzzling, since it *was* the government's job to prove Capone's income.

That night Capone called eight of Chicago's top bookmakers to his Lexington Hotel office. He told them that the next day they would testify for him or they would be out of business. They agreed to testify.

And that was pretty much Al Capone's defense: that he lost when he bet the horses. One bookmaker was asked on cross-examination the names of the horses Capone backed in 1929 at a loss of $10,000 each. He couldn't remember their names.

"Can you give the name of just *one* horse that the defendant bet on?"

"I have five or six in mind, but they just won't come out."

It was a poor and inept defense at best, since it was thought at the time that a taxpayer could deduct gambling losses only to offset winnings, and Fink and Ahern had taken pains to establish that Capone hardly ever won. Moreover, it was a defense that had failed in Jake Guzik's trial for tax evasion. Nor could Capone's lawyers explain his possessions and expenditures over and above his alleged gambling losses. The lack of preparation was pitifully apparent.

In summation the prosecution said that the government was charging that the defendant had an income in excess of $5,000 for the years 1926-29 and had paid no income tax.

"We find him living in Florida like a bejeweled prince in a palatial home. We find that he spent thousands of dollars without even thinking twice. We find him receiving thousands of dollars in telegraphic money orders from Chicago. . . . He told questioners in Florida that Jake Guzik was his financial secretary. On his income of 'secretary,' Guzik has been convicted of income tax fraud. What about the income of his boss, Capone? . . .

"He always had a roll of one-hundred-dollar and five-hundred-dollar bills—a roll 'big enough to choke an ox,' as one witness testified.

Yet when we tried to get from him an idea of his income, we had no help whatever from him. . . .

"Does anybody think that this man did not have a huge income? Why, the idea is ridiculous. Even a child would know better. He had an income that called for his paying to the government a substantial income tax."

Then Capone's attorney Fink addressed the jury for the defense:

"Are they really prosecuting this defendant because of an attempt to defraud the United States on income, or is it just to use that as a means to stow Al Capone away? If the latter, don't you be a party to it. You are the only bulwark that can resist oppression in a time of public excitement. Judges cannot do it. The fathers of this country put this power in the hands of the people. . . .

"The government lawyers have no confidence in the chaff they have presented here. They know that this evidence of spent money does not prove gross income. . . .

"Don't let yourselves be drawn away from the truth by the claim that Al Capone is a bad man. He may be the worst man who ever lived, but there is not a scintilla of evidence that he willfully attempted to defraud the government out of income tax. . . .

"Capone is the kind of man who never fails a friend. He was loved by his followers. Open-handed, generous, a man a bookmaker would trust with a ten-thousand-dollar bet. This does not fit in with the government's picture of a miserly effort to evade income tax. A tinhorn or a piker might try to defraud the government, but not Alphonse Capone."

U.S. District Attorney Johnson made the final summation for the government. Pointing at Capone, he said:

"Who is this man who has become such a glamorous figure? He has been called a Robin Hood by his counsel. Robin Hood took from the strong to feed the weak. Did this Robin Hood buy $8,000 worth of belt buckles for the unemployed? Was his $6,000 meat bill in a few weeks for the hungry? No, it went to the Capone home on Palm Island to feed the guests at nightly poker parties. Did he buy $27 shirts for the shivering men who sleep under Wacker Drive? . . .

"Was Capone the little boy out of the Second Reader who found the pot of gold at the end of the rainbow? If he was not, how did he get the money he spent so lavishly on $12,500 automobiles, $40,000 homes, $27 shirts and $275 diamond-studded belt buckles by the score?"

Judge Wilkerson instructed the jury and at 2:42 P.M. Saturday, October 17, it retired for its deliberations. The jurors returned at 11:00 P.M. Their verdict was guilty.

Sentencing took place a week later. As Capone stood to hear his sentence, he clasped his hands behind his back. His fingers twisted and turned as he waited. It was a complicated sentence and it took 20 minutes to deliver, but it added up to 11 years' imprisonment, fines of $50,000, and court costs of $30,000, the most severe sentence ever given a tax offender.

The U.S. Marshal handcuffed Capone and led him from the courtroom to a freight elevator. In the elevator were other passengers, including undercover agent Lepito-Malone. Capone shook his head. "The only thing that fooled me," he said to Malone, "was your looks. You look like a wop." He managed a sickly smile. "You took your chances," he said, "and I took mine. I lost."

He was removed to Cook County jail. His reign as head of the Outfit had lasted from the day that Hymie Weiss and Bugs Moran tried to kill Johnny Torrio to this day—five years and nine months—not quite two weeks less than a year longer than Johnny Papa had reigned.

On Monday morning his lawyers filed an application for bail, and set about preparing an appeal.

On November 18, 1931, Matt Kolb was in the Morton Inn, a speakeasy he owned in Morton Grove. Two gunmen entered and killed him.

Capone phoned Roger Touhy's brother the next day. "I'm terribly sorry," Al said. "There was a drunken caper and Matt got killed. I couldn't feel worse. I always liked Matt. I'm sending a $100 wreath to the funeral." Capone was calling from the Cook County jail; Judge Wilkerson had denied his application for bail. His appeal was on its way to the District Court of Appeals.

"'Jim,' she began softly, 'I'll be frank. You're not the best dancer in the world. What you need is brushing up on the latest steps. Why don't you get in touch with Arthur Murray?'

"'Arthur Murray!' I exclaimed. 'He teaches dancing by mail. You can't learn that way!'

"'No?' and Marion arched her eyebrows. 'The truth is, that's exactly *the way I learned.'"*

TIME AND CHANCE

In December of 1931 the president of Local 753 of the Milk Wagon Drivers Union, Robert G. "Old Doc" Ritchie, was kidnaped by Murray Humphreys. A ransom of $50,000 cash was demanded of the union for their president's release and it was paid—out of the emergency fund held by Roger Touhy. Two months later the Outfit set up in the milk business as Meadowmoor Dairies, Inc., 1334 South Peoria Street, the corporation chartered with capital of $50,000. The company prospered.

The District Court of Appeals rejected Al Capone's appeal on February 27, 1932. The U.S. Supreme Court rejected his lawyers' application for a writ of certiorari on May 2, which meant that it would not review his case. On May 4 Capone was taken from the Cook County jail and with an auto thief named Vito Morici and six U.S. marshals put on the Dixie Flyer bound for Atlanta. Capone slept that night handcuffed to Morici, sharing the same berth.

At the Atlanta Penitentiary Al Capone was assigned to an eight-man cell, one of whose occupants was Morris "Red" or "Rusty"Rudensky, a safecracker mechanic who had freelanced jobs for Capone in Chicago. His first night in the cell, Capone could not sleep. He woke up Rudensky to talk to him. "Imagine, some creep gets me in a damn tax rap," he said, "and now I suppose they'll be cutting up on the outside for splits. Here I am with a million bucks in half a dozen banks and I'm sitting in a hole like this. Ain't it a helluva deal, Rusty?"

Rudensky, who had long hero-worshipped Capone, felt a mixture of admiration and pity for him. He would wake Capone from his nightmares—"*No, no, no!*"—and shield him as best he could from problems in the yard—taunts of "Where's all the broads and booze now, fat boy?"

About his lawyers Capone would say repeatedly, "They're overpaid dumb bastards who couldn't spring a pickpocket." It was reported he'd sent people to recover his fees from Fink and Ahern. Once

345

he said, "You know, Rusty, I've been crossed! I've shelled out over 200 grand to a big man in Washington who could open the gates from D.C. Not only that, but I've got five of the greatest damn attorneys getting me ready for the spring. But I can't get a word out of any of them!"

He spent hours reading the newspapers and sports magazines or poring over letters from his family. With Rudensky he reminisced about the early days in Chicago, and once Rudensky needled him about Dion O'Banion and Bugs Moran. "Oh, those silly Irish bastards," Capone said. "They have more guts than sense. If we ever all hooked up, I could have been President."

One day he said to the prison's Catholic priest, "Father, I may have made a lot of mistakes, but I never second-guessed myself or the guy who clipped me out in the open."

His work assignment was the shoe repair shop. He heard only from his brother Ralph and his wife Mae, and, occasionally, from his son. His health was deteriorating—though he tried to stay in some sort of shape by playing tennis—and he slowly began to lose confidence that he was going to be released soon.

On a hot Saturday afternoon in mid-August 1934, he and Rudensky were sitting in their cell. Capone's white face looked worried and scared. He held his photograph of his son out to Rudensky. "Rusty," he said, "did you ever really see a better looking con's kid?" He moved uneasily on his bunk. "I mean, I'm getting damn lonesome just looking at shoes and these damn guards. I mean I'm anxious to get out."

His face reddened suddenly, then turned purple, and he slammed the photograph down on his bunk. "Damn it, Rusty, I want action! Where the hell are my big friends? What are those high-paid lawyer sons of bitches doing?"

After the evening meal that night they came to get him. "You're going to the Rock, Al, a nice long ride to Alcatraz."

He fought them with his old-time fury and strength. It took eight guards to remove him from the cell. "My God," he moaned at the last as they overpowered him, "you don't come back from the Rock."

His cellmate's evaluation of him was conventional wisdom:

> Capone, to me, wasn't a big shot gangland giant in the end but a tired, sick, lonely man. Guided in other directions, his imagination, drive and fearlessness might have made him a heroic general, captain of a fleet or mighty business mogul. He had a brilliant knack for organization, which, channeled in the proper direction, would have made him a success in any business operation.

At Alcatraz, where he could not buy favors from other inmates, he was mocked as "the wop with a mop." In 1936 a Texas bank robber, angered because Capone would not loan him $3,000, plunged a pair of barber's scissors into his back. Barbershops have always been dangerous places for gangsters.

On February 5, 1938, Capone failed to fall into line for the mess hall. Seeing that something was seriously wrong with him, the guards left him alone. He finally wandered into the mess hall, a string of saliva hanging from his thick lower lip. He pointed vacantly out the window.

The thread-like corkscrew microorganism (*Treponema pallidum*) had made its way to his brain. The deterioration of his condition could be stopped but the neurological damage could not be reversed. Al Capone was now and forever a syphilitic paretic. As Jake Guzik said sadly, "Al's nutty as a fruitcake."

In January 1939 he was transferred to the Federal Correctional Institution at Terminal Island off San Pedro near Los Angeles. On November 16 at Lewisburg, Pennsylvania, he was released into the custody of his wife Mae and brother Ralph. He had served seven and a half years.

He spent the last seven years of his life at 93 Palm Island in Miami, much of the time sitting on his dock in his bathrobe, holding a fishing pole over the water. In 1930 he had said about Palm Island, "If I could go there and forget it all I would be the happiest man in the world." Now he was and didn't know it.

On January 25, 1947, he died of pneumonia a week after a brain hemorrhage. He was 48 years old. *Qui Riposa.*

Prohibition and two men had been largely responsible for Capone's success in life: Johnny Torrio, who taught him how, and William Hale Thompson, who let him. Between the two of them, Torrio and Thompson illustrated and brought to full truth something the writer George Kibbe Turner had divined about Chicago as long ago as 1907:

> The reputation of Chicago for crime has fastened upon the imagination of the United States as that of no other city has done. . . . Why has that city, year after year, such a flood of violent and adventurous crime? Because of the tremendous and elaborate organizations, financial and political, for creating and attracting and protecting the criminal in Chicago.

Torrio presided over a conference held in NYC in April 1934 that formalized and perfected the working rules and governing structure of the national crime syndicate, the lasting monument to his life's work, though few were aware in his own time or are now that he was the architect. In 1939 he was sentenced to two and a half years in prison for income tax evasion, paroled in mid-April of 1941. Sixteen years later, still toiling on behalf of crime, on April 16, 1957, he sat down in a barber's chair for a shave, suddenly groaned and pitched forward—victim of a coronary attack. He died in the hospital the same day, age 75, in the anonymity he preferred. It was two weeks after his death before the *New York Times* took notice of his passing.

After his defeat by Anton Cermak, Big Bill Thompson attempted yet another political comeback in 1932 to put, as he said, "Tony Cermak back on his pushcart," but it went nowhere. He tried again in 1936 with even less satisfactory results. Discouraged, but not through yet, he declared himself a candidate for mayor of Chicago in 1939 but was humiliated in the primary.

After that he kept close to his hotel room, its closet stocked with whiskey, mailed a monthly check to his estranged wife, Maysie, and was comforted by a young brunette, Ethabelle Green, who had been with him since 1931. He had told her then, "You are just a kid and I am getting on in years. . . . I feel you can give me the happiness that has never been mine. I am confident that it will pay dividends for both of us."

In early 1944 he caught a cold, was put in an oxygen tent, went into a coma, and on March 19 died, age 77. His wife and Ethabelle Green went to court over his $2 million estate, Miss Green finally accepting a $250,000 out-of-court settlement of which, after she paid her lawyers and taxes, $100,000 was left.

A succession of Capone aides has ruled the Outfit since he was sent to jail in 1931, beginning with Frank Nitti, who was released from prison just at the time Big Al was sent to Atlanta. Nitti had a rough start as head of the Outfit because the new mayor of Chicago, Anton Cermak, tried to get him killed. One of Cermak's campaign pledges was that he would rid Chicago of its gangsters.

Anton Cermak was born in Kladno, Bohemia, in 1875. Brought to the United States as a child, he had no formal education beyond the third grade. He worked in the coal mines south of Joliet, Illinois, before coming to Chicago at the age of 16, where he worked as a RR brakeman. He also became a Democratic precinct worker, then organized the United Societies for Local Self-Government, whose ostensible purpose was to keep Chicago a wide-open town. Every brewer and distiller, gambler and gunman, whore and pimp in Chicago was a member.

In 1902 at the age of 27 he became a state legislator, and immediately set up his own real estate and insurance business. He knew in advance where the state would build highways, and so. . . . Businessmen who wanted favors bought their insurance from him, often paying premiums in cash. His real estate firm fortuitously took options on land that the county later bought for forest preserves.

After three terms at Springfield Cermak was a millionaire. By the time he was elected mayor of Chicago his net worth was seven million. When he was president of the Cook County Board of Commissioners (free picnic beer from Roger Touhy), a citizens' group hired an outside engineer to look into contracts he'd pushed through. The consultant said,

"What you need is not an engineer but a grand jury."

On December 19, 1932, Cermak sent Harry Lang and Harry Miller, two tough detective sergeants, to Frank Nitti's office. Miller (one of the four Miller brothers, two of whom Dion O'Banion shot outside a theater in 1924) and Lang were Cermak's bagmen for collection of protection money from the underworld. At 221 North LaSalle Street, they went to room 554 where they found Nitti and five other men.

They searched the men. The diminutive Nitti had no gun. While a third detective sergeant held Nitti by the wrists, Lang shot the ruler of the Outfit twice in the back and once in the neck. Then Lang went into the next room and shot himself in the hand. When newspapermen arrived, Lang claimed Nitti had shot him—first.

Lang and Miller were voted the city's thanks by the City Council and the police department gave them extra compensation and meritorious service awards.

Two days after the shooting, when it became clear that Nitti was not going to die as everyone thought he would, a frightened trio of Cermak, Lang, and Miller entrained for Florida. Nitti learned that Lang had been offered $15,000 by Teddy Newberry, owner of a North Side gambling club, to kill him. On January 7 Newberry's body was found in a ditch near Gary, Indiana. He was wearing the diamond-studded belt buckle given him by Al Capone.

After that inauspicious beginning, Frank Nitti's rule went smoothly enough until he involved the Outfit in a Hollywood extortion racket that turned sour. Facing another prison term and challenged by Paul The Waiter Ricca for his part in the scheme, Nitti went for a drunken afternoon walk on March 19, 1943, along the railroad tracks near his Riverside home and there in a drizzling rain shot himself. He was 58 years old. Nine months before, he had married Edward O'Hare's former secretary. Ricca, once Diamond Joe's head waiter, succeeded him as head of the Outfit.

Edward O'Hare's son Butch graduated from Annapolis in 1937 and became a Navy fighter pilot. His father continued informing for the government after Capone's conviction and the senior O'Hare also became one of Chicago's business leaders, a real estate investor and owner of an insurance agency and two advertising agencies, as well as president of Sportsman's Park race track.

On November 8, 1939 (eight days before Al Capone's early release from prison), O'Hare was driving on Ogden Avenue when a car drew alongside his and two men blasted him with shotguns, killing him outright.

Two years later, on February 20, 1942, with the United States still reeling from the disaster of the surprise attack on Pearl Harbor by the Japanese, his son Butch O'Hare, flying alone over the Pacific at night, shot down five of nine Japanese twin-engine bombers heading for his mother carrier the *Lexington,* and crippled a sixth before he ran out of ammunition. For this feat O'Hare was awarded the Congressional Medal of Honor, President Roosevelt calling his feat "one of the most daring if not the most daring single action in the history of combat aviation."

Butch O'Hare was killed a year later near Tarawa, one of the Gilbert Islands in the Central Pacific. In 1949 Chicago's municipal airport—"The World's Busiest Airport"—was named in his honor; 200,000 Chicagoans attended the ceremonies.

Machine Gun Jack McGurn in three-piece suit (coat off) and spats was killed on the eve of St. Valentine's Day 1936 in a bowling alley on Milwaukee Avenue. His killers left a comic valentine on his body:

> You've lost your job,
> You've lost your dough,
> Your jewels and handsome houses.
> But things could be worse, you know.
> You haven't lost your trousers.

After his North Side gang was absorbed by the Outfit, Bugs Moran was reduced to making a living by robbery. He wound up with a sentence in Leavenworth for robbing a bank in Ansonia, Ohio, and died in prison of lung cancer on February 25, 1957. He received the Last Rites of the Catholic Church while he was fully conscious.

Pig-eyed Frankie McErlane came to an end befitting his life, more or less. In retaliation for his own shooting in January of 1930 he had seen to the death of Dingbat Oberta in March. The coroner found Oberta with a bullet in his head and a tin of aspirins in his pocket. Holding up the aspirins the coroner said, "He died of a headache." Oberta's widow had her husband buried beside his mentor, Big Tim Murphy, who had been her first husband. "They were both good men," she reflected.

In June of the next year the police found McErlane firing a shotgun into the air on South Shore Drive. The street was empty. "They tried to get me," was all McErlane would say.

On October 8, 1931, during Al Capone's trial, McErlane shot and killed his live-in girlfriend, a shoplifter named Elfrieda Rigus, as she sat in the back seat of his car. Beside her body were her German shepherd and her fox terrier, both also shot dead. Exactly a year later, McErlane died of pneumonia in a hospital in downstate Beardstown. Four men had to restrain him as he threshed in his last delirium.

Prohibition ended on December 5, 1933, with the ratification of the 21st Amendment to the Constitution, which repealed the 18th. It had lasted 13 years, 10 months, 18 days, and a few hours. Between Repeal on December 5 and New Year's Eve, the Palmer House hotel bar in Chicago served 130,000 cocktails and glasses of beer. A great thirst was being slaked legally. Herman J. Berghoff, who had an excellent restaurant in the Loop (still there, still excellent), announced a policy: "Ladies will not be served at the bar. We can't handle them when they drink strong liquor."

On February 15, 1933, Giuseppe Zangara, a one-time marksman in the Italian army, shot the mayor of Chicago, Anton Cermak, in Miami, Florida, where the mayor was making a public appearance at the side of President-elect Franklin D. Roosevelt. Cermak died 19 days later. Twenty-second Street—the Street of Whores, the street of the Four Deuces, straight west of which was Capone's stronghold, Cicero—was named Cermak Road in honor of the late mayor.

It is commonly assumed that Zangara's target was FDR and that the assassin missed. John H. Lyle, a Chicago judge during the dry and lawless years, was of a different opinion. His was that the Sicilian Zangara was sent by the Outfit to kill Cermak. In return, the hypochondriac Zangara was promised that his mother would be cared for should he die.

In July of 1933, the British-born, Chicago-raised John "Jake the Barber" Factor, alleged he was kidnaped and held for 12 days until a ransom of $70,000 was paid. The intermediary between Factor's principals and the alleged kidnaping gang was Murray the Camel Humphreys.

At the time, the British government was attempting to extradite Factor to England to serve a prison sentence for an $8 million swindle. Factor had hired expensive legal aid, including two former U.S. senators, to fight his extradition and his case was appealed, finally, in 1933 to the U.S. Supreme Court. Meanwhile, the statute of limitations for extradition was running out. Thus, it was a stroke of good fortune for Jake the Barber that he was kidnaped when he was, notwithstanding his allegedly great personal discomfort.

Factor accused Roger Touhy of masterminding the kidnapers. In a trial distinguished by wholesale perjury by prosecution witnesses, Roger Touhy was found guilty and sentenced to 99 years to be served in Joliet's Stateville Prison.

In 1943 Jake the Barber pled guilty to mail fraud charges in the manipulation of liquor warehouse receipts and served six years of a 10-year sentence. After his release on parole in 1949, he moved to Beverly Hills, California, and paid for a vigorous public relations campaign to establish himself as a reputable real estate investor and philanthropist. (His half-brother Max Factor was a cosmetics tycoon.)

Stateville prisoner No. 8711, Roger Touhy, did hard time. He missed his wife and two sons, of course, but, worse, he knew he was innocent. In 1948 a determined and quixotic Chicago lawyer, Robert B. Johnstone, took up Touhy's cause. Federal court judge John P. Barnes agreed to hear Touhy's writ in 1949. The sixth day of the hearing lawyer

Johnstone collapsed. It was 1953 before the hearing was resumed, with a recovered Johnstone battling for his client just as determinedly as before. Judge Barnes read his 60,000-word decision on August 9, 1954:

> The court finds that John Factor was not kidnaped for ransom, or otherwise . . . , though he was taken as a result of his own connivance. . . . The court finds that Roger Touhy did not kidnap John Factor and, in fact, had no part in the alleged kidnaping of John Factor.

Touhy was free—for 47 hours. The government attorney, while agreeing that Touhy was not guilty, maintained that he had not exhausted his remedies in the state courts. If the law supposes that (per Dickens' Mr. Bumble), the law is a ass, a idiot.

In 1957 Touhy was granted a hearing by the state of Illinois. Until then—though he had been declared innocent—legal technicalities had kept him imprisoned in Stateville. At his 1957 hearing the Illinois Pardon and Parole Board recommended that the governor commute his sentence. This was done, but he was not freed until late 1959. By then he had spent more than a quarter of a century in prison.

While there, with Ray Brennan, a Chicago politics and crime reporter since 1929, Touhy wrote a book about his experiences, *The Stolen Years*. The last sentence in the book is, "My hope is to live out the few years remaining to me in peace and quiet—and freedom—with those I love and respect." *The Stolen Years* was published in the fall of 1959.

On December 16, 1959, just 23 days after he was finally freed from Stateville, as he left his sister's house, Touhy was hit by shotgun blasts. The blasts struck nothing vital, just blew holes through him, and he slowly bled to death; there was no place to put a tourniquet. The publisher of *The Stolen Years* was unable to capitalize on this publicity bonanza because respected philanthropist John Factor was in Chicago to sue Touhy for libel, and he also filed an injunction threatening suit against any bookstore that sold Touhy's book. Some few copies were sold from fringe-of-the-Loop saloons.

Seven months later Jake the Barber Factor sold Murray the Camel Humphreys 400 shares of a life insurance stock at $20 a share. Eight months after this, Factor bought back the stock for $125 a share, a six-for-one return to Humphreys, a $42,000 payoff. After Humphreys' death in 1965 (heart attack), the Internal Revenue Service maintained that tax should have been paid on this sum at the rate for income from services rendered, rather than at the lower capital gains rate. It might be assumed that Touhy's murder was payback for a humiliation in The Arch at Schiller Park 30 years before.

After Touhy's murder, Saul D. Alinsky, the sociologist and community organizer, and a member of the Joliet Stateville prison classification board at the time of Touhy's commitment to the prison, came forward to relate a story he said had "been commonly known for many years in many circles in Chicago." In 1931, with the accession to the mayoralty of Anton J. Cermak, who had promised to drive gangsters from Chicago, a marked increase in mob killings began which lasted till Cermak's death. Most of the victims were from the Outfit.

According to Alinsky, Cermak had forged a community of interests with Roger Touhy to eradicate Outfit mobsters, and offered Touhy the Chicago Police Department as fellow soldiers in this war. When Cermak said he would rid Chicago of gangsters, he meant Outfit mobsters. His plan for crime in Chicago was for city hall to take it over. His assassination was the mob's response. It seems likely.

Bathhouse John Coughlin died in 1938, still alderman for the First Ward he had represented for 46 years. He died in debt largely due to the encroachment of the Outfit on his preserves and his penchant for slow horses. At his death the entrances to City Hall were draped in mourning, black and purple crepe was spread over his council seat, and a vase of roses was placed on his desk.

Guarded by city police and Outfit gunmen, Hinky Dink Kenna spent his last years in his Blackstone Hotel room counting the coins he had hidden there, fearful they would be stolen. The Outfit had forced him to return as First Ward Alderman when Coughlin died. He served till 1944 when, age 85, he retired from that post and also as First Ward Committeeman, which he had been since 1895. Unlike most politicians, he had never liked attending wakes or funerals. When he died in 1947, at the age of 88, there were few mourners at his graveside. As one of his elderly colleagues explained, "If you don't go to other people's funerals, they won't come to yours." He left $1 million, half in cash, to his relatives. All he asked in return was that they erect a $30,000 mausoleum for his wife and himself. His grave and his wife's are marked with $85 headstones.

Al Capone's son, Albert Francis—despite Outfit offers to cut him in on some small action—led an exemplary life. He worked hard at straight jobs and raised four daughters. (His father had left no will or money.) In the late '80s he retired to Florida. His mother, Mae, died about the time he retired.

Highball, the only North Side gang member to survive the carnage of the St. Valentine's Day Massacre in 1929, had to be put down within the year. Something had deranged the dog's mind.

The wages of sin is death—all in God's good time.

Louis Henri Sullivan

Louis Armstrong

CHILD OF THE ROMANS

The dago shovelman sits by the railroad track
Eating a noon meal of bread and bologna.
   A train whirls by, and men and women at tables
   Alive with red roses and yellow jonquils,
   Eat steaks running with brown gravy,
   Strawberries and cream, eclaires and coffee.
The dago shovelman finishes the dry bread and bologna,
Washes it down with a dipper from the water-boy,
And goes back to the second half of a ten-hour day's
   work.
Keeping the road-bed so the roses and jonquils
Shake hardly at all in the cut glass vases
Standing slender on the tables in the dining cars.
                      —Carl Sandburg

Jazz and Chicago School and Prairie Style architecture have been America's only original gifts to the arts—and they came out of Chicago. Yet Chicago is known throughout the world even today not for them, but for Al Capone.

Ralph Capone died peacefully in 1974, age 81. Regarded as a *baccalà*—a lummox—by others in the Outfit, he was never a power in it after his brother went to prison. Jake Guzik died of a heart attack in St. Hubert's Old English Grill on Federal Street, his preferred rendezvous for payoffs, in 1956, age 70. Frank Galluccio, who put the scars on Al Capone's face, died of a heart attack in 1960 in his 60s. Frankie Rio, Al's faithful bodyguard, died of natural causes in the mid-Thirties. Diamond Joe Esposito's waiter, Paul Ricca, who had been head of the outfit, died in 1972, age 75, of natural causes. Sam Giancana (initially recruited by Jack McGurn), who had been head of the Outfit, was executed in his home in 1975, age 67. Tony Accardo (initially recruited by Jack McGurn), who had been head of the Outfit for long periods, died peacefully in 1992, age 86. In three score and ten years of service to the Outfit, he never spent a day in jail.

In the Twenties and Thirties most of the top gangsters were in their 20s. Most of today's top mobsters are older men. For the most part, middle- and high-ranking gangsters are courteous, hospitable, friendly, even courtly and affable—unless you owe them money or they want something from you. But in this last they are not different from other businessmen, though almost all mobsters lack the pretentiousness and arrogance of other, legitimate businessmen—or lawyers or college professors. The head-men mobsters also usually make less than legit CEOs, and they have no employment contracts with golden parachute clauses.

Gangsters can be mean, vindictive, petty, bullying, cruel, ruthless, and deadly killers—but the last goes with their profession. Some are highly literate, like to read, and can wax philosophic. Many are disarmingly sentimental. Many are chiselers. Some are kindly. Some are generous and avuncular. Some are deadbeats and welshers. Some are sadists. Almost none appears to be sinisterly evil. Many are intelligent; others seem not to be. And so on. As with men in other callings, there are all kinds. Up to the present era, the most successful in the United States have been Italians. But in Chicago they never could have made it without the Irish.

In the 1990s the Outfit is as deeply woven into the fabric of Chicago's—and the nation's—identity as ever. Men and women will always want to gamble, copulate, and become intoxicated—whatever their substance of choice—and no matter the laws of their society prohibiting or restricting such conduct. The criminal provides a way and so, as long as there is human life, presumably there will be criminals, a very small minority providing services and goods on demand to a huge majority. The primary biological drives are of course hunger, thirst, sex, but the acquired drives to intoxication and, for some, gambling function like the primary drives. Prohibit any of them and you have trouble—and criminals.

Q: Would you approve of them having machine guns—?
A: Such as the police here have them?
Q: I beg your pardon?
A: Such as the police have them?
Q: Well, would you approve of that?
A: It is necessary. You could not run without them.

That is not a gangster endorsing machine guns, but the frail billionaire Andrew William Mellon, U.S. Secretary of the treasury and the man charged by President Hoover to skewer Al Capone with all due diligence. He is testifying before a Senate Committee, defending his Pittsburgh Coal Company's private police force (aka strikebreakers).

In 1931, as the Great Depression gripped the country ever more cruelly, Mellon purchased 21 paintings from Leningrad's Hermitage Museum, paying the short-of-cash Russian government $6.4 million. A bagatelle for him, while millions went hungry in his native land. During his time as Treasury Secretary, 9,300 U.S. banks failed and a year after he left the post the entire U.S. banking structure collapsed. His own and his family's vast holdings and fortune were unaffected. Andrew William Mellon was about as legit as they get.

An act is criminal depending upon who defines it and how. A 1962 dictionary defines *crime* as: "*1.* an act committed or an omission of duty, injurious to the public welfare, for which punishment is prescribed by law, imposed in a judicial proceeding usually brought in the name of the state. *2.* serious violation of human law. *3.* any offense, esp. one of grave character. *4.* serious wrong-doing; sin." Assuming definitions of crime haven't changed that much in 30 years (not to say since the Ten Commandments), by the dictionary definition, Colosimo, Torrio, and Capone were certainly criminals. But then so were Bathhouse John Coughlin, Hinky Dink Kenna, Johnny Powers, Big Bill Thompson, Police Chief Bill Russell, President Warren Gamaliel Harding, and Chicago Mayor Anton Cermak.

As are our more recent politicians. President Ronald Reagan's appointees outdid President Harding's in corruption, both in scale and disdain and injury to the public welfare, and Reagan, by dozing through the eight years of his Presidency, surely committed that act of omission of duty—enabling his ultra-wealthy sponsors to commit grand acts of larceny and cause international havoc—that was criminal.

A knowing, chronic liar in power or seeking it is by any definition a demagogue and a criminal. Thus, President George Bush. When a man or woman habitually lies to win office or to deceive or mislead his constituency, then because of the position of trust he seeks or holds, he commits a criminal act. Harding lied on a domestic scale; Bush, on a global scale—and that is to say nothing here of George Bush's clear-cut domestic policy except that the significant difference between the Teapot Dome scandal of Harding's time and, say, the savings and loan failures of Reagan-Bush was not the tremendous one of scale, but that the public was never told that the latter *was* a scandal. Only that they must pay for what became no-fault banking, the bail-out of which will cost us, the taxpayers, more than $300 billion.

But we know that politicians lie—and cheat, and steal and kill. And Presidents come and go. The larger question is: What does society define as crime? This question, of course, should be phrased: What does society's ruling elite—its privileged class—define as crime? In the United

States, as in most countries, those acts that threaten the authority or stability of the state are criminal acts. Thus, those who pose this threat are the criminal class, that is, the unemployed underclass and, by simple extension, the employed but poorly paid underclass, as well. (In the 19th century, immigrants and their children made up the greater part of this dangerous underclass; today, ethnic minorities of color do.) Punishment for anti-social acts (ruling-class definition) is imprisonment. Our prisons today are operating at 150 percent capacity and more, though it has yet to be shown that prison rehabilitates or reforms even the occasional individual offender, much less an entire class.

Kenna, Coughlin, Colosimo, Torrio, O'Banion, Weiss, Moran, Capone all came out of the underclass. In crime they found escape from their low status. By virtue of their native talents they became professionals in crime, organized it, and administrated its activities and personnel, acting as a bridge between the upper and lower worlds of their society, useful to both. But always at the last they were rebels—outlaws—and the rulers of the upperworld tolerated them only as long as they were useful and, as well, acquiescent to the often unspoken but clear requirements of the upperworld rulers. Al Capone may have been seen by his countrymen as powerful, and may have himself felt that he was, but when the real rulers of the country decided he was an annoyance to business as usual, they crushed him. J. Pierpont Morgan, possibly the richest man in the world of his time, paid not one red cent of federal income tax between 1929 and 1932, but President Hoover did not tell his treasury secretary, "I want that man Morgan in jail!"

When it is said that there is no justice—that life is not fair—what is meant in societal terms (as distinct from personal) is that there is no justice to be expected from the upperworld. (Southern Italians and Sicilians knew this much further back than their great, great grandfathers.) Those who have will resort to any tyranny to keep what they have and to add more, a point directly opposite to the "liberty and justice for all" taught young people in ninth-grade civics classes.

Crime is not the problem. It is only one consequence. The problem in the United States today, and throughout the world from the beginning of history, is the ruling upperworld and the conditions it imposes on those it rules. Lincoln expressed that idea this way: "As labor is the common burden of our race, so the effort of some to shift their share of the burden onto the shoulders of others is the great durable curse of the race."

When practiced successfully, greed acquires wealth, as we have seen throughout this book, and when adroitly leveraged, wealth can acquire power. Always, of course, at the expense of others, every step of the way, every day of the week.

Successful capitalists understand this intuitively and accept all of its implications willingly, without hesitation. Since they are surviving in grand style, they believe in survival of the fittest. Charles T. Yerkes understood this, as did Colosimo, Torrio, and Capone, as well as Field, Armour, Pullman, Cyrus McCormick, and Samuel Insull.

Anita McCormick came to understand it, and her inherited part in it, and her inability to accept the cost of it to others may have been what finally drove her deeper into the eccentricities to which her family was already predisposed. . . .

In the early 1890s the crusading English journalist William T. Stead had an illuminating interview with the owner of a building in the Levee, a house in which in the wee, still hours of the morning Chicago's doves of the demimonde lay down their weary heads at last to rest, having pleasured a requisite number of males.

> He said he was perfectly willing to let the house to a church for the purpose of a Sunday School if it would pay him as much rent as he received at present. "You see," he said, "they pay me about twice as much as I could get from anybody else."
>
> "Well," I said, "that may be. But if they are using it for purposes of vice?"
>
> "I have nothing to do with that," he replied. "That is not my business, if there is anything wrong it is for the city to look after that. What I have to do is to see to it that I receive my rent."

Stead asked him if he would rent his home to known thieves. "If they would pay me $3 where I would only get $1 from honest tenants, certainly. . . ," was the reply.

Finally, Stead asked him if he would rent to murderers.

> "If they would pay me $3 in the place of $1 which I could get from an ordinary tenant, certainly, I would let it to them directly. I am after the dollar, as every one else is, if they would only say so. . . ."
>
> Here we have asserted, in its baldest and plainest form, the working principle on which the smart man of Chicago acts.

A 1942 one-volume encyclopedia (which, it is assumed, summarized the understandings prevailing then and before) defines capitalism as "the economic system characterized chiefly by the relatively few who, by their ownership of capital, control most of the production, distribution, and credit. . . . Capitalism stresses the individual's freedom to undertake any enterprise, at his own risk, and in his own manner." It "has the sole aim of increasing private profits."

In other words, capitalism is an economic system driven by greed alone ("I am after the dollar, as everyone else is"), and for the benefit of a "relatively few." The definition poses the rhetorical question: From an economic point of view, was there any difference between Chicago's gangsters and its dynasts?

Another and non-rhetorical question: What are, typically, the real-world effects of capitalism? A paradigmatic answer can possibly be found in the fate of the passenger pigeon, the most numerous bird ever to live on earth. The passenger pigeon resembled our mourning dove but it was larger and had a rose-tinted throat and breast, both male and female. Tens of billions of them—billions, not millions—darkened the skies of North America and foraged its forests millennia after millennia. The passenger was also called the *migrating dove* and it could fly at constant speeds of 60 mph, covering 1,000 miles in a day if need be. It numbered 40 percent of the total North American bird population—before forward-looking capitalists of our nation's Gilded Age after the Civil War found that there was a vast commercial market for the bird's cheap and delicious flesh.

At first the harvesting was done by netting, as many as 2,000 at a sweep. To decoy the birds under their giant nets, the trappers captured individual birds and sewed their eyes shut. The blinded birds were then pinned to posts, called *stools*. When their fluttering wings had lured enough of their curious, sighted fellows within range, the net was dropped and the entrapped pigeons had their heads crushed with pincers. The harvesters were pursuing their own particular enterprise at their own risk, in their own manner, for their own profit, and clever fellows they were at it, too.

The blinded decoy birds gave us the term "stool pigeon." Their utterance as they helplessly fluttered their wings was a soft, bell-like murmur, a melodious cooing, with perhaps in it a note of puzzlement, perhaps alarm at the abrupt darkening of their world.

The commercial market for passenger pigeon breasts and thighs was developed to its fullest beginning in the early 1870s. At about the same time, in 1875, gold was discovered in the Black Hills of South Dakota, an event that hastened the betrayal and slaughter of Native Americans—by men pursuing their own enterprise, at their own risk, in their own manner. It was a classic clash of cultures, as well: forward-looking, enterprising capitalists versus complaisant Native Americans who had lived here for millennia upon millennia and, perversely, done nothing to develop the continent's vast resources, content simply to live from the bounty that nature provided.

Less than a century later an overwhelming urge to develop the black gold of Asia prompted forward-looking U.S. capitalists to promote the sending of U.S. troops to Vietnam, there to betray and slaughter the native Vietnamese—on their soil, in their country, half a world away from ours. The only good Indian is a dead Indian was still the thesis. Perhaps that is why U.S. troops sent to Vietnam to kill and maim hundreds of thousands and to be killed and maimed in the tens of thousands called enemy territory "Injun country."

It was a profound blow to national pride when the United States (a country that taught its schoolchildren it had never lost a war—because, implicitly, our cause was always just) had at last to flee Vietnam in defeat. To erase this humiliation, President Reagan's handlers "conquered" tiny Grenada, financed a bloody war in Nicaragua, and made various forays elsewhere in the world.

George Bush, Reagan's successor, disparaged what he termed "that vision thing." (This upset his speech writers, no doubt, since they surely knew that "Where there is no vision the people perish," and may even have been considering having the President mouth that very phrase himself.) But George Bush *did* have a vision—the same vision that has inspired so many of our leaders. President Theodore Roosevelt expressed that vision most clearly in the late 19th century. Progress, he said, is "due solely to the power of the mighty civilized races [by which he meant his own, Anglo-Saxon race] which have not lost the fighting instinct, and which by their expansion are gradually bringing peace to the red wastes where the barbarian peoples of the world hold sway."

Bush sent our military might into the red wastes of the Persian Gulf and in a few days of Operation Desert Storm it rolled up the small country of Iraq. A radiantly triumphant President then proclaimed a New World Order; he did not explain what that would be or how it would differ from the old. He did not have to. "By God, we've kicked the Vietnam syndrome once and for all!" he exulted, authorizing, as the historian Richard Slotkin has observed, "the shedding of blood . . . as a cure for the illness of our imagination."

An objective, impartial observer might conclude that a history of the United States could be written around instances of the triumph of greed over principle and compassion. It is certainly true that in just a few hundred years, because we have often yielded to the promptings of the darkest, greediest souls among us, we have earned the right to be called the most rapacious nation in the annals of mankind. . . . Well, no matter, at least for our present purpose, though we might ask ourselves the question Henry Adams asked himself a century ago at Chicago's Columbian Exposition: Do the American people know where they are driving?

Even though the passenger pigeon had been extensively and excessively hunted, and massacred for sport, as well (a million a year at trapshooting), it still numbered in the billions as late as 1870. Then came the discovery that fortunes could be made by procuring and selling the birds in carload lots for the American table.

First they were netted, as has been described, but then it was found easier and faster—more profitable—to set out quantities of grain soaked in alcohol for them. Their appetite for this treat killed the swift and hardy doves outright. By the millions they slumped to earth, literally dead drunk.

The last passenger pigeon seen in the wild was killed in Pike County, Ohio, on March 24, 1900. Within less than 40 years of capitalism's discovery of the cash value of the superabundant species, it had been exterminated. The very last of all those billions of murmuring, cooing doves died in the Cincinnati Zoo on September 1, 1914, just short of a month after the guns of August began to boom on the Western Front in Europe, presaging the slaughter of millions of humans. This last dove had been hatched in captivity and given the name "Martha." After Martha, dead at age 29, the passenger pigeon was never again seen or heard in the land.

Thomas Mann said, "Very deep is the well of the past. Should we not call it bottomless?"

The history of crime in Chicago, like all human histories, revolves around the ultimates of love, death, sex, money, and power and how the personalities of individuals—and of city and nation—respond to desire and circumstance. An ambitious Jim Colosimo, for example, found favor with political boss Kenna because he was capable and had something to offer the alderman—votes. Because of that and because he was at the right place at the right time, he rose to become vice king of the city. Luck is the first step; after that it's mainly up to you.

One string is unravelled from the fabric of the tapestry, then another, and finally when all are pulled free and examined and studied, there is still something unknowable, especially when those strings are historical events, social forces, and the acts and circumstances of human beings. It is very likely that as the physicist Sir James Jeans said in 1934 of another puzzle, ". . . it may be doubted whether we shall ever properly understand the realities ultimately involved; they may well be so fundamental as to be beyond the grasp of the human mind."

But if we do not try, we can draw no water at all from the well of the past. Johnny Torrio, at the age of 38, succeeded the colorful Colosimo by arranging for his murder. Torrio's task was to organize the realm, expand it, install a system to provide reliable service to customers, and to quell the rivalries among Chicago's contentious bootleggers. He was ideally suited to this task.

If crime and corruption and vice in early 20th-century Chicago can be said to have a hero—it can't—that hero would be Johnny the Fox. He was a murderer, a white slaver, a pimp, a thief, but just as most American-Italian criminal patterns were exaggerations or grotesqueries of aspects of la via vecchia—the old country way—so too was most of Johnny Torrio's way of crime. Torrio believed in honor, vengeance, and solidarity. (Honor if it didn't interfere with business; vengeance if

362

necessary to contribute to business; and solidarity when it served a business purpose.) More, he was an embodiment of the virtues most prized by the contadini. He was, first of all, an *uomo di panza* (lit., a man of belly), a man who knows how to keep things to himself (in his guts); an *uomo segreto*, a secret, private man; but above all, an *uomo di pazienza* (patience).

The man of patience is the man who controls. He is firm; he is constant in all things. He remains aloof from—usually at odds with—the outside society. He has no pretenses. What he has is an inner strength that gives him presence because he waits, he plans, and only at the moment of best chance of success does he strike.

He remembers everything for possible use, learning at the expense of others. He studies their behavior, assesses what will work with them and what probably won't. While his opponents jump and twitch in impatience, he waits, gauging their weaknesses. He knows that *onore* is achieved by being worldly, shrewd, and clever and advancing one's own fortune, not by being good or trusting or acting nobly.

His whole life is one of work and self-denial, of self-reliance and self-control. He does not seek confrontations; he avoids them—unless something of paramount importance is at stake. Otherwise, he maneuvers toward his objective. He is foxy. Above all, he knows what is important, and this gives him dignity and earns him respect.

All this is his manliness, too, and all of these qualities, together with intelligence, Johnny Torrio possessed to a very high degree. He learned from his few failures and mistakes in Chicago, and by the time he left the city he had acquired enough respect among his peers that when, one by one, he proposed the moves that in a comparatively short time established a U.S. national "Mafia"—the Organization—he became, de facto, the Organization's consigliere. At seven years of age Johnny Torrio was swamping out his stepfather's blind pig in Brooklyn; half a century later—quietly—he was one of the most important and wealthy men in a nationwide criminal system—a system his ideas and energy had created.

Of Torrio, as of few other gangsters, it can be said with some certainty that had he been a legitimate businessman he would have been a success. To Elmer Irey, who sent Torrio to jail for two and a half years for tax evasion, the Fox "was the smartest and, I dare say, the best of all the hoodlums. 'Best' referring to talent, not morals." The most knowledgeable chronicler of Chicago crime, Herbert Asbury, characterized Torrio thus: "As an organizer and administrator of underworld affairs Johnny Torrio is unsurpassed in the annals of American crime; he was probably the nearest thing to a real master mind that this country has yet produced."

Torrio was the ruler, and to the ruler those in his realm gave their respect and obedience. But there was little security to life in the realm for anyone, including himself, especially in its earliest, least stable years. Each man in the Outfit depended on all the others, as all the others did on him, yet each man was in competition with every other man and could harm any or all of the rest. The intrigues and conflicts multiplied endlessly.

Those who survived—and for almost five years Torrio survived as ruler—became astute observers of their fellow creatures and developed their understanding of others to a high degree. They thus became highly skilled in dealing with others. Torrio was also a forceful commander, was adept at improvisation, and he possessed a surpassing strategic imagination.

But more than these qualities—which his protegé Capone apparently studied closely as his mentor exercised them—leadership in the time of strife and change that was the early years of Prohibition required taking great risks over and over again. Johnny Torrio came to the realization in his middle age that he did not want to do this anymore. So he turned the empire over to the young Capone, and took his abilities at organization, regulation, consolidation, and supervision back to New York.

The man he selected to succeed himself in Chicago was in many ways his antithesis—a rash-acting 26-year-old roughneck. But because of the additional power he gathered to himself, Capone became the most conspicuous criminal figure of Prohibition times. The circumstances were unique, and as an individual possessing the power he did, Capone was unique. His scope of action, compared to any of his near-peers in Chicago or anywhere else in the nation, was twice or more theirs, and his achievements were nearly absolute. But his rule was not. It, like his mentor's, was always open to challenge, from within and without.

His men followed him because they feared him, because of his loyalty to them, and because he rewarded them, but also because of the attraction of his unpredictable daringness and willingness to leap into action without apparent thought of worst outcomes. Torrio, during his rule, had manipulated people and events as part of long-term strategies; his method did not countenance unpremeditated leaps.

Capone believed he had a gift for taking the right action (which may account for his huge losses at gambling), and because he believed this so strongly, so did his followers. Capone's successes legitimized his rule. He learned to curb his impulsiveness to an extent and he learned to plan, to calculate which courses of action remained to his opponents—their probable intentions and capabilities—and to devise countermeasures to destroy rivals. But he remained a tactician, not a strategist.

His strength and inventiveness carried him, but once the power

364

was consolidated, another man in his position could have sat back in relative safety and managed the realm—as Torrio would have done brilliantly. Capone was incapable of doing this.

Because he was the kind of person he was, Capone created crises for himself, and every encounter became a personal trial; over and over he must prove himself. Just as it did to sports figures such as Jack Dempsey, or Red Grange, or Babe Ruth, every new day presented Capone a tally with no notches in it and he had to prove himself able to triumph and prevail once again. He was incredibly brave (or heedless), impulsive in decision and action, and he seemed to have a sixth sense that alerted him to peril. But as he grew older, the never-ending conflicts and dangers of his life began to wear on him and it is possible that his tax-evasion conviction in 1931 was, in some very small sense, seen as a relief because it removed him from the arena.

His limitations were those of his nature and, initially, his youth: chiefly, reckless impulsiveness. His strengths lay in decisive, dramatic action and an ability—like his mentor Torrio—to understand the strengths, weaknesses, interests, and probable intentions of others. As absolute ruler he not only had to contend with external opposition but also to keep the internal tensions of his own organization balanced and their aims fragmented, to keep the jealousies and rivalries of one faction balanced against the ambitions of another faction so as to hold each in check. He was able to do this and to bring to his rule a precarious equilibrium. Always, however, his rule was based on murder and the fear of murder. As Torrio's had been.

In the larger sphere of the city and nation beyond the Outfit, Capone was seen by most of his countrymen as a great man, a folk hero. In the social circumstances in which he found himself he briefly produced far-reaching effects. This is the sociological definition of a "great man." By the same definition, Genghis Khan, Attila the Hun, Napoleon, and Adolf Hitler were also great men. Leo Tolstoy has told us about great men.

The public of his time accepted Capone as a hero, but why? He was the biggest, boldest, most blatant lawbreaker in the land.

First, because there has always been a scarcely hidden sympathetic complicity in the minds of Americans with the rebel and the outlaw. After all, the country was founded by rebels. This sympathy extends beyond the criminal even to the pillaging capitalist, even to the mortgage-foreclosing banker. Because the tacit assumption is that, given a few breaks, I too could be as powerful as that banker.

Then, also, Capone was seen by many as the heroic leader of a band of valorous brothers resisting an unjust edict—Prohibition. In this view, he *was* Robin Hood and his battles were fought for them, the masses, even though he often fought other bootleggers. As to the latter, the world loves the winner.

Too, the ordinary citizen, whose life was 10 hours a day of drudgery, admired the gangster's seeming freedom, his swagger, bravado, courage. Gangsters seemed the urban, Roaring Twenties' counterparts of the Old West's mythologized gunfighters.

But above all, the time Capone lived in, the Roaring Twenties, thirsted not only for booze but for heroes. Charles A. Lindbergh was the apotheosis. Lindbergh flew the Atlantic alone—and put his life on the line doing it—and won!

But so did Al Capone—and so in a sense did the sports heroes of the era: Dempsey, Grange, Ruth, Helen Wills Moody, Bill Tilden, Gertrude Ederle. Each time they entered the lists, these sports heroes put their reputations on the line—and with their skills and hardihood won. Given a few breaks, the man on the street knew, so could he. . . . If he had been blessed with their talents. But since he hadn't, Dempsey, Grange, Ruth—Al Capone—stood in his stead on the field of valor. They were Davids killing Goliaths, heroes becoming legends, proving that it could be done: One person could make a difference; one individual could triumph even though everyone else stood helpless before the realities of the vast impersonal forces that led from the Great War and careened through the Roaring Twenties to the Great Depression.

One of Ring Lardner's sons, John, put it this way in writing about Lindbergh's solo trans-Atlantic flight:

> His performance was instantly recognized as the climactic stunt of a time of marvelous stunts, of an epoch of noise, hero worship, and the sort of "individualism" which seems to have meant that people were not disposed to look at themselves and their lives, in general, and therefore ran gaping and thirsty to look at anything done by one man or woman that was special and apart from the life they knew. The farther the hero went—whether he went upward, downward, sideways, through air, land, or water, or hand over hand up a flagpole—the better, provided he went alone.

Capone was supremely skilled in his vocation and he achieved early success in it. He lived an outsize life close to the primitive in his animal, instinctual reactions to situations, in his pleasures and passions, in the use of his skills and energy. (This is very nearly the definition of the natural athlete.) Coming from where he came, he captured the popular imagination and the adulation of the masses in the larger world of the Golden Age of the Twenties, triumphing over the invincible because of his special skills and daring. And then the rulers decided he had become excessive—*too* excessive—as a criminal. He was setting a bad example.

When the Roaring Twenties had roared and hiccuped their last, a 10-year moment of extreme lunacy had passed in the country's history. In capsule form, the career of the man Red Grange called "the most impressive man I ever met," the man who took the hardbitten George Halas into camp, C. C. Pyle, illustrates the transition from the Roaring Twenties to the desperate, Depression Thirties.

Red Grange made a million dollars playing football and, as his manager, C. C. Pyle got almost half of it. In 1926 Cash and Carry talked the French tennis queen Suzanne Lenglen into forsaking her amateur status to star for him in a cross-country tour. Pyle guaranteed Mlle. Lenglen $50,000 and cleared $100,000 for himself.

Next he promoted a cross-country marathon foot race, Los Angeles to New York City. Red Grange gave the signal for the start in Los Angeles on March 4, 1928, and 199 runners set off (1,000 had been promised). Pyle traveled ahead of the runners in a luxurious "land yacht." In Chicago, Grange's contract with Pyle came to an end and Red decided not to renew. Cash and Carry had lost his All-America meal ticket.

Fifty-five runners finished the marathon in Madison Square Garden on June 1st. The winner accepted his $25,000 prize and wandered off into a concrete pillar and was knocked cold. Overall, Pyle took a financial bath.

Undaunted, in 1929 he sponsored a second Bunion Derby, as scoffing sportswriters termed it, this time in reverse, NYC to LA. Only 91 runners started and 78 days later the winner accepted his $25,000 prize, went out to watch a sandlot baseball game, and was struck in the head and killed by a foul ball. Pyle took another financial bath.

With fancy footwork he stayed a step ahead of his creditors, put on the Ripley "Believe It or Not" show at the Century of Progress Exhibition in Chicago in 1933-34, and died of a heart attack in 1939, age 55. When the Roaring Twenties ended, so had Pyle's career. Much like Samuel Insull he found that smoke and mirrors do not work forever.

Everything is for sale in the United States, including honor, perhaps beginning with honor. We are a capitalistic country.

The price system operates through demand and supply in competitive markets. Therefore, if you want to jack up the price of your product, you strive to eliminate the competition. The hallmarks of the financial and industrial empires built by J. Pierpont Morgan were a tight, efficient organization centrally controlled, together with the development of shared interests among competitors, leading to a cartel, a syndicate that regulated prices and output. These were exactly also the hallmarks of the empire that Johnny Torrio established. Syndicate crime and cartel capitalism are one and the same, the former perhaps an ultimate version of the latter.

Money is the father of power, the lack of money the mother of misery. As matters stand today, however, the sheer magnitude of the disparity between the very small minority of the ultra-wealthy and the overwhelming majority of the poor has introduced a new and wholly different *quality* into the social equation. In 1890 the richest one percent of the U.S. population of 62-plus million received more income than the poorest 50 percent. A century later—now—the richest one percent (U.S. population quadrupled) receives more income than the poorest 90 percent. We are nearing a time when the country will be peopled by serfs, much as southern Italy was for 500 years (and very nearly is still today). But then, gaining at someone else's expense has always been the essence of capitalism. The rich, a great many of whom have inherited their wealth, and their sons and daughters, too, we have with us, chewing on bones they never made, indolent, idle, conceited, proud of being born into an elite. (When a Marshall Field great-grandson was being groomed to become publisher of the Field family-owned *Chicago Sun-Times* in the middle of this century, a Pulitzer-prizewinning *S-T* reporter was assigned to show him through a Chicago public-housing project. The young Field spied a dime on the stairs. Bending to retrieve it he remarked, only half in jest, "Them as has, gets.")

When carried to extremes, however, certain problems arise for the wealthy in their pursuit of ever more. When a ruling elite denies any freedom of opportunity—including education—to the ruled the likelihood is that a struggle will eventually ensue. Soup kitchens and circuses, Super Bowls and tabloid titillation, drugs and videos, suffice to divert from the real issues of hunger and want for only so long.

In 1993 former U.S. President Jimmy Carter—who published a book for young people that year titled *Talking Peace: A Vision for the Next Generation*—spoke about his concept of human rights, which included ". . . political rights, social rights, as well as economic rights—the right to have a decent home, to have enough food to eat." He said that ". . . when people get desperate with the inability to meet their own family's needs . . . they become inclined to change the government."

The super-rich of our country do not seem—never have seemed—able to grasp that reality. Often they have not even given it lip service; they not only cannot grasp it, but apparently they are unable even to conceive its existence. ("I've got mine, Jack—why should I help some poor sucker who's such a loser he can't find a job?") Many, many times in the past the super-rich of other empires have had cause to rue their inability to see beyond their own riches.

> When Adam delve and Eve span,
> Who was then the gentleman?

The litany of the ills and discontents of our present civilization does not need reinvocation here. You need only pick up a daily newspaper. Is it perhaps not going far enough to suggest that our economic system—capitalism—is the chief responsible underlying agent of these ills, every one, including those most personal?

In another way of life, importance in the community would be determined by judgment, ability, usefulness, and character, and by demonstrated unselfishness and kindness. In this other way of life, the leaders of the people would have no authority, but they would have influence. Others would look to them for leadership because they believed their advice to be sound.

In this other way of life, success would be measured by the good opinion of others. Rank would be dependent upon the things secured and given to the common use. In this other way of life, there would be no need to accumulate goods; everyone would be welcome to all that was needed of the best there was. Everyone would work.

Mankind lived this other way of life roughly a quarter million years, and survived only because it did. Then about 8,000 or so years ago, history tells us, things changed. The earth continued to move in the infinite silences of space as it always had, the rivers ran to the sea as before, but man became clever—and greedy. And so. . . .

Is it possible that mankind has at last overreached itself? That it has become *too* self-sufficient, or so it thinks, *too* clever, and *too* greedy?

One of the multitude of minor scandals of the Reagan-Bush era revolved around the activities of Deborah Gore Dean, a high-ranking staffer at the Department of Housing and Urban Development (HUD). Investigators believed that due to cronyism practiced within the department, and incompetence, fraud, and outright thievery, losses occurred at HUD during the Reagan administration that could reach from $3 billion to $4 billion.

In defense of Ms. Dean and others at HUD accused of mismanagement and favoritism (they were called the "Brat Pack" because of their youth), it should be noted that very few in the department during the Reagan years believed wholeheartedly in the concept of federal housing programs. As they liked to phrase it, theirs was an "ideological antipathy." So if they sabotaged HUD's mandate, they were only doing what they thought was right—and having fun and dispensing favors to friends while doing it. Isn't that what living well and responsibly is all about? Meanwhile, more than half of the poor of this country are spending more than half of their income on housing.

Ms. Dean was for six years a $75,500-a-year executive assistant to HUD's Secretary, Samuel J. Pierce, Jr., a former Reagan campaign

369

aide. Ms. Dean had graduated near the bottom of her class at Georgetown University, and had taken eight years to do it, but her political connections were first-rate. Her father was once head of the Atomic Energy Commission and her mother once lived with former Attorney General John Mitchell, the convicted Watergate felon.

One of Ms. Dean's responsibilities was to approve (or disapprove) applications in a HUD housing rehab program designed to help local housing authorities purchase and renovate buildings as low-income rentals. She okayed mostly projects reported on and developed by consultants to HUD—that is, people she knew or knew of. Reagan's one-time Interior Secretary James G. Watt, for example, got $300,000 as a consultant on a Baltimore project; to earn the money he made several phone calls. The partners in a political consulting firm that worked on the Presidential campaigns of both Reagan and Bush got $326,000 for helping on a Seabrook, New Jersey, project—a project that local officials did not want. Over 15 years one of the partners is to get $15 million in rent subsidies from the unwanted project.

Ms. Dean also arranged and approved some of the projects for which Rick Shelby, a one-time Reagan White House personnel aide, received $700,000 in HUD money. Of one of the rent-subsidy projects he was paid to consult on Shelby said, "I wouldn't hold myself out as an expert in this particular program." Another recipient of HUD money was Ms. Dean's mother's good friend, former Attorney General John Mitchell, who received a $75,000 HUD fee for consulting on departmental matters.

A former special assistant to HUD Secretary Pierce said of Ms. Dean that "She liked power. She liked the idea 'I can call the shots. I can get this for you if I want, I can stomp on you, I can kill you.' That's the kind of thing she liked."

Rising to her own defense Ms. Dean said, "I am absolutely rich, no question about it. I don't need money. My apartment in Washington is one of the nicest in town. I have a Picasso on the wall, for God's sake."

Say goodnight, Gracie. . . . Ms. Dean left HUD early in 1988. The investigation into her activities began a year later. I don't know what finally happened to her. Maybe she went back to school to work on an advanced degree. I stopped hoping for the terrible swift sword of justice for crooked politicians and their slippery favorites about the time I learned that just after the Civil War one of the truly honest Presidents we've had was tried for impeachment, and then later I followed on television the course of events as one of the truly dishonest we've had resigned before he could be so tried, then was given a full Presidential pardon by his successor so that no charges could be brought against him.

Actually, I do know what happened to Ms. Dean. On October 26, 1993, she was convicted of 12 felony counts of defrauding the government, taking a payoff, and lying to Congress. Sentencing was set for January 19 of this year. Max would be 57 years in prison and $3 million in fines. We await to see if Justice is truly blind or, as some say, favors the privileged. Wanna bet?

The conditions that bred crime in the early 1900s in Chicago are breeding crime there today. In what was Little Hell a century ago now stands a shambles of a public housing project begun in 1941, Cabrini-Green. It lies just west of the affluent Gold Coast and has 6,935 residents, nearly all of them African-Americans. Only one in 10 households in the development contains a resident who is employed—today in 1994. The dirt-poor Sicilians a century ago had it much better, by comparison.

Both of our two major national political parties are fond of holding dinners at which individuals, trade groups, political-action committees, and corporations can contribute large sums for "party-building" programs. Since the money is not contributed directly to candidates for office, the sky's the limit on donations. Two years ago a single such dinner, "The President's Dinner," raised $9 million for the Republican party in one evening. Contributions ranged from a low of $1,500 to a high of $400,000, which sum was contributed by a corporation executive.

Because contributors not only got dinner but were promised special, individual access to President Bush and to key officials of his administration and to the entire Republican membership of the House and Senate, the dinner came in for some criticism as catering to monied interests. A White House spokesman put the matter into its proper perspective:

> "We don't believe it's buying influence, but it certainly—it's buying access to the system, yes. When you contribute to the political parties and the political system, you are supporting the process in America, you're supporting the political process, you're buying into the political process as a participant."

Unfortunately for those of us who can only afford to buy into the political process by voting, the President's spokesman had confused our putative democracy with our plutocracy.

Did the nation learn anything from its Great Experiment, as President Hoover termed Prohibition? (Hoover's words were: "a great social and economic experiment, noble in motive. . . ." The President's own preferred hard-likker drink during Prohibition was the sloe gin fizz.) Did the nation learn that if you want to increase the popularity of and encourage illicit traffic in a pleasure substance, one way is to ban it? That you thereby increase profit in it as well?

Perhaps. With religion having lost much of its appeal as an opiate

371

for the masses, maybe it was decided that drugs themselves would do. Perhaps all along presidents Bush and Reagan, and their sponsors, had a certain hidden agenda. . . . Hey! Things *do* happen. Better a fire in *their* brains than a fire in *our* streets.

As for gambling, it seems by these '90s to have achieved respectability in the land, though the proliferation of state lotteries does not seem to have eased any state's financial problems—and the lotteries have become, in effect, a regressive tax on the poor.

Chicago's 1990s mayor wants casino gambling in the city; it would be "family entertainment," though—not "gaming" and certainly not "gambling."

Supporters of the mayor in this civic crusade have not stressed (or even mentioned, would you believe it?) that such legalization is the precursor to a rising violent crime rate (a rate already at an all-time high in Chicago), a rising rate of homelessness, and a rising rate of corruption among city officials. (Cf. Atlantic City on all these counts.) As for the casino industry's promised jobs, they will be entry-level, minimum-wage, counter-smile jobs. And say, is that a gangster lurking behind that pillar over there? . . . Have a nice day.

With respect to the violent crime rate, if you really wanted to curb violence in the streets, you'd ban handguns. Our Presidents don't endorse this; our Congress talks and does little. Yet despite the sloganeering of the National Rifle Association, it *is* guns that kill people. Very few humans can throw a pellet of metal with the velocity needed to pierce the flesh of another human without the propellant aid of a gun. . . . But they're only killing each other, aren't they. Just like the gangsters.

The same curious—because far less than determined—resolution characterized the Reagan-Bush approach to combatting the AIDS epidemic. (But AIDS victims, too, are only killing themselves—aren't they?) That is to say—in sum—for a dozen years—1980-92—the people of privilege in the United States ruled autocratically, selfishly, and shortsightedly in what they presumed was their own and sole best interest. The most damaging consequences of this policy were found, as always, in the economic sphere. What was comparatively new about it was that it was done quite openly, with an attitude of "Why damn you! What are you made for but to be plundered?"

This is not the place to attempt to explain that or why it was tolerated—even welcomed—by the majority of U.S. citizens, but in a way what happened in the Greedy Eighties to the citizens of the United States was no more strange than what the citizenry of Chicago permitted their municipal government to foist on them in the Roaring Twenties.

The foregoing is perhaps relevant and meaningful when considering the interdependent histories of Torrio, Capone, Chicago, and the United States. In Torrio's and Capone's time and in ours.

. . . Sometimes you wonder why they put history into the books that nobody reads.

In the Roaring Twenties the Irish-Americans of Chicago had a preponderance of the city's political jobs, including those on its police force, and the Italian-Americans had most of its best gangland jobs. The Irish and the Italians worked together—at least up to a point. If they had not, the gangsters would never have succeeded as they did.

There is a theory that because the Irish and the Italians were Roman Catholics—with that religion's structure of confession, penance, expiation, and forgiveness—they were predisposed to break laws imposed on them by an unjust ruling class. . . . Possibly. What is certain is that Sicilians and southern Italians came to the United States with a long history of responding to misgovernment, oppression, and exploitation with contempt for officials of the government and the enforcers of the law.

In Chicago, and in the nation as a whole, however, the percentage of Italians who worked at crime was less than the percentage for any other nationality. Italians were also low on the scale of incidence of alcoholism—and very high on the scale of mental stability.

At the turn of the century, the percentage of pauperism among Italian-Americans was the lowest of all ethnic groups in America. (It was highest among the Irish.) This, while Italians were lowest on the job ladder. Italians considered it degrading to be an object of charity; therefore, they took care of each other. That was their way of life.

The Italian man walked with an erect, proud posture, eyes fixed and penetrating. He knew who he was and what he stood for. The Italian woman held herself close to the home, the source of all that gave meaning to life—that and work. The Italians of past generations made things with their hands. That is what they considered honest labor—making something or doing something with their hands. Even today the percentage of Italians in the professions and in white-collar jobs is low compared with that of other nationalities.

Work was considered moral training for the young. It was a time of a sterner, simpler ethic. *Poveri si, ma perche lagnusi?* Poor yes, but why lazy?

The Italian gangster was false, to be sure, to most of the traditions of his people. The gangster spoke of honor and respect, and killed or was killed in betrayal. But the bigshot Italian gangster *was* the consummate capitalist. And compared to his legitimate counterparts, the Italian gangster had guts to spare.

And so this account of the Wicked City and its leading citizens ends, but not before recalling that when in the very late 19th century "Cap" Streeter—a squatter off Chicago's Gold Coast—was criticized for illegally selling beer and liquor on Sunday in his "District" (land built up from a sand bar in Lake Michigan after his boat grounded on it), the Captain replied, "This here is a frontier town and it's got to go through its red-blooded youth. A church and a WCTU never growed a big town yet!" (The 186 acres Cap Streeter was finally evicted from by the dry goods and real estate millionaire Potter Palmer is today worth more than $1.5 billion.)

Theodore Dreiser wrote of his cherished city that it was "the Babylon, the Troy, the Nineveh of a younger day. Here came the gaping West and the hopeful East to see. Here hungry men, raw from the shops and fields, idylls and romances in their minds, builded them an empire crying glory in the mud."

Half a century later, Chicago's other great writer, Nelson Algren, wrote that you had to know

> . . . that the call girl, the dope peddler, the hoodlum, the beggar, the thief, didn't invent their trades. That we don't have much complaint about the gangster because all he is doing is doing what we say is right: he is going to get all he can, by any means he can, because it isn't how you get it that counts and nobody is going to ask how.

And he said that "Chicago is perhaps the most universal of all cities, of all cities the one most like man himself in getting back on its feet, wiping off the blood and grinning around the board, asking, 'What did he hit me with?'"

And then, after long consideration of his city on the make, he said of it: "There may be lovelier lovelies, but never a lovely so real."

Nothing, however, so finds the spirit of Chicago, I think, as the reply made by Bertha Honoré Palmer—a silk stocking, no less—when she was asked what "art" was. Mrs. Palmer, who was born in Kentucky, was Chicago's social leader for most of the years after her marriage in 1871 at the age of 21 to the 44-year-old Potter Palmer until her death in 1918. She was a close friend of the painter Mary Cassatt—and of Jane Addams. Among her many accomplishments was that of introducing the French Impressionists to the United States. She was one of the first and became one of the greatest collectors of the work of Claude Monet. Her bequests are the foundation of the Chicago Art Institute's outstanding collection of Impressionists. So she had the credentials.

"What is art?" she mused. "In my limited conception it is the work of some genius graced with extraordinary proclivities not given to ordinary mortals." She thought a moment more, then added, "Speaking of art, my husband can spit over a freight car."

. . . Bella, molto bella.

Bertha Honoré Palmer, 1893 (oil on canvas by Anders Zorn; photograph © 1993, The Art Institute of Chicago. All Rights Reserved)

BIBLIOGRAPHY

Books

Allsop, Kenneth. *The Bootleggers*. Arlington House, 1961, 1968.

Andrews, Wayne. *Battle for Chicago*. Harcourt, Brace, 1946.

Ansley, Clarke F., ed. *The Columbia Encyclopedia*. Columbia University Press, 1942.

Asbury, Herbert. *Gem of the Prairie*. Knopf, 1940.

Asbury, Herbert. *The Great Illusion*. Doubleday, 1950.

Armstrong, Louis. *Satchmo*. Da Capo Press, 1954.

Asinof, Eliot. *Eight Men Out*. Holt, Rinehart and Winston, 1963.

Barnard, Harry. *"Eagle Forgotten": The Life of John Peter Altgeld*. Bobbs-Merrill, 1938.

Barnhart, C. L., ed. *The American College Dictionary*. Random House, 1958.

Becker, Stephen. *Marshall Field III*. Simon and Schuster, 1964.

Berendt, Joachim E. *The Jazz Book*. Lawrence Hill, 1953.

Boardman, Barrington. *Flappers, Bootleggers, "Typhoid Mary," & the Bomb*. Harper and Row, 1988.

Boettiger, John. *Jake Lingle*. E. P. Dutton, 1931.

Bonanno, Joseph, with Sergio Lalli. *A Man of Honor*. Simon and Schuster, 1983.

Bowden, Charles, and Lew Kreinberg. *Street Signs Chicago*. Chicago Review Press, 1981.

Brashler, William. *The Don: The Life and Death of Sam Giancana*. Harper and Row, 1977.

Browning, Frank, and John Gerassi. *The American Way of Crime*. G. P. Putnam's Sons, 1980.

Burns, Walter Noble. *The One Way Ride*. Doubleday, Doran, 1931.

Carpenter, Harry. *Boxing: An Illustrated History*. Crescent Books, 1982.

Cohen, Mickey, with John Peer Nugent. *Mickey Cohen*. Prentice-Hall, 1975.

Collier, James Lincoln. *Louis Armstrong: An American Genius*. Oxford University Press, 1983.

Cook, Fred J. *The Secret Rulers*. Duell, Sloan and Pearce, 1966.

Cressey, Donald R. *Theft of the Nation*. Harper and Row, 1969.

Davis, John H. *Mafia Kingfish*. McGraw-Hill, 1989.

Day, David. *The Doomsday Book of Animals*. Viking, 1981.

Dedmon, Emmett. *Fabulous Chicago*. Atheneum, 1981.

Demaris, Ovid. *Captive City*. Lyle Stuart, 1969.

Dempsey, Jack, with Barbara Piattelli Dempsey. *Dempsey*. Harper and Row, 1977.

Dreiser, Theodore. *A Book About Myself*. Boni and Liveright, 1922.

Dreiser, Theodore. *Sister Carrie*. Doubleday and Page, 1900.

Dreiser, Theodore. *The Titan*. John Lane, 1914.

Dreiser, Vera, with Brett Howard. *My Uncle Theodore*. Nash Publishing, 1976.

Duffey, Bernard. *The Chicago Renaissance in American Letters*. Michigan State University Press, 1956.

Elias, Norbert. *The Court Society*. Pantheon, 1969.

Elias, Robert H. *Theodore Dreiser: Apostle of Nature*. Knopf, 1949.

Farr, Finis. *Chicago*. Arlington House, 1973.

Fleischer, Nat, Sam Andre, and Nat Loubet. *A Pictorial History of Boxing*. Bonanza, 1981.

Fox, Stephen. *Blood and Power*. William Morrow, 1989.

Frampton, Kenneth. *Modern Architecture*. Oxford University Press, 1980.

Frazier, Nancy. *Louis Sullivan and the Chicago School*. Crescent Books, 1991.

Furer, Howard B. *Chicago*. Oceana Publications, 1974.

Gambino, Richard. *Blood of My Blood: The Dilemma of the Italian-Americans*. Doubleday, 1974.

George, Peter. *The Emergence of Industrial America*. State University of New York Press, Albany, 1982.

Giancana, Antoinette, and Thomas C. Renner. *Mafia Princess*. William Morrow, 1984.

Gosch, Martin A., and Richard Hammer. *The Last Testament of Lucky Luciano*. Little, Brown, 1974.

Halas, George. *Halas by Halas*. McGraw-Hill, 1979.

Halper, Albert, ed. *The Chicago Crime Book*. World, 1967.

Hansen, Harry. *The Chicago*. Farrar and Rinehart, 1942.

Harrington, Michael. *The Accidental Century*. Macmillan, 1965.

Harrison, Gilbert A. *A Timeless Affair*. University of Chicago Press, 1979.

Hecht, Ben. *A Child of the Century*. Simon and Schuster, 1954.

Heise, Kenan. *The Chicagoization of America 1893-1917*. Chicago Historical Bookworks, 1990.

Heise, Kenan, and Mark Frazel. *Hands on Chicago*. Bonus Books, 1987.

Hermann, Charles H. *Recollections of Life & Doings in Chicago*. Normandie House, 1945.

Hibbeler, Ray. *Upstairs at the Everleigh Club*. Volitant Books, n.d.

Hollatz, Tom. *Gangster Holidays*. North Star Press of St. Cloud, 1989.

Horan, James D. *The Desperate Years*. Bonanza Books, 1962.

Jones, Max, and John Chilton. *Louis: The Louis Armstrong Story 1900-1971*. Little, Brown, 1971.

Keepnews, Orrin, and Bill Grauer, Jr. *A Pictorial History of Jazz*. Crown, 1955.

Kenney, William Howland. *Chicago Jazz: A Cultural History, 1904-1930*. Oxford University Press, 1993.

Kimball, Nell. *Nell Kimball: Her Life as an American Madam*. 1970.

Kobler, John. *Capone*. Putnam's, 1971.

Kohn, Aaron. *The Kohn Report: Crime and Politics in Chicago*. Independent Voters of Illinois, 1953.

Kramer, Dale. *Chicago Renaissance: The Literary Life in the Midwest 1900-1930*. Appleton-Century, 1966.

Lacey, Robert. *Little Man: Meyer Lansky and the Gangster Life*. Little, Brown, 1991.

Lait, Jack, and Lee Mortimer. *Chicago Confidential*. Crown, 1950.

Landesco, John. *Organized Crime in Chicago*. University of Chicago Press, 1968.

Lardner, John. *The World of John Lardner*. Simon and Schuster, 1961.

Lens, Sidney. *The Labor Wars*. Doubleday, 1973.

Lewis, Lloyd, and Henry Justin Smith. *Chicago: The History of Its Reputation*. Harcourt, Brace, 1929.

Liebling, A. J. *Chicago: The Second City*. Knopf, 1952.

Longstreet, Stephen. *Chicago: 1860-1919*. David McKay, 1973.

Lowe, David. *Lost Chicago*. American Legacy Press, 1985.

Lyden, Jacki, and Chet Jakus. *Landmarks and Legends of Uptown*. 1980.

Lyle, John H. *The Dry and Lawless Years*. Prentice-Hall, 1960.

Lyman, Robert Hunt, ed. *The 1929 World Almanac Book of Facts*. Workman, 1929.

Mark, Norman. *Mayors, Madams, and Madmen*. Chicago Review Press, 1979.

Masters, Edgar Lee. *The Tale of Chicago*. Putnam's, 1933.

McDonald, Forrest. *Insull*. University of Chicago Press, 1962.

McPhaul, Jack. *Johnny Torrio*. Arlington House, 1970.

Meeker, Arthur. *Chicago, with Love*. Knopf, 1955.

Mezzrow, Milton, and Bernard Wolfe. *Really the Blues*. Random House, 1946.

Murray, George. *The Legacy of Al Capone*. Putnam's, 1975.

Mustain, Gene, and Jerry Capeci. *Murder Machine*. Dutton, 1992.

Nelli, Humbert S. *Italians in Chicago*. Oxford University Press, 1970.

Ness, Eliot, with Oscar Fraley. *The Untouchables*. Messner, 1957.

Norris, Frank. *The Pit*. Doubleday, Page, 1903.

Morgan, John. *Prince of Crime*. Stein and Day, 1985.

O'Connor. *Mellon's Millions*. John Day, 1933.

Pasley, Fred D. *Al Capone*. Garden City, 1930.

Paul, Sherman. *Louis Sullivan*. Prentice-Hall, 1962.

Peterson, Virgil W. *Barbarians in Our Midst*. Little, Brown, 1952.

Poole, Ernest. *Giants Gone*. Whittlesey House, London, 1943.

Puzo, Mario. *The Fortunate Pilgrim*. Fawcett Crest Books, 1964.

Rathet, Mike, and Don R. Smith. *Their Deeds and Dogged Faith*. Balsam Press, 1984.

Reid, E. *The Grim Reaper*. Henry Regnery Co., 1969.

Roberts, Randy. *Jack Dempsey*. Louisiana State University Press, 1979.

Roemer, William F., Jr. *War of the Godfathers*. Donald I. Fine, 1990.

Ross, Shelley. *Fall from Grace*. Ballantine Books, 1988.

Rudensky, Morris, and John Riley. *The Gonif*. Piper Company, 1970.

Sann, Paul. *American Panorama*. Crown, 1980.

Sann, Paul. *Kill the Dutchman*. Arlington House, 1971.

Sann, Paul. *The Lawless Decade*. Crown, 1957.

Sautter, R. Craig, ed. *Floyd Dell*. December Press, 1994.

Schoenberg, Robert J. *Mr. Capone*. William Morrow, 1992.

Shay, Art. *Nelson Algren's Chicago*. University of Illinois Press, 1988.

Siegel, Ronald K. *Intoxication*. E. P. Dutton, 1989.

Sinclair, Upton. *The Jungle*. 1906.

Sawyers, June Skinner. *Chicago Portraits*. Loyola University Press, 1991.

Smith, Alson J. *Chicago's Left Bank*. Henry Regnery, 1953.

Smith, Dwight C., Jr. *The Mafia Mystique*. Basic Books, 1975.

Smith, Red. *To Absent Friends*. Atheneum, 1982.

Spiering, Frank. *The Man Who Got Capone*. Bobbs-Merrill, 1976.

Stead, William T. *If Christ Came to Chicago*. Laird and Lee, 1894.

Stearns, Marshall W. *The Story of Jazz*. Oxford University Press, 1956.

Stokes, W. Royal. *The Jazz Scene*. Oxford University Press, 1991

Sugar, Bert Randolph. *The 100 Greatest Boxers of All Time*. Bonanza Books, 1984.

Sullivan, Edward Dean. *Chicago Surrenders*. Vanguard Press, 1930.

Tafel, Edgar. *Apprentice to Genius*. McGraw-Hill, 1979.

Talese, Gay. *Unto the Sons*. Knopf, 1992.

Tirro, Frank. *Jazz: A History*. W. W. Norton, 1977.

Tomasi, Silvan M., and Madeline H. Engel, ed. *The Italian Experience in the United States*. Center for Migration Studies, 1970.

Touhy, Roger, with Ray Brennan. *The Stolen Years*. Pennington Press, 1959.

Twombly, Robert. *Louis Sullivan*. Viking Penguin, 1986.

Veblen, Thorstein. *The Theory of the Leisure Class*. Macmillan, 1899, 1912.

Viskochil, Larry A. *Chicago at the Turn of the Century in Photographs*. Dover, 1984.

Wakenknecht, Edward. *Chicago*. University of Oklahoma Press, 1964.

Wallek, Lee. *The Mafia Manager*. December Press, 1991.

Washburn, Charles. *Come into My Parlor: A Biography of the Aristocratic Everleigh Sisters of Chicago*. Knickerbocker, 1936.

Wendt, Lloyd, and Herman Kogan. *Big Bill of Chicago*. Bobbs-Marrill, 1953.

Wendt, Lloyd, and Herman Kogan. *Lords of the Levee*. Bobbs-Merrill, 1943.

Williams, Martin. *The Jazz Tradition*. Grove, 1959.

Wilson, Colin. *A Criminal History of America*. Putnam's, 1984.

Wilson, Robert, and Dorothy Chamberlain. *The Otis Ferguson Reader*. December Press, 1982.

Wolf, George, and Joseph DiMona. *Frank Costello*. William Morrow, 1974.

Woodford, Jack. *The Autobiography of Jack Woodford*. Woodford Memorial Editions, 1962.

Woodford, Jack. *My Years with Capone*. Woodford Memorial Editions, 1985.
Zorbaugh, Harvey Warren. *The Gold Coast and the Slum*. University of Chicago Press, 1929.

Articles

Abramson, Jill, and Edward T. Pound. "The Brat Pack." *Wall Street Journal*, June 26, 1989.

Amman, Emile. "Driving Miss Edith." *Spring 52*, 1992.

"Ex-HUD aide guilty of lying to Congress." Associated Press, Oct. 27, 1993..

Baumann, Edward. "The Haymarket Bomber." *Chicago Tribune Magazine*, April 27, 1986.

Bernstein, Elizabeth. "Kosher-Style Capones." *JUF News*, June 1993 (Sivan 5753).

Biemiller, Lawrence. "Slowly and Deliberately Roosevelt U. Is Restoring One of the Masterpieces of American Architecture." *Chronicle of Higher Education*, March 13, 1991.

Buenker, John D. "Chicago's Ethnics and the Politics of Accommodation." *Chicago History*, Fall 1974.

Bushnell, George. "Hunger in Chicago, then and now." *Chicago Tribune*, April 24, 1984.

"Cleaning House at HUD—And then Some." *Business Week*, July 10, 1989.

"White House defends big fundraising dinner." *Chicago Tribune*, April 29, 1992.

Collin, Dorothy. "No Welcome Mats Here." *Chicago Tribune*, Nov. 7, 1980.

Cordts, Michael. "Village Needs Sugar Daddy." *Chicago Sun-Times*, June 17, 1984.

Doctorow, E. L. "Standards." *Harper's Magazine*, 1991.

Doherty, James. "Valley Kills Italian Leader." *Chicago Tribune*, March 22, 1928.

Egan, Msgr. John J. "A Gamble We can't Afford." *Chicago Tribune*, June 1, 1992.

Fanning, Charles F., Jr. "Mr. Dooley's Bridgeport Chronicle." *Chicago History*, Spring 1972.

Franklin, H. Bruce. "John Wayne's World." *In These Times*, August 9, 1993.

Gapp, Paul. "Burnham's Fair City." *Chicago Tribune*, May 24, 1992.

Gapp, Paul. "Frank Lloyd Wright: 'Deity of Design.'" *Chicago Tribune*, Feb. 9, 1992.

Griffin, Richard T. "Sin-drenched Revels at the Infamous First Ward Ball." *Smithsonian*, Nov. 1976.

Grossman, Ron. "Even Sin Strips Have Redeeming Value—for Land." *Chicago Tribune*, May 26, 1985.

Grossman, Ron. "The World's Fair and the fair sex." *Chicago Tribune*, April 18, 1993.

"Chicago Architecture." *Harper's Magazine*, 1891.

"Chicago—The Main Exhibit." *Harper's Magazine*, 1892.

"Chicago's Gentle Side." *Harper's Magazine*, 1893.

"Glimpses of Western Architecture." *Harper's Magazine*, 1891.

"The Geology of Chicago." *Harper's Magazine*, 1890.

"Shades of the Great West—Chicago." *Harper's Magazine*, 1888.

Hellie, Richard. "Our descent into neofeudalism." *Chicago Tribune*, Oct. 20, 1992.

Holtzman, Jerome. "Rose's Hall Ban Hits 'Shoeless Joe' Again." *Chicago Tribune*, Feb. 5, 1991.

Holtzman, Jerome. "Weaver Case Seems to Be Lost in Limbo." *Chicago Tribune*, Jan. 12, 1992.

Kamin, Blair. "City on the plain." *Chicago Tribune*, May 16, 1993.

Koziol, Ronald, and George Estep. "New Insight on St. Valentine Killing." *Chicago Tribune*, Feb. 14, 1983.

Le Sueur, Meridel. "Women on the Breadlines." *New Masses*, Jan. 1932.

McCarron, John. "Real school crisis: Suburban dropouts." *Chicago Tribune*, Sept. 12, 1993.

Miller, Scott. "The Assassination of Jake Lingle." *Reader*, March 20, 1981.

Nashe, Jay Robert. "St. Valentine's Day, 1929." *Reader*, Feb. 9, 1979.
Nelli, Humbert S. "John Powers and the Italians." *Journal of American History*, June 1970.
Patton, Phil. "Sell the cookstove if necessary, but come to the Fair." *Smithsonian*, June 1993.
Petacque, Art, and Hugh Hough. "Out Front." *Chicago Tribune*, Feb. 11, 1979.
Reardon, Patrick T. "Burnham quote: Well, it may be." *Chicago Tribune*, Jan. 1, 1992.
Reich, Howard. "Hotter near the lake." *Chicago Tribune Magazine*, Sept. 5, 1993.
Reich, Howard. "Legends on the line." *Chicago Tribune*, Oct. 31, 1993.
Roback, Diane. "Talking Peace with President Carter." *Publishers Weekly*, Aug. 2, 1993.
Stefansson, Vilhjalmur. "Lessons in Living from the Stone Age." *Harper's Magazine*, 1939.
Tuomey, Timothy J. and Magdalene. "St. Joseph's tables." *Chicago Tribune*, March 20, 1992.
Turner, George Kibbe. "The City of Chicago: A Study of the Great Immoralities." *McClure's Magazine*, April 1907.
Vanderbilt, Cornelius, Jr. "How Al Capone Would Run This Country." *Liberty*, Sept. 17, 1931.
Wood, Morrison. "A Half Century of the Culinary Arts in Chicago." *Chicago History*, Spring 1972.
Zemitsch, W. Paul. "Anton Cermak's Chicago." *Chicago Tribune*, March 20, 1983.
Zulkey, Edward J. "The Ladies Everleigh." *Chicago Tribune Magazine*, Jan. 21, 1979.

PHOTO CREDITS

Pages *ix* and 124, Jane Addams Memorial Collection, Special Collections, The University Library, The University of Illinois at Chicago

Pages *x*, 108, 116, 144, 152, 176, 180, 216, 228, 238, 250, 292, and 332, The Chicago Historical Society. The authors wish to thank Eileen Flanagan of the Society for her invaluable assistance in obtaining these photographs.

Page 12, Historic Pullman Foundation Archives (Pullman), and Library of Congress (Field)

Pages 40, 90, and 204, Italian American Collection, Special Collections, The University Library, The University of Illinois at Chicago

Pages 48, 72, 160, 354 (Sullivan), *Chicago Tribune*

Page 192, National Archives

Page 354, The Bettmann Archive (Armstrong)

INDEX

383

Harrison, Carter, Jr., 5-6, 78, 98, 103, 110, 111, 140
Hastings, Mary, 30, 85
Hayden, Sophia, 32
Healy, Daniel, 222
Heath, Monroe, 16
Hecht, Ben, 62, 117, 253, 323
Hedlin, David, 167
Heeney, Willie, 269-70
Hein, Mel, 232
Heinan, Jack, 241
Heitler, Mike, 240
Hemingway, Ernest, 62
Henderson, Fletcher, 288, 289
Henry, Arthur, 63, 64-65, 67
Herrick, Mother, 74
Herrmann, Urbine J., 225-26
Heydler, John, 111
Heyer, Adam, 295
Highball, 294, 295, 353
Hines, Earl, 285-86, 288, 289
Hirohito, Emperor, 190
Hitler, Adolf, 190, 365
Hodes, Art, 287
Hoff, Max, 301
Hoffman, Peter B., 149, 167, 177, 217
Hogarty, Joe, 104
Holabird, William, 28
Hoover, Henry, 200
Hoover, Herbert, 264, 298, 313, 337, 356, 358, 371
Houdini, Harry, 205
Howard, Joseph, 168, 170, 196, 239
Howells, William Dean, 62
Hubbard, Gurdon, 26
Hubbard, Major, 188
Hughes, Michael, 244, 248, 268
Humphreys, Murray, 206, 271, 272, 273, 295, 312, 336, 345, 351, 352
Hunt, Sam, 241, 299
Hunter, Alberta, 246
Hyman, Elaine, 70

Insull, Samuel, 6, 218, 221, 243-44, 307-10, 359, 367
Irey, Elmer L., 249, 264, 312, 337, 340, 363

Jackson, Joe, 112, 113
Jackson, Tony, 246
Jacobs, Benjamin, 213
James, Henry, 331

Jeans, James, 362
Jenney, William LeBaron, 28, 29
Johnson, Andrew, 370
Johnson, Ban, 111
Johnson, Bunk, 279, 280
Johnson, Enoch, 301
Johnson, George E. Q., 334, 337, 340, 343
Johnson, Jack, 79, 94, 96, 140
Johnson, Lonnie, 289
Johnson, Robert, 291
Johnstone, Robert B., 351-52
Jolson, Al, 89, 247
Joyce, James, 70, 185
Jung, Karl Gustav, 184

Kearns, Jack, 94-96, 230-31, 233-34
Kelly, Paul, 99-100
Kenna, Michael, 4, 7-11, 55-56, 77, 81-82, 84, 97, 103-4, 111, 138, 141, 197, 242, 248, 253, 328, 353, 357, 358, 362
Kennedy, Joseph, 243
Ketchell, Stanley, 76
Kipling, Rudyard, 28, 64
Klenha, Joseph Z., 166-67, 196
Klimas, Leo, 293
Kolb, Matt, 269, 299, 311, 315, 324, 344
Koncil, Frank, 209, 212, 214-15, 219
Kouryoumdjouglou, Mme., 310
Krenn, Edward, 185, 188
Krupa, Gene, 290

Lake, Frankie, 121, 123, 177, 217, 264
Lala, Pete, 281
LaMantio, Angelo, 248
Lame Jimmy, 81
Landis, Kenesaw Mountain, 112, 114, 141, 273
Lang, Harry, 349
Lannigan, Jim, 286
Lansky, Meyer, 243, 301, 302
Lardner, John, 366
Lardner, Ring, 76, 109, 113, 115, 366
LaRocca, Nick, 282
Lawrence, Clark, 190
Lazar, Sam, 301
Lazia, John, 301
Leiter, Joseph, 16-17
Leiter, Levi Z., 13, 14
Lenglen, Suzanne, 367
Lepito, Michael. See *Malone, Michael*
Lespinasse, Victor D., 187